# THE ARCHITECTURAL MEDAL

# The Architectural

## ENGLAND IN THE

An annotated catalogue, with accompanying illustrations and biographical notes on architects and medallists. Based on the collection of architectural medals in the British Museum.

JEREMY TAYLOR

No. 106a
Bank of England
Architect: Sir John Soane

# Medal
## NINETEENTH CENTURY

A COLONNADE BOOK

Published by British Museum Publications Limited

Colonnade Books are published by British Museum Publications Ltd, and are offered as contributions to the enjoyment, study, and understanding of art, archaeology and history.
The same publishers also produce the official publications of the British Museum.


ISBN 0 7141 0840 5

Published by British Museum Publications Ltd, 6 Bedford Square, London WC1B 3RA

Designed by Bernard Crossland
Typeset in Linotron Caledonia 14/16pt and 11/12pt
and printed in Great Britain by J. W. Arrowsmith, Bristol BS3 2NT

# CONTENTS


Preface vii

Abbreviations x

Note on Numbering, Indexing, and Cross-referencing xii

1 INTRODUCTION 1

*Reasons for striking medals* 5

*'View' of architecture provided by the medal* 19

*Medallic design* 24

2 BUILDINGS PORTRAYED 35

3 CATALOGUE OF MEDALS 43

4 ARCHITECTS and DESIGNERS 183

5 MEDALLISTS, SCULPTORS, and PUBLISHERS 211

Index of places and persons 229

# PREFACE

The present work has as its primary aim the compilation of a first catalogue of architectural medals for the period 1800–1900. Not only was this a time of unparalleled building activity in England, but it was also a century that fostered an equally dramatic expansion of interest in the production of commemorative medals. Three main sections support the numismatic material: details and dates of *buildings* depicted; biographies of *architects and designers* referred to; biographies of *medallic artists* whose works are listed. In addition, reference is made in the introductory essay to the 'reasons why' medals might be commissioned. For the main sections, basic published references have been provided to allow the reader, whether architect, numismatist, or historian, an easy access to more specialised information. Many of the medals, together with detailed inscriptions, relate to obscure buildings and little known architects; a suprisingly large number of these buildings have now been destroyed or altered. It is hoped therefore that the entries, together with the medallic illustrations, will provide a useful source of material for the student of architectural history, as well as offering a record for numismatic studies.

In preparing the catalogue, I have found that the most relevant existing work was *Medals and Medallions relating to Architects*, published privately by L. J. Eidlitz, New York, 1927. Although this is centred around the theme of the architect, and covers the wider field of Europe and America, it contains many plates and cross-references; I have accordingly noted these against present medal entries wherever relevant. I am indebted to Mr Graham Pollard, Keeper of Coins and Medals at the Fitzwilliam Museum, Cambridge, for drawing my attention to this rare book at an early stage in my work. In obtaining much other reference material I have been most grateful for all the help given to me by the librarian of the Institute of Advanced Architectural Studies, University of York, Mr Keith Parker.

Many of the buildings portrayed in the catalogue have been demolished or considerably altered; others may not hitherto have been thought of sufficient merit or interest to figure in any of the standard reference books. For a variety of such obscure buildings, searches for evidence of dating, location, or architect, have been ably assisted by many local librarians and their staff; I would like to take this opportunity to thank them for the care and attention which they have devoted to my detailed queries. Additional architectural information has also been given to me by the Librarian of the RIBA; the Librarian of the London Hospital Medical College; the Archivist of the GLC Record Office; the Archivist of Liverpool University; the Headmaster and the Archivist of Charterhouse School; Mr J. Algie, Mr Howard Colvin CBE, Mr Denis Evinson, Mr Peter Howell, Mr Keith Howes, Fr Francis Keegan, Mr John Roper, Mr L. Sutton, and Miss Corinne Wilson. In finalising the architectural aspects of this work I am especially grateful to Dr Derek Linstrum for reading through the whole of the text, and for making many valuable suggestions and contributions.

The majority of medals which form the basis of this catalogue are in the permanent collection at the British Museum. I would like to acknowledge the very considerable assistance that has been afforded to me by Mr Kenneth Jenkins, Keeper of the Department of Coins and Medals, and by members of his staff at the British Museum; in particular I would like to record my gratitude to Mrs Joan Martin whose detailed searches have helped me to establish much of the material in the medallic list, and whose untiring checking of numismatic sources and references has been a healthy corrective to my architectural interests. Some medals have been added to the British Museum material; these come from private collections, and also from items in the Leeds City Museum. In the latter case the source is indicated with the relevant entry, and I am grateful to Miss Elizabeth Pirie for her assistance. Other medallic information has been helpfully supplied by Mr Graham Dyer of the Royal Mint Museum. For the assembly of all the material, both architectural as well as medallic, my thanks are also very much due to my wife for so diligently and patiently creating an accurate typescript out of the many separate manuscript entries and inscriptions.

Although it is intended that this initial volume should present a general view of the nineteenth-century English architectural medal, it is also recognised that various yet unrecorded or unclassified medals can be expected to be identified—particularly in local museums and collections, and often of lesser-known buildings. An implicit aim throughout this work has therefore been to set out the system of numbering of the catalogue, and the structuring of the text, so as to allow for new material to be easily added.

All photographs are by the author, except for No. 111a by courtesy of the Royal Mint Museum, No. 187a by courtesy of the Gloucester City Museum, No. 154a by Ray Gardner, and photos of those medals shown as from the former Watt Collection, which are by courtesy of the Trustees of the British Museum.

JEREMY TAYLOR

*January 1977*
*York*

# ABBREVIATIONS

| | |
|---|---|
| *Arch. Mag.* | *Architectural Magazine*, ed. J. C. Loudon, vols 1–5. London, 1834–38. |
| *AR* | *Architectural Review*, 1897–. |
| Beulah | 'The Medals of the Art Union of London', by G. K. Beulah, in *British Numismatic Journal*, xxxvi (1967), 179–85 with plates. |
| BM | British Museum. |
| *BNJ* | *British Numismatic Journal*, 1903–. |
| *British Sculpture* | Catalogue of exhibition at The Fine Art Society Ltd, *British Sculpture 1850–1914*. London, 1968. |
| *Builder* | *The Builder Magazine*, 1843–. |
| Clarke | *Church Builders of the Nineteenth Century*, B. F. L. Clarke. London, 1938 (reprinted, Newton Abbot, 1969). |
| Colvin | *A Biographical Dictionary of English Architects 1660–1840*, H. M. Colvin. London, 1954. |
| del. | delineate. |
| dem or D | demolished. |
| Eidlitz | *Medals and Medallions relating to Architects*, R. J. Eidlitz. New York, privately printed, 1927. |
| fec. or F | fecit. |
| Ferriday | *Victorian Architecture*, P. Ferriday ed. London, 1963. |
| Forrer | *Biographical Dictionary of Medallists*, L. Forrer. Vols i–viii, London, 1904– (reprinted Franklin, New York, 1970). |
| *GM* | *The Gentleman's Magazine*, 1736–1877. |
| Grant | 'British Medals since 1760', by M. H. Grant, in *BNJ* xxii (1934–7), 267–93; xxiii (1938–41), 119–52, and 321–52. |
| Grueber | 'English Personal Medals from 1760', by H. A. Grueber, in *Numismatic Chronicle*, serially 1887–94. |
| Gunnis | *Dictionary of British Sculptors 1660–1851*, R. Gunnis. London, 1951. |
| Hawkins | 'Dictionary of British Makers of Metallic Tickets, and Counters', Parts I, II, III, by R. N. P. Hawkins, in *Seaby Coin and Medal Bulletin*, serially, 1960, 1966–67, 1968. |
| Hitchcock | *Early Victorian Architecture in Britain*, Henry-Russell Hitchcock, vols 1 and 2. London, 1954. |

| | |
|---|---|
| Hocking | *Catalogue of the Coins, Tokens, Medals, Dies & Seals in the Museum of the Royal Mint*, vol. ii, by W. J. Hocking, London, 1910 (section related to medals, pp. 145–318). |
| IBA | Institute of British Architects. |
| *Kings Arcadia* | *The Kings Arcadia: Inigo Jones and the Stuart Court*; catalogue of exhibition at the Banqueting House, Arts Council of Great Britain. London, 1973. |
| *Marble Halls* | *Marble Halls*, drawings and models for Victorian secular building; catalogue of exhibition at the Victoria and Albert Museum. London, 1973. (References are to catalogue numbers.) |
| *Med. Ill.* | *Medallic Illustrations of the History of Great Britain and Ireland*, E. Hawkins. Two vols. London, 1885, reprinted 1969. |
| Norris | 'Some Birmingham Medallists' by D. M. Norris, in *Birm. Archaeol. Soc. Trans.* (1951), 71–75. |
| *Num. Chron.* | *Numismatic Chronicle*, 1838–. |
| Pevsner | *The Buildings of England*, N. Pevsner, *et al.* Harmondsworth, 1951–. |
| Pollard | *Renaissance Medals* (from Samuel H. Kress collection) G. F. Hill, revised by Graham Pollard. London, 1967. |
| Port | *Six Hundred New Churches*, M. H. Port. London, 1961. |
| qv. | for which see separate entry. |
| RA | Royal Academy. |
| RIBA | Royal Institute of British Architects. |
| *RIBA Dwgs Coll.* | *Catalogue of the Drawings Collection of the Royal Institute of British Architects*, volumes as published. London, 1969– |
| *RIBAJ* | *Journal of the Royal Institute of British Architects*, 1893–. (Preceded by Transactions, and Sessional Papers, 1835–. |
| Seaborne | *The English School, its Architecture and Organisation 1370–1870*, Malcolm Seaborne. London, 1971. |
| *Survey of London* | *Survey of London*, GLC (in succession to LCC). London, vol. 1–, 1900–. |
| V & A | Victoria and Albert Museum. |
| *VCH* | *The Victoria History of the Counties of England.* Oxford, 1900–. |
| Ware | *A Short Dictionary of British Architects*, D. Ware, London, 1967. |
| Willis & Clark | *The Architectural History of the University of Cambridge*, R. Willis and J. W. Clark. Vols i–iv. Cambridge, 1886. |

# Note on NUMBERING, INDEXING, and CROSS-REFERENCING

**a** Buildings shown on medals are listed sequentially by date of their completion. This forms the basis for arranging the catalogue of medals (Section 3) and for the sequence of *key identification numbers* of buildings, and medals related to them. For example, St Paul's Cathedral, which was completed 1710, is catalogue No. 39 and medals of it listed 39a, 39b, 39c, . . . etc.

**b** An *index of buildings*, in date order of completion, is provided at Section 2 as a guide to the medallic catalogue. The index at the end of the book provides access to place and building names, as well as names of architects, medallists, patrons, etc.

**c** A cross-reference for the Architects of buildings shown, and of Medallists concerned, is provided by the *biographical entries* (Sections 4 and 5). Here buildings by an architect which are depicted on a medal are listed below the entry; similarly, medallists who have produced architectural medals have the buildings concerned listed below their entries. In both these cases the *key identification number* is given with the building to allow rapid reference to the catalogue.

# INTRODUCTION 1

Buildings have always provided an obvious subject for interpretation by the designer of coins, medals, or tokens; the numismatic history of Imperial Rome demonstrates, for instance, a generous record of the important contemporary temples and the most useful public works. By the time of the Italian Renaissance, architectural themes had been redefined to illustrate more local and factional interests and to include such new building forms as Alberti's church at Rimini for Sigismondo Malatesta (medallist after Matteo de Pasti),[1] or the centralised chapel proposed *c.* 1460 by Filarete for Francesco Sforza, Duke of Milan (medallist Sperandio of Mantua).[2] By the eighteenth century the focus in Italy had changed again with some outstanding examples of the architectural medal being provided by the Papal series, e.g. the elevation of the new east front of St John Lateran by the architect Galilei, shown on a 1733 medal of Pope Clement XII (medallist O. Hamerani).[3]

It was with the history of medallic illustration of buildings in mind, and with a topical relevance to the still popular Grand Tour, that the newly formed Institute of British Architects included the following advice to correspondents and travellers in a pamphlet of 1836:

> Another source of information is ancient coins and medals, which frequently represent upon the reverse some building, the erection

1. Pollard No. 66. The medal also shows the dome to a larger space (never built). See Wittkower, *Architectural Principles in the Age of Humanism*, Tiranti, 1952, 33–35, where this church is discussed; the medal reverse is illustrated pl. 15a.

2. Pollard No. 115. The subject of this medal is discussed in N. Pevsner, *An Outline of European Architecture*, Harmondsworth, 1960, 184, 185, together with a reconstruction of the plan, fig. 129. Pevsner attributes the design to the Florentine architect Antonio Filarete (d. 1470).

3. Eidlitz No. 438, pl. 53.

> of which they are designed to commemorate. Series of these have been chronologically arranged at Rome and sold in sets. From them Piranesi and other architectural writers have derived authority for the restoration of many ancient buildings.

The co-secretary of the Institute in its formative years, and the probable author of that comment, was the architect T. L. Donaldson. In 1859 he published the first complete book on the subject of architectural medals: *Architectura Numismatica* or 'the Architectural Medals of Classical Antiquity'. Donaldson summarised his aim in this book as:

> . . . to convey to my professional brethren, the members of the Royal Institute of British Architects, an impression of the rich treasury of reference, which medals offer; and to explain some of the pecularities relating to them, which have been variously described by different writers, who from want of the technical knowledge of our art, have misunderstood some of the features. . .

And those 'features' meant for Donaldson the elements of 'correct' building in a classical style. Significantly he dedicated the volume to Lord Palmerston, then Foreign Secretary, as 'The enlightened advocate of classical architecture'—and it was Palmerston who, just returned to office as Foreign Secretary, again that year (1859) rejected Gilbert Scott's gothic design for the new Foreign Office building and instructed Scott to rework it in a classical format. So Donaldson's book on medals can also be related, if distantly, to the famous 'Battle of the Styles' which had been so exercising the architectural profession in the middle of the nineteenth century.

If however, instead of taking the products of Greece and Rome as evidence in an argument about styles, we look at Donaldson's own century, the nineteenth, what do the 'architectural' medals in England at that time record? And what do they tell us about the building stock, the architectural preoccupations, and the medallic art? The medals which comprise this catalogue (Section 3), and therefore provide the evidence for examining such questions, have been compiled within the following limits:

1. Medals (as opposed to tokens or advertising checks and medallets) which were produced in England during the nineteenth century, or which portray relevant English architectural subjects during that period.

2. Medals which show buildings as a primary item on the obverse or reverse; for these the architect may, or may not, be known. (Decisions may have to be taken as to whether to exclude buildings which are 'incidental' only, in say a topographical view, or those more in the class of monuments than buildings.)

3. Structures and works which, although not by architects, are commonly understood as 'works in architecture', e.g. as set out in Colvin's *Dictionary of English Architects*. Examples included under this category are London Bridge, by the engineer John Rennie, and the Menai Strait railway bridge, which although by the engineer Robert Stephenson, had an important contribution to the masonry design by the architect Francis Thompson. (In most cases, however, engineering and railway works, e.g. the Thames Tunnel, or a railway viaduct, are excluded.)

4. Portraits of architects themselves, e.g. the portrait medal by J. S. and A. B. Wyon of 1865 struck to mark the retirement of T. L. Donaldson as Professor of Architecture at University College London. (There are few nineteenth-century medals in this category.)

On the above basis for selection the catalogue lists some four hundred medals; between them they illustrate by means of views, elevations, or interiors a total of 232 different works of architecture. These consist of two main groups:

(*a*) Those completed PRIOR to the nineteenth century (26 per cent of the total).

(*b*) Those completed DURING the nineteenth century and comprising such types as Educational (22 per cent), Churches (16 per cent), Civic (9 per cent), Commercial (8 per cent), Welfare (8 per cent).

Some buildings in these groups may be recorded by only one medal of one material, while others, particularly 'popular' subjects such as the 1851 Exhibition Building, or the new Royal Exchange, may be shown on twenty or thirty different architectural medals—each in turn with variants of the metal used for the striking.

If one selects those medals showing main categories of buildings completed during the nineteenth century (i.e. group (*b*) above), what sort of 'profile' does this give of architectural and medallic activity during the period? The new buildings which were commemorated for each decade were:

| | | | | | | | | | | |
|---|---|---|---|---|---|---|---|---|---|---|
| from: | 1800 | 1810 | 1820 | 1830 | 1840 | 1850 | 1860 | 1870 | 1880 | 1890 |
| buildings: | 5 | 10 | 28 | 30 | 33 | 15 | 9 | 11 | 19 | 15 |

The noticeably empty period of the 1800s and 1810s was recalled by Professor Donaldson (writing in 1867): 'In the first quarter of the present century our art was at a very low ebb. The long and dreadful struggle with France had absorbed all the nations resources. We had no spare money to bestow upon architecture, properly so called; the Government confined its expenditure to buildings required for the commonest purposes, raised in the most economical manner and with ordinary materials. The speculative builder superseded the accomplished architect, and erected, for the nobility and gentry, rows of square boxes of brick or stucco houses as mansions, without any pretension to effective decoration or dignified aspect'.[1]

An apparently bleak start to the century was, however, rapidly to turn into that period of unparalleled building activity and urban development fostered by the Industrial Revolution. This activity, with its new building types, was not only mirrored by the production of architectural medals, but the medals themselves could now be more easily and cheaply produced by new and improved technology. The first surge of building clearly recorded by the medal was the impact of the £1 million allocated by the State under the Church Building Act of 1818 (administered by the Church Commissioners) and manifested in the Commissioners' churches of the 1820s (e.g. medals Nos. 80, 83, 88, 89). By the end of the next decade, the area of activity influencing medallic production had changed to highlight the Proprietary and Grammar Schools which were built to meet the needs of middle-class education (e.g. medals Nos. 116, 120, 140). Then from the 1850s onwards the three main themes of civic pride, commercial activity and educational provision emerge as steady subject areas for the medallist.

In addition to such contemporary buildings the nineteenth-century medal also portrayed buildings completed in earlier centuries (group (*a*) above and see pp. 35 to 37 in Section 2). For instance, the architectural heritage of medieval cathedrals which the nineteenth century began to appreciate, with the aid of such books as John Britton's *Cathedral Antiquities* of 1818. Reflecting this particular awareness and demand there

1. *RIBA Sessional Papers*, 4 November, 1867, 2.

were two main sets of medals depicting cathedrals: from 1835 on a set of ten medals by J. Davis of Birmingham (see p. 216), and in the 1850s five medals by J. Wiener of Brussels (see p. 224); both sets are notable for combining exterior and interior views as obverse and reverse. Additionally there were individual medals showing cathedrals and medieval churches, as well as those depicting secular buildings deemed important as 'monuments'; the latter might perhaps be combined with the portrait of the architect as a tribute, e.g. Sir William Chambers, *Rev.* Somerset House, in the Art Union Series (No. 52).

Rather more common amongst medals showing architecture prior to the nineteenth century, were those lesser-known buildings that were redefined, or converted, for a new use. For example, the house that the builder Henry Emlyn had designed at Old Windsor, *c.* 1785, which in the 1860s was converted to become Beaumont Roman Catholic College; a medal struck to relate to this new use shows the double columns of the portico originally designed to follow Emlyn's strange proposal for a 'British Order of Architecture' (see No. 55 and p. 191). A similar example shows the original sixteenth-century gatehouse of the Shireburn family house at Stonyhurst, absorbed, by the date of the mid-nineteenth-century medal, into an enlarged range of school buildings.

## REASONS FOR STRIKING MEDALS

If one now takes all these nineteenth-century medals together, i.e. those portraying both contemporary buildings and those showing older works, what are some of the reasons why they were commissioned? One particularly clear statement on how an architectural medal came about is recorded in a letter to J. C. Loudon's *Architectural Magazine* of 1837. In this Charles Fowler, the architect of Covent Garden and Hungerford markets, writes of his competition winning design for the new market at Exeter which had just been completed that year:

> The accompanying medal [*see* No. 118a] has been struck to commemorate the erection of the Western Market at Exeter. It is engraved by Mr. B. Wyon; and, therefore, it will no doubt be esteemed as a work of fine art, independently of any interest it may possess as an architectural memorial. In this latter respect, it may (be) observed, as a remarkable coincidence, that, in excavating for the foundations of the new building a great number of Roman coins and other antiquities were discovered; and amongst them a

medal struck on an occasion precisely similar; viz. the erection of a meat market at Rome by Nero; having on the reverse the representation of a building two stories high, crowned with a cupola and inscribed MAC: AUG: This circumstance first suggested the idea of striking the present medal, which in execution greatly surpasses its Roman prototype; it might be added, that this mode of commemorating the erection of public buildings, besides being warranted by the ancients, is desirable in itself, as being likely to outlast all other records, and as giving employment to the medallic art which so well deserves encouragement.[1]

Coin of Nero found at Exeter; from Shortt—see note 2 below. Approx. 30 mm diameter.

What of the Roman coin of the time of Nero? Here there is an interesting architectural link: Charles Fowler was a co-secretary of the IBA with Donaldson during the years 1836–39, and pl. 72 in *Architectura Numismatica* is undoubtedly the same as the coin described as found on the Exeter site, and illustrates what Fowler termed 'a remarkable coincidence'.[2] What the Roman coin showed was, according to Donaldson's interpretation, a circular building erected in the centre of an open court, to house the statue of the emperor; on either side are different porticos representing, as a 'convention', the forum or enclosing court.

The choice of Benjamin Wyon as designer for the Exeter medal appears also to follow on from T. L. Donaldson's activity at the newly founded

1. *Arch. Mag.* iv, London, 1837, 312.

2. Donaldson describes and interprets the coin in *Architectura Numismatica*, 267–69. His idealised drawing omits the inscription and amends the building. The coin is discussed, and more accurately illustrated, by W. T. P. Shortt in *Roman and Other Antiquities of Exeter*, 1840, 47, pl. 111, No. 33.

No. 118a

Plate 72 in *Architectura Numismatica*

Institute, for in 1836 Wyon had completed the commission for the IBA's first medal (in bronze and silver) to Donaldson's own design. As well as Wyon's signature, the medal is also signed T.L.D. DIR(exit) and bears the motto which he had invented: FOR THE USE OF CITIZENS, FOR THE BEAUTY OF TOWNS. The temple front is modelled on a fifth-century BC type (e.g. Temple of Zeus at Olympia) but has been amended by Donaldson to symbolise architecture both in the tympanum and with the crowning statues (see No. 24a).

This carefully recorded account of the Exeter medal represents a first important category of reason why medals portraying buildings might be struck, i.e.: *Recording stages in the life of the building fabric.* Certainly in the case of the Exeter market Fowler was correct in his estimate that a medal showing the newly completed building would act as a permanent record; the market was destroyed by fire in 1942 and the medal now provides a true elevation not published elsewhere. The medal also represented the completion of a new and particularly nineteenth-century building type, and in the case of Exeter one that was put up by the city as part of several urgent 'improvements' following a bad outbreak of cholera. The medal therefore can also be seen to record the completion stage in terms of planning achievement and aspirations, as well as civic pride; and for most nineteenth-century architectural medals the same complexity of motive may well be discovered.

A very common reason for a medal was to mark the laying of a foundation stone. Here there is the problem for the medallist that he must hope to portray the building as it will be completed. In this respect many works of architecture shown on medals are deficient as records of 'completion', for the designer may well have wished to make alterations during the construction stages (e.g. the competition design approved for the Houses of Parliament when compared to Barry's finally realised solution). However as records of interim stages in the design process such medals may now be of considerable value to the architectural historian and provide a useful source for illustrations. An example of this can be seen in the medal, signed by T. Webb, marking the foundation stone ceremony for Christ Church, Colmore Row, Birmingham, in 1805 (No. 65a). The obverse is a well-executed portrait of George III—for which the medal is nowadays best known—and this gives the impression that he attended the ceremony. Perhaps he was expected at one stage, as indicated by the *Gentleman's Magazine* of that year, but it was the Earl of Dartmouth who laid the stone and '. . . the occasion was one of much rejoicing, and as a permanent record of the event a medal was struck . . .'.[1] The reverse shows a very poorly delineated view of the church, designed by the Birmingham Surveyor Charles Norton; when finally completed in 1814 the medallist's impression had been overtaken by events, for the cupola was replaced by a tall spire.

During the life of the building fabric there may be occasions when it is restored, upgraded, or adapted. A record of this is provided by Stothard's medal of Windsor Castle of 1828.[2] When George IV decided to take up residence at Windsor in 1823 he found the buildings dilapidated and inconvenient; as a result, several architects were asked to submit designs and finally Jeffry Wyatt (one of a prolific architectural family) was selected on the basis of his proposals. From then until his death in 1840 his principal work was at Windsor, and the design of today is essentially as he converted and rebuilt it. The medal shows the emphatic 'gothicising' which Wyatville[3] applied, the creation of a new entrance by duplicating a single existing tower, and the extra height with battlements given to the Keep and buildings of the Upper Ward. The medal was struck to mark the completion of the first stage in 1828—the creation of new apartments for the King and his official move to Windsor. The obverse has a good portrait

1. *GM*, 1805, August, p. 766, October, p. 915.

2. An earlier eighteenth-century example had been J. Kirk's medal showing Alnwick Castle restored in 1766.

3. He was allowed to change his name by Royal Warrant to distinguish himself from other architects in the family.

of George IV, and for this rebuilding he represents client and patron, as well as monarch.

There is of course one final stage in the history of a building fabric that also receives medallic note—that of its destruction or dismantling. Destruction by fire is noted on several medals, for example that commemorating the 'old' Royal Exchange burnt down in 1838, but less common is the building shown to commemorate its purposeful dismantling. The best-known example of this is the large uniface lead medal of 1878 which showed Temple Bar, removed that year to allow for the widening of the Strand; it was struck from the lead taken from the roof. By contrast, a much more obscure example of dismantling commemorated showed St Michael's Church, Bath, built 1742 and taken down in 1835 in order to allow for a fashionable gothic replacement by the then City Architect G. Manners. A companion medal showing the proposed replacement church was also struck in the same year; both were early architectural medal designs by J. Davis of Birmingham.

A second category of reasons for striking architectural medals can comprise those: *Marking an event related to, or made to relate to, the use of the building.* A visit by a monarch, or a member of the royal family, was a common theme. A fine medal by William Wyon was commissioned by the City of London to mark the visit of the young Queen Victoria to the Guildhall in 1837. This shows the main entrance façade to the Guildhall, as rebuilt by the City Architect George Dance in 1789 (see p. 18). Later in Queen Victoria's reign her two Jubilees of 1887 and 1897 were the occasion of a variety of medals showing buildings. Some, such as that showing the sixteenth-century City of London church of St Giles, Cripplegate, were a loyal gesture from the parish. Other medal patrons, e.g. the congregation of Tintwistle Church, Cheshire, built 1837, took the occasion to note their own jubilee as well, or to record a new building that conveniently coincided with a Jubilee year.

A different category of event was fund raising. A view of Birmingham General Hospital (built in the 1780s) appears on medals of the 1820s to mark the Triennial Music Festival. These music festivals raised money to support free beds in the Hospital and to help with a programme of building extension; at the same time they reflected a growing interest in the arts from the rapidly developing town of Birmingham. Initially the only place for these concerts was at the Royal Hotel assembly room—already in the 1820s far too small. As a result there was considerable pressure to provide a large auditorium incorporated into a Town Hall.

PLATE 1

No. 108b
BIRMINGHAM TOWN HALL
Architects: Hansom & Welch

The result was the first major example of the many nineteenth-century Town Hall buildings that were to become a recurrent theme in the century's architecture and which (like Birmingham) had as their main reason the provision of an auditorium to serve an expanding urban population. The opening in 1834 of the Birmingham Town Hall (a competition design by the then unknown architectural partnership of Hansom & Welch) was marked by a grand music festival, and the striking of a large number of medals which, between them, showed interior and exterior views and recorded the principal dimensions (Plate 1). Later in the century medals were to be produced for the opening of other important civic buildings at Liverpool (architect H. Elmes), Leeds (architect C. Brodrick), and Manchester (architect A. Waterhouse).

Other occasions or events which might provide a reason for an architectural medal included political or educational meetings, anniversaries, e.g. celebrations of foundation, thanksgiving services. At Leeds the medal which had been struck to mark the visit of Queen Victoria, for the opening of the Town Hall in 1858, was to be reused eight years later with a different obverse to record the reform rally held by John Bright (see No. 175b). For schools, the anniversary of an establishment provided a suitable theme for the medallist; of many examples one of the finest, and most original, appeared late in the nineteenth century to commemorate the five hundredth year of Winchester College (No. 27a). Several medals relate to services in St Paul's Cathedral and its unique and symbolic role in the nation's life; early in the 1800s it appears on medals commemorating services held in connection with the Peace of Amiens, and for a return to health of George III. The finest example of this type was however to be the large bronze by J. S. and A. B. Wyon produced to mark the thanksgiving service for the recovery of the Prince of Wales in 1882 (No. 39k); this shows the Cathedral interior with the assembled congregation.

One other general category suggests reasons why architectural subjects were to appear on medals: *To celebrate the form of a building for its associations.* Medals were produced by schools, hospitals, and institutions to be used as prizes or for an award. Here a medal originally produced for a specific occasion might be reused with modifications, e.g. that showing the Bank of England and a portrait of Sir John Soane, which was later used as a RIBA prize. Alternatively, the medal would provide the opportunity to note the date of foundation; for instance that showing Charing Cross hospital notes the 1818 foundation date, shows the existing 1830s building and was apparently provided for award in the 1840s.

PLATE 2

No. 165f
GREAT EXHIBITION BUILDING, 1851
Designer: Sir Joseph Paxton

Those medals produced for private schools often show an earlier, existing, building taken over for the school, together with the foundation date of the school as an institution.

The sudden expansion of towns and cities during the Victorian age, the ease of travel brought about by the railways, and the novelty and variety of new building types, meant that for many people the medal could also provide a memento of a memorable visit or occasion. The thirty-three architectural medals showing the structure for the Great Exhibition of 1851 in Hyde Park (the 'Crystal Palace') represent the greatest variety and number for any one nineteenth-century building (Plate 2). The majority were produced on white metal to act as mementos for the enormous crowds, many of whom had never visited London before, let alone set eyes on such a range of exhibits. The rebuilt, and much enlarged, Crystal Palace at Sydenham, and the 1862 Exhibition building at South Kensington, also prompted many similar medals to be produced to commemorate a visit. Publishers appear to have been quick to realise what would prove a popular subject, and to have found it profitable to meet the demand. Ironically the use of the cheaper white metal for such strikings, the longer runs, and the apparently ephemeral quality of such medals, has often meant their preservation due to the very fact that they have not been re-sold or circulated.

Although medallets and checks directly advertising firms and their products are not included in this catalogue, certain medals which portray buildings did so with the motive of encouraging the medallic art or, more prosaically, encouraging medallic trade. An unusual bronze medal of *c.* 1823 combines both these elements in showing Charles Jones's Repository of the Arts (or Pantechnatheca) built in central Birmingham. The building (No. 76), with its interior arcade, seems to have functioned not only for the retail sale of works of art and medals, but also as a form of 'design centre' where buyers from abroad could see collected together many of the local Birmingham products, including the products of the many local medallists. At a very different level from this example, it was with the aim of reviving interest in the medallists' art, and to encourage British die-engravers, that the Art Union planned its medallic series in 1842, and commissioned William Wyon both to undertake the inaugural medal and to act as consultant. Ultimately this series was to include six items showing famous architects and their works.

A common thread running through these three main categories of medal (i.e. those recording building stages, those marking events, and

No. 34a
BANQUETING HOUSE, WHITEHALL
Architect: Inigo Jones

those celebrating form for its associations) is that in some cases medals also belong to sequences or series; for example, medals illustrating buildings of a particular type, such as the group showing new Commissioners' churches in the Midlands area during the 1820s. Alternatively a series may show one building where similar events take place, e.g. the series for the Cambridge publisher J. Peters, marking the installation of University of Cambridge Chancellors. These show portrait busts and on the reverse alternatives of exterior, or interior, of James Gibbs's Senate House.

In the case of the Art-Union Series (which produced thirty medals between 1846 and 1887) the aim was to produce a 'medallic History of British Art'; those medals which depict an architect have, on each reverse, one of his best-known buildings in recognition of his achievement as a designer (Plates 3, 4). Perhaps the most dramatic example in the series is the high relief portrait of Sir John Vanbrugh with, reverse, the entrance front of the centre block of Blenheim Palace; the medal is one of Benjamin Wyon's finest, and the modelling of the building elevation is of superb quality (Plate 5).

The equally well-known sequence of medals issued by the City of London during the nineteenth century marked historic events in the City's life. The first of these was for the opening of London Bridge, and the next to provide a building subject was the fourth in the sequence, for Queen Victoria's visit to the Guildhall (Plate 6).[1] One notable medal in the series was that to mark the opening of the new Coal Exchange by Prince Albert in 1849; not only is this another outstanding medal by Benjamin Wyon, but the building, designed by the City Architect J. B. Bunning, has now come to be recognised as one of the major architectural monuments of the Early Victorian Era. As with so many fine nineteenth-century subjects the medal now depicts a Victorian building demolished for redevelopment—albeit in this case amidst considerable protest.

1. By 1902 the series totalled twenty-nine items. A list of architectural subjects is given on p. 215.

PLATE 4

No. 52a
SOMERSET HOUSE, STRAND
Architect: Sir William Chambers

No. 42a
BLENHEIM PALACE
Architect: Sir John Vanbrugh

No. 53b
LONDON, GUILDHALL
S. ENTRANCE FAÇADE
Architect: George Dance

## 'VIEW' OF ARCHITECTURE PROVIDED BY THE MEDAL

Some of the categories of building types have been outlined, as well as likely reasons for commissioning of medals. But what do these medals provide as a particular 'view' of the architecture of the nineteenth century, and what sort of architectural information do they contain?

Apart from the actual illustration of the building, and the internal evidence which this may provide, the most useful supporting material will be provided by the inscription—particularly as a record of dates and building history for local buildings. A typical example is shown in the medal of the Argyle Chapel, Bath, where the inscription gives ERECTED 1789, FIRST ENLARGEMENT 1804, SECOND ENLARGEMENT 1821 (i.e. the elevation shown, by the architect H. E. Goodridge) while the obverse portrait indicates the medal as of 1841, and therefore prior to further alterations in the 1850s. Alternatively, the medal may provide a profusion of technical detail—for instance in the case of the 1851 Exhibition building in Hyde Park, where one inscription gives LENGTH 1848 F, WIDTH 456 F, HEIGHT 64 F, EXHIBITION SURFACE 21 ACRES, CONTRACT FOR USE £79,800 IF RETAINED £150,000 DESIGNED BY JOS. PAXTON Esq FRS, while another notes the 2,244 IRON GIRDERS, 3,300 COLUMNS, 202 MILES OF SASH BAR used in this first large-scale prefabricated structure. For social conditions, reference has already been made to the efforts to improve public health and sanitation at Exeter following a cholera outbreak; the ravages of cholera in early nineteenth-century England, together with the need for new welfare building types, are attested to on a medal showing the Bilston Cholera Orphan School: IN THE YEAR 1832 POPULATION OF BILSTON 14,492/PERSONS ATTACKED BY CHOLERA 3568/PERSONS WHO PERISHED BY CHOLERA 742/THE FIRST CASE AUGUST 3 THE LAST DEATH SEP. 18. Elsewhere background events such as these, the personalities involved in the organisation and funding of the building, and the responsible designers, are all set out at some length and are often supplemented by portraits of founders and patrons.

At a different level, nineteenth-century architectural medals provide a useful mirror to that preoccupation with styles which was an important part of the polemic of the first half of the century (and which has been mentioned earlier in relation to *Architectura Numismatica*). For instance, medals of the 1820s illustrate such buildings as the Freemasons' Hall, Bath, and the 'adopted' design for the University of London, both in a correct classical style by William Wilkins, the dedicated protagonist of

PLATE 7

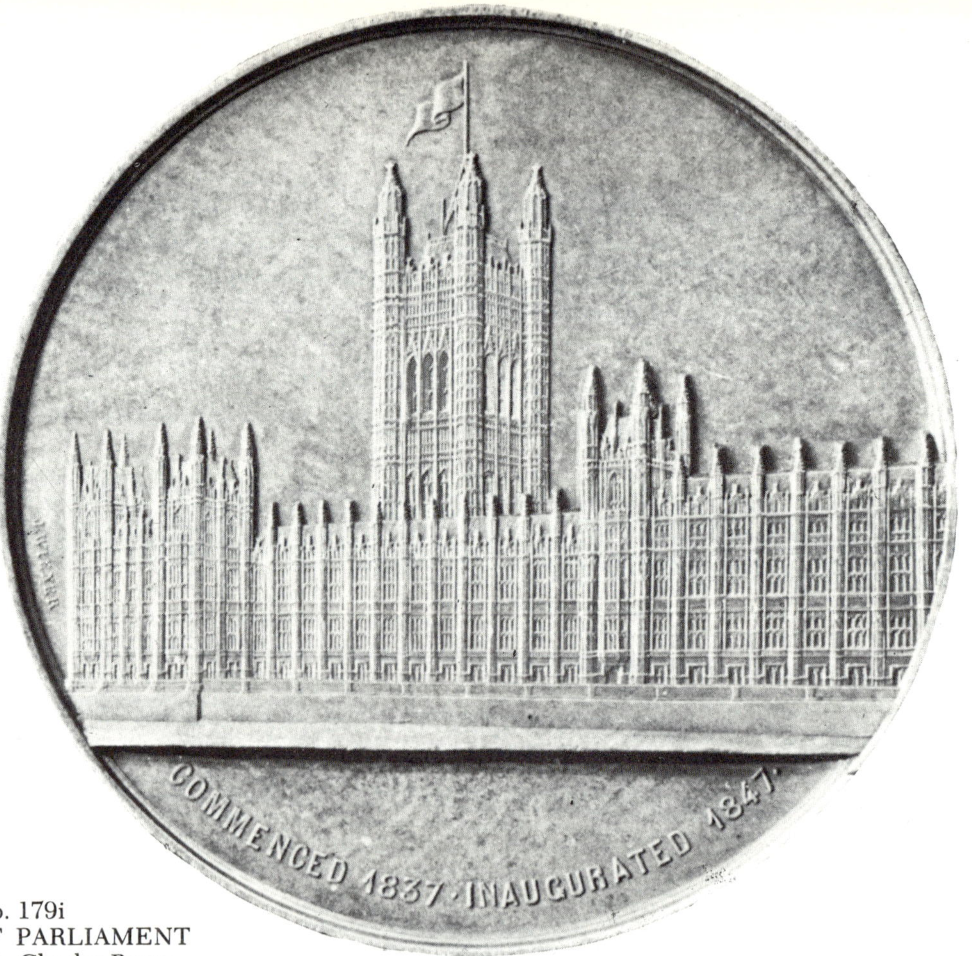


No. 179i
HOUSES OF PARLIAMENT
Architect: Sir Charles Barry
with A. W. N. Pugin

the Greek revival. By contrast the same decade is also able to show Nash's Royal Pavilion at Brighton (in a style contemporaries called 'Indian gothic') or the 'Perpendicular' style so widely used for the Commissioners' churches, e.g. by the architects Francis Goodwin or Thomas Rickman (author of the treatise which first established the nomenclature of gothic architecture). The 1830s provide one of the great neo-classical monuments, the Euston Arch by Philip Hardwick, as well as the Gothic revival church at Brighton and King Edward VI school at Birmingham, both by Charles Barry. In the latter case Barry was assisted by A. W. N. Pugin, in whom the Gothic cause had found its great prophet. The ideas inherent in such writings as his *Contrasts* (and initially put into practice at Oscott Chapel, see medal No. 124a) were to convert to Pugin's 'true principles' of Gothic one of the century's most famous and prolific architects—Sir Gilbert Scott. The church of St Giles, Camberwell, by Scott, is shown on a medal of 1844 and serves as a reminder of the coming variety of Victorian gothic designs that medallists would be required to illustrate. Buildings as diverse as Manchester Town Hall, Truro Cathedral, or Tower Bridge were all to be depicted; perhaps the finest example of an 'exuberant' gothic design shown on a medal being that by Joseph Moore to mark the opening of the Birmingham & Midland Institute extension in 1881 (see No. 200a).

Quite a different viewpoint on the century's architecture comes via those buildings that proved the most 'popular' as medal subjects (not however that such popularity necessarily reflected a great work of architecture). An early example was Birmingham Town Hall, and this was followed soon after by the King Edward VI Grammar School, Birmingham (1833–37). The latter design was the first large gothic revival building in the town centre and represented a considerable innovation for its time; the medals all depict the New Street elevation with the stepped buttresses, 'perpendicular' windows, and oriels to the end bays. The year before its completion the school's architect, Charles Barry (again with assistance from Pugin), had won the competition for the new Houses of Parliament—ultimately one of the century's masterpieces (Plate 7). At the opening of the House of Lords in 1847 the building was then only partly complete, but a large number of medals were struck with the views conveniently based on Barry's final competition drawings of 1836; these show clearly how this original design had been related to the elevational treatment of the Birmingham School.

Another 'popular' subject was the Royal Exchange in London. In 1838, the seventeenth-century building on Cornhill (designed soon after the

PLATE 8

No. 39h
ST PAUL'S CATHEDRAL
Architect: Sir Christopher Wren

Fire of London by Edward Jarman) was burnt down, and a first group of medals were issued to record its demise. Following one of the many abortive architectural competitions that were so common in the nineteenth century, a design by William Tite was selected; further medals were then provided showing the portico of the new Exchange, both as proposed when Prince Albert laid the foundation stone in 1842, and also as completed for the opening by Queen Victoria in 1844.

The other popular architectural subjects were the structures housing the 1851 and 1862 London exhibitions and the enlarged 'Crystal Palace' rebuilt at Sydenham as part of a permanent entertainment complex. For the 1851 building especially, the medals describe in detail the unprecedented construction, and pay note to the designer, engineer, and contractor, as well as the role played by Prince Albert in realising a grand concept.

The designers whose buildings are represented on these most 'popular' medals were the little known Hansom & Welch; Charles Barry assisted by A. W. N. Pugin; the businessman/architect William Tite; the engineer/designers Joseph Paxton and Francis Fowke. If one adds to these all those buildings and their designers listed in Sections 2 and 4 it will be seen that the medallic profile of nineteenth-century architecture is, not surprisingly, an extremely uneven one with many omissions. For instance, an important work in a major city, St George's Hall, Liverpool (by H. L. Elmes, completed by C. R. Cockerell), is represented by a remarkably insignificant medal with the building only glimpsed in the background to the allegory. No medallic record appears to exist of such key nineteenth-century works as the British Museum (architect Sir Robert Smirke) or the Law Courts (architect G. E. Street), nor of buildings by such prominent names as W. Burges, W. Butterfield, E. W. Godwin, or A. Salvin. On the other hand the same lists provided by the medallic material offer a less traditional view and one that presents many little known buildings only now being properly described and assessed in the architectural history of the nineteenth century. The designers of such works shown on medals include J. B. Bunning, J. H. Chamberlain, R. D. Chantrell, F. Fowke, C. Fowler, F. Goodwin, Sir Horace Jones, T. Rickman, E. R. Robson, C. H. Townsend, J. W. Wild, and T. H. Wyatt.

As well as this picture of architects and designers built up from the illustrations of their buildings, one other viewpoint on them was able to be provided by the medallist: the personal portrait medal. Although few in number, the most important group belong to the sequence commissioned by the Art Union (see p. 212). Typical of these can be instanced the profile portrait head—the most commonly successful format—of Sir Christopher Wren engraved by W. Wilson (Plate 8); this appears to be after a contemporary marble bust by Edward Pierce made when Wren was aged forty, i.e. soon after his knighthood in 1673, and the year of his first proposal for St. Paul's. Another memorial medal, but in this case of a nineteenth-century designer, was the portrait head of Captain Francis Fowke RE (d. 1865—the designer of the 1862 Exhibition building, and also of the initial scheme for the Albert Hall); this was sculpted by G. Morgan for use as a prize medal of the Corps of Royal Engineers (see p. 192).

Although personal tributes to designers during their lifetime were rare—the medal of Professor T. L. Donaldson is an example (see p. 190)—one occasion in the nineteenth-century was outstanding. This was the formal presentation in March 1835 of a specially designed gold medal to Sir John Soane, then aged eighty-one and the senior architect in the profession. The year before, he had finally retired from his appointment as architect to the Bank of England. This building, which was Soane's great work, is shown in part on the medal reverse (Frontispiece) by the so-called 'Tivoli corner' of the screen wall which surrounded the whole site; the building with its famous domed interiors was almost totally destroyed by the reconstruction of the 1930s, an event described by Pevsner as 'the worst individual loss suffered by London architecture in the first half of the twentieth century'. The medal obverse shows the portrait of Sir John Soane by W. Wyon. The presentation, on behalf of his fellow architects, was made to Soane at his home in Lincoln's Inn Fields, now Sir John Soane's Museum.

But these were of course prominent architects, and by contrast the great mass of architectural medals portray buildings for which perhaps only half will now have an identifiable architect. In some cases the medal itself, and its inscription, may prove one helpful link in any attribution—particularly where obscure local firms are involved.

## MEDALLIC DESIGN

Attention has so far been focused on the likely context for commissioning architectural medals, and on the view of architecture in the nineteenth century created by the buildings—the subject matter—which they portray. But what of the manner in which builders have been portrayed, i.e. the methods and the sources that have been employed by the medallist.

ST. PAUL'S CATHEDRAL
Medal by G. D. Gaab of Augsburg

The representation of a building usually comprises an exterior or an interior, a part or a detail, or, in some Continental examples, a plan. For the exterior, one approach is to use the artist's view, the perspective sketch—but that this can go very wrong is shown in the 1807 view of St Paul's Cathedral (No. 39b; p. 63); and it is undoubtedly difficult even in more skilled hands, such as Wiener's 1849 exterior of St Paul's (No. 39i; p. 64) which displays an awkwardness, both in the perspective of the North Transept and in the junction between dome, drum, and crossing. It is even worth questioning whether for the truly architectural (as opposed to the topographical) medal an exterior 'view' can ever hope to be entirely successful unless some degree of selection or 'conventionalism' is used.[1]

For the nineteenth-century architectural medal the most obvious convention to use was to present a true elevation in high relief, i.e. an elevation as designed and drawn by the architect on his board, and in effect as he would shadow it in to gain the final modelled effect of that part of the building. It was this approach to St Paul's that had been used by Gaab for his fine eighteenth-century medal. It was also the approach used by B. Wyon for the west elevation of St Paul's shown on the reverse of the Art Union medal (No. 39h) in 1849—considered by the *Art Journal* at the time as 'one of the most successful medallic representations of a building ever executed' (Plate 8).[2] In one sense an ideal viewpoint, but also

1. For the Roman coin or medal depicting a temple front a usual 'conventionalism' was to open out the central pair of columns to allow the figure of the deity within to be portrayed.

2. *Art Journal*, 1850, 191.

PLATE 9

No. 13d
YORK MINSTER

allowing the medallist the extra option for a selected part of the building only to be shown. It was this format which was to be used by both William and Benjamin Wyon for their finest architectural medals.

If we now turn to the portrayal of the interior, there was one nineteenth-century medallist, Jacques Wiener, who constantly achieved outstanding effects of accurate detail and perspective—especially in relation to cathedral interiors. His interior of St Paul's cathedral (No. 39i) demonstrates a precision and delicacy of touch never quite equalled by the interiors of the earlier Davis series of cathedrals, while his York Minster interior (1854)—a typical gothic Wiener interior—shows the degree to which such medallic illustrations allow of enlargement without noticeable distortion (Plate 9).

Other than cathedral and church subjects, an interior was only occasionally attempted. To mark the opening in 1847 of the House of Lords, medals showed the interior (e.g. No. 179c)—a view which acts as a tribute both to one of Pugin's most successful and mature decorative schemes and to his collaboration with Barry. The opening of two other notable nineteenth-century interiors, the London Coal Exchange (1849, Plate 10) and the new Guildhall Council Chamber (1884, Plate 11), were both marked with particularly fine, large, bronze medals in the City of London series. In these cases the architectural view is formed by a half section through the centralised space, with the perspective developed about a centre point within the frame; details of mural decoration, carved wood panelling, and floor inlay are all carefully delineated.

Mention has already been made of the way in which Barry's 1836 competition design for the Houses of Parliament was still used ten years later to provide an illustration for medallists commemorating an event in the partly completed building. This question of source illustrations used by the designers of architectural medals presents an interesting area of study in relation to the architects' drawings for the buildings concerned. For instance, the 1838 silver medal of Oscott College, Birmingham, shows on the reverse the interior of the new chapel as fitted out by Pugin in a 'correct' gothic manner (Plate 12); the medallic illustration apparently copies, line for line, Pugin's own etching of the scene based on his design proposals for the client.[1]

There are of course many examples of medals showing the design as initially proposed on the architect's drawing, although the building as

1. Etching of 1837, illustrated in P. Stanton, *Pugin*, 1971, 34.

PLATE 10

No. 161c
LONDON, THE COAL EXCHANGE
Architect: J. B. Bunning

No. 206a
LONDON
GUILDHALL COUNCIL CHAMBER
Architect: Sir Horace Jones

PLATE 12

No. 124a
BIRMINGHAM, ST MARY'S COLLEGE,
NEW OSCOTT
Architect: Joseph Potter
Chapel interior: A. W. N. Pugin

finally completed was to be considerably revised, e.g. Christ Church, Birmingham. The approved design by William Wilkins for the University of London, shown on the 1826 medal, indicates subsidiary domes at the ends of the main block—while a pencil sketch by Wilkins of about the same date shows a different solution (see p. 94). So the medal may provide on some occasions both design variations that help in its own dating, together with further information on interim design stages. Medal views may also be based on contemporary drawing or book illustrations and can now, in the twentieth century, provide a reference to alterations in detail. An example of this is shown by Wiener's interior view of Winchester Cathedral nave, usually dated about 1856 (No. 11b). The view shows a most interesting classical choir screen apparently taken down over thirty years before, in 1820, but clearly shown on an engraving in J. Britton's *Cathedral Antiquities* of 1818 from a very similar viewpoint; so Wiener's delineation of cathedrals could apparently be based on books such as the one quoted. (Today the screen is of considerable interest as an extant, though dismantled, work of Inigo Jones of *c.* 1636–40; see p. 49.)

The production of nineteenth-century medals involved the same process as that for the manufacturing of coins, i.e. stamping out or 'striking'. For this steel dies were engraved, and then hardened, to provide for the obverse and for the reverse; the resultant striking under great pressure enabled that fine detail to be obtained which is the essential ingredient of the more precise architectural medals. (The older, simpler, process of casting is demonstrated by No. 63a, a cast silver medal of 1810 showing the proposed Huntington chapel.) The most sympathetic material for the struck medal is undoubtedly bronze and its colour, surface finish, and ability to take detail all meant its use for the best architectural pieces, e.g. those by the Art Union and the City of London—both series with issues of several hundreds per medal—or for individual items such as the 1838 medal of the Euston Arch by G. R. Collis. The Art-Union series also provided a limited number of each medal in the more expensive, but not necessarily more pleasing, alternative of silver; a variety of other presentation or prize medals are also noted in the catalogue as of silver or occasionally gold (e.g. that presented to Queen Victoria at the opening of Aston Hall, Birmingham; see p. 59), or issued with a gilt finish. However, the bulk of nineteenth-century architectural medals is provided by the cheaper alternative of white metal alloy which (if not damaged) can prove quite a satisfactory means of simple recording; it also provided a cheap alternative material to issue alongside a more expensive striking in bronze.

No. 146x
LONDON, ROYAL EXCHANGE
Architect: Sir William Tite

Often some of the century's finest and largest buildings—if at all commemorated by a medal—have only been the subject of a white metal striking as a popular souvenir, and nothing has been commissioned of the quality of a presentation bronze by one of the Wyon family, by Joseph Moore, or by Wiener. Other materials much less commonly employed were copper, brass and lead. Where the latter was used for the large struck uniface medal of Temple Bar (No. 37a), it was issued in a brass case with glass cover to prevent this essentially soft metal from accidental damage; for the crude Holborn Restaurant medal (No. 207a) the lead was 'bronzed' in imitation of the more expensive metal.

By the nineteenth century the technology of die engraving had been advanced to the point where steel dies were able to be cut mechanically using a 'Reducing Machine'.[1] This in principle meant that a larger model could be provided, for instance in plaster,[2] and the Reducing Machine could then be used to cut dies from this at the final reduced scale chosen for the medal.[3] The high sculptural relief obtained for fine quality Victorian medals such as W. Wyon's portrait of Thomas Gresham, with reverse the Royal Exchange (Plate 13), was achieved in this way. Although in the first half of the century such techniques were essentially the preserve of the die-engraver, the use of the Reducing Machine logically implied the production of a medal die from any sculpted material. With further technical improvements in the process, sculptors became increasingly interested and involved in this field of medallic design during the 1880s. Additionally new stylistic ideas on medal design, together with related experiments on the surface treatment of bronze, were being developed by a younger generation of continental artists such as J. C. Chaplain and L.-O. Roty. Two of the later architectural medals which demonstrate these influences on English artists, and show the typically softer modelling and less literal interpretation of building form, are those in the 1890s for Winchester College (No. 27a by George Frampton) and Tower Bridge (No. 225a by Frank Bowcher).

1. Matthew Boulton had such a machine in use at his Soho works, Birmingham. For a discussion of this, and the Reducing Machine at the Royal Mint, see J. G. Pollard, 'Matthew Boulton and the Reducing Machine in England', in *Num. Chron.* 1971, 311–17.

2. Or from a plaster cast of a portrait modelled in wax. Such portraits are discussed in E. J. Pyke, *A Biographical Dictionary of Wax Modellers*, Oxford, 1973.

3. With nineteenth-century machines much depended on the skill of the operator; the tracer and cutting tool each traverse backward and forward in parallel motion (across model or die), and so allow the cutting tool to reproduce every indentation and contour of the original model. Some hand finishing would then be required. See Pollard in *Num. Chron.*, op. cit.

The list of medallists and sculptors involved with the architectural subject area (Section 5) is dominated by two main themes: (*a*) The number of die-engravers employed or practising in and around the Birmingham area, especially during the first half of the century and (*b*) the importance of the Wyon family with their many appointments, and continuing employment, at the Royal Mint, London. Of those in the first group, from Birmingham, the most 'prolific' in relation to different building subjects portrayed were: Allen & Moore, succeeded by Joseph Moore of the partnership practising on his own, Joseph Davis, Thomas Halliday, and John Ottley. For the second group the important individuals were: William Wyon, his cousin Benjamin, and Joseph Shepherd and Alfred Benjamin (sons of Benjamin whose joint signature is on a later group of medals of the 1870s and 1880s).

The eminence of Birmingham as a centre for coin and medal production had been well established in the 1790s by the partnership of Matthew Boulton with James Watt, and the use of the latter's steam-powered coin presses for their Soho Mint at the Birmingham suburb of Handsworth. This manufactury was later to become the Soho Foundry, but nineteenth-century coining was also developed further, with Boulton-designed machinery, at Ralph Heaton's works ('The Mint', Birmingham, see p. 150). The preparation of dies for the mass production of coins and medals in such new mechanised works as Boulton's called for a force of highly skilled die-sinkers and medallists; as a result a centre of expertise developed around this Birmingham industry during the early nineteenth century, with many of the individual craftsmen and artists setting up on their own after initial experience under key figures like Boulton. The impact of this locally is clearly expressed in the large number of medals listed which refer to buildings of Birmingham and the surrounding Midlands area.

By contrast with this Birmingham 'school', and its many practitioners, the Wyons were to remain a small closely linked family dynasty whose members were consistently able to fill the top posts at the Royal Mint, London, by sheer force of their outstanding artistic ability. And it is on the basis of the Wyons' work (with many architectural examples related to the City of London and the patronage of the Art Union) that any criteria for artistic excellence must inevitably be set up when assessing the quality of architectural medals in the nineteenth century.

# BUILDINGS PORTRAYED 2

The buildings listed are all depicted on medals given in the detailed catalogue (see Section 3). The ordering of this index is as the catalogue, i.e. by *date order of completion of the buildings.* The exception to this is for any buildings prior to the seventeenth century; such buildings are arranged in three separate groups (*a*) Cathedrals (alphabetical), (*b*) Churches, (*c*) Other types of building. Each building entry is prefaced by its *key identification number.*

Each entry is followed by the *dates of the building's construction*; these are taken as from foundation stone laying to opening or consecration. Such information is in some instances clearly given on the medal inscription, alternatively dates are established from basic references such as Colvin's *Biographical Dictionary of English Architects*, or Pevsner's *Buildings of England* series.

Where buildings have been destroyed or demolished (D), undergone major alteration (A), or been restored or rebuilt (R), this is noted together with the relevant dates. These entries all refer to occurrences taking place after the date of the view on the medal. A total of 232 completed works are portrayed, of these 65 have been demolished, and a further 29 have undergone major rebuilding or alteration.

*Buildings prior to the seventeenth century*

(a) **Cathedrals** (in alphabetical order)

| | |
|---|---|
| 1. Canterbury Cathedral | *12th to 19th centuries* |
| 2. Chichester Cathedral | *12th century onwards* |
| 3. Durham Cathedral | *11th to 15th centuries* |
| 4. Ely Cathedral | *12th to 14th centuries* |
| 5. Gloucester Cathedral | *13th to 15th centuries* |

| | | | |
|---|---|---|---|
| 6. | Lichfield Cathedral | *13th to 14th centuries (restored 1788–95)* | |
| 7. | Lincoln Cathedral | *12th to 15th centuries* | |
| 8. | London, Westminster Abbey | *13th to 18th centuries* | |
| 9. | Oxford Cathedral | *12th to 15th centuries* | |
| 10. | Salisbury Cathedral | *13th to 14th centuries* | |
| 11. | Winchester Cathedral | *11th to 15th centuries* | |
| 12. | Worcester Cathedral | *11th to 14th centuries* | |
| 13. | York Minster | *13th to 15th centuries* | |

**(b) Churches**

| | | | |
|---|---|---|---|
| 14. | Nantwich, Cheshire, St Mary's Church | *14th century* | |
| 15. | Shepton Mallet, Somerset, St Peter and St Paul | *to 14th century* | |
| 16. | Nether Alderley, Cheshire, St Mary's Church | *late 14th century* | A 1878 |
| 17. | Bridport, Dorset, St Mary's Church | *14th/15th century* | |
| 18. | Coventry, West Midlands, St Michael's Church | *14th/15th century* | D 1940 |
| 19. | Coventry, West Midlands, St John's Church | *15th century* | |
| 20. | Newcastle upon Tyne, St Nicholas's Church | *15th century* | |
| 21. | Sherborne, Dorset, Abbey Church | *to end 15th century* | |
| 22. | London, St Giles Church, Cripplegate | *c. 1545–50* | R 1960s |
| 23. | Preston, Lancs., St John's Church | *16th century* | D 1853 |

**(c) Other buildings**

| | | | |
|---|---|---|---|
| 24. | Temple (Allegorical) | *as fifth century* BC | |
| 25. | Dover Castle, Kent | *1168 to 13th century* | |
| 26. | Bodiam Castle, East Sussex | *1385 on* | R 1919 |
| 27. | Winchester College, Hants., Chapel | *c. 1387–94* | |
| 28. | Stratford-upon-Avon, Warwicks, Shakespeare's House | *?16th century on* | R 1858 |
| 29. | Cambridge, Christ's College Gateway | *c. 1505 on* | |
| 30. | Evesham, Heref. and Worcs., Bell Tower | *1513 on* | |
| 31. | Eton College, Berks., School Yard | *15th century and c. 1520* | |
| 32. | Rothwell, Northants, Market House | *1578* | |
| 33. | Stonyhurst College, Lancs., Gatehouse | *1592–c. 1595* | |

## *Buildings of the seventeenth century*

| | | | |
|---|---|---|---|
| 34. | London, Banqueting House, Whitehall | *1619–22* | |
| 35. | Birmingham, West Midlands, Aston Hall | *c. 1635* | |
| 36. | London, Royal Exchange, Cornhill | *1667–71* | D 1838 |
| 37. | London, Temple Bar, Strand | *1672* | D 1878 |
| 38. | Bromsgrove, Heref. and Worcs., Edward VI's Grammar School | *c.1695* | A 1859 |

## *Buildings of the eighteenth century*

| | | |
|---|---|---|
| 39. London, St Paul's Cathedral | *1675–1710* | |
| 40. Kettering, Northants, Baptist Mission House | *?c. 1710* | |
| 41. Birmingham, St Philip's Church, Colmore Row | *1710–15* | |
| 42. Woodstock, Oxon., Blenheim Palace | *1705–20* | |
| 43. London, Lambeth, Stockwell Park School | *? before 1730* | D 1882 |
| 44. Sedgley Park School, West Midlands | *? before 1730* | |
| 45. Cambridge, Cambs., Senate House | *1722–30* | |
| 46. Bath, Avon, St Michael's (old) Church | *1742* | D 1835 |
| 47. Bath, Avon, Prior Park, Combe Down | *1735–c. 1750* | |
| 48. Warrington, Cheshire, Bank Hall | *c. 1750* | |
| 49. London, The London Hospital, Whitechapel Road | *1752–57* | A 1890 |
| 50. Ackworth, West Yorks., Ackworth School | *1758 on* | |
| 51. Birmingham, St John's Church, Deritend | *1735 and 1762* | D 1961 |
| 52. London, Somerset House, Strand | *1776–86* | |
| 53. London, Guildhall, South entrance façade | *1788–89* | R 1909 |
| 54. Birmingham, General Hospital, Sumner Lane | *1766–90* | D *c.* 1897 |
| 55. Old Windsor, Berks., Beaumont Lodge | *1790* | |
| 56. Chelmsford, Essex, Shire Hall | *1789–91* | |
| 57. Birmingham, Blue Coat School | *1792–94* | D 1935 |
| 58. Birmingham, Old Meeting House | *1795* | D 1881 |

## *Buildings of the nineteenth century*

| | | |
|---|---|---|
| 59. London, Charterhouse School, Finsbury | *1802–3* | D 1872 |
| 60. Old Hall Green, Herts., St Edmund's College | *1795 to 1805* | |
| 61. Birmingham, Baptist Meeting House, Cannon Street | *1806* | D 1879 |
| 62. Stockport, Greater Manchester, Sunday School | *1805–6* | |
| 63. London, Providence Chapel, Gray's Inn Lane | *1810* | D |
| 64. London, Hackney Parochial Schools | *1811* | |
| 65. Birmingham, Christ Church, Colmore Row | *1805–14* | D 1899 |
| 66. Macclesfield, Cheshire, Sunday School | *1813–14* | |
| 67. London, Waterloo Bridge, | *1811–17* | D 1938 |
| 68. Stockport, Greater Manchester, St Mary's Church | *1813–17* | |
| 69. Dudley, West Midlands, St Thomas' Church | *1816–18* | |
| 70. Bath, Avon, Freemasons Hall, York Street | *1817–19* | |
| 71. Bath, Avon, Bathwick Hill House | *c. 1820* | |
| 72. Birmingham, Carrs Lane Chapel | *1819–20* | A 1876 |
| 73. London, Harrow School, 'Old Schools' building | *1819–20* | |
| 74. Bath, Avon, Argyle Chapel, Bathwick | *1821* | A 1852 |
| 75. Brighton, East Sussex, The Royal Pavilion | *1815–21* | |
| 76. Birmingham, 'Pantechnatheca', New Street | *c. 1823* | D |
| 77. London, Hackney, London Orphan Asylum | *c. 1823* | |
| 78. Birmingham, Holy Trinity Church, Bordesley | *1820–23* | |
| 79. Brighton, East Sussex, Chain Pier | *1823* | D 1896 |

| | | | |
|---|---|---|---|
| 80. | Ashton-under-Lyne, Greater Manchester, St Peter's Church | *1821–24* | |
| 81. | Kidderminster, Heref. and Worcs., St George's Church | *1821–24* | R 1925 |
| 82. | Liverpool, Infirmary, Brownlow Street | *1822–24* | D 1887 |
| 83. | London, Southwark, St George's Church, Wells Way | *1822–24* | A 1893 |
| 84. | Nr Atherstone, Warwicks., Grendon Hall | *c. 1825* | D 1933 |
| 85. | Doncaster, South Yorks., New Betting Rooms | *1826* | |
| 86. | Southsea, Hants, St Paul's School | *1826* | D |
| 87. | London, Lambeth, British Orphan Asylum | *c. 1827–* | D |
| 88. | Birmingham, St Peter's Church, Dale End | *1825–27* | R 1837, D 1899 |
| 89. | Leicester, St George's Church | *1823–27* | R 1922 |
| 90. | London, St Peter's Church, Eaton Square | *1824–27* | |
| 91. | Brighton, East Sussex, St Peter's Church | *1824–28* | A 1900 |
| 92. | West Bromwich, West Midlands, Christ Church | *1821–28* | A 1884 |
| 93. | Birmingham, School of Medicine, Snow Hill | *1828–29* | D 1852 |
| 94. | Darwen, Lancs., Holy Trinity Church | *1827–29* | |
| 95. | Doncaster, South Yorks., Prospect House | *1829* | D 1936 |
| 96. | London, Christ's Hospital School, Great Hall | *1829* | D 1903 |
| 97. | London, University College, Gower Street | *1827–29* | |
| 98. | Stoke-on-Trent, Staffs., St Peter's Church | *1826–29* | |
| 99. | London, Pimlico Grammar School, Ebury Street | *1830* | A 19th century |
| 100. | Sheffield, South Yorks., St Mary's Church, Bramhall Lane | *1826–30* | R 1957 |
| 101. | Wolverhampton, West Midlands, St George's Church | *1828–30* | |
| 102. | London Bridge | *1825–31* | D 1970 |
| 103. | Leamington, Warwicks., Beech Lawn House | *1832* | D 1946 |
| 104. | Bilston, West Midlands, Cholera Orphan School | *1833* | D *c.* 1960 |
| 105. | Birmingham, St John's Church, Perry Bar | *1831–33* | A 1887 |
| 106. | London, Bank of England, Threadneedle Street | *1788–1833* | A 1924–39 |
| 107. | Swinton, Greater Manchester, St Peter's School | *1833* | D 1866 |
| 108. | Birmingham, Town Hall | *1832–34* | A 1835 on |
| 109. | London, Charing Cross Hospital, Strand | *1831–34* | A *c.* 1880 |
| 110. | Oldham, Greater Manchester, Blue Coat School | *1829–34* | |
| 111. | Manchester, Royal Institution, Mosley Street | *1824–35* | |
| 112. | Birmingham, Cemetery Chapel, Key Hill | *1835–36* | |
| 113. | Liverpool Railway Station, entrance screen | *1835–36* | D *c.* 1870 |
| 114. | Newark, Notts., Christ Church | *1836* | |
| 115. | Bath, Avon, St Michael's Church, Broad Street | *1835–37* | |
| 116. | Birmingham, King Edward VI Grammar School, New Street | *1833–37* | D 1936 |
| 117. | Dorking, Surrey, St Martin's Church | *1837* | D 1872 |
| 118. | Exeter, Devon, Lower Market | *1835–37* | D 1942 |
| 119. | Liverpool, Mechanics Institution, Mount Street | *1835–37* | |
| 120. | London, City of London School, Milk Street | *1835–37* | D *c.* 1890 |
| 121. | Tintwistle, Derbs., Christ Church | *1837* | |
| 122. | Walsall Wood, West Midlands, St John's Church | *1837* | A 1886 and 1895 |

| | | | |
|---|---|---|---|
| 123. | Birmingham, Bishop Ryder Memorial Church | *1837–38* | D 1960 |
| 124. | Birmingham, St Mary's College, New Oscott | *1835–38* | |
| 125. | London, Euston Station, the 'Euston Arch' | *1836–38* | D 1962 |
| 126. | London, Southwark, St Saviour's School | *c. 1838–39* | D *c.* 1950 |
| 127. | London, Wesleyan Centenary Hall, Bishopsgate | *1839–40* | D 1969 |
| 128. | Frome, Somerset, Sunday School Room | *1840* | |
| 129. | London, Philosophical Institution, Beaumont Square | *1840* | D 1937 |
| 130. | Sheffield, South Yorks., Wesley College | *1837–40* | |
| 131. | Windsor Castle, Berks., | *1824–40* | |
| 132. | Leeds, West Yorks., St Peter's Church | *1839–41* | |
| 133. | London, South Islington and Pentonville Schools | *1841* | |
| 134. | London, Christ Church, Streatham | *1840–41* | |
| 135. | Macclesfield, Cheshire, Christ Church School | *1841* | |
| 136. | Birmingham, St Philip's National School | *1842* | D 1880s |
| 137. | Dudley, West Midlands, St James' School | *1842* | |
| 138. | Gt Ayton, North Yorks., Ayton School | *c. 1817 and 1842 on* | |
| 139. | Birmingham, Hebrew National School, Hurst Street | *1843* | D *c.* 1856 |
| 140. | Cheltenham, Gloucs., Cheltenham Proprietary College | *1842–43* | |
| 141. | Liverpool, Collegiate Institution, Everton | *1840–43* | |
| 142. | London, Infant Orphan Asylum, Wanstead | *1841–43* | |
| 143. | London, The Nelson Monument, Trafalgar Square | *1840–43* | |
| 144. | Brown Edge, Staffs., St Anne's Church | *1844* | A 1854 |
| 145. | Gloucester, Gloucs., St James Parochial Schools | *1844* | |
| 146. | London, City, Royal Exchange, Cornhill | *1842–44* | |
| 147. | London, St Giles Church, Camberwell Church Street | *1842–44* | |
| 148. | Liverpool, Royal Infirmary Medical School, Dover Street | *1844–45* | D 1950s |
| 149. | Liverpool, St Mary's Church (Roman Catholic), Highfield Street | *1844–45* | D 1940s |
| 150. | London, Lincoln's Inn, New Hall and Library | *1843–45* | |
| 151. | Sheffield, South Yorks., Mount St Mary's College | *1842–45* | A 1859 and 1890 |
| 152. | Birmingham, St Andrew's Church, Bordesley | *1844–46* | R 1901 |
| 153. | London, Brompton Hospital, Fulham Road | *1844–46* | |
| 154. | Wilton, Wilts., St Mary and St Nicholas | *1843–46* | |
| 155. | Worsley, Greater Manchester, Worsley Hall | *1840–46* | D 20th century |
| 156. | Bootle, Merseyside, St Mary's Church | *1827 and 1847* | D 1940 |
| 157. | London, The Orphan Working School, Haverstock Hill | *c. 1847* | D *c.* 1947 |
| 158. | Birmingham, Church and Cemetery, Warstone Lane | *1847–48* | D 1954 |
| 159. | Liverpool, Sailors' Home, Canning Place | *1846–48* | D 1973 |
| 160. | London, Governesses Benevolent Institution, Kentish Town | *1848–49* | |
| 161. | London, The Coal Exchange, Lower Thames Street | *1847–49* | D 1962 |
| 162. | London, Southwark, Licensed Victuallers' Asylum 'The Ladies Wing' | *1849* | |
| 163. | Richmond, North Yorks., School | *1849* | |

| | | | |
|---|---|---|---|
| 164. | Menai Strait, Britannia Tubular Bridge | *1846–50* | A 1970s |
| 165. | London, Great Exhibition Building, Hyde Park | *1850–51* | D 1852 |
| 166. | London, Victoria Park Hospital, Bethnal Green | *1851 on* | |
| 167. | Birmingham, General Institution for the Blind | *1851–52* | |
| 168. | London, Twickenham, Police Orphanage, Wellesley-House | *1852–63* | D 1971 |
| 169. | Wolverhampton, West Midlands, Orphan Asylum | *1853* | |
| 170. | Liverpool, St George's Hall | *1842–54* | |
| 171. | London, 'The Crystal Palace', Sydenham | *1852–54* | D 1936 |
| 172. | Lancaster, Lancs., Royal Grammar School | *1851–55* | |
| 173. | Manchester, Art Treasures Exhibition building | *1856–57* | D |
| 174. | Derby, Derbs., St Michael's Church, Queen Street | *1858* | |
| 175. | Leeds, West Yorks., Town Hall | *1853–58* | |
| 176. | Walsall, West Midlands, St John's Church, Pleck Road | *1857–58* | D 1976 |
| 177. | Oxford, Oxon., University Gymnasium, Alfred Street | *1858–59* | |
| 178. | Birmingham, The Mint, Icknield Street | *c. 1860* | |
| 179. | London, The Houses of Parliament | *1840–60* | |
| 180. | London, Horticultural Society Buildings, Kensington | *1861* | D 1889 on |
| 181. | London, Merchant Seamen's Orphan Asylum, Wanstead | *1861* | |
| 182. | London, International Exhibition Building, Kensington | *1861–62* | D 1864 |
| 183. | Blackpool, Lancs., North Pier | *1862–63* | |
| 184. | Lancaster, Lancs., Ripley Hospital | *1856–64* | A 20th century |
| 185. | London, Guildhall, hall interior | *1864–65* | R 1940s |
| 186. | Bewdley, Heref. and Worcs., Wyre Hill Schools | *1868* | |
| 187. | Gretton Green, Gloucs., Christ Church | *1867–68* | |
| 188. | Chester, Cheshire, Town Hall | *1864–69* | |
| 189. | London, The Albert Hall, Kensington | *1867–71* | |
| 190. | Saltaire, West Yorks, The Institute | *1867–71* | |
| 191. | Tunbridge Wells, Kent, St John's Church | *1858 and 1871* | A 1896 |
| 192. | Godalming, Surrey, Charterhouse School | *1870–72* | |
| 193. | Manchester, St Thomas's Girls School, Ardwick | *1872* | |
| 194. | Winchester, Hants, Guildhall | *1871–73* | |
| 195. | Blackburn, Lancs., Library and Museum | *1872–74* | |
| 196. | London, Alexandra Palace, Wood Green | *1874–75* | A 20th century |
| 197. | Manchester, Town Hall | *1868–77* | |
| 198. | Derby, Derbs., Library and Museum | *1878–79* | |
| 199. | Birmingham, The Mason Science College | *1875–80* | D 1960s |
| 200. | Birmingham, Birmingham & Midland Institute extension | *1881* | D 1960s |
| 201. | Bradford, West Yorks., Technical College | *1880–82* | |
| 202. | London, City of London School for Boys, Victoria Embankment | *1881–82* | |
| 203. | Worcester, Heref. and Worcs., Exhibition Building | *1864 on and 1882* | |
| 204. | Huddersfield, West Yorks., Technical School and Mechanics Institution | *1881–83* | |

| | | | |
|---|---|---|---|
| 205. | Oldham, Lancs., Library and Museum | *1881–83* | |
| [19]. | Coventry, West Midlands, St John's Schools (ref. St John's Church of 15th century) | *1884* | D 1964 |
| 206. | London, Guildhall, New Council Chamber | *1883–84* | D 1940s |
| 207. | London, Holborn Restaurant | *1883–85* | D 1955 |
| 208. | London, The Albert Palace, Battersea Park | *1885* | D *c.* 1890 |
| 209. | Wolverhampton, West Midlands, Art Gallery | *1883–85* | |
| 210. | Burnley, Lancs., Burnley & District Hospital | *1884–86* | |
| 211. | Hindley, Greater Manchester, Library and Museum | *1887* | |
| 212. | London, New College, Finchley Road | *1887* | |
| 213. | London, 'The Peoples Palace', Mile End Road | *1885–87* | |
| 214. | London, National Liberal Club, Whitehall Place | *1884–87* | |
| 215. | Manchester, Jubilee Exhibition Buildings | *1886–87* | D |
| 216. | Truro, Cornwall, Truro Cathedral | *1880–87* | compl. 1910 |
| 217. | Harrogate, North Yorks., Royal Bath Hospital | *1888–89* | |
| 218. | Birmingham, Victoria Law Courts | *1887–91* | |
| 219. | Kettering, Northants, School | *1892* | |
| 220. | Bristol, Avon, Exhibition Building | *1893* | D 1894 |
| 221. | London, Imperial Institute, Kensington | *1887–93* | D 1960s |
| 222. | Blackpool, Lancs., The Tower | *1891–94* | |
| 223. | Colne, Lancs., Town Hall | *1894* | |
| 224. | London, Bishopsgate Institute | *1894* | |
| 225. | London, Tower Bridge | *1886–94* | |
| 226. | Halifax, West Yorks., Municipal Technical School | *1893–95* | |
| 227. | London, Cripplegate Institute, Golden Lane | *1894–96* | |
| 228. | Bilston, West Midlands, Technical, Science, and Art School | *1897* | |
| 228. | Bilston, West Midlands, Waterworks | *1897* | |
| 229. | London, St Gabriel's Church, Warwick Square | *1854 and 1897* | |
| 230. | Northwich, Cheshire, Verdin Technical School | *1897* | |
| 231. | Bristol, Avon, Cabot Memorial Tower, Brandon Hill | *1897–98* | |

# CATALOGUE OF MEDALS 3

Medals forming the catalogue are entered under the *building* to which they relate, and the sequence of buildings is organised by the date of their completion.

Each medal has a *key identification number* and this is shown to the left of the entry. This key number is provided by the *index number of the particular building*, together with a suffix specific to each medal, e.g. St Paul's Cathedral is building index No. 39 and medals of it are listed 39a, 39b, 39c, . . . etc. For 'complex' entries comprising many medals, e.g. the Royal Exchange, these are grouped by medallists, and by date order of striking.

The system is designed to relate the catalogue number to the building subject matter, and to allow for any further medals of a building, or any new building entry, to be added into the numbering sequence.

If a medallist's name or initials are recorded on the inscription, reference should be made to the biographical entries (Section 5) for dates and details of work, and for cross reference to other architectural medals by the same author.

The dates indicated for the striking of medals (shown below each entry) are from internal evidence wherever possible, e.g. inscription or building details. Where other information is not available, dates are suggested on Grant's listing, and this is given as ( )$^{G}$. When there are several medals relating to a building, these are arranged by date, by medallist, and by size. Medals in the British Museum collection are marked (BM) and if different versions are available from other public collections these are indicated. References are also given to the Eidlitz catalogue, together with plate numbers. Where photographs are held at the BM of medals in the former Watt Collection, these are shown as the source.

## ARCHITECTURAL NOTES

These are provided to amplify any architectural information on the medals and, wherever possible to identify the architect(s) concerned. Separate biographies of architects' names are provided (Section 4) and are intended to be read in conjunction with the building entry.

Notes are compiled to identify the building shown on the medal and to relate to the particular view, elevation, or interior chosen by the medallist. These notes are also intended to provide the reader with basic reference books selected for ease of access, e.g. the invaluable guides in the *Buildings of England* series (ed. N. Pevsner) which provide details of location and building history; H.-R. Hitchcock's monumental work on *Early Victorian Architecture in Britain*; or B. F. L. Clarke on *Church Builders of the Nineteenth Century*. In addition key books with useful bibliographies are noted for specific topics, e.g. *Wren* by M. Whinney, or *Pugin* by P. Stanton.

To relate to the architectural notes an illustration is given of the building concerned. For this the obverse or reverse of one of the medals listed has been selected; this is at actual size unless otherwise stated.

Addresses for buildings are related to the new structure of English counties and metropolitan counties established in the local government reorganisation of 1974.

1a

CANTERBURY, Kent, **The Cathedral** *12th to 19th centuries*

**1a** *Obv.* View from south-west. CANTERBURY CATHEDRAL—DEDICATED BY PERMISSION TO H.R.H. PRINCE ALBERT. Signed, J. DAVIS MEDALLIST BIRM$^{M}$

*Rev.* Interior. VIEW IN THE NAVE. Around, CANTERBURY CATHEDRAL.

Bronze, White Metal, 60 mm. ?1840s (BM)

**1b** *Obv.* View from south-west, showing identical towers to west front. In exergue, CANTERBURY CATHEDRAL WITH THE NORTH WESTERN NEW TOWER. Signed, on base of scene, DAVIS, and on exergue bar, PUBLISHED BY HENRY WARD CANTERBURY.

*Rev.* Interior view, to east end. THE CHOIR OF CANTERBURY CATHEDRAL.

Bronze, White Metal, 51 mm. *c.*1841 (BM)

The present structure started with the rebuilding of the choir (1175–78) under the master mason William of Sens. This was extended eastwards (1179–84) to form the shrine of St Thomas à Becket. A major rebuilding of the nave and transepts (1391–1468), in the Perpendicular style, was followed by the south-west tower (1424–34) and the central tower

(1494–1503). The north-west tower of Archbishop Lanfranc's church of 1077 survived until it was replaced (1832–41) by a replica of the south-west tower; this design, and a complete restoration of the fabric, was carried out by the cathedral surveyor George Austin. The new north-west tower is shown on both medals above; these are *c.* 1841 and probably commemorate its completion.

See: Pevsner, ed. J. Newman, *NE and E Kent*, 164 ff.

CHICHESTER, West Sussex, **The Cathedral** *12th century on*

**2a** *Obv.* View from north-east. In exergue, CHICHESTER CATHEDRAL. Signed, I. BARKER 1844.

*Rev.* View on axis. In exergue, CHICHESTER CROSS. Signed, I. BARKER 1844.

Bronze, White Metal, 60 mm. 1844 (BM)

The earlier, Norman, parts of the cathedral were consecrated in 1184. The fine central spire was added in the fifteenth century but, together with the tower, collapsed in 1861 (i.e. after the medal above). They were restored in replica by Sir G. G. Scott. The reverse of the medal shows Bishop Story's Market Cross (1501); its original purpose was similar to that of a market hall cf. the cross at Salisbury.

See: Pevsner, *Sussex*, 128 ff.

2a

DURHAM, Durham, **The Cathedral** *11th to 15th centuries*

**3a** *Obv.* View of Cathedral and hillside. DURHAM CATHEDRAL.

Bronze (uniface), 25 mm. 18--? (BM)

The cathedral was essentially completed between 1093 and 1133. Historically and technically it is of great interest for the use of rib vaults in the chancel (*c.* 1104) and the nave (1130). The crossing tower was added in 1465–90. In a spectacular setting, together with castle and monastery, Durham is 'one of the great experiences of Europe to the eyes of those who appreciate architecture and to the minds of those who understand architecture' (Pevsner). Restorations in 1795 by James Wyatt, and in 1870–76 by Sir G. G. Scott.

See: Pevsner, *Durham*, 77 ff.

3a

ELY, Cambs., **The Cathedral** *12th to 14th centuries*

**4a** *Obv.* View of WEST FRONT OF ELY CATHEDRAL. Signed in exergue, JOSEPH DAVIS MEDALLIST BIRM[M].

*Rev.* Interior looking towards east end. WEST VIEW OF THE CHOIR. Below, ELY CATHEDRAL.

Bronze, 60 mm. *c.*1840 (BM)

The architectural details are identical to those on the medal below; however here the dedication to H.R.H. Prince Albert is missing (see note, p. 216).

4a

**4b** *Obv.* View of WEST FRONT OF ELY CATHEDRAL. In exergue, DEDICATED BY PERMISSION TO H:R:H: PRINCE ALBERT. Signed, J. DAVIS BIRM$^{M}$.

*Rev.* Interior, looking towards east end. WEST VIEW OF THE CHOIR. Below, ELY CATHEDRAL.

White Metal, 60 mm. 1840s

A rebuilding of the nave towards the west end, with its unusual west tower, was completed *c.* 1200; the tower originally had a stone spire which was replaced by the tall octagon storey in the later fourteenth-century. The two most famous elements at Ely are, however, the larger octagon which forms the lantern of the central crossing (1322–48, after the original crossing tower collapsed) and the highly glazed, rectangular, Lady Chapel (1322–53). There was a restoration by Sir G. G. Scott in 1847, following one by James Essex in the 1750s which had been unusually careful for its time.

See: Pevsner, *Cambs.* 339.

5a

GLOUCESTER, Gloucs., **The Cathedral** *13th to 15th centuries*

**5a** *Obv.* View from south-west. GLOUCESTER CATHEDRAL — — DEDICATED BY PERMISSION TO H.R.H. PRINCE ALBERT. Signed, J. DAVIS MEDALIST BIRM$^{M}$

*Rev.* Interior view. THE CHOIR GLOUCESTER CATHEDRAL.

Bronze, 61 mm. ?1840s (BM, Restrike)

A rebuilding of the cathedral began in 1089. The nave was consecrated in 1121, and its stone vaulting completed in 1242. After 1327, when the body of Edward II was brought to Gloucester, the cathedral became a place of pilgrimage and was able to afford a further rebuilding programme. The south transept was transformed (1331–37) to the new perpendicular style and proved influential in the development of English gothic architecture. This perpendicular rebuilding continued into the fifteenth century and included the fine fan vaulting to the cloisters, and the magnificent east window. Restoration in the nineteenth century was by Sir G. G. Scott, who removed anything not gothic.

See: Pevsner, ed., D. Verey, *Gloucs: Vale and Forest of Dean,* 198 ff.

6a

LICHFIELD, Staffs., **The Cathedral**

*13th to 14th centuries, Res. 1788–95*

**6a** *Obv.* View from west end. LICHFIELD CATHEDRAL DEDICATED BY PERMISSION TO H:R:H: PRINCE ALBERT. Signed, J. DAVIS BIRM.

*Rev.* Interior view. THE CHOIR LICHFIELD CATHEDRAL.

Bronze, 60 mm. ?1840s (BM)

The main building period was from *c.* 1200; the west front dates from *c.* 1280 onwards; the crossing tower is *c.* 1300 and west spires 1320–30. The cathedral was damaged in the Civil War and the spire was restored 1661–69. In 1788 James Wyatt began a major restoration—his first—with the local Joseph Potter, senior, as his executant architect. The medal shows the cathedral as it was when Pugin visited it in 1834 and wrote abusively: 'This monster of architectural depravity—this pest of cathedral architecture—has been here. Need I say more?' There were further restorations by Sir G. G. Scott, and his son, from 1857 to 1901.

See: Pevsner, *Staffs.* 174 ff.

LINCOLN, Lincolnshire, **The Cathedral** *12th to 15th centuries*

**7a** *Obv.* View from north-west. In exergue, LINCOLN CATHEDRAL — · — DEDICATED BY PERMISSION TO H.R.H. PRINCE ALBERT — J. DAVIS. MEDALLIST BIRM$^{M}$

*Rev.* View within choir, towards organ screen. INTERIOR OF LINCOLN CATHEDRAL.

Bronze, 60 mm. 1840s (BM)

**7b** *Obv.* View from south-west of LINCOLN CATHEDRAL. Signed, in exergue, J. WIENER F. BRUSSELS ELKINGTON & C. LONDON.

*Rev.* Interior of nave looking towards crossing, screen, and organ. Below, FOUNDED 1085. BURNT 1141. OFTEN REBUILT 1135–1250. SOUTH TRANSEPT 1306.

Bronze, 60 mm. 1856 (BM)

Like Durham, on a spectacular hill site. The cathedral has an impressive silhouette which, during the Middle Ages, had spires on each of the three towers. The main building periods were *c.* 1072–92, and then 1141 to 1280, with the towers added in the fourteen and fifthteenth centuries. The turrets and parapets on the central tower were added by James Essex during his restoration in the 1760s. The interior view on the Davis medal (above) shows only the west part of the choir; behind, at the east end, is the Presbytery or 'Angel Choir' (1256–80).

See: Pevsner, *Lincs.* 81 ff.; Thomas H. Cocke, 'James Essex, cathedral restorer', in *Architectural History*, 18, 1975, pp. 12–22.

7a

LONDON, **Westminster Abbey** *13th to 18th century*

**8a** *Obv.* View of west front. WESTMINSTER ABBEY. In exergue, DEDICATED BY PERMISSION TO H:R:H: PRINCE ALBERT. J. DAVIS. MEDALLIST. BIRM$^{M}$

*Rev.* Interior view towards crossing and chancel. THE CHOIR WESTMINSTER ABBEY.

Bronze, 60 mm. ?1840s (BM)

**8b** *Obv.* Perspective view of exterior with west façade and towers. Around WESTMINSTER ABBEY. Signed J. WIENER F BRUSSELS.

*Rev.* Interior of Henry VII's Chapel. Left panel: THE PRESENT CHURCH CONSTRUCTED 1220–1285. RESTORED END OF XVII CENTURY. Right panel: WESTMINSTER HALL BUILT 1397. THE CHAPEL OF HENRY VII COMMENCED 1503 RESTORED 1809. Below, ST PETER'S CHURCH FOUNDED ABOUT 612. REBUILT AND ERECTED AN ABBEY 958 AND 1049–1066. Signed, ELKINGTON SC. LONDON.

Bronze, 59 mm. 1856 (BM)

One of Weiner series of English Cathedrals (see p.224)

The foundation stone of the present abbey church was laid in 1245; by 1269 the chancel, transepts and first five bays of nave (the choir shown on

8b

the Davis medal above) were ready for the body of St Edward the Confessor to be re-enshrined. This rebuilding, on a much nobler scale, was initiated for Henry III, and culminated in a redesigning of the rest of the nave, still in a thirteenth-century style, by Henry Yevele (from 1375 on). The chapel of Henry VII was added to the east end in 1503–12, and was the work of the masons Robert and William Vertue;[1] it was built as a mausoleum for the King and took the place of an earlier Lady Chapel. The final major addition was the building of the two west towers (1734–45) by Nicholas Hawksmoor and his successor as Surveyor, John James. Between 1809 and 1813 James Wyatt refaced Henry VII's chapel, and during the nineteenth century restorers included Blore, G. G. Scott, and Pearson.

See: Pevsner, *London 1*, 337.

1. But see Walter C. Leedy, 'The design of the vaulting of Henry VII's Chapel, Westminster: a reappraisal', in *Architectural History*, 18, 1975, pp. 5–11, where Robert Janyns Jnr is suggested as a more likely designer.

9a

OXFORD, Oxon., **Christ Church Cathedral** *12th to 15th centuries*

**9a** *Obv.* View of exterior. OXFORD CATHEDRAL. Below, DEDICATED BY PERMISSION TO H:R:H: PRINCE ALBERT. Signed, J. DAVIS BIRM^M

*Rev.* Interior, showing pendant vault. THE CHOIR OXFORD CATHEDRAL.

Bronze, 61 mm. ?1840s (BM)

**9b** *Obv.* View of THE MARTYRS' MEMORIAL OXFORD. Below, 1843. Signed around, JOS^H DAVIS BIRM^M.

*Rev.* Interior showing pendant vault. THE CHOIR OXFORD CATHEDRAL (as No. 9a above).

Bronze, 61 mm. ?1840s (BM)

Building of the Priory church started in the twelfth century with the Norman choir; it was here that the system of tall round piers and arches was established. The stone pendant vault which finally completed the choir (see medals) is *c.* 1500, similar to that of the Divinity School, Oxford, by the mason William Orchard. In the sixteenth century the nave was shortened to make possible the building of Tom Quad at Christ Church. The Cathedral forms an integral part of the College buildings, and the view on the medal is the north front from the Deanery garden. Restorations were carried out in 1870–76 by Sir G. G. Scott, who was also the designer of the Martyrs' Memorial in St Giles, Oxford, shown on the obverse of No. 9b; this was erected 1841–43 and is based on the Eleanor Cross at Waltham Cross, Herts.

See: Pevsner and Sherwood, *Oxford*, 115 ff.

SALISBURY, Wilts., **The Cathedral** *13th to 14th centuries*

**10a** *Obv.* View across the Close, from the south-west. SALISBURY CATHEDRAL. Signed on exergue bar, HALLIDAY. F. In exergue, BENNETT. DIREX.

*Rev.* Interior. THE CHOIR OF SALISBURY CATHEDRAL. Signed, BENNETT DIREX.

White Metal, 50 mm. 1830$^{G}$ (BM)

**10b** *Obv.* View across Cathedral Close. SALISBURY CATHEDRAL.

*Rev.* Mitre, with sprays of oak and laurel leaves below. SALISBURY DIOCESAN BOARD OF EDUCATION.

White Metal, 51 mm. mid-nineteenth century (BM)

The plan and unity of Salisbury is the ideal of the Early English cathedral. It was built in a short space of time (1220–58), and had its superb 404 ft spire added in the 1330s; it was concern for the safety of this spire which brought Wren, in his capacity as a mathematician, to design a scheme for its strengthening in 1668. A typical late eighteenth-century 'improvement' of the cathedral was carried out by James Wyatt from 1789, only to be followed in 1863 by Sir G. G. Scott who 'swept away as much Wyatt as he could and replaced it by Scott'.

See: Pevsner, *Wilts.* 350.

10b

WINCHESTER, Hants, **The Cathedral** *11th to 15th centuries*

**11a** *Obv.* View of WEST FRONT WINCHESTER CATHEDRAL. Signed, BENNETT SARUM.

*Rev.* Interior. THE CHOIR WINCHESTER CATHEDRAL.

White Metal, 50 mm. ?1820s to 1840s (BM)

**11b** *Obv.* View from north-west of exterior. In exergue, WINCHESTER CATHEDRAL FOUNDED AT THE EPOCH OF THE SAXON KINGS. THE PRESENT CATHEDRAL BUILT 1079–1093. THE NAVES AND THE AISLES CONSTRUCTED BY WYKEHAM 1370–1400. Signed, ELKINGTON & CO. LONDON.

*Rev.* Interior view looking down nave towards screen, which has classical details and pediment. Signed below, J. WIENER F. BRUXELLES.

Bronze, 59 mm. 1856 (BM)

At 556 ft, the external length is the longest of any gothic cathedral in Europe. Of the Norman abbey foundation, built 1079–98, there only remains the transepts; the Norman nave and choir were restyled (1345–1404) by William of Wykeham (see No. 27a) and his successors with a veneer of Perpendicular, and with a vaulted roof. The stone screen shown on the Wiener medal (above) is that given by Charles I when he visited the Cathedral in 1635; it was designed by Inigo Jones, and when completed *c.* 1640 the two niches held statues by Le Sueur. This screen was dismantled in 1820 and much of it is still in existence.[1]

See: Pevsner, *Hants.*, 661 ff.; J. M. G. Blakiston, 'The Inigo Jones Screen', Part I in *Winchester Cathedral Record*, 1976, 10–16.

1. The correct date of dismantling has been established by Mr Blakiston. The centre portion of the screen is in the Museum of Archaeology and Ethnology, Cambridge; the remaining pieces and the statues of James I and Charles I are in the Cathedral at Winchester.

11b

WORCESTER, Hereford and Worcester, **The Cathedral**
*11th to 14th centuries*

**12a** *Obv.* View from north-east, of exterior. WORCESTER CATHEDRAL —·— DEDICATED BY PERMISSION TO H.R.H. PRINCE ALBERT. Signed, JOS. DAVIS MEDALLIST BIRM.

*Rev.* Interior view. THE CHOIR AND PRESBYTERY WORCESTER CATHEDRAL.

Bronze, 61 mm. ?1840s (BM, Restrike)

12a

The present building was begun in 1084, and a circular Norman chapter house remains from that period. The new east end (seen on the medal) was begun in 1224. The nave, cloisters and crossing tower are Decorated and Perpendicular. There were extensive restorations in 1857, and then in 1864–74 (by G. G. Scott). 'Let it be said at once that the surface of the exterior is entirely mid–Victorian and that many windows are too' (Pevsner).

See: Pevsner, *Worcs.* 295 ff.

YORK, North Yorks. **The Minster** *13th to 15th centuries*

**13a** *Obv.* View of Minster from south-west. In exergue, YORK MINSTER. Signed, BARBER CATTLE & NORTH.

*Rev.* View of Keep, with wooden drawbridge, guards etc. Around, CLIFFORDS TOWER. In exergue, BLOWN UP AD 1684.

Bronze, White Metal, 45 mm. ?1820s (BM)

Clifford's Tower was built *c.* 1250–75, on the mound of one of William the Conqueror's two castles at York.

**13b** *Obv.* View of Minster from south-west. In exergue, YORK MINSTER 1825. Signed, BARBER CATTLE & NORTH.

*Rev.* View down choir to east end. In exergue, THE CHOIR OF YORK MINSTER DESTROYED BY FIRE FEB$^{RY}$ 2$^{ND}$ 1829.

White Metal, 45 mm. 1829 (BM)

**13c** *Obv.* View from south-west of YORK CATHEDRAL. Signed, J. DAVIS MEDALLIST BIRM$^{M}$.

*Rev.* Interior view, looking down choir towards the east window. CHOIR OF YORK CATHEDRAL.

Bronze, 61 mm. ?1835–40 (see p. 216.) (BM)

**13d** *Obv.* View showing twin towers of west end, and Decorated west window. In exergue, YORK CATHEDRAL BUILT 630–642. BURNT 1069. REBUILT 1070 AGAIN BURNT 1137. RECONSTRUCTED 1171–1361. RESTORATION FINISHED 1832. Signed, J. WIENER F. and ELKINGTON & CO LONDON.

*Rev.* Interior view of nave, looking towards west window. Signed in exergue, J. WIENER BRUXELLES.

Bronze, 59 mm. (See also Plate 9.) 1854 (BM)

13c

Rebuilt between 1230 and 1475, York has the largest area of any English medieval cathedral. The fine windows include: the north transept lancets (the 'Five Sisters') of *c.* 1253; the great west window with its

13d

flowing tracery of 1338 (see 13d above); the east window, designed, built and glazed in only three years (1405–8 by John Thornton of Coventry). The main crossing tower is early fifteenth century, and the west towers 1433–75. In the nineteenth century Sir Robert Smirke rebuilt the wooden choir vaults after a fire (see above) and in 1840, after another fire, Sydney Smirke rebuilt the nave vaulting.

See: Pevsner, *York and E Riding*, 75 ff.

NANTWICH, Cheshire, **St Mary's Church** *14th century*

**14a** *Obv.* View of church. CHURCH SUNDAY SCHOOL. In exergue, NANTWICH.

*Rev.* Dove holding olive branch in beak and flying to right. Legend: AS THE WATERS COVER THE SEA. REWARD OF MERIT.

Bronze, 47 mm. ?before 1850s (BM)

A large essentially fourteenth-century church, with an octagonal crossing tower. Restored in 1854–61 by Sir G. G. Scott who confidently replaced a Decorated doorway and a Perpendicular window on the west front with his favourite late thirteenth-century style. The medal antedates this and shows what he destroyed.

See: Pevsner, *Cheshire*, 285.

14a

SHEPTON MALLET, Somerset, **Church of St Peter and St Paul** *to 14th century (and 1837)*

**15a** *Obv.* Side view of church. Around, THE POOR HAVE THE GOSPEL PREACHED TO THEM. MATT. XI, 5. Signed on bar, T. W. INGRAM. BIRM., and below exergue bar, C. WAINWRIGHT ARCH$^{\text{T}}$

*Rev.* Inscription, around, SHEPTON MALLET CHURCH ENLARGED A.D. 1837 · 700 FREE SITTINGS GIVEN TO THE POOR FOR EVER · In centre, RECTOR REV$^{\text{D}}$ W. P. T. WICKHAM. — · — CURATE REV$^{\text{D}}$ F. T. NEW. — · — CHA$^{\text{S}}$ WAINWRIGHT THO$^{\text{S}}$ MILLARD CH. WARDENS.

Bronze, 48 mm. 1837 (BM)

The medal view shows the fine Somerset west tower of the late fourteenth century, and the south aisle as widened, along with the north aisle, in 1837. The medal gives the architect for this rebuilding as C. Wainwright. The nave has an outstanding example of a 'wagon roof'.

See: Pevsner, *N Somerset*, 255.

15a

16a

NETHER ALDERLEY, Cheshire, **St Mary's Church** *late 14th century*

**16a** *Obv.* View of church from south-east. 1. MACC. 7. 37. Signed, HALLIDAY S.

*Rev.* Wreath with inscription around, SUPERIOR MERIT ALDERLEY. Within, REV$^{D}$ EDWARD STANLEY TO (left blank) 3. JOHN 4.

White Metal, 45 mm. ?1810s to 1830s (BM)

Much of the fabric of the late fourteenth-century church, shown on the medal, was pulled down and rebuilt in a drastic reconstruction of 1877–78 by Paley & Austin. (The chancel had been demolished in 1851 and rebuilt 1856 by Cuffley and Starkey.) The dominant west tower is of local red sandstone, and is similar in design to that at Mobberley. The elaborate seventeenth-century Stanley memorial pew, entered by a flight of steps from outside the building, still remains following the alterations. The Revd Edward Stanley (see reverse) was rector 1805–37.

See: Raymond Richards, *Old Cheshire Churches*, London, 1947, 18–22; Pevsner and E. Hubbard, *Cheshire*, 291, 292.

17a

BRIDPORT, Dorset, **St Mary's Church** *14th/15th century*

**17a** *Obv.* View of church. Legend: TE DEUM LAUDAMUS. In exergue, E. J. L. B. HENSLOWE, RECTOR. THE FEAR OF THE LORD IS THE BEGINNING OF WISDOM.

*Rev.* Inscription: BRIDPORT PARISH CHURCH SUNDAY SCHOOLS. In centre, in eleven lines: INSTITUTED JANUARY 1$^{ST}$ 1788 THIS MEDAL WAS STRUCK TO COMMEMORATE THEIR CENTENARY SUNDAY, JANUARY 1$^{ST}$ 1888 SUPERINTENDENTS BOYS. T. B. BAKER GIRLS. G. WHETHAM 2$^{ND}$ DIVISION E. M. VIVIAN.

Bronze, White Metal, 39 mm. 1888 (BM)

Essentially Early English and Perpendicular. Two west bays of nave and chancel added in 1858–60 by John Hicks of Dorchester.

See: Pevsner ed., J. Newman, *Dorset*, 109.

18a

COVENTRY, West Midlands, **St Michael's Church** *14th/15th century*

**18a** *Obv.* North-east view of church with tower and spire. ST MICHAELS CHURCH. Signed, W. WYON.

*Rev.* Interior view. THE CHANCEL.

Bronze, 38 mm. ?1820s to 1840s (BM)

Only the superb 300-ft tower and spire remains of this large town church (designated cathedral in 1918) built in the late fourteenth and early fifteenth centuries. The medal interior view shows a classical altar screen removed in the nineteenth-century restorations.

COVENTRY, West Midlands, **St John's Church** *15th century*

**19a** *Obv.* View of restored church. Around on border, S. JOHN'S CHURCH COVENTRY · REOPENED AFTER RESTORATION 1877 ·

*Rev.* Elevation of school building. Around on border, S. JOHN'S SCHOOLS COVENTRY · ERECTED 1884 · Illustrated following entry 205.

White Metal, 44 mm. 1884 (BM)

Most of the present red sandstone church is fifteenth-century Perpendicular. The church was restored in 1877 (see medal) by Sir G. G. Scott. The medal reverse marks the opening of St John's Schools, built in a strange Elizabethan Early English mixture (see p.168).

See: Pevsner, *Warwicks.*, 261, St John's Church.

19a

NEWCASTLE UPON TYNE, Tyne and Wear, **St Nicholas Church** (now the Cathedral of St Nicholas) *15th century*

**20a** *Obv.* Top part of west tower and 'crown'. Around, INDOCTI DISCANT ET AMENT MEMINISSE PERITI.

*Rev.* Inscription: THIS MEDAL WAS STRUCK FOR THE EXHIBITION OF OBJECTS CONNECTED WITH ART, MANUFACTURE AND SCIENCE AT NEWCASTLE UPON TYNE 1840.

Bronze, 41 mm. 1840 (BM)

St Nicholas was a parish church until 1882, when it was designated a cathedral. The building is largely fourteenth and fifteenth century. The remarkable stone spire (or 'crown') shown on the medal is *c.* 1437–70, and is earlier than similar designs at St Giles Cathedral, Edinburgh (*c.* 1495) and Kings College, Aberdeen (*c.* 1500).

See: Pevsner, *Northumberland*, 224; a paper by W. H. Wood in *RIBAJ*, 30 September 1905, 619–33, discusses and illustrates in detail the construction of the tower and spire.

20a

SHERBORNE, Dorset, **The Abbey Church** *15th century*

**21a** *Obv.* View of church from south-east. Around top, HOW AMIABLE ARE THY TABERNACLES, O LORD OF HOSTS! P$^{S}$ 84 V.1. In exergue, SHERBORNE CHURCH. Signed on base of scene, ALLEN & MOORE. F.

*Rev.* At top dove in flight, with sprig in its beak. Below, crown on Bible. Inscription in centre, RESTORATION COMMENCED JULY 1849.

Copper, 39 mm. 1849

Formerly part of the monastic buildings; it was sold to the town in 1540 to become the parish church. Most of the south view of the church shown on the medal is Perpendicular of *c.* 1420 on; some Norman work remains in the south transept. Restored in 1849–58 by R. C. Carpenter (d. 1855) and his partner Slater.

See: Pevsner and Newman, *Dorset*, 368 ff.

21a

22a

LONDON, City, **St Giles Cripplegate** *c. 1545–50*

**22a** *Obv.* Head of Queen to left, wearing tiara and veil. Around on border, [crown] VICTORIA [crown] QUEEN OF GREAT BRITAIN AND IRELAND: EMPRESS OF INDIA ASCENDED THE THRONE 1837 JUBILEE 1887.

*Rev.* View of church, from the south. Around, · ST GILES [cross] CRIPPLEGATE · IN COMMEMORATION OF THE QUEEN'S JUBILEE. In exergue, THIS MEDAL WAS STRUCK BY ALBERT BARFF. M.A. VICAR JOHN. J. BADDELEY LEONARD. W. CUBITT CHURCHWARDENS.

Bronze, 44 mm. 1887

A large gothic, Perpendicular, parish church of late date, i.e. *c.* 1545–50; the top of the tower was raised and cased in brick, 1682–84, by John Bridges (as shown on the medal). The church was gutted during the 1940s but has been restored as part of the City's Barbican scheme.

23a

PRESTON, Lancs., **St John the Divine,** Church Street *16th century*

**23a** *Obv.* View of church. IN COMMEMORATION OF THE JUBILEE HELD AT PRESTON 1822.

*Rev.* Emblazoned shields (the arms of Preston). Around, NICH$^{S}$ GRIMSHAW ESQ$^{RE}$ MAYOR OF PRESTON AT THE GUILDS OF 1802 & 1822.

Bronze, White Metal, 35 mm. 1822 (BM)

This 1822 medal shows, albeit crudely, the sixteenth-century church demolished in 1853 to make way for the present building (by E. H. Shellard of 1853–55). The original structure had fallen into decay during the eighteenth century, and by 1811 the tower had to be pulled down to the level of the roof as unsafe; the tower was then rebuilt in 1814, and the chancel rebuilt in 1817.

See: *VCH*, *Lancs.*, 7, 81–82, pl. facing p. 80.

24a

TEMPLE (Allegorical: IBA Medal) *type of 5th century* BC

**24a** *Obv.* Doric temple front, with arms of IBA in a roundel in the tympanum along with symbols of architecture, column capitals etc. Around, VSVI CIVIVM DECORI VRBIVM. In exergue, MDCCCXXXIV. Signed, T.L.D. DIR. B. WYON F.

*Rev.* Within a raised border, a wreath and inscription: INSTITVTE OF BRITISH ARCHITECTS.

Silver, Bronze, 57 mm 1836[1] (BM)

The inauguration of the Institute of British Architects in the year 1834 is commemorated on their first medal; it shows a Greek temple front of the peripteral hexastyle type, as for instance the Temple of Zeus, Olympia (*c.* 460 BC). The portico design was, however, suitably amended by T. L. Donaldson (qv), then secretary of the IBA, to symbolise Architecture (the medal is signed T.L.D.). The roundel in the tympanum has on it a column flanked by lions (cf. the Lion Gate at Mycenae, Greece) which Donaldson created as the emblem of the newly formed Institute; he also invented its motto which provides the surrounding inscription.

1. The first presentation of this medal was made at an IBA meeting on 18 July 1836; it was received by George Godwin for his prize essay on the Nature of Concrete. The President, Earl de Grey, noted that the medallist Benjamin Wyon was in the audience. See *Arch. Mag.* iii, 1836, 391–2.

CAMBRIDGE, Cambs., **Christs College, Gateway,** St Andrews Street *c. 1505 on*

**29a** *Obv.* Bust to left. GEORGIUS III · PIUS FORTIS DEFENSOR FIDEI.

*Rev.* View of college buildings, with entrance gateway, from street. Above, OB STUDIA THEOLOGIAE FELICITER INSTITUTA. In exergue, COLL. CHRISTI PIETATIS ERGO D. ALUMNUS OLIM BEILBY PORTEUS EPISC. LOND. 1808. Signed, I. PHILLP F. on exergue bar.

Bronze, 49 mm. 1808 (BM)

29a

**29b** As above but reverse has view from further away, and tree and wall to right. Signed, I.P. FEC only.

Bronze, 49 mm. 1808 (BM)

**29c** *Obv.* Bust to left. GEORGIUS III. PIUS FORTIS DEFENSOR FIDEI. Signed below bust, I PHILLP FEC.

*Rev.* Elevation of main gate with college arms over. On scroll, OB INSIGNE IN S.S. PUBLICE LEGENDIS ELOQUIUM. In exergue, COLL. CHRISTI PIETATIS ERGO D. ALUMNUS OLIM BEILBY PORTEUS EPISC. LOND. 1808.

Bronze, 42 mm. 1808 (BM)

Refounded by Lady Margaret Beaufort, mother of Henry VII, in 1505. The showpiece gateway and street façade were built shortly after this (cf. the gateway at St John's College for the same founder). The appearance of the original street front was changed by ashlar refacing between 1714 and 1739, and by alterations to the windows.

See: Pevsner, *Cambridge*, 39; Royal Commission on Historical Monuments, *City of Cambridge, 1*, HMSO, 1959, 25 ff.

EVESHAM, Hereford and Worcs., **Bell Tower,** Abbey Precinct *1513 on*

**30a** *Obv.* Bust of Queen, to left, with 'jubilee' crown. VICTORIA QUEEN AND EMPRESS * JUBILEE 1887 *. Signed on truncation, B & A.

*Rev.* Perpendicular style tower. BOROUGH OF EVESHAM.

White Metal, 38 mm. 1887 (BM)

30a

Abbot Lichfield's freestanding campanile is of 1513 or later. It is richly decorated with panelling, battlements, pinnacles, etc., and formed one of the elements of the Evesham Abbey precinct.

See: Pevsner, *Worcs.* 145.

ETON COLLEGE, Berks., **School Yard** *15th and 16th centuries*

**31a** *Obv.* Within framed panel: View of Lupton's Range, with statue of Henry VI in foreground. Below, ETON COLLEGE. Signed around border, THE EDUCATIONAL SUPPLY ASSOCIATION L$^{TD}$ LONDON.

*Rev.* Wreath and scrolls around. Inscription in centre: AWARDED FOR GENERAL IMPROVEMENT.

Bronze, 44 mm. 1852$^{G}$ (Watt Coll.)

31a

The medal shows Lupton's Gatehouse and Range built of brick in 1517–*c.* 1520. To the right is the College Chapel (1449–75), and in the centre of School Yard is a statue of the founder, Henry VI, by Francis Bird (1719).

See: Pevsner, *Bucks.* 120 ff.

32a

ROTHWELL, Northants, **Market House** *1578*

**32a** *Obv.* View of the Market House. ROTHWELL BOARD SCHOOL. Signed in exergue, SPINK & SON LONDON.

*Rev.* Inscription: AWARDED, and on central panel, TO ——— FOR REGULAR ATTENDANCE.

White Metal, 38 mm. ?1890s (Watt Coll.)

The medal shows the market house built for Sir Thomas Tresham by William Grumbold. The agreement for this was dated 1578. Grumbold was one of a family of Northants freemasons, whose best-known member was to be Robert Grumbold (1639–1720), the mason of Sir Christopher Wren's Trinity College Library, Cambridge. The Rothwell market house remained incomplete until 1895, when it was finally roofed to the design of the architect J. A. Gotch.[1]

See: Pevsner, *Northants.* (2nd ed.), 393, pl. 78.

1. Gotch had published in 1883, *A complete account of the buildings erected in Northamptonshire by Sir Thomas Tresham 1575–1605.* In 1894 he produced the two lavishly illustrated folio volumes of *Architecture of the Renaissance in England*; this gives (vol. 1, p. 39 and pl. 53) a plan of the Rothwell market house and a photograph prior to roofing.

33b

STONYHURST, Lancs., **Stonyhurst College, Gateway** *1592–c.1595*

**33a** *Obv.* Elevation of gateway to college buildings. RELIGIONI AVITAE. In exergue, COLL · STONYHVRST. Signed T.H.F. at base of gateway.

*Rev.* Three busts with symbols of music and learning, a globe etc. Above, irradiating these, I H S and +. In exergue, PRINCIBUS · RR · PP · Q. Around on border, HAEC · OLIM · MEMI · NISSE · IVVABIT. Signed, HALLIDAY FECIT.

Silver, 53 mm. ?1830s or 1840s (BM)

**33b** *Obv.* Elevation of gateway (as above No. 33a).

*Rev.* Two trees growing together into one. In exergue, PRINCIBVS SS · CG · Q. Around on border, CRESCENT · ILLAE · CRESCETIS · HONORES.

Silver, White Metal, 44 mm. ?1830s or 1840s (BM)

**33c** *Obv.* Madonna blessing Father and Son. On border, + B·M·V· IMM · CONC. STUDIORUM · PATRONA + COLL· S · ALOYS ·

*Rev.* Elevation of main front with central gateway and pinnacles of tower in background. On border + RELIGIONI · ET · LITTERIS + AUDOMARI · 1592 · LEODII · 1773 · STONYHURST · 1794.

Silver, 54 mm. ?nineteenth century (Watt Coll.)

The gateway and range to the south of it was built as a house for the Shireburn family 1592–*c* 1595; Baroque cupolas were added to the gateway in 1712. The house was sold to the Society of Jesus in 1794, and the range to the north of the gateway added 1843–56 as part of the school expansion.

See: Pevsner, *N Lancs.* 239–45; *VCH, Lancs.* 7, 4 ff, illus. facing p. 8.

LONDON, Westminster, **Banqueting House,** Whitehall *1619–22*

**34a** *Obv.* Bust with cap, to left. INIGO JONES. Signed C.F. CARTER F.

*Rev.* Elevation to Whitehall, shown freestanding. BANQUETING HOUSE WHITEHALL 1616. Edge inscription ART — UNION OF LONDON 1849.

Silver, Bronze, 54 mm. 1852 (Eidlitz 611, pl. 68.) (BM)

The portrait is based on a bust by Michael Rysbrack made for Lord Burlington, and now in the Chatsworth collection (see Plate 3).

The date on the Art-Union medal is incorrect. The second banqueting house was destroyed by fire on 12 January 1619 and Inigo Jones's famous, and influential, design was built in 1619–22. The interior is a single double cube space, developed from the idea of a Roman basilica; Rubens' painted ceiling on 'the apotheosis of James I' was added in 1635. To the exterior the serenity of proportion, and the scholarly reworking of Palladio's design, must have come as a revelation to the crowded medieval London of the time. As originally built the basement was of honey-coloured stone, the upper walls were of a brownish stone, and only the enriched details were in white Portland stone. This emphasis was changed in 1829, when Sir John Soane completed a total refacing in Portland stone.[1]

See: J. Summerson, *Inigo Jones*, 1966; Catalogue, *The Kings Arcadia*, Arts Council, 1973; P. Palme, *The Triumph of Peace*, 1957.

1. Wren proposed to incorporate a transformed Banqueting House into his Whitehall Palace Scheme of *c.* 1694. See: M. Whinney, *Wren*, 1971, 181.

34a

BIRMINGHAM, West Midlands, **Aston Hall** *c. 1635*

**35a** *Obv.* Cameo bust, to left, of Queen Victoria. On banneret; GOD SAVE THE QUEEN. Below, inscription: TO COMMEMORATE THE VISIT OF HER MAJESTY QUEEN VICTORIA TO BIRMINGHAM ON THE $15^{TH}$ JUNE 1858 TO OPEN ASTON HALL & PARK AS A PLACE OF PUBLIC RECREATION. — JOHN RATCLIFF, ESQ MAYOR.

*Rev.* Front view of Aston Hall. Around, ASTON HALL. ERECTED 1620. In exergue, BOUGHT (WITH 43 ACRES OF PARK) BY THE PEOPLE OF BIRMINGHAM. Signed on bar, J. MOORE F.

Bronze, White Metal, 44 mm. 1858 (BM)

(A gold impression was presented to Queen Victoria: see *Forrer*, 4, 136.)

**35b** *Obv.* Cameo head of Queen Victoria, wearing tiara, in central frame of oak leaves. VICTORIA REGINA. Either side on banner, GOD SAVE THE QUEEN. Around above, TO COMMEMORATE THE VISIT OF HER MOST GRACIOUS MAJESTY TO BIRMINGHAM ON THE $15^{\underline{TH}}$ JUNE 1858, below, TO OPEN ASTON HALL AND PARK AS A PLACE OF PUBLIC RECREATION. — JOHN RATCLIFF ESQ. MAYOR.

*Rev.* View of main front. Above, ASTON HALL, BEGAN 1618. COMPLETED 1635. Below, BOUGHT (WITH 43 ACRES OF PARK) BY THE PEOPLE OF BIRMINGHAM. Signed, J. MOORE F. BIRMINGHAM.

Bronze, White Metal, 55 mm. 1858 (BM)

**35c** *Obv.* Head of Queen to left. Around, HER M.G.M. QUEEN VICTORIA VISITED BIRMINGHAM JUNE 15. 1858 FOR THE PURPOSE OF OPENING ASTON HALL & PARK · THEY HAVING BEEN PURCHASED BY THE INHABITANTS AS A PLACE FOR RECREATION ·:· JOHN RATCLIFF ESQ: MAYOR.

*Rev.* View of main front. ASTON HALL. Below, ERECTED A.D. 1620. Signed, OTTLEY.

White Metal, 45 mm. 1858 (BM)

**35d** *Obv.* Portrait head to right, surrounded by wreath of oak leaves, roses, thistles and shamrocks. HER MOST GRACIOUS MAJESTY QUEEN VICTORIA. Signed, OTTLEY BIRM:.

*Rev.* View of main front of building, with projecting wings. ASTON HALL ERECTED 1618–35. Above, H.M.G. MAJESTY QUEEN VICTORIA VISITED BIRMINGHAM TO INAUGURATE ASTON HALL & PARK AS A PLACE FOR RECRFATION. JUNE 15TH 1858. Signed on bar, OTTLEY BIRM. Around on inside of rim, a decorated fillet.

Bronze, White Metal, 74 mm. 1858 (BM)

**35e** *Obv.* Conjoint heads, to left. VICTORIA D:G:BRIT:REG:F:D:. ALBERT PRINCE CONSORT. Signed OTTLEY.

*Rev.* View of main front of building (as above No. 35d).

Bronze, 74 mm. 1858 (BM)

An early Jacobean house, cf. Audley End or Hatfield. There exist drawings of the house, in a slightly different form, by John Thorpe (*c.* 1563–1655) but he cannot be assumed to be the designer. Built of dark red brick with stone dressing, and with the typical stonework details of the period.

See: *VCH Warwicks.* 7, 61, and plan; Pevsner, *Warwicks.* 149.

35d

LONDON, City, **Royal Exchange,** Cornhill *1667–71*

**36a** *Obv.* Elevation to Cornhill. Around, ROYAL EXCHANGE. Below, BUILT · BY · S$^{R}$ · THO · GRESHAM · 1566 DESTROYED · BY · THE · FIRE · OF · LONDON REBUILT · 1669 · AGAIN · BURNT · JAN$^{RY}$ · 10 · 1838. Signed, I · BARBER · FECIT on ribbon PUB · BY · GRIFFIN & HYAMS · CORNHILL.

*Rev.* Queen Elizabeth I surrounded by courtiers; in exergue legend in five lines: QUEEN · ELIZABETH · PROCLAIMING THE · BURSE · TO · BE · CALLED THE · ROYAL · EXCHANGE · FOR · EVER · 1570.

Bronze, White Metal, 61 mm. 1838 (BM)

**[146d]** *Obv.* View of new Royal Exchange.

*Rev.* Elevation to Cornhill.[1] Around, ROYAL EXCHANGE. Below, BUILT BY S$^{R}$ THOS$^{S}$ GRESHAM 1566 DESTROYED BY THE FIRE OF LONDON REBUILT 1669. AGAIN BURNT JAN$^{Y}$. 10 1838. Signed, HALLIDAY. F: around below, PUBLISHED BY HYAM HYAMS CORNHILL.

White Metal, 61 mm. 1842 (BM)

146d

Rebuilt after the Great Fire of London to the design of one of the City Surveyors, Edward Jarman. The plan had an open court, covered arcades, and a main building front to Cornhill (shown on the medal as restored in the eighteenth century by George Dance (qv)). The statues either side of the central entrance are of Charles I and Charles II by Bushnell.[2] The attic storey, over the four giant Corinthian three-quarter columns, had two sculptured panels; one of these represents Queen Elizabeth proclaiming the original building, i.e. the subject of the medal reverse above. Destroyed by fire 1838 and replaced by Sir William Tite's design (No. 146).

See: Britton and Pugin, *Illustrations of the Public Buildings of London*, 1825–28, vol. i, 292.

1. Although the obverse of this medal is superficially similar to I. Barber's elevation (above) there are many minor differences, e.g. the cupola is shown in perspective; the arcades are filled in by glazing bars; the ground level is not textured.
2. John Bushnell, d. 1701. The statues are now at the Old Bailey. See: Gunnis, 72, 73.

LONDON, City, **Temple Bar,** Strand/Fleet Street *1672*

**37a** *Obv.* West elevation (to Strand). Around, TEMPLE BAR: ERECTED 1672, DEMOLISHED 1878: THIS EFFIGY OF IT WAS STRUCK FROM THE LEAD FORMERLY ON THE ROOF. Monogram HJ on shield. On scroll, SIR C.WREN ARCH$^{T}$. Signed on exergue bar: CH & J MABEY SCULP: FOOT & TEBAY FECIT.

Uniface: Lead, 100 mm. 1878 (BM)

The design is similar to the drawing on the title-page of vol. ii of Britton and Pugin's *Public Buildings of London.* The monogram HJ may refer to the City Architect in 1878, (Sir) Horace Jones. Copies of this medal exist in a decorated brass case, with a glass cover.

The Bar stood at the Strand/Fleet Street boundary of the Cities of Westminster and London. Built by the master masons Thomas Knight (*c.* 1637–80) and Joshua Marshall (1629–78), but often attributed to Wren. The statues of the King and Queen made for Temple Bar in 1670

37a

were the first public works of the sculptor John Bushnell.[1] The Bar, which was of Portland stone, was dismantled in 1878 to allow for traffic widening in conjunction with the building of the Law Courts; it has been re-erected at Theobalds Park, Cheshunt, Hertfordshire.

See: Colvin, 349, 704; Pevsner, *Herts.* 247.

1. Gunnis, 72.

BROMSGROVE, Hereford and Worcester, **King Edward VI Grammar School** *c. 1695*

38a

**38a** *Obv.* Façade of brick building with pitched roof. Below, GRAMMAR SCHOOL OF KING EDW$^{D}$ VI$^{th}$ BROMSGROVE.

White Metal (uniface), 36 mm. 18?? (BM)

The oldest building of Bromsgrove School (refounded in 1693); it contained the original schoolroom. Of *c.* 1695, but the attractive red brick design was harshly altered in 1859 by the addition of a third storey dormitory. It is now adapted for use as study rooms.[1]

See: Pevsner, *Worcs.* 111; *VCH*, *Worcs.* 3, 19; H. E. M. Icely, *Bromsgrove School through four centuries*, Oxford, 1953, 29, 65, 35pl.

1. I am grateful to Mr J. D. H. Hedley for his notes on the Cookes House building. The School has no record of what this medal was struck for, or its date; it could, however, relate to the extensive 'Tercentenary' celebrations of 1853.

LONDON, City, **St Paul's Cathedral** *1675–1710*

**39a** *Obv.* Figure representing Peace crowning George III, dressed as a warrior. Around, REGNO PACEM OBTULIT. In exergue, SUPER PACE RATA DIE 27 MART 11. Signed, HANCOCK.

*Rev.* Perspective view of St Paul's from north-west. Around, DEO GLORIAM REFERT. Below PAX CELEBRATA DIE 1 JUN 11 MDCCCII. Signed K & K (Kempson & Kindon) and H (Hancock).

Silver Gilt, Bronze, 49 mm. 1802 (Eidlitz 1074, pl. 121) (BM)

39b

**39b** *Obv.* Bust, to right, of George III. GOD SAVE THE KING. Signed HALLIDAY F.

*Rev.* Perspective view of St Paul's from north-west. CHURCH AND KING MDCCCVII.

White Metal, gilded, 47 mm. With glass cover in silver ring inscribed, MANUFACTURED BY EDWARD THOMASON, BIRMINGHAM. 1807

**39c** *Obv.* Bust, to right, of George III. GOD SAVE THE KING. Signed K & K below bust.

*Rev.* Perspective view of St Paul's from north-west. KING AND CONSTITUTION. In exergue, MDCCCVII.

Silver, 42 mm. 1807 (BM)

**39d** *Obv.* As above No. 39c.

*Rev.* Perspective view of St Paul's from north-west. CHURCH & KING. In exergue, MDCCCVII.

White Metal, 42 mm. 1807 (BM)

**39e** *Obv.* Plenty, blindfolded, stands on a wheel amidst clouds while her cornucopia dispenses coins. Around, WEALTH AND INDEPENDENCE.

*Rev.* West fronts of St Paul's and Westminster Abbey placed side by side. THE CONSTITUTION 1821.

Brass, 45 mm. 1821 (BM)

**39f** *Obv.* View of cathedral. Around, S$^{T}$ PAUL'S CATHEDRAL LONDON. In exergue, NORTH-WEST VIEW. Signed JOS$^{H}$ DAVIS BIRMINGHAM.

*Rev.* View of nave looking towards crossing. INTERIOR OF S$^{T}$ PAUL'S THE NAVE AND CHOIR.

Bronze, White Metal, 60 mm. 1835 (Eidlitz 1076, pl. 121) (BM)

One of the Davis series of English cathedrals (see p. 216).

**39g** *Obv.* Exterior view. ST PAULS CATHEDRAL LONDON. Signed, DAVIS BIRM.

*Rev.* Inscription: ST PAUL'S CATHEDRAL — A CHRISTIAN CHURCH IS SUPPOSED TO HAVE BEEN FOUNDED HERE ON THE FIRST INTRODUCTION OF CHRISTIANITY IN THE SECOND CEN-TURY AND TO HAVE BEEN DESTROYED IN THE DIOCLESION PERSECUTION; IT WAS REBUILT ON THE CONVERSION OF ETHELBERT ABOUT A.D. 610 AND DESTROYED BY FIRE A.D. 1086. THE REBUILDING WAS COMMENCED BY MAURICE THEN BISHOP OF LONDON & THE CONSECRATION TOOK PLACE IN 1240, ALTHOUGH NOT COMPLETED BEFORE 1315, WHICH BUILDING WAS AGAIN DESTROYED IN THE GREAT FIRE OF 1666. THE PRESENT FABRICK WAS COMMENCED IN 1675, DIVINE SERVICE FIRST PERFORMED DEC. 2 1697 AND THE CHURCH COMPLETED IN 1710, WHICH WITH ITS EMBELLISHMENTS COST UPWARDS OF £736,000. IT IS IN LENGTH 500 F$^{T}$ BREADTH 285 F$^{T}$ HEIGHT TO THE TOP OF THE CROSS 340 F$^{T}$

Bronze, 44 mm. ?1840s (Eidlitz 1077)

39h

**39h** *Obv.* Profile portrait to right. WREN. Signed, W. WILSON SC.
*Rev.* West elevation of St Paul's. CHRISTOPHER WREN ARCHITECT — MDCCX. Below, SI MONUMENTUM REQUIRIS CIRCUMSPICE. Signed B.WYON S.
Edge Inscription ART-UNION OF LONDON 1846.
Bronze, 59 mm. 1849–50 (Eidlitz 1078, pl. 121) (BM)

One of the Art-Union series depicting artists, architects and their works; issued in silver or bronze (see p. 212, and Plate 8). The Latin quotation on the reverse is the well-known epitaph on the tomb of Wren, who is buried in the crypt of the cathedral. For date of striking see Beulah, p. 182.

**39i** *Obv.* Perspective view of exterior from north-west. Below, ST PAUL'S CATHEDRAL LONDON. Signed, J. WIENER F.
*Rev.* Interior of cathedral, from nave towards choir and altar. Below, FOUNDED VII CENTURY. BURNT XI CENTURY. REBUILT IN STONE XII AND XIII CENT$^{Y}$ AGAIN BURNT 1666. REBUILT IN ITS PRESENT STATE 1675–1710. ARCHIT. CHRIST. WREN. Signed J. WIENER F.
Bronze, 59 mm. 1849 (Eidlitz 1075, pl. 121) (BM)

This is one of the Wiener series of English cathedrals (see p. 224); there is a variant in the BM with the reverse inscription in French.

39i

**39j** *Obv.* View of St Paul's from south-west. Signed in exergue, W. J. TAYLOR LONDON.

*Rev.* Wreath of leaves. Around, NATIONAL THANKSGIVING FOR THE RECOVERY OF H.R.H. THE PRINCE OF WALES · In centre: — ST PAUL'S CATHEDRAL FEB:27:1872 —.

White Metal, 35 mm. 1872 (BM)

**39k** *Obv.* Allegorical setting: The Prince of Wales and Queen Victoria welcomed by the City of London, supported by Britannia, at the West Portico of St Paul's Cathedral. Below, I WAS GLAD WHEN THEY SAID UNTO ME LET US GO INTO THE HOUSE OF THE LORD. Signed, J. S. & A. B. WYON SC.

*Rev.* Interior of St Paul's Cathedral with assembled congregation. Flanked by Royal Arms (left) and City Arms (right) on shields. On border of interior, NATIONAL THANKSGIVING FOR THE RECOVERY OF H.R.H. THE PRINCE OF WALES ST PAUL'S LONDON. Below 27 FEB 1872. Signed, J. S. & A. B. WYON SC.

Bronze, 76 mm. 1872 (BM)

One of the City of London series (see p. 214). In presentation case with gilt lettering.

39k

**39l** *Obv.* Head to left. ALBERT EDWARD PRINCE OF WALES. Below, BORN NOV 9 1841.

*Rev.* Exterior view. ST PAUL'S CATHEDRAL. Below, LONDON 1872.

Bronze, 23 mm. Edge milled. 1872 (Eidlitz 1079, pl. 121)

**39m** *Obv.* View of St Paul's Cathedral from south-west.

*Rev.* View of Tower Bridge. River Thames and ships in foreground.

Brass, 24 mm. ?1894 (BM)

Of 1894, or after, as Tower Bridge is shown completed (see No. 225a).

**39n** *Obv.* View of Cathedral from north-west. On scroll, MAY NATIONAL EDUCATION EVER FLOURISH. In exergue, five lines (but no inscription).

*Rev.* Crown on bible. MONITORS MEDAL.

Bronze, White Metal, 45 mm. 18 . . (BM)

**39o** *Obv.* Elevation of west end of St Paul's with dome in background. Rim beaded. Around, ST PAUL'S CATHEDRAL. Below, LONDON.

*Rev.* Inscription: FOUNDED 1675 FINISHED 1710 — * — SIR CHRISTOPHER WREN ARCHITECT.

Bronze, 32 mm. 18 . . (BM)

Sir Christopher Wren's 'Great' Model of 1673 proposed a centralised plan, but the concept proved liturgically unacceptable. A compromise design was then given the Royal Warrant in 1675; this was modified during building to provide the outer walls of the aisles with a second storey 'screen' wall above them. The increased height changed the whole character of the building, by giving an impression of size lacking in the 'Warrant' design, and by concealing the traditional Gothic cathedral profile of lower aisles and flying buttresses. The two-storey classical screen (cf. the Banqueting House of 1622, No. 34) is shown on the medals together with the very Baroque west towers (1705–8) and the dome (*c.* 1706–10). The pediment to the west front contains a relief 'The Conversion of St Paul' by the sculptor Francis Bird, and the exterior carving includes outstanding work by Grinling Gibbons and Caius Gabriel Cibber. The interior view (No. 39k) shows the choir before the installation of G. F. Bodley's high altar and reredos, 1886–88 (destroyed in 1940 and replaced by the present baldachino in the 1950s).

See: M. Whinney, *Wren*, 1971, 81–132; Pevsner, *London 1*, 111 ff.

KETTERING, Northants, **Baptist Mission House,** Lower Street *?c. 1710*

**40a** *Obv.* View of Mission House. BAPTIST MISSION JUBILEE 1842. In exergue, THE HOUSE AT KETTERING IN WHICH THE BAPTIST MISSIONARY SOCIETY WAS FORMED OCT. 2$^{nd}$ 1792. Signed on exergue bar, DAVIS BIRM.

*Rev.* Inscription: NOT BY MIGHT, NOT BY POWER, BUT BY MY SPIRIT SAITH THE LORD. ZECH. C. 4. V. 6. In centre, an open Bible, surrounded by five portrait busts within roundels labelled, CAREY FULLER PEARCE RYLAND SUTCLIFF.

Bronze, 39 mm. 1842 (BM)

40b

**40b** *Obv.* View of Mission House. JUBILEE OF BAPTIST MISSION. Below, FORMED AT KETTERING OCT$^{R}$ 2$^{ND}$ 1792. Signed, J. TAYLOR BIRM:

*Rev.* Two portrait busts, side by side. CAREY AND THOMAS THE FIRST MISSIONARIES.

White Metal, 43 mm. 1842 (BM)

**40c** *Obv.* View of Mission House. BAPTIST MISSION CENTENARY 1792–1892. In exergue, THE HOUSE AT KETTERING IN WHICH THE BAPTIST MISSIONARY SOCIETY WAS FORMED OCT 2$^{ND}$ 1792.

*Rev.* Inscription: CAREY FULLER MARSHMAN WARD. In centre, an open Bible, surrounded by four roundels within which are: views of AFRICA (top) INDIA (left) CHINA (right), and objects of slavery WEST INDIES EMANCIPATION (below).

White Metal, 45 mm. 1892 (BM)

A handsome seven-bay, double-fronted early eighteenth-century house. Built of stone, rendered and painted, with a Collyweston slate roof. It is now owned by the Baptist Missionary Society.

See: Pevsner, *Northants*, 265.

BIRMINGHAM, West Midlands, **St Philip's Church**, Colmore Row (now St Philip's Cathedral) *1710–15*

41a

**41a** *Obv.* View of church from east end. Around, S$^{T}$ PHILIP'S CHURCH BIRMINGHAM. CONSECRATED 4$^{TH}$ OCT. 1715. Signed H on ground.

*Rev.* Crown on HOLY BIBLE. Around, COMMEMORATION MEDAL 4$^{TH}$ OCT$^{R}$ 1815*.

Bronze, White Metal, 46 mm. 1815 (BM)

**41b** *Obv.* Bust to left. EDM. OUTRAM D.D. Signed around, MODELED BY HOLLINS THOMASON & JONES · D ·

*Rev.* View of church from east end (as above obverse, No. 41a).

Bronze, 46 mm. ?1822 (BM)

Grant gives 1822 for a medal of this description by Hollins & Halliday. Built in 1710–15, with the tower completed 1725. It was Thomas Archer's first major commission and it reflects his study abroad, particularly of the Italian Baroque works of Bernini and Borromini. This is most apparent in the west end and tower (cf. the west towers of St Paul's Cathedral). The chancel was extended (1883–84) by the local architect J. A. Chatwin. St Philip's was given cathedral status in 1905.

See: Pevsner, *Warwicks.* 106; Marcus Whiffen, *Stuart and Georgian Churches*, London, 1948, 23, 24.

WOODSTOCK, Oxon., **Blenheim Palace** *1705–20*

**42a** *Obv.* Bust facing. SIR JOHN VANBRUGH. Signed, BENJ. WYON SC.

*Rev.* Portico and nine-bay central block shown in elevation. BLENHEIM. Signed, BENJ. WYON SC. Edge inscription: ART UNION OF LONDON 1855.

Bronze, 55 mm. 1856 (BM)

This fine medal of Blenheim and its architect is one of the Art-Union series (see p. 213, and Plate 5). The portrait is based upon the painting of Vanbrugh, aged about forty, by Sir Godfrey Kneller in the National Portrait Gallery. The image is, however, reversed.

Commissioned in 1705 from Sir John Vanbrugh, whose architectural work already included Castle Howard, Yorks. The design for Blenheim allowed him to create a palace on a heroic scale, and to develop a personal interpretation of Baroque 'Movement' by arranging large building elements for effects of recession and projection. The medal shows part of the north (courtyard) front of the main block, and isolates the centre

42a

section; behind the entrance portico lies a great hall (70 ft long, 45 ft wide, 67 ft high) which provides the approach to the saloon and state apartments. As assistant to Vanbrugh, 1705–16 (and later as sole architect to the Duchess of Marlborough), Nicholas Hawksmoor's role in the design of Blenheim is an important one, and this aspect is discussed in the references given.

See: L. Whistler, *The Imagination of Vanbrugh*, 1954, 83 ff.; Pevsner, *Oxon.*, 459–75; D. Green, *Blenheim Palace*, 1951.

LONDON, Lambeth, **Stockwell Park School** *?before 1730*

43a

**43a** *Obv.* View of school house, within grounds. STOCKWELL PARK. Around, on border, a wreath of leaves.

*Rev.* A young boy, carrying a book and a laurel spray. In the background the sunrise. Around, SUA PRÆMIA LAUDI.

Bronze, White Metal, 41 mm. 1820[G] (BM)

Carlisle attributes this medal to W. Wyon in his *Memoir of the Life and Works*, p. 164. It is also given in Forrer's list of Wyon's medals (vol. 6, p. 650 ff.) with no date known. The Survey of London information (below) suggests this might be a prize medal struck at the opening of the school.

John Angell (d. 1784) had built the large brick Stockwell Park House in the early 1700s. After his death (and by 1826) this was turned into a school. The house was pulled down in 1882 when Benedict and Speenham Roads were made.

See: *Survey of London*, vol. 26; E. Walford, *Old and New London*, 1897, vol. 6, p. 329.

SEDGLEY, West Midlands, **Sedgley Park School** *?before 1730*

44a

**44a** *Obv.* View of formal central block with older, adjoining, wings. SEDGLEY PARK. Below, ESTABLISHED IN 1762. Signed, WYON. F.

*Rev.* A roman tripod, with olive branch to either side. THE REWARD OF MERIT.

Bronze, White Metal, 42 mm. ?1799 (BM)

Grant gives this as T. Wyon Sen. in 1799. The medal was originated by the Revd. John Kirk, a former chaplain at Sedgley Park, and the reverse is copied from a silver medal he had received in Rome from Cardinal Corsini.[1]

44b

**44b** *Obv.* School from similar viewpoint to above, but wing buildings have been improved and windows altered. Around, on scrolls, SEDGLEY PARK; below · ESTABLISHED · 1763 ·

*Rev.* Inscription around: BENE FUNDATA EST DOMUS DOMINI SUPRA FIRMAN PETRAM with quatrefoil design in centre.

Bronze, 43 mm. 1863[G] (BM)

The style of this medal suggests a mid-nineteenth-century date; Grant relates it to the centenary of the school.

Sedgley Park School was established in 1763, as a Roman Catholic Seminary, in Park Hall, the former home of the first Viscount Dudley and Ward. It continued as a school until 1866. The main block shown on the medal views of Park Hall is described by Pevsner as late seventeenth-century or a very conservative eighteenth-century design. Brick with a frontispiece of three stages with attached columns. The later medal shows several 'improvements', e.g. the rebuilt left-hand block, and the sash windows to the wing buildings to replace earlier arched openings with industrial type fenestration.

See: Pevsner, *Staffs.* 232.

1. M. Perkins, in *Blocksidge's Dudley Almanack*, 1910, 81–82. The medals were conferred at Christmas each year to the best scholars. The date 1762 is an error for 1763 (see No. 44b) discovered after striking.

CAMBRIDGE, Cambs., **Senate House** *1722–30*

45a

45b

**45a** *Obv.* Bust to left of Marquis of Camden. Around, JOAN : JEFFREYS MARCH : CAMDEN : NOBILISS : ACAD : CANTAB : CANCELL : 1835.

*Rev.* Interior of Senate House, from entrance, with columns supporting balcony on either side. Above, angel with garland. Below, DEUM TIMETO : REGEM HONORATO : VIRTUTEM COLITO : DISCIPLINIS BONIS OPERAM DATO.

Silver, Bronze, White Metal, 44 mm. 1835[1] (BM)

**45b** *Obv.* Head of Duke of Northumberland.[2] Around, PRINCEPS ILLUSTRISS : HUGO PERCY NORTUMB : DUX ACAD : CANTAB CANCELL : 1842.

*Rev.* Exterior of Senate House from court, with graduates in cap and gown in procession. Above, arms of Duke of Northumberland, ESPERANCE EN DIEU. Below, SENATE HOUSE and coat of arms of University ALMA MATER CANTABRIGIA.

Silver, Bronze, 44 mm. 1842 (BM)

**45c** *Obv.* Head of Duke of Northumberland (as above No. 45b).

*Rev.* Interior of Senate House (as above No. 45a).

Silver, Bronze, 44 mm. 1842 (BM)

**45d** *Obv.* Bust of Prince Albert. Around, PRINCEPS CELSISSIMUS ALBERTUS ACAD : CANTAB : CANCELL. 1847.

*Rev.* Interior of Senate House (as above No. 45a).

Bronze, 44 mm. 1847 (BM)

**45e** *Obv.* Bust of Duke of Devonshire. Around, PRINCEPS ILLUSTRISS : GULIELMUS CAVENDISH DEVONIÆ DUX ACAD : CANTAB : CANCELL : 1862.

*Rev.* Interior of Senate House (as above No. 45a).

Silver, glazed, 44 mm. 1862 (BM)

These medals were published in Cambridge by J. Peters to celebrate the installation of University Chancellors at the Senate House; they may have been struck by Ottley (see p. 220).[3] The 1835 medal for the Marquess of Camden (1759–1840) is described by H. A. Grueber in *Num. Chron.* 1888, 265; it is incorrectly stated that the 'new Senate House' was opened in 1835. It was in fact opened by the ceremonies of Public Commencement 6 July 1730 (Willis & Clark, iii, p. 54).

Designed by James Gibbs as one element in his unrealised scheme of Senate House, Library, and Registry forming an open quadrangle. Built of Portland stone it combines Palladianism with Gibbs's experience in Rome under Carlo Fontana. The medallic views of the interior show the single rectangular space, with galleries along three sides and a coffered plaster ceiling (by the Italians Artari and Bagutti).

See: Pevsner, *Cambs.* 164.

1. Hocking, vol. ii, p. 254, no. 65, lists this as a work of William Wyon, although the medal is unsigned and there remains no real evidence for the attribution. All the medals in this series are of similar format with a common reverse (the interior); that of the Duke of Northumberland of 1842 is specifically referred to in *GM,* 1842, p. 182, as published by James Peters.

2. The *GM,* op. cit., was extremely critical of this medal: 'The workmanship is indifferently good, but the design is poor indeed. This betrays itself in the Duke's dress particularly in the arrangement of the collar of the Garter which also wants its distinctive pendant of St George. The silent Senate-house, with its procession of eleven figures and one spectator, is little characteristic of the thronging installation; but the most objectionable feature is the mode in which the field is cut up, and tastelessly arranged. Even the Duke's achievement is not correct. Besides the omission of his customary quartering of Percy, his sinister supporter is given as a unicorn, whereas he uses in that place a lion with four affrontée. His motto is spread out above the achievement, instead of being placed upon the label below his shield, which is yet there, but awkwardly left empty. This motto being french together with the words "Senate House" in English and "Alma Mater Cantabrigia" in latin, make an unnecessary and injudicious mixture of languages. We have frequently observed the poverty of invention and want of taste in our medallists; but we hope that the School of Design will effect a change in this most lasting, as well as the more evanescent forms of art.'

3. Grant, in *BNJ,* xxiii, 131n.; E. A. Barnard, 'Cambridge Installation Medals 1835–1862', in *Notes and Queries,* vol. 183, 29 August 1942, 122–4, records that the Camden installation medal was advertised by Peters in the *Cambridge Chronicle,* and described as being made at Soho, Birmingham. Peters later advertised the Albert installation medal, 1847, as having an effigy taken from a miniature by (Sir William) Ross.

BATH, Avon, **St Michael's (Old) Church,** Broad Street *1742*

46a

**46a** *Obv.* South elevation of church in classical style. ST MICHAEL'S OLD CHURCH BATH ERECTED 1742. TAKEN DOWN 1835. Signed, DAVIS BIRM.

*Rev.* Inscription: IN MEMORY OF THE REV$^{D}$ JOHN RICHARDS OB$^{T}$ APRIL. 15. 1825 WHOSE FAITH FOLLOW HEB. XIII. 7.

Bronze, 38 mm. 1835 (BM)

Companion piece to No. 115a.

By the Bath mason John Harvey, who secured the appointment rather than the better-known John Wood (qv). The church, skilfully fitted into a cramped site, was entered by the south portico (shown on the medal); this opened into a single south aisle with segmental ends. The design was duly criticised by Wood in his *Essay Towards a Description of Bath.* Demolished in 1835 to make way for G. P. Manners's gothic design (No. 115).

See: W. Ison, *The Georgian Buildings of Bath,* 1948, 70, 71.

BATH, Avon, **Prior Park,** Combe Down (now Prior Park School)
*1735–c. 1750*

**47a** *Obv.* View of building, with main portico, and landscaped terraces and stairs in foreground. PRIOR PARK. Signed, HALLIDAY. F.

*Rev.* Shield, with SS. Peter and Paul seated to either side. Above the dove of the Holy spirit. Motto: ITA DESIDERAT ANIMA MEA.

Silver, 51 mm. $1839^{G}$ (BM)

47a

Designed by John Wood, the elder, for Ralph Allen as a grand villa in the manner of Palladio. The main block of local stone (the south front is shown on the medal) was to be linked by curved one-storey arcades to pavilion blocks, but the latter were never correctly built.[1] Further changes were made in 1830, when Prior Park became a Roman Catholic boarding school (cf. medal reverse). In 1836 the Bath architect H. E. Goodridge added the elaborate outer staircase to the south front.

See: Pevsner, *N. Somerset,* 113.

1. The completion of Prior Park was handed over to Richard Jones, the clerk of works, following a quarrel between architect and client.

WARRINGTON, Cheshire, **Bank Hall** (now the Town Hall, Sankey Street) *c. 1750*

**48a** *Obv.* View of former 'Bank House' with two-storey, three-bay portico.

*Rev.* Inscription: NEW TOWN HALL AND BANK PARK OPENED $20^{TH}$ JUNE 1873.

Bronze gilt, 32 mm. 1873 (BM)

48a

Built by James Gibbs *c.* 1750 as a country house on the edge of town. 'The finest house of its date in S. Lancs' (Pevsner). The outer three bays of the façade are of exposed brick, the middle three rendered to imitate rusticated ashlar. The house is flanked by detached service wings with pedimented central sections.

See: Pevsner, *S Lancs.*, 413; *AR* lxiv (1928), 30–31 for drawings.

LONDON, Tower Hamlets, **The London Hospital,** Whitechapel Road
*1752–57*

**49a** *Obv.* North elevation of three-storey hospital building, with central and wing blocks slightly emphasised. On border around, PRESENTED BY THE GOVERNORS OF THE LONDON HOSPITAL. In exergue, FOUNDED 1740. Signed B. WYON S.

*Rev.* Wreath and Aesculapian symbol in central panel. Border around blank (for inscription?).

White Metal, 36 mm. *c.* 1840[1] (Watt Coll. 1339)

49a

The hospital moved to Whitechapel in 1757 and the architect of its new building (1752–57) was Boulton Mainwaring. His initial block of twenty-three bays (see medal) had additions built behind it in the eighteenth and nineteenth centuries; further extensions were then made to the left (1876) and right (1866; dem. 1974). The central portion of Mainwaring's design was extended outwards in 1890, to the design of Roland Plumbe, and the front elevation raised to four storeys.

1. Although there is no mention of this medal in the hospital records, it is believed to mark the 'First Centenary' (1740–1840). I am grateful to the Revd A. C. C. Courtauld, and to the Librarian of the London Hospital Medical College, for information on the building history.

50a

ACKWORTH, West Yorks. (near Pontefract), **Ackworth School** *1758 on*

**50a** *Obv.* Bust to right. D$^{R}$ JOHN FOTHERGILL, FOUNDER OF ACKWORTH SCHOOL BORN 1712 – DIED 1780. Signed on truncation JOS$^{H}$ MOORE. F.

*Rev.* View of grounds, and school buildings. ACKWORTH SCHOOL FOUNDED 1779. Around on border. IN COMMEMORATION OF THE CENTENNIAL OF ACKWORTH SCHOOL. 1879.

White Metal, 51 mm. 1879 (BM)

Built on a grand scale, 1758 on, by the Governors of the London Foundling Hospital. Bought 1778 by Dr John Fothergill (see medal obverse) and opened as a Friends School 1779. The centre block is connected by semicircular linking colonnades to side wings each of thirteen bays.[1]

See: Pevsner, *Yorks., W Riding,* 71; M. Seaborne, *The English School,* 1971, 113, 114, and pl. 104. E. Vipont, *Ackworth School,* 1959.

1. Vipont, *op. cit.,* 19, gives the name of the designer as 'Watson'; the east wing with cupola was completed 1758, the rest of the building by 1765.

51a

BIRMINGHAM, West Midlands, **St John the Baptist,** Deritend High Street *1735 and 1762*

**51a** *Obv.* View of church.

*Rev.* Legend: DERITEND & BORDESLEY SUNDAY SCHOOLS. In centre, MERIT.

Bronze, 38 mm. 18–– (BM)

A rectangular brick church, with a tower (added in 1762) of two stages topped by a balustrade and urns at the angles. This stood on the south side of Deritend High Street and replaced a fourteenth-century building. Restored in 1891 to have 800 sittings; sold to City authorities in 1939; demolished in 1961.

See: *VCH, Warwicks.,* vol. 7, 364, 365 and illus.

LONDON, Westminster, **Somerset House,** Strand *1776–86*

**52a** *Obv.* Profile portrait, to right, of architect. CHAMBERS 1725–1796. Signed on truncation, B. WYON; below, AFTER WESTMACOTT.

*Rev.* Elevation to Strand of nine-bay entrance block. Below, SOMERSET HOUSE 1781 SIR WILLIAM CHAMBERS R.A. ARCHITECT. Signed, B. WYON. Edge inscription ART-UNION of LONDON 1857.

Bronze, 55 mm. 1857 (Eidlitz 240, pl. 10) (BM)

52a

Issued as one of Art-Union series (see p. 212, and Plate 4). See also: H. A. Grueber in *Num. Chron.* 1888, 281, 282. The medal gives incorrect dates for Chambers (1723–96). The portrait is based on a bust exhibited at the Royal Academy in 1797 by Sir Richard Westmacott (1775–1856); this is now in Sir John Soane's Museum.[1]

Built, under an Act of 1775, as a great new administrative centre to house official and academic bodies. Designed by Sir William Chambers, the Surveyor General, and completed in the nineteenth century by Sir Robert Smirke (eastern extension for Kings' College), and Sir James Pennethorne (western extension to Waterloo Bridge). Chambers decided on a central courtyard, approached through a block of narrow frontage which was to house the learned societies, including the Royal Academy and Society of Antiquaries. It is the Strand façade of this entrance block that is shown on the medal; it was complete by 1781 and incorporated sculpture by fellow Academicians Bacon, Carlini, and Wilton.

See: Pevsner, *London 1*, 284–87; J. Harris, *Sir William Chambers*, 1970, 96–106.

1. See J. Harris, op. cit. p. 173; this reference attributes the Art-Union medal in error to William Wyon.

LONDON, City, **Guildhall, South Entrance Façade** *1788–89*

**53a** *Obv.* Head of Queen Victoria to left, with hair plaited. VICTORIA. Signed on truncation, W. WYON.

*Rev.* Façade. In exergue, THE QUEEN VISITS THE CITY OF LONDON NOV 9 1837.

Silver, Bronze, 21 mm. 1837 (BM)

To mark the presence of the Queen at the Mayoralty Banquet at Guildhall.

**53b** *Obv.* Profile portrait to left of Queen Victoria, wearing tiara. Around, VICTORIA REGINA. Signed W. WYON R. A.

*Rev.* Entrance façade of Guildhall. Below, IN HONOUR OF HER MAJESTY'S VISIT TO THE CORPORATION OF LONDON 9TH NOV: 1837.

Silver, Bronze, 54 mm. 1838 (BM)

53b

One of the medals issued during the nineteenth century by the Corporation of the City of London (see p. 214, and Plate 6). The portrait of the young Queen subsequently became famous as that used on the first postage stamp, the Penny Black.[1]

**53c** *Obv.* Entrance façade of Guildhall. Below, GUILDHALL LONDON 1837.

*Rev.* Inscription: IN HONOR [*sic*] OF HER MAJESTY'S VISIT TO THE CORPORATION OF LONDON 9$^{TH}$ NOVEMBER 1837.

Silver, Bronze, 51mm. 1838 (Royal Mint Museum)

Given in Hocking (ii), p. 221, nos. 6–7, as by B. Wyon. The execution of the Guildhall elevation is identical to that of the W. Wyon medal above (No. 53b). The difference in size of the obverse of No. 53c to the reverse of No. 53b is due to the addition of an extra moulding within the rim of the latter.

The work of George Dance. The quasi-Oriental character of this new south façade, later to be mocked by Pugin in his *Contrasts*, can be related to Dance's interest in the publication *Select Views of India* (1786) by his friend William Hodges.[2] The façade is also 'suprisingly daredevil in its mixing of Gothic and classical motifs' (Pevsner); however, as a design this was only following the example of an existing gothic porch of 1430, and one which by the eighteenth century had had classical motifs superimposed on it.[3] Unpopular as it was to become in the nineteenth century, Dance's solution can now be said to have conserved some of the essence of a very cherished local scene. The east side of the façade was torn down in the 1870s, but restored again in 1909, and the work happily survives intact.

See: Pevsner, *London 1,* 171; D. Stroud, *George Dance,* 1971, 119 ff.

1. *Num. Chron.*, pp. 192–94, describes how this medal was commissioned by the City's Royal Entertainments Committee *following* the event, and prompted by the small medal (No. 53a above) which Wyon had already published; it was this Committee which made 'humble application' requesting the Queen to sit for her portrait.
2. This influence is discussed in Stroud, op. cit. 119–20.
3. See C. M. Barron, *The Medieval Guildhall of London*, 1974, 27, pls 7, 8.

BIRMINGHAM, West Midlands, **General Hospital,** Summer Lane *1766–90*

54a

**54a** *Obv.* Main front of hospital and flanking pavilions; behind wall. Irradiated above: THE GENERAL HOSPITAL BIRMINGHAM.

*Rev.* Inscription: BIRMINGHAM MUSICAL FESTIVAL FOR THE BENEFIT OF THE GENERAL HOSPITAL OCTOBER 7. 8. 9. & 10. 1823 — PATRON HIS MOST EXCELLENT MAJESTY — PRESIDENT THE R$^{T}$ HON$^{BLE}$ EARL TALBOT — VICE PRESIDENTS D. OF DEVONSHIRE. M. OF STAFFORD. M. OF ANGLESEY. EARLS. OF DENBIGH. PLYMOUTH. DARTMOUTH. AYLESFORD. WARWICK. CORNWALLIS BISHOP OF LICHFIELD & COVENTRY. CRAVEN. HARROWBY. BRADFORD. BEAUCHAMP. HOWE. CLONMELL. GOWER. VIS$^{S}$ DUDLEY & WARD ANSON. GRANVILLE. NEWPORT. LORD BISHOP OF OXFORD. LORDS WILLOUGHBY DE BROKE. MIDDLETON. BAGOT. CALTHORPE. — SKIPWITH. LAWLEY. WROTTESLEY. M.P. WINNINGTON M.P. HARTOPP. PEEL. BART$^{S}$ DUGDALE M.P. LAWLEY M.P. LITTLETON M.P.

INGE. LEGGE. ESQ$^{S}$ REV. L. GARDNER D.D. RECTOR OF S$^{T}$ PHILIPS CHURCH.

White Metal, 64 mm. 1823 (BM)

(Note the format as Church series, e.g. St Peter's, Dale End, No. 88a.)

**54b** *Obv.* Main front of hospital and flanking pavilions behind wall. Irradiated above: THE GENERAL HOSPITAL BIRMINGHAM.

*Rev.* Inscription within wreath; musical symbols below: BIRMINGHAM MUSICAL FESTIVAL FOR THE BENEFIT OF THE GENERAL HOSPITAL OCTOBER 3.4.5. & 6. 1826 PATRON THE KINGS MOST EXCELLENT MAJESTY PRESIDENT THE RIGHT HONOURABLE EARL HOWE. Signed, OTTLEY.

Bronze, 64 mm. 1826 (BM)

**54c** *Obv.* Main front of hospital. (As above No. 54a.)

*Rev.* Inscription around: BIRMINGHAM MUSICAL FESTIVAL and musical symbols. In centre a tabulation of: YEAR | RECEIPTS | EXPENSES | PROCEEDS from 1784 to 1829.

White Metal, 64 mm. 1829 (BM)

The first part of the hospital was a three-storey brick block of 1766–79; two wings in the same style were added in 1790 (see medal obverse).[1] In 1768 a series of concerts had been given to raise finances for the hospital; from 1796 this developed into a regular Triennial Musical Festival. The medals above give details of these festivals, and were perhaps sold in aid of them. Prior to the 1830s the festivals were held in the assembly rooms of the Royal Hotel; only after the building of Birmingham Town Hall (see No. 108) were full orchestral performances made possible. The building was replaced by a new General Hospital completed 1897.

See: *VCH, Warwicks.*, vol. 7, 43, 218, illus. opp. p. 327.

1. J. T. Bunce, *The Birmingham General Hospital & Triennial Musical Festivals*, 1858, notes that, 'A plan for the building having been obtained from a Mr Vyse . . . ' the construction started in 1766. Due to lack of funds the building lay partly complete from 1769 to 1776 'a miserable object of ruin and dilapidation' (R. K. Dent, *The Making of Birmingham*, 1894, 117).

OLD WINDSOR, Berks., **Beaumont Lodge** *1790*

**55a** *Obv.* Elevation of the former Beaumont Lodge with three-storey central portico. COLL STI. STANISLAI BEAUMONT. Below, NON AD CADUCA SED AD ÆTERNA.

*Rev.* Within panels, the Virgin, flanked by cherubic heads and wings. Around, SEDES SAPIENTIÆ ORA PRO NOBIS.

Silver, 56 mm. ?1860s (BM)

55a

An earlier house 'improved' by Henry Emlyn of Windsor, and completed by 1790. The portico incorporated Emlyn's own invention, the soon forgotten 'British Order' of architecture. The medal obverse shows his use of coupled columns growing out of a common base—the point of splitting being covered by the symbol of the Order of the Garter. The house was bought by the Society of Jesus in 1854, and a school established there in 1861; it is for this school that the medal was struck.

See: Pevsner, *Berks.* 189; S. Blutman, *Beaumont Lodge and the British Order* (in H. Colvin and J. Harris, eds, *The Country Seat*, 1970, 181 ff.).

56a

CHELMSFORD, Essex, **Shire Hall,** Tindal Square *1789–91*

**56a** *Obv.* View of main front. Below on scroll, SHIRE HALL.

*Rev.* Inscription: CHELMSFORD POLYTECHNIC EXHIBITION MAY 1848.

White Metal, 29 mm. 1848 (BM)

**56b** *Obv.* Elevation of main front, with three-bay pediment. In exergue, COUNTY HALL CHELMSFORD. Signed, PINCHES LONDON.

*Rev.* Cow with sheep in background; below, a plough. Around, TO COMMEMORATE THE VISIT OF THE ROYAL AGRICULTURAL SOCIETY OF ENGLAND. In exergue, JULY 1856. Signed on bar, PINCHES LONDON.

White Metal, 51 mm. 1856 (BM)

By John Johnson, County Surveyor. Built of Portland stone, with four attached giant columns. Coade stone relief plaques above the middle windows by the elder Bacon.

See: Pevsner, *Essex*, 117.

57a

BIRMINGHAM, West Midlands, **Blue Coat School,** St Philip's Churchyard *1792–94*

**57a** *Obv.* View of four-storey school buildings. BLUE COAT CHARITY SCHOOL BIRMINGHAM. Signed in script, OTTLEY.

*Rev.* Inscription: FOR THE EDUCATION AND SUPPORT OF BOYS AND GIRLS PARISHONERS OF BIRMINGHAM AND MEMBERS OF THE ESTABLISHED CHURCH WAS ERECTED A.D. 1724 AND ENLARGED A.D. 1794. — THIS MEDAL WAS STRUCK TO COMMEMORATE THE CELEBRATION OF THE CENTENARY $4^{th}$ AUGUST 1824 BY ORDER OF THE COMMITTEE. — THOMAS MOLE CHAIRMAN.

Bronze, 48 mm. 1824 (BM)

The building shown on the medal is that rebuilt 1792–94 by John Rawsthorne. It stood on the east side of St Philip's Churchyard and was demolished 1935 when the Blue Coat School moved out to the suburb of Harbourne.

See: Pevsner, *Warwicks.*, 186.

58a

BIRMINGHAM, West Midlands, **Old Meeting House,** Old Meeting House Street *1795*

**58a** *Obv.* Exterior: elevation of five bays. OLD MEETING-HOUSE BIRMINGHAM.

*Rev.* Inscription: SUNDAY SCHOOLS FIFTIETH ANNIVERSARY WISDOM IS BETTER THAN STRENGTH 1837.

Bronze, 38 mm. 1837 (BM)

A new brick chapel was completed 1795 to replace an earlier dissenters (i.e. Presbyterian/Unitarian) building burnt in 1791. The chapel was entered via a recessed porch behind the arched openings; there were three galleries internally and seating for 870. Sold in 1881, and demolished to make way for New Street Station.

See: *VCH, Warwicks.*, vol. 7, 476, illus. opp. p. 411.

LONDON, Islington, **Charterhouse School** *1802–3*

**59a** *Obv.* Elevation of five-bay Charterhouse School building. ΓΡΑΜΜΑΤΙΚΗΙ ΕΤΕΙ $\overline{A\omega\gamma}$.[1]

*Rev.* Wreath around. Inscription in centre: CARTHVSIANI HONORIS CAVSA.

Silver, 36 mm. 1816ᴳ (Watt Coll.)*

59a

The award was instituted in 1816. This specimen* has an edge inscription JOSEPH WILLIAM ALLAN GR.IAMB 1819; Allan was both Gold and Silver Medallist for 1819 and retained this Silver version for his Greek Iambics.

The elevation shown is of the brick-built schoolroom known as 'Big School'. Designed by William Pilkington, it was completed in 1803 on the raised ground that marked the debris of the northern range of the Cloisters of the Carthusian monastery. The design consisted of a single large space with a central octagonal lantern light; within this space a complex layout of seating and desks allowed for several classes with four 'horseshoe' arrangements related to masters' desks. The building, together with the later classrooms added at either end, was demolished in 1872 when the school moved to Godalming (see No. 192); parts of the façade, which had been inscribed with the names of former pupils, were transferred to this new site.[2]

1. This inscription appeared on a stone above the central doorway; it gives the date 1803 ( $\overline{A\omega\gamma}$ ) and the dedication 'to grammar'. Details of this and of the award, together with views of the building, are given in *Memorials of Charterhouse*, by C. W. Radclyffe, published James Moore, London, 1844 (no pp. nos).

2. I am indebted to the Headmaster and Archivist of Charterhouse School for much of the information related to this building. A contemporary print entitled 'New Grammar School at the Charter House', 1836, is in the Crace Collection at the BM (Portfolio xxvi, No. 29).

OLD HALL GREEN, Herts., **St Edmund's College** 1795–1805

**60a** *Obv.* East façade of college. COLLEGIUM SANCTI EDMUNDI MDCCCV.

*Rev.* Symbolic religious scene with two draped female figures; in the background St Edmund's College. In exergue, RELIGIONI AC BONIS ARTIBUS. Signed H & L and on exergue bar P.W.F.

Silver, White Metal, 52 mm. 1805 (BM)

60a

The college was built as a Roman Catholic seminary, to replace the old English College at Douai. The main centre block (1795–99) is of brick, by the architect James Taylor of Islington. The medal date coincides with the addition of the two-storeyed wings; the north wing contained a Chapel, and the south wing a refectory.[1] An important later addition to the college buildings was a large new chapel, completed in 1853 in the gothic style, by A. W. N. Pugin (qv).

See: Pevsner, *Hertfordshire,* 182–84.

1. The original design had been for the wings to lie at right angles to the main block: see Bernard Ward, *St Edmund's College Chapel*, 1903, 18. James Taylor disapproved of the design of the wings as shown and had nothing to do with their erection. A local builder, Mr Bangs, undertook the work. (Information from Mr Peter Howell and Mr Denis Evinson.)

61a

BIRMINGHAM, West Midlands, **Baptist Meeting House,** Cannon Street *1806*

**61a** *Obv.* Elevation of main façade of four bays. Two central bays have entrance with single, central column. On border: BAPTIST MEETING HOUSE CANNON STREET BIRMINGHAM DIMENSIONS 70 FEET BY 45 FEET. In exergue, THE FIRST BUILDING ERECTED 1738 ENLARGED 1763. AND 1780. PRESENT EDIFICE ERECTED 1806. Signed, DAVIS.

*Rev.* Around on border, inscription: THE FIRST PARTICULAR BAPTIST CHURCH IN BIRMINGHAM FORMED IN HIGH STREET, AUGUST 24. 1737. In centre, THIS MEDAL COMMEMORATES THE FIRST CENTENARY OF THE BAPTIST CHURCH, CANNON $S^T$ BIRMINGHAM, AUGUST 24. 1837 — NUMBER OF MEMBERS AT THE FORMATION OF THE CHURCH SEVENTEEN. PRESENT NUMBER OF MEMBERS 742 — PASTOR THE $REV^D$ THOMAS SWAN. — DEACONS, OWEN JOHNSON. JAMES ROOM. JAMES C. PERRY. $WILL^M$ WILLCOX. JOHN WHITEHOUSE SHOWELL. — NOT UNTO US O LORD, NOT UNTO US, BUT UNTC THY NAME GIVE GLORY. PSALM 115. V 1.

Bronze, White Metal, 51 mm. 1837 (BM)

This square red brick chapel, with its recessed porch and Tuscan stone columns, replaced the original building in 1806. It was the 'mother church' of the Birmingham Baptists and provided 840 sittings. Demolished after 1879 for town improvements in Cannon Street.

See: *VCH, Warwicks.*, vol. 7, 436.

STOCKPORT, Greater Manchester, **Sunday School,** Duke Street. *1805–6*

**62a** *Obv.* Façade of building. STOCKPORT SUNDAY SCHOOL. In exergue—(space for name) TRUSTEE. Signed, FAULKNER F.

*Rev.* Legend with sprays of laurel and oak: ERECTED ANNO DOMINI 1805 BY VOLUNTARY SUBSCRIPTION FOR THE EDUCATION & RELIGIOUS INSTRUCTION OF THE CHILDREN OF THE LABOURING POOR.

Silver glazed, 52 mm. over-all. 1805 (BM)

**62b** Similar to No. 62a above, but no artist's signature
Bronze, 51 mm. 1805 (BM)

**62c** *Obv.* Bust of Joseph Mayer three-quarter facing to left. Semicircular legend: STOCKPORT SUNDAY SCHOOL CENTENNIAL CELEBRATION 1884 (etc etc) THE LAST SURVIVOR OF THE FOUNDERS (etc etc).

*Rev.* View of building with more foreground than previous two medals. STOCKPORT SUNDAY SCHOOL CENTENNIAL CELEBRATION 1884. In exergue, ANNUAL EXPENDITURE £800 REGISTERED SCHOLARS 96000 REGISTERED TEACHERS 5500. Signed, OTTLEY $BIRM^M$.

White Metal, 54 mm. 1884 (BM)

A brick building of 1805–6; enlarged in 1835–36, and with a Centenary Hall attached in 1905–9. Cf. a similar large four-storey block at Macclesfield of 1813/14 (No. 66) also with its entrances left and right.

See: Pevsner, *Cheshire,* 342.

62b

LONDON, Camden, **Providence Chapel**, Gray's Inn Lane *1810*

**63a** *Obv.* Bust to left. Around, REV. W. HUNTINGTON. S.S. CHAPEL GRAYS INN LANE.

*Rev.* Façade of chapel. Above, PROVIDENCE CHAPEL. In exergue, NOV. 21. 1810 and hallmark.

Silver, 48 mm. 1810 (BM)

The façade shown is the design for a new Providence Chapel (built 1810 onwards) on the east side of Gray's Inn Lane, to replace the first 'Providence Chapel' in Great Titchfield Street. The latter was built by the eccentric preacher Revd. William Huntington S.S.;[1] when it burnt down his congregation raised £10,000 for this larger building. It has since been demolished. The medal, which is cast and chased, was made at the time Huntington started his rebuilding subscription (see H. A. Grueber, *Num. Chron.* 1892, 318).

1. These letters, which appear on the medal obverse were explained by Huntington: 'As I cannot get a D.D. for want of cash, neither can I get an M.A. for want of learning, therefore I am compelled to fly for refuge to S.S., by which I mean Sinner Saved.'

63a

LONDON, Hackney, **Hackney Parochial Schools**, Chatham Place *1811*

**64a** *Obv.* Façade of entrance block. Around HACKNEY FREE AND PAROCHIAL SCHOOLS.

*Rev.* Inscription around, THE GIFT OF BARRY SEDGWICK ESQ: (In centre, surrounded by wreath, space for inscription).

Silver, 40 mm. 18-- (Watt Coll.)[1]

The medal shows the former charity school of 1811, nine bays, brick built, the centre suitably emphasised.

See: Pevsner, *London 2*, 168.

1. This copy presented 1892.

64a

BIRMINGHAM, West Midlands, **Christ Church**, Colmore Row and New Street *1805–14*

**65a** *Obv.* Bust of George III to right. Around, GEORGIUS III · D : G · BRITANNIARUM REX · F · D. Signed WEBB F.

*Rev.* View of church with domed tower over portico. Around, ÆD : XTI : LAP : PRIM : ANG : P : C : GEO : III : FIDEI COLUMEN · PRÆSIDIUM : DECUS. In exergue, BIRM : XI · CAL : AUG : MDCCCV.

Gold, Silver, and Bronze, 42 mm. 1805 (BM)

Built from a design by the Birmingham surveyor Charles Norton. The medal marks the laying of the foundation stone in 1805; the tower and spire were completed in 1814. The church was of stone, with a three-bay Doric west portico, and a west tower surmounted by an octagonal belfry and octagonal spire. The medal view, although of poor execution, shows an early design with a cupola. Christ Church occupied a commanding central site at the junction of Colmore Row and New Street; it was demolished in 1899. Despite the inference of the medal inscription, the foundation stone was laid on 22 July 1805 by the Earl of Dartmouth (representing the King). In describing the event the *Gentleman's*

65a

*Magazine* noted that the medal 'was generally circulated, and many of them worn, with blue ribbons, at the breasts of the spectators'.[1]

See: *VCH, Warwicks.* 381 and illus.; Colvin, 419, 420.

1. *GM*, August, p. 766, October, p. 915. See also summary of these notes and reference to a second (? unpublished) medal in *Birmingham Weekly Post*, 27 February 1897 (Local Notes and Queries); this article indicates that the gold copy of No. 65a in the BM had been presented to George III.

66a

MACCLESFIELD, Cheshire, **Sunday School,** Roe Street *1813–14*

**66a** *Obv.* Bust of John Whitaker three-quarter facing to right. JOHN WHITAKER ESQ. BORN NOV[R] 24[TH] 1772. DIED OCT[R] 29[TH] 1820.

*Rev.* View of house. MACCLESFIELD SUNDAY SCHOOL. In exergue, FOUNDED MAY 6[TH] 1796 JUBILEE CELEBRATED MAY 6[TH] 1846. Signed, ALLEN & MOORE BIRM[M].

White Metal glazed, 48 mm. 1846 (BM)

An impressively large brick building of 1813–14 (cf. the earlier Stockport Sunday School No. 62). The monument shown in front of the school is of 1846 and commemorates the founder John Whitaker, as does the medal obverse of the same year.

See: Pevsner, *Cheshire*, 269.

67a

LONDON, Westminster, **Waterloo Bridge** *1811–17*

**67a** *Obv.* Bust to left. GEORGE P. REGENT.

*Rev.* Elevation. WATERLOO BRIDGE, below, JUNE 18. 1817.

Silver, 20 mm. 1817 (BM)

Forrer, vol. 6, 650 ff, gives the medallist as William Wyon (joint production with Thomas Wyon Jnr).

The medal commemorates the opening of the new Strand Bridge (named 'Waterloo' in 1816) by the Prince Regent.[1] Designed by John Rennie, it was of nine arches, with pairs of Doric columns placed at each springing point to carry a continuous entablature. But the impressive scale 'was dictated by the structure not by the designer's handling of detail. Hence its sheer magnificence' (J. Summerson, *Georgian London*, 224). Demolished in 1938.

1. Hocking, vol. ii, 248 notes that the Prince Regent distributed a medal by T. Wyon Jnr to mark the ceremony; the number struck for this was 4,200 (the medal design was: *Obv.* Laureated bust of Prince Regent, *Rev.* Royal Standard. Silver, 27 mm.).

68a

STOCKPORT, Greater Manchester, **St Mary's Church,** Market Place *1813–17*

**68a** *Obv.* View of church from west end, with tower in centre. In exergue, I. MACC : 7. 37. Signed on exergue bar, HALLIDAY F.

*Rev.* Inscription: THE PARISH CHURCH OF STOCKPORT WAS CONSECRATED JULY 4. 1817. BY THE RIGHT REV[D] GEO. HENRY LAW D.D. LORD BISHOP OF CHESTER.

Bronze, White Metal, 45 mm. 1817 (BM)

Rebuilt in 1813 onwards, to the design of Lewis Wyatt, but keeping the existing Decorated chancel with its monument to a rector of 1334. The medal shows the new west tower and the Perpendicular gothic style chosen by Wyatt; the sides of the church have two tiers of windows.

See: Pevsner, *Cheshire*, 339.

DUDLEY, West Midlands, **St Thomas's Church,** High Street *1816–18*

**69a** *Obv.* Façade of west end of church with spire. Around ΟΝΤΟΣ ΑΚΡΟΓΟΝΙΑΙΟϒ ΑϒΤΟϒ ΙΗΣΟϒΧΡΙΣΤΟϒ.[1] Signed on exergue bar HALLIDAY F. In exergue EPH. II. XX.

*Rev.* Inscription THE FOUNDATION STONE OF S$^{T}$ THOMAS$^{S}$ CHURCH, DUDLEY LAID OCTOBER · XXV MDCCCXVI.

White Metal, 43 mm. 1816 (BM)

69a

By William Brooks. The medal view shows the west front and indicates the unusual junction of tower to nave by a special angled bay. Built in a Perpendicular style in 1816–18.

See: Pevsner, *Staffs.*, 121.

1. 'Jesus Christ himself being the chief corner stone'; Eph. 2. v. 20.

BATH, Avon, **Freemason's Hall,** York Street (now the Friends Meeting House) *1817–19*

**70a** *Obv.* Portrait bust. H.R.H. FRED$^{K}$ DUKE OF SUSSEX M.W. G.M.

*Rev.* Elevation of building. FREE MASON'S HALL · A · L · 5817. In exergue, DEDICATED SEP$^{R}$ 23 1819.

White Metal, 38 mm. 1819 (BM)

70a

A Greek revival design by William Wilkins. The front has a projecting three-bay portico with fluted Ionic columns.

See: Pevsner, *N Somerset*, 110.

BATH, Avon, **Bathwick Hill House,** Bathwick Hill *c. 1820*

**71a** *Obv.* View of three-bay, two-storey house. BATHWICK HILL SCHOOL ONE MILE FROM THE CITY OF BATH CONDUCTED BY — GEORGE CLARKE.

*Rev.* Inscription, around blank central panel: HONORÆST PRÆMIUM VIRTUTIS.

White Metal, 45 mm. ? 1820s (BM)

71a

The development of Bathwick, as an extension of Bath, dates from the 1790s and was prefaced by the building of Pulteney Bridge. The medal shows Bathwick Hill House, of *c.* 1820, by H. E. Goodridge who was responsible for much of the later work in the Bathwick area. The house was used for Bathwick-Hill School until *c.* 1853, when it last appeared in the Bath directories amongst the 'Gentlemen's Academies'.[1]

1. An advertisement for the school, with some indication of Mr George Clarke's regime, is given in: Charles Clark, *Bath Annual Directory and Almanack*, 1849.

BIRMINGHAM, West Midlands, **Carrs Lane Chapel** (Congregational Chapel) *1819–20*

**72a** *Obv.* Upper part of façade of Carrs Lane Chapel. Above, HOSANNA, clouds at each side, cornerstone in foreground. In exergue, DEPOSITED XXX JULY MDCCCXIX. Signed, WHITWELL D. HALLIDAY F.

*Rev.* Inscription around: BY VOLUNTARY SUBSCRIPTION. In centre, INDEPENDENT MEETING HOUSE CARRS LANE BIRMINGHAM — CAPACITY 2100 SEATS — JOHN ANGEL JAMES MINISTER — S.T. [*sic*] WHITWELL ARCHITECT.

Bronze, 54 mm. 1819 (Eidlitz 1069, pl. 118) (BM)

72b

**72b** *Obv.* Façade of Carrs Lane Chapel, irradiated, and with HOSANNA across it. Clouds at each side and cornerstone in foreground. In exergue, DEPOSITED JULY XXX MDCCCXIX. Signed, WHITWELL. D. HALLIDAY. F.

*Rev.* Inscription (as above No. 72a).

White Metal, 54 mm. 1819 (BM)

A large brick building, with Greek revival elements, which was the third chapel on this site, 1819–20, by the architect T. S. Whitwell,[1] who signs the elevation on the medal D(elineate). Internally there are galleries on three sides and an impressive Ionic colonnade on the east wall. In 1876 the chapel underwent a major rebuilding and a new façade was substituted.

See: Pevsner, *Warwicks.* 113; *VCH, Warwicks.*, vol. 7, 448.

1. The medal reverse gives his initials incorrectly.

LONDON, Harrow, **Harrow School, 'Old Schools' Building.** *1819–20*

73a

**73a** *Obv.* Elevation of 'Old Schools' building. Below, STET FORTUNA DOMUS. Signed, W.W. below exergue bar.

*Rev.* Within laurel wreath, inscription: IN MEMORIAM ISABELLAE CONIVGIS RICARDVS GREGORY HARROVIENSIS HARROVIENSIBUS PROPOSVIT M.S. MDCCCXXXVIII.

Bronze, 45 mm. 1846[1] (BM)

The medal shows the 'Old Schools' building as enlarged by C. R. Cockerell. This was his first completed work after setting up in practice, and is a remarkably successful conservation exercise in a 'Tudor' style. The left-hand wing contains the old Fourth Form Room of 1615; the right-hand wing and entrance link are completely new, of 1819–20, and provided a Speech Room. Cockerell unified the two halves by means of oriel windows, stepped gables, and a refacing of the old brickwork.

See: Pevsner, *Middlesex*, 101; M. Seaborne, *The English School*, 1971, 58 (with plan) and pls 55, 56.

1. Forrer, vol. 6, 683, gives the 'Gregory Medal' as 1846 by W. Wyon.

BATH, Avon, **Argyle Chapel,** Argyle Street, Bathwick (now Congregational Church) *1821*

**74a** *Obv.* Bust to left. Around THE REV[D] WILLIAM JAY COMPLETED A PASTORATE OF FIFTY YEARS JAN[Y] 30. 1841. Signed on truncation, S.K.

*Rev.* Elevation. ARGYLE CHAPEL BATH ERECTED 1789. FIRST ENLARGEMENT 1804. SECOND ENLARGEMENT 1821.

Bronze, 49 mm. 1841 (BM)

The medal shows the Grecian façade of 1821, with Ionic columns 'in antis', by H. E. Goodridge. This was part of his rebuilding of the 1789 chapel (designed by Baldwin, who developed much of Bathwick New Town). In 1852 the street façade was to be further altered.

See: Pevsner, *N. Somerset*, 109, 110.

74a

BRIGHTON, East Sussex, **The Royal Pavilion** *1815–21*

**75a** *Obv.* Head of Queen Victoria, to left. VICTORIA D.G. BRITTANIARUM REGINA F.D. Signed, LANGRIDGE BRIGHTON DIREX.

*Rev.* View of buildings and domed pavilions. THE ROYAL PAVILION BRIGHTON. In exergue, royal coat of arms radiated.

Bronze, 57 mm. 1837 (BM)

The medal, which celebrates Queen Victoria's accession, shows the Royal Pavilion as enlarged and remodelled by John Nash between 1815 and 1821. Nash converted Henry Holland's earlier house (of 1787) to bring it into line with current theories on the Picturesque; to do this he restyled it with a mixture of oriental motifs given the contemporary label of 'Indian Gothic' (cf. Sezincote, *c.* 1800). At the same time he added completely new outer blocks (see left and right on medal view) to provide the larger rooms required. Nash's client, King George IV, quickly tired of his creation and by 1824 was already involved with a much more extensive remodelling—that at Windsor Castle by Jeffry Wyatville (see No. 131).

See: Pevsner, *E Sussex*, 438 ff.

75a

BIRMINGHAM, West Midlands, **'Pantechnatheca'**, New Street *1823*

**76a** *Obv.* Elevation of two-storey building of seven bays with ground floor shops and central arcade. Around, REPOSITORY OF ALL THE ARTS. In exergue panel, CHARLES JONES BIRMINGHAM; on building cornice, ΠΑΝΤΕΙΧΝΗΘΗΚΗ; on lintel, GOLD & SILVER PLATE JONES BRONZES GEMS MEDALS. Signed at rim, FAULKNER F.

*Rev.* Allegorical scene of art crowned by two graces. Signed in exergue, FAULKNER F.

Bronze, 64 mm. 1823[1] (BM)

This building was established by Charles Jones in 1823 to provide showrooms in which Birmingham manufacturers could display their

1. Grant and Forrer both give 1821 for the date of this medal, i.e. two years before the recorded completion of the building. The BM copy is entered under the year 1828.

76a

products. These appear to have acted as an early 'Design Centre' for buyers visiting Birmingham, as well as providing for retail purchases. The medal shows how a central arcade ran through the building at ground floor level, behind the Doric columns on the street front.

See: *VCH, Warwicks.*, vol. 7, 114, pl. opp. p. 107.

LONDON, Hackney, **London Orphan Asylum,** Linscott Road, Clapton (now the Salvation Army Congress Hall) *c. 1823*

77a

**77a** *Obv.* View of central block with three-bay portico, and pavilion buildings. Below, LONDON ORPHAN ASYLUM CLAPTON. Signed, TAYLOR BIRM.

*Rev.* Wreath. (Blank for inscription).

Silver, 38 mm. ?1820s to 1840s (Watt Coll.)[1]

By W. S. Inman, *c.* 1823. The medal shows three two-storey blocks with linking colonnades. The central block has a giant Tuscan portico.

See: Pevsner, *London 2*, 171.

1. This copy presented 1854.

BIRMINGHAM, West Midlands, **Holy Trinity Church,** Camp Hill, Bordesley *1820–23*

78a

**78a** *Obv.* View of chapel. TRINITY CHAPEL BORDESLEY.

*Rev.* Inscription: THIS CHAPEL WAS ERECTED BY HIS MAJESTY'S COMMISSIONERS FOR BUILDING NEW CHURCHES UPON A SITE WHICH WITH TWO ADJOINING HOUSES AND BURIAL GROUND WAS PURCHASED AND FENCED BY VOLUNTARY CONTRIBUTIONS THE CEREMONIAL STONE WAS LAID BY THE RIGHT HONORABLE OTHER EARL OF PLYMOUTH ON THE 29TH DAY OF SEPTEMBER A·D· 1820 AND THE CONSECRATION BY THE RIGHT REVEREND GEORGE HENRY LAW D.D. LORD BISHOP OF CHESTER TOOK PLACE ON THE 23 DAY OF JANUARY A·D· 1823 REV$^{D}$ SAMUEL CRANE B·A· MINISTER FRANCIS

GOODWIN ARCHITECT LONDON JOHN WALTHEW BUILDER BIRMINGHAM MESS[RS] WETHERHEAD & C[O] IRONFOUNDERS DERBY THOMAS MOLE ESQ[R] HON SECRETARY.

Bronze, 64 mm. 1823 (Eidlitz 466, pl. 53) (BM)

A rectangular stone Commissioners' church, 1820–23, by Francis Goodwin. In his favourite Perpendicular style (as was his design for St Philip, Stepney, analysed by the Commissioners as a 'model' church). Inside a single space with galleries to three sides supported on cast-iron columns. A large rose window on the east wall with cast-iron tracery.

See: Pevsner, *Warwicks.* 131; M. H. Port in *Architectural History,* vol. 1, 1958, 60–72, also *Six Hundred New Churches*, 1961, 71–72, 138.

BRIGHTON (BRIGHTHELMSTONE), East Sussex, **Royal Pier** (or **'Chain' Pier**) *1823*

**79a** *Obv.* Bust of George IV to right. GEORGIUS IIII D : G : BRITANNIAR : REX F : D : Signed, B. WYON SC.

*Rev.* View of the chain pier. BRIGHTHELMSTONE ROYAL PIER. In exergue, DESIGNED & ERECTED BY SAMUEL BROWN ESQ : COMMANDER IN HIS MAJESTY'S NAVY 1823 — PUBLISHED BY T. WYON & SON.

Bronze, 52 mm. 1823 (BM)

79a

An early medal of Benjamin Wyon's and apparently the first of his on which a structure is shown (Wyon's London Bridge, 1831, is a very similar composition). The medal shows the series of suspension spans whose chains gave the pier its popular name; the hollow supporting towers were of cast iron and each concealed a small shop. Built initially as a landing stage for cross-Channel boats, it rapidly became a fashionable promenade and established a pattern for future 'pleasure' piers. It collapsed in a storm in 1896.

ASHTON-UNDER-LYNE, Greater Manchester, **St Peter's Church,** Manchester Road *1821–24*

**80a** *Obv.* Façade. Above, ST PETER'S CHURCH. Below, ASHTON UNDER LYNE. Inner legend, GLORY TO GOD IN THE HIGHEST.

*Rev.* THE CEREMONIAL STONE OF THIS CHURCH, DEDICATED TO ST PETER, WAS LAID ON THE 24 DAY OCTOBER, A.D. 1821. BY THE RIGHT REVEREND, GEORGE HENRY LAW. D · D. THE LORD BISHOP OF CHESTER. THE AREA OF THE CHURCH, WILL BE 142 FEET LONG, BY 65 FEET WIDE, AND WILL BE CAPABLE OF CONTAINING 1800 PERSONS. THE HEIGHT OF THE TOWER WILL BE 128 FEET. THE SITE OF THE CHURCH AND BURIAL GROUND, PART OF THE DEMESNE OF ASHTON UNDER LYNE, CONTAINING 15680 SQUARE YARDS, WAS PRESENTED BY GEORGE HARRY. EARL OF STAMFORD & WARRINGTON. PATRON OF THE RECTORY, AND LORD OF THE MANOR OF ASHTON UNDER LYNE. — FRANCIS · GOODWIN. ARCHITECT. LONDON. — WILLIAM & GEORGE BROADHEAD, MASONS. SAMUEL MOSS, CARPENTER. ASHTON UNDER LYNE.

Bronze, 64 mm. 1821 (Eidlitz 465, pl. 53) (BM)

Another large and ambitious Commissioners' church from Francis

80a

Goodwin. Perpendicular again and, as at Kidderminster (No. 81), he develops a pinnacled west tower with an open bell stage. Interior one space, i.e. no aisles, but with galleries.

See: Pevsner, *S Lancs.* 69; Port, *Six Hundred New Churches*, 89 ff., 132.

KIDDERMINSTER, Hereford and Worcester, **St George's Church**

*1821–24*

**81a** *Obv.* West elevation. Around on border, ST GEORGES CHAPEL KIDDERMINSTER; within, GLORY TO GOD IN THE HIGHEST.

*Rev.* Inscription: THE BRICK FOUNDATIONS WERE COMMENCED ON THE CORONATION DAY OF HIS MAJESTY GEORGE IV THE CEREMONIAL STONE IS TO BE LAID ON THE 28TH DAY OF AUGUST IN THE SAME YEAR BY THE VENERABLE THE ARCHDEACON ONSLOW VICAR OF KIDDERMINSTER THE AREA OF THE CHAPEL TO BE 93 FEET LONG BY 60 FEET WIDE AND IS INTENDED TO ACCOM-MODATE TWO THOUSAND PERSONS, ONE HALF PART TO CONSIST OF FREE SEATS. THE TOWER WILL BE 135 FEET HIGH, AND THE ESTIMATED EXPENCE OF THE STRUCTURE WITH THE ENCLOSURE OF THE BURIAL GROUND £18000, OF WHICH £3000 WILL BE APPROPRIATED TO THE BUILDING, AND THE RESIDUE TO THE ENDOWMENT. THE FURTHER EXPENCES WILL BE DEFRAY'D BY A GRANT FROM THE PARLIAMENTIARY [*sic*] FUND. THE SITE AND BURIAL GROUND HAVE BEEN PROVIDED BY THE PARISH. — FRANCIS · GOODWIN ARCHITECT LONDON.

Bronze, 64 mm. 1821 (Eidlitz 463) (BM)

81a

**81b** *Obv.* As above No. 81a.

*Rev.* Inscription: THE FOUNDATIONS WERE BEGUN JULY XIX. AD. MDCCCXXI. THE CORONATION DAY OF HIS MAJESTY GEORGE IV. THE FIRST STONE WAS LAID THE XXVIII DAY OF AUGUST IN THE SAME YEAR BY THE VENERABLE R. F. ONSLOW. MA. ARCHDEACON OF THE DIOCESE AND VICAR OF KIDDERMINSTER. THE CHAPEL AND BURIAL GROUND WERE CONSECRATED THE XIII DAY OF SEPTEMBER. AD. MDCCCXXIV. BY THE RIGHT REVEREND FHW CORNEWALL. DD. LORD BISHOP OF WORCESTER. THE EXPENCE OF ERECTING THIS CHAPEL WAS DEFRAYED PART-LY BY A GRANT FROM PARLIAMENT UNDER ACTS PASSED IN THE 58 & 59 YEARS OF GEORGE 3 & PARTLY BY A VOLUNTARY SUBSCRIPTION OF 2000L FROM THE INHABITANTS OF THE TOWN & NEIGHBOURHOOD OF KIDDERMINSTER IT CONTAINS 2000 SITTINGS OF WHICH 1200 ARE APPROPRIATED TO THE ACCOMMODATION OF THE POOR & IT IS BUILT UPON A SITE WHICH TOGETHER WITH A SPACIOUS BURIAL GROUND ADJOINING WAS PROVIDED AT THE EXPENCE OF THE PARISH — FRANCIS GOODWIN ARCHITECT — Signed in script, OTTLEY.

Bronze, 64 mm. 1824 (BM)

'A fine stately church of the Commissioners' type' (Pevsner). 1821–24 by Francis Goodwin. Perpendicular and (cf. Bordesley No. 78) has a rose window with cast-iron tracery on the east wall. Interior gutted by fire 1922 and rebuilt by Sir Giles G. Scott.

See: Pevsner, *Worcs.* 206; Port, *Six Hundred New Churches*, 42, 72 ff., 138.

LIVERPOOL, Merseyside, **Infirmary,** Brownlow Street *1822–24*

**82a** *Obv.* Main elevation to building. Around, OF THE MOST HIGH COMETH HEALING. In exergue, NEW INFIRMARY LIVERPOOL. Signed on bar, HALLIDAY F.

*Rev.* Inscription: THIS MEDAL INTENDED TO AID THE FUNDS OF THE LIVERPOOL INFIRMARY IS RESPECTFULLY DEDICATED TO THE LADIES PATRONESSES OF THE CHARITY BY THE PUBLISHER THO$^{S}$ WOOLFIELD BAZAAR CHURCH STREET SEP. 1831.

White Metal, 48 mm. 1831 (BM)

The medal shows the nine-bay front of the Royal Infirmary of 1822–24. It has a seven-bay centre of giant unfluted Ionic columns and is typical of the Grecian style of its Liverpool architect John Foster Jnr. Demolished in 1887, and replaced by Alfred Waterhouse's gothic design.

See: Q. Hughes, *Seaport*, 1964, 95.

82a

LONDON, Southwark, **St George's Church**, Wells Way (formerly in Surrey) *1822–24*

**83a** *Obv.* Façade. ST GEORGE'S CHURCH CAMBERWELL SURREY. In exergue, FRANCIS BEDFORD ARCHITECT. Signed, E. CROSS F.

*Rev.* Inscription: THE FIRST STONE OF THIS CHURCH WAS LAID BY THE RIGHT REVEREND FATHER IN GOD GEO · TOMLINE D · D · LORD BISHOP OF WINCHESTER ON THE 23$^{D}$ · DAY OF APRIL IN THE YEAR

83a

OF OUR LORD 1822 IN THE THIRD YEAR OF THE REIGN OF KING GEORGE THE IV · THE REV$^{D}$. EDWARD SMYTH VICAR HEN$^{Y}$ GOOCH · RICH$^{D}$ BILLITER · THO$^{S}$ TURK CHURCHWARDENS · CHURCH COMMITTEE · JAMES JACKS R$^{T}$ BYGRAVE CHARLES DODD JOSEPH WARD PETER DAVEY W. PINCHBACK W · G · MEYMOTT ISAAC RICE JOHN BRETT W$^{M}$ WHIFFIN SAM$^{L}$ LILLEY ROB$^{T}$ CURTIS ROB$^{T}$ HOWARD ROB$^{T}$ YOUNG GEO · ATHEARN JN$^{O}$ SKIPPER WILLIAM FRY JOS$^{H}$ FIDLER CHA$^{S}$ BRUCE W$^{M}$ VIZARD JA$^{S}$ FISHER J$^{S}$ HALLETT CHR$^{R}$ MASON ROBERT SMALL · TREASURER GEO · SPENCE · SEC$^{Y}$

Silver, 59 mm. 1822 (Eidlitz 61, pl. 18) (BM)

A Commissioners' church of 1822–24 by Francis Bedford. A hexastyle Greek Doric portico, with a square west tower set back behind it. Cf. the architect's similar church St John, Waterloo Road, Lambeth. Altered in 1893 and 1909.

See: Pevsner, *London 2*, 76; Port, *Six Hundred New Churches*, 134.

84a

Near ATHERSTONE, Warwicks, **Grendon Hall** *c. 1825*

**84a** *Obv.* Portrait head to right. SIR GEORGE CHETWYND BAR$^{T}$. Signed, B. WYON S.

*Rev.* View of house, in Jacobean style. GRENDON HALL. Below, coat of arms, 1833. On edge motto, QUOD DEUS VULT FIET. Signed, B. WYON.

Silver, 34 mm. 1833$^{G}$ (BM)

Rebuilt for Sir George Chetwynd (1783–1850) by Joseph Potter of Lichfield. There are drawings in the V & A by Potter dated 1825 (see Colvin, p. 470). The medal shows the rebuilt exterior with a mixture of early and late seventeenth-century motifs. Chetwynd was known to numismatists for his collection of tradesmen's tokens (see H. A. Grueber, *Num. Chron.*, 1890, 56). Pulled down in 1933.[1]

1. *VCH, Warwicks.*, vol. 4, 75.

85a

DONCASTER, South Yorks., **New Betting Rooms,** High Street *1826*

**85a** *Obv.* Façade of single-storey building with two Ionic columns; trophy of racing horse on balustrade. NEW BETTING ROOMS DONCASTER.

*Rev.* Racehorses with jockeys, ESTABLISHED 1826. Signed, T. W. INGRAM. BIRM$^{M}$

White Metal, 35 mm. 1826 (BM)

Built in 1826 to the design of the local architects Woodhead and Hurst. A contemporary account in the *Sporting Gazette* reported: 'The building presents to the street a neat front with columns and pilasters of the Ionic order, from the small temple on the River Illysus, at Athens. By ascending three steps you enter a loggia 25ft. long and 14ft. wide serving as an approach to the large room, which is 90ft long, 23ft. wide and 20ft. high.' Beyond were two smaller rooms that have recently been demolished. The building is now to be restored.

SOUTHSEA, Hants, **St Paul's School,** St Paul's Square *1826*

**86a** *Obv.* Elevation of five-bay classical building; coupled columns to either side of entrance porch. ST PAUL'S SCHOOL SOUTHSEA. Below, INSTITUTED A D 1825.

*Rev.* Wreath. (Blank for inscription).

Silver, White Metal, 51 mm. ? 1826 (Watt Coll.)[1] (BM)

86a

Southsea's first church, St Paul (1820–22 gothic), had been designed by Francis Goodwin (qv). St Paul's School was founded in 1825 by a society of one hundred persons taking subscriptions of £25 each.[2] Tenders were invited the same year and the school opened on 1 August 1826.[3] The architect was Jacob Owen, who in 1827–28 built All Saints', Mile End, Portsea.[4] The school, which was at the corner of King Street, was sold in 1850 to become a Baptist Chapel, and has since been demolished.

1. This copy presented 1841.
2. A. N. Y. Howell, *Notes on the Topography of Portsmouth*, 1913.
3. See *Hampshire Telegraph*, 5 December 1825 and 1 August 1826. Mr Owen, and a Mr Adams, are given as the architects.
4. Both St Paul's, Southsea, and All Saints', Portsea, were Commissioners' churches. See Port, p. 132 (and p. 72 where Goodwin's failure to secure this second commission at Portsea is discussed).

LONDON, Lambeth, **British Orphan Asylum,** Clapham Rise *c. 1827 on*

**87a** *Obv.* Façade of three-storey building with BRITISH ORPHAN ASYLUM on parapet panel. In exergue, CLAPHAM RISE.

*Rev.* Inscription: BRITISH ORPHAN ASYLUM UNDER THE PATRONAGE OF THEIR MAJESTIES INSTITUTED 1827.

White Metal, 38 mm. ? 1830s (BM)

87a

Clapham Rise was a favourite area in the early nineteenth century for charitable institutions. The building occupied by the British Orphan Asylum stood on the west side of Clapham Rise Road (a continuation of the High Street). An illustration of the orphanage 'From 1834 to 1863'[1]—i.e. when the Asylum is recorded as occupying the building[2]—shows certain marked alterations from the medal view.[3] These include a widening to six bays and no break forward of the central three bays. In 1863 the orphanage moved to new premises in Slough, and the building was then taken over for the Home for Incurables until 1894. Since demolished.

1. In the Minet Library of the Borough of Lambeth; I am indebted to the Borough Archivist for details of this.
2. The *Clapham Gazette* for July 1863 stated that the orphanage had been there for twenty-nine years. The date of the medal, and of completion, may therefore be *c.* 1834.
3. It appears however to be derived from the same basic design.

88a

BIRMINGHAM, West Midlands, **St. Peter's Church,** Dale End *1825–27*

**88a** *Obv.* Façade. S$^{T}$ PETERS CHURCH BIRMINGHAM. Signed, OTTLEY MEDALLIST.

*Rev.* Inscription: THE FOUNDATION WAS BEGUN THE 11 DAY OF MAY MDCCCXXV. THE FIRST STONE WAS LAID THE XXVI DAY OF JULY MDCCCXXV BY THE REV. CHARLES CURTIS REV. LAURENCE GARDNER D D. AND JAMES TAYLOR ESQ. THE LOCAL COMMISSIONERS FOR BUILDING CHURCHES IN THIS DISTRICT. — THE CHURCH WAS CONSECRATED THE X DAY OF AUGUST MDCCCXXVII BY THE HON$^{BLE}$ & RIGHT REV. HENRY RYDER D.D. LORD BISHOP OF THE DIOCESE. — THE TOTAL COST OF ERECTING THE CHURCH AMOUNTED TO L13087.12.3 BEING L 882.10.8 LESS THAN THE APPROVED ESTIMATE WHICH SUM TOGETHER WITH L3718.0.0 THE COST OF THE SITE WAS DEFRAYED BY HIS MAJESTYS COMMISSIONERS FOR BUILDING NEW CHURCHES OUT OF THE PARLIAMENTARY GRANT OF L1.000.000. — THE CHURCH CONTAINS 1903 SITTINGS OF WHICH 1381 ARE APPROPRIATED TO THE ACCOMMODATION OF THE POOR. — REV. L. GARDNER D.D. RECTOR OF THE PARISH REV. A. J. CLARKE A.M. MINISTER I. W. WHATELEY AND JOHN COPE ESQ$^{RS}$ CHURCHWARDENS. — RICKMAN & HUTCHINSON ARCH$^{TS}$

Bronze, White Metal, 64 mm. 1827 (Eidlitz 831, pl. 86) (BM)

**88b** *Obv.* Façade of St. Peter's, Dale End. THOU ART PETER AND UPON THIS ROCK I WILL BUILD MY CHURCH. In exergue, CONSECRATED. AUG$^{T}$ 10 1827.

*Rev.* Inscription: THE HON$^{BLE}$ & R$^{T}$ REV$^{D}$ HENRY RYDER LORD BISHOP OF LICHFIELD & COVENTRY — REV$^{D}$ L. GARDNER. D.D. RECTOR OF S$^{T}$ PHILIP'S BIRMINGHAM. — RICKMAN & HUTCHINSON. ARCH$^{TS}$.

White Metal, 41 mm. 1827 (Eidlitz 832, pl. 86) (BM)

By Rickman and Hutchinson. A Greek revival design built in 1825–27 and one of only three of Rickman's fifty-four churches that was not gothic. St. Peter's was gutted by fire in 1831, and restored in 1837 by Charles Edge (who was then completing Birmingham Town Hall, see No. 108). Closed for demolition in 1899.

See: Port, *Six Hundred New Churches*, 60 ff., 138.

89a

LEICESTER, Leics., **St George's Church** *1823–27*

**89a** *Obv.* Façade. S$^{T}$ GEORGE'S LEICESTER.

*Rev.* Inscription: THE CEREMONIAL STONE OF THIS CHURCH WAS LAID ON FRIDAY THE 29 AUGUST 1823 IN THE FOURTH YEAR OF THE REIGN OF HIS MAJESTY GEORGE THE IV. BY THE RIGHT HONORABLE RICHARD WILLIAM PENN EARL HOWE. LENGTH OF THE CHURCH 92 FEET, BREADTH 64 FEET, HEIGHT OF THE TOWER AND SPIRE 170 FEET. THE EXPENCE OF ERECTING THE CHURCH IS DEFRAYED BY HIS MAJESTYS COMMISSIONERS FOR BUILDING ADDITIONAL CHURCHES IN POPULOUS PARISHES & THE SITE PURCHASED BY VOLUNTARY CONTRIBUTIONS. WILLIAM PARSONS ARCHITECT LEICESTER. THE HON. & RIGHT REV. GEO. PELHAM D.D LORD

BISHOP OF LINCOLN. THE VENERABLE T. PARKINSON D.D. ARCHDEACON OF LEICESTER & CHAIRMAN OF THE DISTRICT BOARD · JOHN STOCKDALE HARDY HON · SECRETARY ·

Bronze, White Metal, 64 mm. 1823 (Eidlitz 740, pl. 89) (BM)

By William Parsons. A big church in the Perpendicular style, built 1823–27, and originally having a spire to the west tower (see medal). Destroyed by fire 1911, and rebuilt 1912 by W. D. Caroe.

See: Pevsner, *Leics.* 143; Port, *Six Hundred New Churches,* 134.

LONDON, Westminster, **St Peter's Church,** Eaton Square *1824–27*

**90a** *Obv.* Portrait bust of Queen Victoria,[1] to left. VICTORIA REGINA.

*Rev.* View of church and west portico. S$^{T}$ PETER'S EATON SQ$^{RE}$; in field, THE REV. JOHN STORRS. In exergue, TO COMMEMORATE THE 60$^{TH}$ YEAR OF HER MAJESTY'S REIGN 1837–1897.

Lead, bronzed, 78 mm. 1897 (BM)

By Henry Hakewill, 1824–27. Built with a giant Ionic portico after his first gothic design was rejected. Gutted by fire in 1836 but completely rebuilt from the original drawings by his son J. H. Hakewill. What was a simple interior with three galleries was 'fiercely normanised' by Sir Arthur Blomfield in 1872–73.

See: Pevsner, *London 1,* 434; Port, *Six Hundred New Churches,* 136.

1. Grant gives this as 'after Sir T. Brock'.

90a

91a

BRIGHTON, East Sussex, **St Peter's Church,** Victoria Gardens *1824–28*

**91a** *Obv.* Exterior; view from the north-east, with tower in background. Around, S[T] PETER'S CHURCH BRIGHTON. In exergue, DEDICATED BY PERMISSION TO THE REV H. M. WAGNER A.M. VICAR OF BRIGHTON.

*Rev.* Interior looking towards the east end. Left, INTERIOR OF, right, THE CHURCH. In exergue, PUB. BY J. LANGRIDGE BRIGHTON.

Bronze, 57 mm. 1830[1] (BM)

An early building by (Sir) Charles Barry. Won in competition 1823 and built in that period in the 1820s to which most of his churches belong. A basic Commissioners' plan, with Perpendicular decoration, and a west tower in two stages—the top stage set back behind four pinnacles. The medal shows this upper stage, and also Barry's polygonal apse which was removed (1900) to allow G. Somers Clarke to add a large chancel.

See: Pevsner, *E. Sussex*, 435; Port, *Six Hundred New Churches*, 162.

1. Given by W. Wroth, 'English personal medals in the British Museum, 1760–1886', in *Num. Chron.* 6, 1886.

92a

WEST BROMWICH, West Midlands, **Christ Church,** High Street *1821–28*

**92a** *Obv.* Façade. CHRIST CHURCH WEST BROMWICH. Inner legend, GLORY TO GOD IN THE HIGHEST.

*Rev.* Inscription: THE FIRST STONE OF THIS CHURCH WAS LAID, BY THE RIGHT HONORABLE, THE EARL OF DARTMOUTH, ON THE 25 DAY OF SEPTEMBER, IN THE YEAR OF OUR LORD, 1821, AND THE SECOND YEAR OF THE REIGN OF HIS MAJESTY KING GEORGE THE IV. LENGTH OF THE CHURCH 130 FEET. BREADTH 56 FEET. HEIGHT OF THE TOWER 114 FEET. — FRANCIS GOODWIN ARCHITECT LONDON — JOHN HEDGE BUILDER, LITTLE COMPTON STREET, SOHO, LONDON.

Bronze, White Metal, 64 mm. 1821 (Eidlitz 464, pl. 53) (BM)

The fourth of the similarly designed medals showing Commissioners' Churches designed by Francis Goodwin (cf. Bordesley, No. 78; Ashton-under-Lyne, No. 80; Kidderminster, No. 81). The West Bromwich church is of the same group, but was not completed until much later in 1828. It was altered in 1878–84.

See: Pevsner, *Staffs.* 301; Port, *Six Hundred New Churches*, 51, 77, 136.

93a

BIRMINGHAM, West Midlands, **School of Medicine,** Snow Hill *1828–29*

**93a** *Obv.* Façade, with inscription on entablature: SCHOOL OF MEDICINE. Around, SCHOLA MEDICINÆ BIRMINGHAMIENSIS. In exergue, ANNO DOMINI M.D.CCC.XXVIII INSTITUTA. Signed, on base of building T.W.I.

*Rev.* Wreath. Around, MACTE NOVA VIRTUTE. In centre, JUVENEM INGENUUM HOC PRÆMIO DONAVIT. Signed at rim, T. W. INGRAM.

Bronze, 51 mm. 1828 (BM)

The medal shows the two-storey street façade, to Snow Hill, of the first Birmingham School of Medicine and Surgery. This had been established by the efforts of the surgeon W. Sands Fox, FRS, and the building (containing lecture theatre, museum, library and offices) was opened in October 1829.[1] It was sold in 1834, and demolished 1852 to make way for Snow Hill station. The School of Medicine moved to a site in Paradise Street in 1834, and by 1843 had become Queens College; at this stage a Gothic Revival building, influenced by the King Edward VI Grammar School (No. 116), was put up (1843–45) to designs of the architects Drury and Bateman.

See: *VCH, Warwicks.*, vol. 7, 44, 339.

1. J. T. Morrison, *William Sands Cox and the Birmingham Medical School* [n.d.], 32, 33. There is a note on p. 43 that from 1828 two prize medals were awarded annually.

DARWEN, Lancs., **Holy Trinity Church** *1827–29*

**94a** *Obv.* View of exterior. Below, TRINITY CHURCH DARWEN. Around, THEY SHALL PROSPER THAT LOVE THEE. 122 PS V. 6.
*Rev.* Inscription: TRINITY CHURCH UNITED SUNDAY SCHOOLS SICK CLUB INSTITUTED JULY 1832. Around, BELOVED, LET US LOVE ONE ANOTHER. 1. EP. JOHN. CHAP. IV. V. 7.
White Metal, 38 mm. 1832 (BM)

94a

Designed by Thomas Rickman in a correct Perpendicular style (1827–29). One of the many Commissioners' churches of that period with a west tower and a polygonal apse.

See: Pevsner, *N Lancs.* 112; Port, *Six Hundred New Churches*, 134.

DONCASTER, South Yorks., **Prospect House,** Thorne Road *1829*

**95a** *Obv.* View of school building with children playing in foreground. R. GRAHAM'S PROSPECT HOUSE ACADEMY. Below, DONCASTER ESTABLISHED 1804. Signed, OTTLEY.
*Rev.* Inscription: THE REWARD OF MERIT (and blank for details).
Bronze, White Metal, 48 mm. ? 1829 (BM)

95a

Built by Robert Graham to house his academy, which had outgrown various other premises since its establishment *c.* 1810.[1] The building shown was opened 27 July 1829; it is possibly a work of Messrs Woodhead and Hurst (qv) who were the only practising architects in Doncaster at that time. Graham was forced to sell the house *c.* 1840 and it was renamed Highfield House; it later became the Vicarage of St George's church. Demolished in 1936.

1. 1804 on the inscription may refer to Graham's entry into the teaching profession.

LONDON, City, **Christ's Hospital School, Great Hall,** Newgate Street *1825–29*

**96a** *Obv.* Portrait head to left. WILLIAM THOMPSON M.P. PRESIDENT 1839. Signed on truncation, B. WYON.
*Rev.* Elevation. CHRIST'S HOSPITAL MATHEMATICAL PRIZE.
Bronze, 41 mm. 1839 (BM)

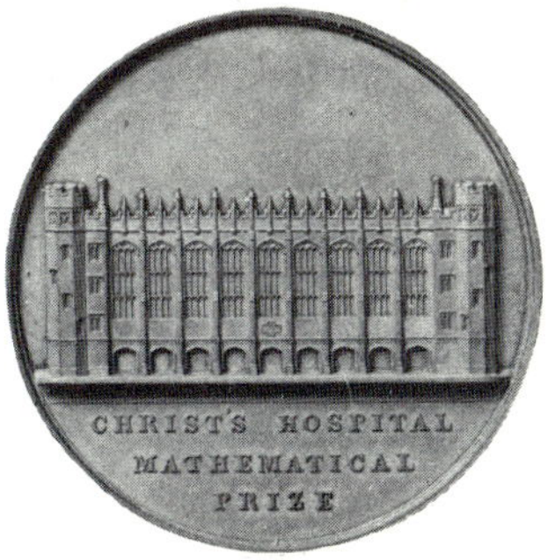

96a

Part of a major redevelopment in the 1820s and 1830s of this London school (founded 1552 with a grant of land at Grey Friars). The architect to Christ's Hospital was John Shaw Snr; his gothic 'Great Hall' was built in 1825–29, and provided, according to one writer in 1842, 'next to Westminster Hall, the noblest room in the metropolis'. All these buildings were demolished in 1902 when the school moved to Horsham in Sussex.

See: M. Seaborne, *The English School*, 175, pl. 153.

LONDON, Camden, **University College,** Gower Street *1827–29*

**97a** *Obv.* View of main range of buildings, with central portico and dome, and proposed wing buildings. Around on border, DESIGN ADOPTED BY THE COUNCIL FOR THE UNIVERSITY OF LONDON 1826. Below exergue bar, W. WILKINS M.A. ARC$^{T}$.

97a

*Rev.* Inscription: around on border: HISTORY. POLITICAL ECONOMY. MEDICAL SCIENCES. LANGUAGE. MATHEMATICS. PHYSICS. MENTAL SCIENCE. MORAL SCIENCES. In centre, COUNCIL HON. JAMES ABERCROMBIE M.P. RIGHT HON. LORD AUCKLAND. ALEXANDER BARING ESQ. M.P. GEORGE BIRKBECK M.D. HENRY BROUGHAM ESQ. M.P. F.R.S. THOMAS CAMPBELL ESQ. RIGHT HON. VISCOUNT DUDLEY AND WARD. ISAAC LYON GOLDSMID ESQ. OLINTHUS G. GREGORY LL.D. GEORGE GROTE JUN ESQ. JOSEPH HUME ESQ M.P. F.R.S. MOST NOBLE THE MARQUIS OF LANSDOWNE F.R.S. ZACHARY MACAULY ESQ. F.R.S. SIR JAMES MACKINTOSH M.P. F.R.S. JAMES MILL ESQ. HIS GRACE THE DUKE OF NORFOLK. LORD JOHN RUSSELL M.P. BENJAMIN SHAW ESQ. JOHN SMITH ESQ. M.P. WILLIAM TOOKE ESQ. F.R.S. HENRY WARBURTON ESQ. F.R.S. HENRY WAYMOUTH ESQ. JOHN WHISHAW ESQ. F.R.S. THOMAS WILSON ESQ.

Copper plated silver, 81 mm. 1826[1] (BM)

In the early 1820s the idea of a metropolitan, non-sectarian, University for London was proposed by such freethinkers as Jeremy Bentham and Henry Brougham. A site was purchased in Gower Street in 1825 and drawings advertised for in the press. The 'adopted design' was that of William Wilkins; it was published in 1826 and the proposed elevation illustrated on this medal is of the same year. The medal elevation differs from a drawing by Wilkins,[2] and a later engraving in *Metropolitan Improvements,*[3] which both show the two subsidiary domes brought forward to the ends of the wings and combined with curved porticos.[4] Ultimately only the main range, portico, and the central dome of Wilkins's scheme were built.[5] Wings were not added until 1869–81 (by Hayter Lewis, in a suitably harmonizing style). The name was changed to University College in 1836.[6]

See: Pevsner, *London 2,* 210.

1. Forrer, vol. 6, 79, gives 'Foundation 1826' as by Edward Thomason.
2. See *RIBAJ*, 14 January 1933, p. 150.
3. Shepherd & Elmes, *Metropolitan Improvements*, 1827–28, p. 125.
4. Medal view shows domes at junction of main range and wing blocks.
5. The executed design was by Wilkins with J. Gandy-Deering.
6. A reaction to the University of London foundation was the creation of the Anglican 'Kings College'; the government gave them a site adjoining Somerset House on the understanding that their architect, Sir Robert Smirke, completed Chambers' design (see No. 52).

STOKE-ON-TRENT, Staffs., **St Peter's Church** *1826–29*

**98a** *Obv.* View of church. Legend S$^{T}$ PETER'S CHURCH STOKE UPON TRENT. Signed OTTLEY BIRM$^{M}$.

*Rev.* Within a cartouche St Peter standing facing, with hands resting on shoulders of small child. Around cartouche, SAINT + PETER'S + CHURCH + AND + SCHOOLS + STOKE UPON TRENT. Legend, FOR REGULAR ATTENDANCE — AT THE SUNDAY SCHOOL.

White Metal, 46 mm. ? 1850s (BM)

Another Commissioners' church of 1826–29 by Trubshaw & Johnson. Perpendicular, with a west tower and a two-bay chancel projection. The medal format, by Ottley, is identical with that of St Michael, Derby (No. 174) and suggests a date of issue close to 1858.

See: Pevsner, *Staffs.* 262.

98a

LONDON, Westminster, **Pimlico Grammar School,** Ebury Street *1830*

**99a** *Obv.* Single-storey façade, with central door in screen wall, and double height Doric portico. PIMLICO GRAMMAR SCHOOL. Below FOUNDED 1829 — · — LORD VISC$^{T}$ MILTON PRESIDENT.

*Rev.* Within a wreath — · — PALMAM QUI MERUIT FERAT — · —.

Bronze, 48 mm. ?1830 (BM)

By J. P. Gandy-Deering, who collaborated with Wilkins on the Greek revival design of University of London (No. 97). The medal elevation shows a giant Doric portico, with columns 'in antis', an engaged screen wall, and rooms off left and right. The foundation stone[1] was laid by Viscount Milton (see medal obverse) in 1830. By the 1850s the building was in use for the Pimlico Literary Institute; it is now incorporated into a terrace of nineteenth-century houses and has had extra floors added to the corner bays.

See: Pevsner, *London 1*, 505.

1. Existing above the doorway. It reads: HVIVSCE AEDIFICII PRIMUM LAPIDEM POSUIT VIR HONARITISSIMUS VICECOMES MILTON PRID ID MAII MDCCCXXX QUOD OPUS SUSCEPTUM AD PUERORUM INSTUTIONEM CHRISTI FIDE MORIBUS ARTIBUS AC LITERIS SPIRITVS SACROSANCTVS SECVNDET. I am grateful to Mrs Joan Martin for obtaining this information. She has suggested an attribution of the medal to W. Wyon.

99a

SHEFFIELD, South Yorks., **St Mary's Church,** Bramhall Lane *1826–30*

**100a** *Obv.*. Bust of Queen Victoria to left, wearing small 'jubilee' crown and veil. VICTORIA QUEEN AND EMPRESS · DIAMOND JUBILEE 1897 ·

*Rev.* View of church. Around S$^{T}$ MARY'S CHURCH SUNDAY SCHOOL. SHEFFIELD. In exergue, REV R.H. HAMMOND VICAR.

Bronze, 31 mm. 1897 (BM)

By Joseph and Robert Potter, 1826–30. Perpendicular style, with a short chancel. Bombed, but rebuilt in 1957.

See: Pevsner, *Yorks; W. Riding*, 458; Port, *Six Hundred New Churches*, 138.

100a

101a

WOLVERHAMPTON, West Midlands, **St George's Church,** Bilston Road *1828–30*

**101a** *Obv.* West façade, with spire, of church. Around, GLORY TO GOD IN THE HIGHEST. On border, S$^{T}$ GEORGE'S CHURCH WOLVERHAMPTON.

*Rev.* Inscription: THE FIRST STONE OF THIS CHURCH WAS LAID AUGUST 18$^{TH}$ IN THE NINTH YEAR OF THE REIGN OF HIS MOST GRACIOUS MAJESTY KING GEORGE THE IV. A.D. 1828, BY THE HON$^{BLE}$ & VERY REV$^{D}$. H L HOBART D.D. DEAN OF WINDSOR & WOLVERHAMPTON. THE EXPENCE OF ERECTING THE CHURCH WAS DEFRAYED PARTLY BY A GRANT FROM PARLIAMENT UNDER ACTS PASSED IN 58 & 59$^{TH}$ YEARS OF THE REIGN OF HIS LATE MAJESTY KING GEORGE III AND PARTLY BY A VOLUNTARY SUBSCRIPTION OF L 3300 FROM THE INHABITANTS OF THE TOWN & NEIGHBOURHOOD OF WOLVERHAMPTON. IT CONTAINS 2300 SITTINGS OF WHICH 1300 ARE APPROPRIATED TO THE ACCOMMODATION OF THE POOR AND IT IS BUILT ON A SITE WHICH TOGETHER WITH THE SPACIOUS BURIAL GROUND CONTAINING 14520 SQUARE YARDS WAS PROVIDED BY RATES UPON THE INHABITANTS OF THE TOWNSHIP. — JAMES MORGAN ARCHITECT LONDON. Signed in script, OTTLEY MEDALLIST.

Bronze, 64 mm. 1828 (BM)

**101b** *Obv.* West façade, with spire, of church.

As above No. 101a but with, in exergue, in script, MORGAN ARCHITECT.

*Rev.* Inscription: THE FOUNDATIONS WERE BEGUN JULY 21$^{ST}$ A.D. 1828. THE FIRST STONE WAS LAID ON THE 18$^{TH}$ DAY OF AUGUST IN THE NINTH YEAR OF THE REIGN OF HIS MAJESTY GEORGE IV. BY THE HON$^{BLE}$ & VERY REV.$^{D}$ H.L. HOBART D.D. DEAN OF WINDSOR & WOLVERHAMPTON. THE EXPENCE OF ERECTING THE CHURCH WAS DEFRAYED PARTLY BY A GRANT FROM PARLIAMENT & PARTLY BY A VOLUNTARY SUBSCRIPTION OF L 3300 FROM THE INHABITANTS OF THE TOWN & NEIGHBOURHOOD OF WOLVERHAMPTON. IT CONTAINS 2300 SITTINGS OF WHICH 1300 ARE FOR THE POOR. Signed in script, OTTLEY MEDALLIST.

Silver, 45 mm. 1828 (BM)

A Commissioners' church by James Morgan, 1828–30, which combined a classical form with a medieval spire. The medal design by Ottley appears identical with those (unsigned) for Commissioners churches by the architect Francis Goodwin, e.g. Bordesley (No. 78).

See: Pevsner, *Worcs.* 315; Port, *Six Hundred New Churches*, 162.

102a

LONDON, City, **London Bridge** *1825–31*

**102a** *Obv.* Portrait head to right. WILLIAM THE FOURTH. Signed, BENJ. WYON F.

*Rev.* Elevation of new bridge; river shown with wavelets. LONDON BRIDGE COMMENCED 15 JUNE 1825 OPENED 1 AUGUST 1831. Signed, BENJ. WYON F.

Bronze, White Metal, 51 mm. 1831 (BM)

**102b** *Obv.* View of new five-arched bridge, with ships. LENGTH 928 FT, WIDTH 56 FT, CARRIAGEWAY 36 FT, In exergue WATERWAY 692 FT, CENTRE ARCH 152, SIDE ARCHES 140, EXTREME 130, HEIGHT 55.

*Rev.* Inscription: NEW LONDON BRIDGE FIRST STONE WAS LAID BY THE RT HON THE LORD MAYOR JOHN GARRATT ESQ^R ON THE 15 JUNE 1825 AND THE BRIDGE OPENED BY THEIR MAJESTIES THE 1^ST AUG 1831 COST 506,000 POUNDS.

Brass, 28 mm. 1831 (BM)

**102c** *Obv.* View of new bridge with St Paul's beyond. Around, CARRIAGE WAY 33½ F^T In exergue, LENGTH OF BRIDGE 782 F^T CENTRE ARCH 150 SIDE ARCH 14 [?].

*Rev.* Inscription: THE FIRST STONE OF THE NEW LONDON BRIDGE WAS LAID BY JOHN GARRATT ESQ^R. LORD MAYOR OF LONDON ON THE 14 OF MARCH 1824[*sic*][1] AND OPEN'D BY THEIR MAJESTIES AUGUST 1^ST 1831.

Brass, 28 mm. 1831 (BM)

The last major work of the engineer John Rennie, who submitted the design to the City of London in 1821. After a competition won in 1823 by the architect Charles Fowler (qv) had been set aside, Rennie's design of a five-arch bridge was built in 1825–31 by his son (Sir) John Rennie. The bridge was opened by William IV with great ceremony on 1 August 1831; on his arrival by river he was presented with a gold medal commemorating the event.[2] Rennie's London Bridge, which replaced the many spans of the medieval bridge founded in 1209, was widened in 1904 and then demolished to make way for the present bridge (1968–72). The facing stonework has been rebuilt at a site in Arizona, U.S.A.

1. This is a confusion with the date of commencement of preliminary works: piling for the foundations started 15 March 1824. When the coffer dams were completed the first stone was laid 15 June 1825. See: C. Welch, *History of the Tower Bridge*, 1894, 129.

2. This is given as 'by William Wyon, of the Royal Mint' in C. Welch, *The History of Tower Bridge*, London, 1894, 132. The book provides an excellent history of the medieval bridge.

LEAMINGTON, Warwicks., **Beech Lawn House**, Warwick Street *1832*

**103a** *Obv.* Dr Jephson seated by a writing table, facing to right. Around HENRY JEPHSON ESQUIRE M.D.

*Rev.* View of main front of house, with driveway in foreground. Around top, BEECH LAWN LEAMINGTON. In exergue, THE RESIDENCE OF H. JEPHSON ESQ. M.D. Signed below in script, OTTLEY.

White Metal, 51 mm. 1846 (Illustrated in Forrer, vol. 4, 337).

103b

**103b** *Obv.* Bust of Dr Jephson, facing to left. Around, HENRY JEPHSON ESQUIRE M.D.

*Rev.* View of main front of house, etc. (as above).

Silver, Bronze,* White Metal,* Copper, 51 mm. 1846 (BM)*

These medals, by Ottley, were sold at Leamington to commemorate the opening of the Jephson Gardens on 12 May 1846 (see H. G. Clarke, *Royal Leamington Spa*, 1947, 93 and illus. p. 95).

A large early nineteenth-century Leamington villa that reflects the town's sudden expansion in the 1820s and 1830s. This was due to the popularity of its Spa Waters—and the part played by the notable Dr Jephson (1798–1878), who was to Leamington what Dr Russell was to Brighton. The medal shows the house and consulting rooms, by William Startin, which Dr Jephson had built for himself in 1832. The view is identical with that given on p. 243 of *The Spas of England*, vol. 2, by A. B. Granville, published 1841 (reprint edition, 1971, Adams & Dart). After the death of Dr Jephson the house became a 'Ladies College & High School'; it was demolished in 1946.

BILSTON, West Midlands, **Cholera Orphan School,** Prouds Lane *1833*

104a

**104a** *Obv.* Elevation of building. CHOLERA ORPHAN SCHOOL. In exergue, OPENED AUGUST. 5. 1833 NUMBER OF ORPHANS 450 BY CHOLERA UNDER 12 YEARS OF AGE. Signed, OTTLEY.

*Rev.* Inscription: ERECTED & SUPPORTED FROM A FUND SUBSCRIBED BY THE BRITISH NATION FOR THE RELIEF OF SUFFERERS BY CHOLERA AT BILSTON IN THE YEAR 1832 POPULATION 14492 PERSONS ATTACKED BY CHOLERA 3568 PERSONS WHO PERISHED 742 THE FIRST CASE AUGUST 3 THE LAST DEATH SEP. 18 AMOUNT OF CONTRIBUTIONS $8536^{L}..8^{S}..7^{D}$ — · — W. LEIGH. A.M. INCUMBENT.

Bronze, 45 mm. 1833 (BM)

The Cholera Orphan School, which cost £400, was opened a year after the epidemic began: 'Previous to the opening several hundred neat and well executed medals had been prepared . . . to commemorate the sad event, and one of them was suspended, by a black riband, round the neck of each child'.[1] The Revd William Leigh (see medal reverse), of St Leonard's Bilston,[2] was a campaigner for cholera 'reform' and author of *Cholera in Bilston*, Wolverhampton, 1833. The building was demolished *c.* 1960.

1. William White, *History, Gazeteer and Directory of Staffordshire*, Sheffield, 1834, 224–5 (I am grateful to Mr John Roper for this reference).

2. Which had recently been rebuilt by Francis Goodwin (qv); he was also the architect of Bilston Parish Church (1827–29).

BIRMINGHAM, West Midlands, **St John's Church,** Church Road, Perry Bar *1831–33*

**105a** *Obv.* View of church. S. W. VIEW OF ST JOHN'S CHURCH. In exergue, PERRY BAR. Signed in script, OTTLEY.

*Rev.* Inscription: ST JOHN'S CHURCH. PERRY BARR IN THE PARISH OF HANDSWORTH. & COUNTY OF STAFFORD. WAS ERECTED & ENDOWED AT THE SOLE COST OF JOHN GOUGH ESQUIRE OF PERRY HALL. THE FIRST STONE OF THIS EDIFICE (CONTAINING 450 SITTINGS, OF WHICH 150 ARE FREE) WAS LAID. APRIL. 18 1831. & THE CONSECRATION OF IT BY THE LORD BISHOP OF LICHFIELD & COVENTRY, TOOK PLACE AUGST 6. 1833. FRANCIS E. TURNOUR MINISTER. W. H. OSBORN. G. L. PROUD CHURCHWARDENS THOMAS LANE FREER RECTOR OF HANDSWORTH.

Bronze, 45 mm. 1833 (BM)

105a

Gothic style, in stone, with strangely emphasised battlements. A chancel and transepts were added *c.* 1887. The inscription indicated that this was not a Commissioners' church.

See: Pevsner, *Warwicks.* 195.

LONDON, City, **Bank of England,** Threadneedle Street *1788–1833*

**106a** *Obv.* Portrait head, to right, of the architect, JOHN SOANE. Signed, W. WYON A.R.A. MINT.

*Rev.* Elevation of 'Tivoli Corner' of Bank Building. Around on border, A TRIBUTE OF RESPECT FROM THE BRITISH ARCHITECTS. Below, MDCCCXXXIV.

Gold, Silver,* Bronze,* 58 mm. 1835 (Eidlitz 952, pl. 112) (See also Frontispiece.) (BM)*

It was this medal, in gold, which was presented to Sir John Soane in March 1835, following donations in 1834 by 350 subscribers (see Frontispiece). It marked the esteem in which he was held as the senior member of his profession. The occasion was celebrated in Soane's London house (now Sir John Soane's Museum, Lincoln's Inn Fields) and the presentation made by Sir Jeffry Wyatville RA.[1] The medal reverse shows the so-called 'Tivoli Corner' of John Soane's new building for the Bank of England (1788–1833). This north-west corner of the screen wall, at the junction of Princes Street and Lothbury, was completed 1805 and used a Corinthian order deriving from the Temple of Vesta at Tivoli. Although the screen wall remains, the building of Sir Herbert Baker's huge block on the site (1923–33) destroyed Soane's outstanding interiors with their system of shallow domes and rooflights.[2]

106a

See: D. Stroud, *The Architecture of Sir John Soane,* 65, 66, and pls. 65–92; Pevsner, *London 1,* 164–67.

1. Then next senior in the profession to Soane. See D. Linstrum, *Sir Jeffry Wyatville,* 1972, p. 1 for a note of this unique event. A version of the medal, with collar, has been used by the RIBA as an annual student award.

2. 'The worst individual loss suffered by London architecture in the first half of the C20'. Pevsner, op. cit., p. 164; and see H. Hobhouse, *Lost London,* 197.

107a

SWINTON, Greater Manchester, **St Peter's School** *1833*

**107a** *Obv.* View of School with foundation date on wall 1833. ERECTED BY VOLUNTARY SUBSCRIPTIONS 1833. In exergue, SAINT PETERS SCHOOL.

*Rev.* Inscription: JUBILEE HELD SEPTEMBER 8, 1883. SAINT PETERS CHURCH SWINTON, and within, a further legend, IN COMMEMORATION OF THE FIFTIETH ANNIVERSARY OF THE FIRST SUNDAY SCHOOL BUILT IN CONNECTION WITH.

White Metal, 38 mm. 1883 (BM)

The building shown was opened in April 1833, as the first for school purposes in Swinton. In 1835 an Infant's day school was opened in the room below the Sunday School room.[1] Demolished 1866, to make way for the Church of St Peter by G. E. Street (qv.) on the same site.

1. See Dennis Fletcher, *Swinton Church and Parish,* 1929.

BIRMINGHAM, West Midlands, **Town Hall,** Paradise Street
*1832–34 (altered 1835 on)*

**108a** *Obv.* View of BIRMINGHAM TOWN HALL, radiated. In exergue, EREC$^{D}$ MDCCCXXXIV BY HANSOM & WELCH. Signed, E. AVERN F.

*Rev.* Female figure with lyre and attributes of music. Legend: MUSIC FESTIVAL HELD IN THE TOWN HALL BIRM$^{M}$ 1834. Signed in exergue, E. AVERN F.

White Metal, 49 mm. 1834 (Eidlitz 498)(BM)

108b

**108b** *Obv.* View of BIRMINGHAM TOWN HALL. In exergue, EXTREME LENGTH 166 FEET, WIDTH 104 FEET, HEIGHT 83 FEET. — FIRST — MUSICAL FESTIVAL OCT. 1834. Signed, HALLIDAY.

*Rev.* Interior of the hall. At left, INTERIOR VIEW. At right, OF THE HALL. In exergue, LENGTH 140 FEET BREADTH 65 FEET HEIGHT 65 F$^{T}$. HANSOM & WELCH ARCHT$^{S}$.

Bronze, White Metal, 49 mm. 1834 (Eidlitz 500, pl. 57) (BM)

(See also Plate 1.)

**108c** *Obv.* View of BIRMINGHAM TOWN HALL. In exergue, HANSOM & WELCH ARCHITECTS.

*Rev.* Inscription: EXTREME LENGTH 166 FEET. WIDTH 104 HEIGHT 83. LENGTH OF HALL 140 FEET. WIDTH 65. HEIGHT 65. WILL CONTAIN 8000 PERSONS. THE FIRST MUSICAL FESTIVAL HELD IN THE HALL OCTOBER 1834. PRESIDENT THE RIGHT HON$^{L}$ THE EARL OF AYLESFORD.

Bronze, 38 mm. 1834 (Eidlitz 499, pl. 57) (BM)

**108d** *Obv.* View of the BIRMINGHAM TOWN HALL. At bottom, 1834. Below the building, HANSOM & WELCH ARCH$^{TS}$.

*Rev.* Inscription: THE COMMITTEE APPOINTED TO SUPERINTEND THE ERECTING OF THE BUILDING — WILL. BEALE ESQ. THOMAS CLARK ESQ. I. W. CROMPTON ESQ. S. T. GALTON ESQ. P. M. JAMES ESQ. THOMAS LEE ESQ. OLIVER MASON ESQ. JOSEPH MOORE ESQ. JAMES PEARSON ESQ. WILL. PHIPSON ESQ. THEODORE PRICE ESQ.

CHARLES SHAW ESQ. TIMOTHY SMITH ESQ. HENRY SMITH ESQ. RICHARD SPOONER ESQ. SIR EDWARD THOMASON KT JOHN TURNER ESQ. JOSEPH WALKER ESQ. — JOHN ARNOLD ESQ. AND WILLIAM HAINES ESQ. SOL^S — THE GRAND MUSICAL FESTIVALS FOR THE BENEFIT OF THE GENERAL HOSPITAL WILL BE HELD IN THIS MARBLE HALL. THE SIZE OF THE MUSIC ROOM IS IN LENGTH 140 FEET, IN WIDTH 65 FEET, IN HEIGHT 65 FEET; THE ORGAN IS THE MOST POWERFULL ONE IN EUROPE, AND IS 40 FEET WIDE AND 45 FEET HIGH. —

Silver, Bronze, White Metal, 73 mm.
1834 (Eidlitz 497, pl. 57) (BM)

**108e** *Obv.* View of TOWN HALL BIRMINGHAM. In exergue, OPENED 1834, ENLARGED 1837 — LENGTH OF BUILDING 173 F^T WIDTH 104 F^T HEIGHT 83 F^T — HANSOM & WELCH. ARCHT^S Signed, DAVIS BIRM.

*Rev.* View of interior. Legend: INTERIOR VIEW OF THE HALL FROM THE GREAT GALLERY. In exergue, LENGTH OF THE ROOM, 155 FEET BREADTH, 65 FEET HEIGHT, 65 FEET —

Bronze, White Metal, 51 mm. 1837 (Eidlitz 502, pl. 57) (BM)

**108f** *Obv.* View of town hall (as obverse of No. 108b, above).

*Rev.* Elevation. BIRMINGHAM FREE GRAMMAR SCHOOL. In exergue, FOUNDED BY KING EDWARD VI. 1552 PRESENT EDIFICE FINISHED 1837 — LENGTH IN FRONT 174 FEET 125 FEET IN FLANK 60 FEET IN HEIGHT — Signed, T. HALLIDAY. F.

White Metal, 49 mm. 1837 (Eidlitz 501, pl. 57)

Reverse is as obverse of No. 116c, for Birmingham King Edward VI Grammar School.

The young, and then little-known, architects were J. A. Hansom and his partner E. Welch. They won a hurried 1830 competition[1] with a fine classical revival design based on the Temple of Castor and Pollux in the Roman Forum. It is built of brick and faced with Anglesey marble. Although the building was sufficiently complete for it to be opened in 1834, the contracting costs brought the architects to bankruptcy. From 1835 Charles Edge was appointed the architect in charge; he lengthened the building by two columns (i.e. to fifteen, not the thirteen shown on the medals) to gain space for a large organ given by the musical committee of the General Hospital (see No. 54). Several of the medals commemorate the music festival of 1834; it was the housing of this established triennial festival[2] that had provided one of the main pressures for building a Town Hall. The interior (shown on Nos. 108b, 108e) was considerably altered by Sir Charles Allom in 1926–27.

See: Pevsner, *Warwicks.* 113, 114; *VCH Warwicks.*, vol. 7, 43, 327.

1. Only two months were allowed. Other entrants included Barry, Rickman.
2. See p. 75.

109a

LONDON, Westminster, **Charing Cross Hospital,** Agar Street, Strand *1831–34*

**109a** *Obv.* Elevation of three storeys, with pediment to central five bays. CHARING CROSS HOSPITAL LONDON. In exergue, FOUNDED 1818. Signed, B. WYON S.

*Rev.* Laurel wreath. In centre, — — space for inscription. Legend around: SCHOLA MEDICINAE PALMAM PRAECLARIOR AUFERT.

Bronze, 58 mm. 1843$^{G}$ (BM)

By Decimus Burton. The hospital formed part of of the west Strand improvements planned by Nash to relate to his Trafalgar Square layout of the 1820s. The medal shows the building without the extra fourth floor that was constructed later. For the south (end) façade, a successful semicircular addition was devised to articulate the corner facing the Strand.[1]

See: Pevsner, *London 1*, 272.

1. Illustrated in *Survey of London*, vol. xx, pl. 38a.

110a

OLDHAM, Greater Manchester, **Blue Coat School,** Horsedge Street *1829–34*

**110a** *Obv.* Elevation of building, with forecourt. OLDHAM BLUE-COAT SCHOOL. In exergue, THE CEREMONIAL STONE WAS LAID BY THO$^{S}$ BARKER ESQ$^{RE}$ APRIL 20 $^{TH}$ 1829. — RICH$^{D}$ LANE. ARCHITECT. Signed on bar, T.H.F.

*Rev.* Wreath, as border. Inscription: ERECTED BY PUBLIC SUBSCRIPTION, AND ENDOWED BY THE WILL OF THE LATE THOMAS HENSHAW ESQ$^{R}$ FOR THE MAINTENANCE AND EDUCATION OF POOR CHILDREN.

Bronze, White Metal, 54 mm. 1829 (BM)

By Richard Lane of Manchester. Built in 1829–34. The medal shows the seventeen-bay main front with pinnacles, battlements, and a 'Tudor' style then normal for educational institutions.[1]

See: Pevsner, *S Lancs.* 357.

1. Cf. Lane's more exaggerated romanticism in the composition of the Deaf & Dumb School & Blind Asylum, Old Trafford (1834–37); this is illustrated in C. Stewart, *The Stones of Manchester*, p. 21.

111a

MANCHESTER, **Royal Institution,** Mosley Street (now the City Art Gallery) *1824–35*

**111a** *Obv.* Bust to right. B. A. HEYWOOD.[1] Signed, on truncation W. WYON A.R.A. MINT.

*Rev.* Elevation of Royal Institution building. INSTITVTVM REGIVM MANCVNIENSE; below, MDCCCXXIII.

Silver, 51 mm.

See Hocking, ii, 293 no. 25. *c.* 1824 (Royal Mint Museum)

The Manchester Royal Institution was designed by Charles Barry following a limited competition (in 1824) and was completed in 1835;

his solution was preferred to the submissions of Francis Goodwin (qv.), J. B. Papworth, John Foster Jnr (qv.), and Lewis Wyatt (qv.). Hitchcock, i, 38 refers to it as one of the best examples of the Grecian museums that were characteristic of the early nineteenth century: 'It illustrates better than do any of the churches the young architect's capabilities as an academic designer'.

See: Pevsner, *S Lancs.* 284.

1. Forrer, vol. 6, 650 ff., notes that Sir Benjamin Heywood (1793–1865) was the donor of this medal.

BIRMINGHAM, West Midlands, **Cemetery Chapel,** Key Hill
*1835–36*

112a

**112a** *Obv.* View of the cemetery and chapel. Above, S.W. VIEW OF THE BIRMINGHAM CEMETERY. In exergue, CHA$^{S}$ EDGE. ARCHITECT W. SMITH. BUILDER. Signed, OTTLEY.

*Rev.* Inscription: THE FIRST STONE OF THIS CHAPEL FOR FUNERAL SERVICES WAS LAID BY P. M. JAMES ESQ$^{R}$ HIGH BAILIFF AND THO$^{S}$ TYNDALL ESQ$^{R}$ LOW BAILIFF OF THIS BOROUGH. ASSISTED BY THE REV$^{D}$ J.A. JAMES AND THE REV$^{D}$ THO$^{S}$ MORGAN, ON THE 14 DAY OF JULY IN THE YEAR OF OUR LORD 1835 AND THE 6 YEAR OF THE REIGN OF HIS MAJESTY KING WILLIAM THE FOURTH. — DIRECTORS GEO$^{R}$ GOODWIN. JOS$^{H}$ ROCK. JACOB POPE. RICH$^{D}$ HASLUCK. CHA$^{S}$ EDGE. W. R. MARSTON. WILL$^{M}$ ROOM. BENJ$^{N}$ HUDSON. WILL$^{M}$ ROBERTSON.

Bronze, White Metal, 44 mm. 1835 (Eidlitz 373, pl. 42) (BM)

Chapel designed by Charles Edge, in 1835, as a Greek temple with a Doric portico.

See: Pevsner, *Warwicks.* 140.

LIVERPOOL, Merseyside, **Lime Street Railway Station, Entrance Screen**
*1835–36*

113a

**113a** *Obv.* Elevation of main entrance to station. NEW GRAND ENTRANCE OF THE RAILWAY STATION AT LIVERPOOL — Signed, T. HALLIDAY: FECIT:

*Rev.* View of viaduct, with town in background. PART OF THE VIADUCT OF 28 ARCHES AT BIRMINGHAM. Below ON THE LIVERPOOL, MANCHESTER & BIRMINGHAM GRAND JUNCTION RAILWAY OPENED. JULY. 4. 1837. Signed, HALLIDAY. F.

White Metal, 48 mm. 1837 (BM)

**113b** *Obv.* Elevation of main entrance to station. GRAND FACADE OF THE NEW RAILWAY STATION LIVERPOOL —

*Rev.* View of railway viaduct crossing landscape with river. VIADUCT OVER THE VALLEY OF THE WEAVER. Below, PUBLISHED TO COMMEMORATE THE OPENING OF THE GRAND JUNCTION RAILWAY JULY. 4. 1837 BY W.B. PROMOLI LATE THO$^{S}$ WOOLFIELD CHURCH STREET LIVERPOOL — Signed T. HALLIDAY. FECIT.

White Metal, 55 mm. 1837 (BM)

The medals show the entrance façade by John Foster Jnr, for the original Lime Street Station (opened in 1836). This was the first attempt at monumental expression in a railway station; it used a Roman triumphal arch theme, and screened the train sheds designed by John Cunningham (qv.). The latter were rebuilt in 1846–50 in conjunction with new buildings by Sir William Tite (qv.); Foster's screen was finally demolished *c.* 1870 to make way for a station hotel by Alfred Waterhouse (qv.).

See: H.-R. Hitchcock, *Early Victorian Architecture*, 496, 497, pl. xv3.

114a

NEWARK, Notts., **Christ Church,** Lombard Street *1836*

**114a** *Obv.* View of church. JULY 1836. In exergue, CHRIST CHURCH NEWARK. Signed, OTTLEY.

*Rev.* Inscription: ERECTED BY VOLUNTARY CONTRIBUTION UNDER 1 & 2 W.IV.C. 38 — JAMES THORPE ESQ$^{RE}$ MAYOR. On scroll, 2 CHRONICLES C. VI. V. 40. 41. 42

White Metal, 50 mm. 1836 (BM)

A simple rectangular plan, 1836, in the Early English 'lancet' window style, by J. D. Paine.

See: Pevsner, *Notts.* 110.

115a

BATH, Avon, **St Michael's Church,** Broad Street *1835–37*

**115a** *Obv.* View of new gothic style church with spire. ST MICHAEL'S CHURCH BATH FIRST STONE LAID APRIL 21. 1835. Signed, DAVIS BIRM.

*Rev.* Inscription: THIS CHURCH ERECTED TO THE GLORY OF THE TRIUNE JEHOVAH, AND FOR THE ETERNAL GOOD OF SOULS, WAS BUILT BY VOLUNTARY SUBSCRIPTION EPH.11.20.21.

Bronze, 38 mm. 1835 (BM)

A Gothic replacement for the classical design of 1742, which was pulled down (see No. 46). The new St Michael of 1835–37 is by G. P. Manners (the City Architect), and the medal shows its strange west tower, with huge lancets and polygonal flanking porches.

See: Pevsner, *N. Somerset,* 107.

BIRMINGHAM, West Midlands, **King Edward VI Grammar School,** New Street *1833–37*

**116a** *Obv.* Bust of Edward VI facing right. EDVARDUS VI. LAUS DEO.

*Rev.* Elevation of FREE GRAMMAR SCHOOL BIRMINGHAM. In exergue, FOUNDED BY KING EDWARD VI. A.D. 1552 REBUILT 1707. PRESENT EDIFICE ERECTED 1836 REV. FRANCIS JEUNE D.C.L. REV. SYDNEY GEDGE M.A. MASTERS. C. BARRY ARCHITECT. Signed, DAVIS.

Bronze, White Metal, 51 mm.
1837 (Eidlitz 50, pl. 5; *Med. Ill.* i, p. 59, No. 11) (BM)

**116b** *Obv.* Elevation of BIRMINGHAM FREE GRAMMAR SCHOOL. Below, FOUNDED BY KING EDWARD VI. A.D. 1552 REBUILT 1707 PRESENT EDIFICE ERECTED 1836 LENGTH 174 FEET HEIGHT 60 FEET C. BARRY ARCHT. Signed, T.H.F.

*Rev.* Bust, half left, of Edward VI in central roundel. EDVARD. VI D.G. ANG. PR. ET HIB. REX. Around on a wide border, THIS SCHOOL WAS ENDOWED BY EDWARD VI FOR THE INSTRUCTION OF THE YOUTH OF BIRMING$^{M}$ & NEIGHBOURHOOD IN GRAMMAR. In panel, PATER MELIORIS EVI. Around below, PRESENT MASTERS REV. FRANCIS JEUNE D.C.L. REV. SIDNEY GEDGE M.A. — ESTIMATED COST OF THE PRESENT BUILDING £35000.

White Metal, 41 mm. 1837 (*Med. Ill.* i, p. 60, No. 14) (BM)

**116c** *Obv.* Elevation of BIRMINGHAM FREE GRAMMAR SCHOOL. Below, FOUNDED BY KING EDWARD VI. 1552 PRESENT EDIFICE FINISHED 1837 — LENGTH IN FRONT 174 FEET 125 FEET IN FLANK 60 FEET HEIGHT — Signed, T. HALLIDAY F.

*Rev.* Bust, half left, of Edward VI in central roundel. EDVARD.VI D.G. ANG. PR. ET HIB. REX. Around on wide border at top, THIS SCHOOL WAS ENDOWED BY EDWARD VI. FOR THE INSTRUCTION OF THE YOUTH OF BIRMINGHAM & NEIGHBOURHOOD IN GRAMMAR On scroll, PATER MELIORIS EVI. Around below, PRESENT MASTERS REV. FRANCIS JEUNE D.C.L. REV. SIDNEY GEDGE M.A. UNDER THE MANAGEMENT OF 20 GOVERNORS — C. BARRY ARCHT. ESTIMATED COST OF THE PRESENT BUILDING £35000.

Bronze, 48 mm. 1837 (*Med. Ill.* i, p. 60, No. 13) (BM)

**116d** *Obv.* Elevation of BIRMINGHAM FREE GRAMMAR SCHOOL. In exergue, FOUNDED BY KING EDWARD VI. A.D. 1552 REBUILT 1707. PRESENT EDIFICE ERECTED 1836 — LENGTH IN FRONT 174 FEET 125 FEET IN FLANK 60 FEET IN HEIGHT — C. BARRY ARCHITECT. Signed HALLIDAY. F.

*Rev.* Bust of Edward VI to left, laurel branches below. PATER MELIORIS EVI, above. EDVARDVS VI·D·G·ANG· FR· ET HIB· REX· around bust. THIS SCHOOL WAS ENDOWED BY EDWARD VI. WITH LANDS AND HOUSES PRODUCING £41 PER ANNUM. WHICH NOW PRODUCE UPWARDS OF £4000 PER AN. FOR THE INSTRUCTION OF THE YOUTH OF BIRMINGHAM AND NEIGHBOURHOOD IN GRAMMAR UNDER THE MANAGEMENT OF 20 GOVERNORS. — PRESENT MASTERS REV. FRANCIS JEUNE D.C.L. REV. SYDNEY GEDGE M.A. — ESTIMATED COST OF THE PRESENT BUILDING £35000.

Bronze, White Metal, 63 mm. 1837 (Eidlitz 49, pl. 5; *Med. Ill.* i, p. 59, No. 12) (BM)

116d

This was the first gothic Revival building to appear in central Birmingham. The architect was Charles Barry, and the medal shows the Perpendicular tracery, buttresses and pinnacles of the main façade to New Street. Barry had worked on the design from 1833, and in 1835 hired the young A. W. N. Pugin (qv.) to help with the detailing of furniture, ceiling decoration, bosses, pendants, etc.[1] It was this collaboration, and the development of Birmingham themes, that flowered in Barry's competition winning design for the Houses of Parliament at the end of the same year (see No. 179c). The school moved to Edgbaston in 1936, and Barry's building was demolished.

See: M. Seaborne, *The English School*, 176 plan, pl. 159; H.-R. Hitchcock, *Early Victorian Architecture*, 48.

1. P. Stanton, *Pugin*, 1970, 21.

DORKING, Surrey, **St Martin's Church** *1835–37*

117a

**117a** *Obv.* View of church. Around, AN HABITATION FOR THE MIGHTY GOD OF JACOB. In exergue ST MARTIN'S DORKING.

*Rev.* Inscription around: TO THE GLORY OF GOD AND FOR THE SALVATION OF MAN. In centre, ERECTED BY VOLUNTARY CONTRIBUTION AND OPENED FOR DIVINE WORSHIP BY THE LORD BISHOP OF WINCHESTER JULY. 18. 1837. — THE REV. J. JOYCE. M.A. VICAR THE REV. S. ISAACSON. CURATE. — MR J. CHEESMAN MR J. MARTYR CHURCHWARDENS — MR S. BOTHWELL BUILDER.

Bronze, 34 mm. 1837 (BM)

By William McIntosh Brookes. The gothic church shown on the medal was built 1835–37, but demolished in 1872 to be replaced by the present building by H. Woodyer.

EXETER, Devon, **Lower Market,** New Street *1835–37*

118a

**118a** *Obv.* Elevation to street. MEAT & CORN MARKET. Below, FOUNDED BY THE CHAMBER MDCCCXXXV C. FOWLER ARCHT

*Rev.* Arms of the City of Exeter. Around, COMPLETED BY THE COUNCIL OF EXETER MDCCCXXXVII. Signed B. WYON F.

Bronze, 38 mm. 1837 (BM)

The medal shows the south elevation of the meat market designed by Charles Fowler after a competition win in 1834. Stylistically similar to his earlier Hungerford market, it was a rare application, in England, of the theories of the French rationalist architect J. N. L. Durand. The building was one of several city improvements following a severe cholera outbreak; it was destroyed in 1942. The idea of commemorating the market with a medal occurred to the architect when a Roman coin of the time of Nero, also depicting a meat market, was dug up during site excavation (see p. 6).[1] This appears to be the coin which is illustrated as No. 72, and described on pp. 267 ff., in *Architectura Numismatica* by Fowler's friend and colleague T. L. Donaldson (qv.).[2]

See: J. R. B. Taylor in *AR*, March 1964, 174, 180.

1. See Fowler's account in *Arch. Mag.* iv, 1837, 312. The Exeter medal should be compared with Eidlitz 733, pl. 85, where an earlier medal of 1824 (by E. Dubois) illustrates E. N. Pagot's Cornmarket at Orleans, designed in a similar rationalist style.
2. Fowler was co-secretary of the IBA with Donaldson between 1836 and 1839.

LIVERPOOL, Merseyside, **Mechanics Institution,** Mount Street (now High School for Boys) *1835–37*

**119a** *Obv.* Portrait head to left. WILLIAM ROSCOE. Signed: on truncation I GIESON, with below CLINT. F, and around, CLEMENTS L'POOL DIREXIT.

*Rev.* Façade. ROSCOE PRIZE MEDAL LIVERPOOL MECHANICS INSTITUTION. Signed below exergue bar, CARTER. F. MAYER. DIR.

Bronze, 46 mm. ?1837 (BM)

119a

By A. H. Holme, after a competition in 1835.[1] Ashlar faced, of two floors, with a portico of two pairs of giant Ionic columns. The building provided the membership of 1,200 with a horseshoe plan lecture room, library, committee and reading rooms, classrooms, workshops and accompanying caretaker's flat.

See: Pevsner, *S Lancs.* 182; M. Seaborne, *The English School,* 190 (plan), 191.

1. *Arch. Mag.* ii, 1835, 317 suggests that J. A. Picton was given the job of combining the entries of the first three, i.e. Holme, Alderson, and Picton; however iv, 1837, 402 makes clear Picton's role as supervisor only.

LONDON, City, **City of London School,** Milk Street *1835–37*

**120a** *Obv.* Entrance elevation facing Milk Street. Around, CITY OF LONDON SCHOOL. Below, FOUNDED BY THE CORPORATION 1834. Signed, J. B. BUNNING ARCH. B.WYON F.

*Rev.* Allegorical scene: Knowledge seated; before her stands a youth with book. Above, City of London arms, at sides symbols of learning. A plaque in centre inscribed: JOHN CARPENTER 1447. Around, FOR THE RELIGOUS AND VIRTUOUS EDUCATION OF BOYS & THEIR INSTRUCTION IN LITERATURE & USEFUL KNOWLEDGE. Signed in exergue, B. WYON F.

Silver, Bronze, 57 mm. 1837 (Eidlitz 159, pl. 18) (BM)

120a

This medal was struck in 1837; a letter from Benjamin Wyon dated December 1837, in *Num. Chron.* ii, 182, discussed an accompanying reproduction. There are variants with heraldic compositions on the reverse. These were used for School prize medals at a later date. See records (in BM) of Watt Collection Nos. 982, 992: Arithmetical prize 1845 and English prize 1868.

Built (1835–37) by using funds from a charity endowed by John Carpenter, a Town Clerk of London in the fifteenth century (see medal reverse). The building was designed by J. B. Bunning on the site of the former Honey Lane Market in Cheapside. It was an innovatory school design for its time and provided a science laboratory (one of the earliest in the country), a number of different classrooms, and a semi-circular assembly theatre (cf. Liverpool Mechanics Institution No. 119 which was another building to reflect the reform movement in education of the 1820s).[1] The medal shows the main elevation to Milk Street for which Bunning used a Perpendicular style, with overtones of a college gateway. The school moved to a larger building on the Embankment in 1882 (see No. 202) and, after being used as a clubhouse, Bunning's building was demolished.

See: M. Seaborne, *The English School,* 183–85 incl. plan.

1. The protagonist of the movement was Lord Brougham, who laid the foundation stone of both schools.

121a

TINTWISTLE, Derbyshire, **Christ Church** *1837*

**121a** *Obv.* Bust of Queen Victoria to left, wearing 'jubilee' crown and laurel wreath. Around, QUEEN VICTORIA BORN MAY $24^{TH}$ 1819 ASCENDED THE THRONE $20^{TH}$ JUNE 1837 · Signed, PINCHES LONDON.

*Rev.* View of church with tower at west end. Around, CHRIST CHURCH TINTWISTLE CHESHIRE · JUBILEE MEDAL 1887 · In exergue, CONSECRATED OCT $10^{TH}$ 1837.

Bronze, White Metal, 36 mm. 1887 (BM)

See: Pevsner, *Cheshire,* 364.

122a

WALSALL WOOD, West Midlands, **St John's Church** *1837*

**122a** *Obv.* View of church. AN HABITATION FOR THE MIGHTY GOD OF JACOB. In exergue, $S^{T}$ JOHN'S WALSALL WOOD. Signed, DAVIS BIRM.

*Rev.* Inscription: THIS CHURCH ERECTED TO THE GLORY OF THE TRIUNE JEHOVAH, AND FOR THE ETERNAL GOOD OF SOULS, WAS BUILT BY VOLUNTARY SUBSCRIPTION. — CONSECRATED AUG. 22. 1837. — EPH. 11.20. 21.

Bronze, 38 mm. 1837 (BM)

By Isaac Highway, 1837. The plain church shown on the medal was enlarged in 1886 and 1895.

See: Pevsner, *Staffs.* 297.

123a

BIRMINGHAM, West Midlands, **Bishop Ryder Memorial Church,** Gem Street *1837–38*

**123a** *Obv.* Portrait bust to right. HENRY RYDER D.D. BISHOP OF LICHFIELD & COVENTRY 1824–36. Signed, P. HOLLINS. INV. T. W. INGRAM. SC.

*Rev.* View of west end of church. BISHOP RYDER'S CHURCH CONSECRATED DEC. 18. 1838 BIRMINGHAM.

White Metal, 44 mm. 1838 (BM)

A gothic design in red brick and stone of 1837–38, by Thomas Rickman (assisted by R. C. Hussey). The medal shows the tall, pinnacled, west tower with octagonal bell storey. The church was demolished in 1960.

See: H.-R. Hitchcock, *Early Victorian Architecture,* pl. iii, 15.

BIRMINGHAM, West Midlands, **St Mary's College,** New Oscott *1835–38*

**124a** *Obv.* Perspective view of college buildings. Around, COLLEGIVM. SANCTÆ. MARI. L.DE. OSCOTT. Below, OB EXTRUCTUM SEMINARIVM ET ECCLESIAM DEDICATAM ANNO SALVTIS. M. C|Ↄ .CCC.XXX.VIII. Signed H + SS EXC D + R FECIT.

*Rev.* Interior of chapel. VIRGINI DEIPARÆ.

Silver, 56 mm. 1838 (Watt. Coll.)

124a

The medal obverse shows the Tudor-style exterior of red brick with its stone dressings (see Plate 12); the designer was Joseph Potter of Lichfield, who also acted as contractor for the new buildings (1835–38). In 1837 A. W. N. Pugin was introduced to this Roman Catholic theological college, and promptly set out to put his recently published *Contrasts* into practice. He prepared a scheme for decorating and furnishing the Chapel interior (within the structure being built by Potter); this was carried out and the medal reverse shows an excellent copy of Pugin's etching of 1837.

See: Pevsner, *Warwicks.* 196–99; P. Stanton, *Pugin,* 1971, 34, pl. 10.

LONDON, Camden, **Euston Station, the 'Euston Arch'** *1836–38*

**125a** *Obv.* Elevation of Doric Portico — the 'Euston Arch'. LONDON AND BIRMINGHAM RAILWAY. In exergue, ENTRANCE FRONT OF THE LONDON STATION — HEIGHT TO THE TOP OF THE PEDIMENT 72$^{FT}$ HEIGHT OF ENTABLATURE 16 $^{FT}$ HEIGHT OF COLUMNS 44 $^{FT}$ LOWER DIAM$^{R}$ OF COL$^{S}$ 8$^{FT}$ 6 $^{IN}$ UPPER DIAM$^{R}$ OF COL$^{S}$ 6 $^{FT}$ 4 $^{IN}$ — PHILIP HARDWICK ESQ$^{R}$ F · R · S· ARCHITECT· Signed, G. R. COLLIS BIRM$^{M}$

*Rev.* Inscription: THE DIRECTORS OF THE LONDON & BIRMINGHAM RAILWAY COMPANY — 1838 — G. C. GLYN ESQ$^{R}$ CHAIRMAN. J. F. LEDSAM ESQ$^{R}$ DEPUTY CHAIRMAN G. P. BARCLAY ESQ. I. B. BOOTHBY ESQ. E. CALVERT ESQ. T. COOKE ESQ. E. CROPPER ESQ. R. GARNETT ESQ. P. S$^{T}$ L. GRENFELL E$^{SQ}$ D. HODGSON ESQ. H. HOULDSWORTH E$^{SQ}$ T. LOWE ESQ W. PHIPSON ESQ. I. L. PREVOST ESQ. T. W. RATHBONE ESQ. HENRY ROWLES ESQ. JOSEPH STURGE ESQ. T. TOOKE ESQ. J. WALKER ESQ. H$^{Y}$ WARRE ESQ. E. WILSON ESQ. T. YOUNG ESQ. — RICH$^{D}$ CREED ESQ$^{R}$ CAPT$^{N}$ C. R. MOORSOM R.N SECRETARIES ROB$^{T}$ STEPHENSON ESQ. ENGINEER IN CHIEF —

Bronze, 73 mm. 1838 (Eidlitz 503, pl. 57) (BM)

**125b** *Obv.* Head of George IV to right. GULIELMUS IIII REX PATRONUS ILLUSTRISSIMUS. Signed, G.R. COLLIS FECIT.

*Rev.* Elevation of Doric Portico — as obverse of No. 125a above.

White Metal, 73 mm. 1838 (Eidlitz 504)

Details of this medal are quoted by Eidlitz; he leaves Gulielmus IIII as 'George IV'.

125a

This fine Doric 'propylaeum', or gateway, was designed on a heroic scale by Philip Hardwick. Symbolically it represented the early railway age, as the entrance to the first railway station in the world in a capital city. Functionally it acted, with its four smaller adjacent lodges, as a screen to the station sheds[1] (cf. Foster's screen at Liverpool No. 113). The 'Euston Arch' did not stand in its comparative isolation for long, and the terminus buildings were much enlarged by Hardwick's son (P. C. Hardwick) in 1846–49. It was demolished, amidst considerable national protest, in 1962.

See: H.-R. Hitchcock, *Early Victorian Architecture*, 500, 501, pl. xv 6–8; *Marble Halls*, p. 153.

1. By Robert Stephenson, whose name is on the reverse of No. 125a.

LONDON, Southwark, **St Saviour's School,** Summer Street *c. 1838–39*

126a

**126a** *Obv.* Bust to left of Queen Elizabeth I. On border, ALUMNO OPTIME MERITO PRAEFECTI D.D.

*Rev.* View of school building. SCHOLA S. SALVATORIS COND. Below, ELIZABETHA REG. 1562 RENOV. VICTORIA REG 1839. Signed C. EDMONDS ARCHT. W. J. TAYLOR F.

Silver, 42 mm. 1839 (*Med. Ill.* i, p. 110, No. 38) (BM)

The buildings shown are of brick with stone dressings; designed by Christopher Edmonds, *c.* 1838–39. Their Tudor domestic style appropriately rehoused, on a new South Bank site,[1] the grammar school founded under Queen Elizabeth and previously located near Green Dragon Court. By the end of the nineteenth century the school buildings were hemmed in by factories and warehouses, and the attendance had dropped to twenty-three. In 1899 St Saviour's was united with St Olave's Grammar School and the building then became a church day school.[2] It was badly damaged by bombing in the 1940s and has since been demolished.

1. Next to St Peter, Bankside by the same architect (1839 destroyed 1940)
2. *Survey of London,* vol. xxii, *Bankside,* 92.

LONDON, City, **Wesleyan Centenary Hall,** Bishopsgate Street Within *1839–40*

**127a** *Obv.* Portrait bust of John Wesley to left, wearing preacher's bands. Around, JOHN WESLEY, M.A. BORN JUNE 14TH 1703. DIED MARCH 2ND 1791. Signed on truncation, CARTER F.

*Rev.* Elevation of five bays, three storeys high, with a giant order standing on a rusticated base. Around, CENTENARY OF WESLEYAN METHODISM, 1839. "THE WORLD IS MY PARISH". Below elevation, CENTENARY HALL AND MISSION HOUSE LONDON.

Bronze, White Metal, 48 mm. 1839 (Leeds City Museum) (BM)

127a

Forrer, vol. 8, 325, gives P. Champ as publisher and W. J. Taylor, London, as die engraver for these medals to mark the centenary on 25 October 1839.

**127b** Medal as above, except 65 mm. in White Metal (Leeds City Museum)

Between the two outer pilasters of the façade four attached Corinthian columns carry the enriched entablature; the medal does not, however, show a crowning pediment which was constructed above this projecting centre section.[1] Designed by the London architect William Fuller Pocock (1779–1849),[2] it was largely a rebuilding in 1839–40 of the London Tavern site in Bishopsgate.[3] In 1904 much of the accommodation not required by the Methodist Missionary Society was rented to the Bank of India;[4] the latter continued in possession until 1969 when the building was demolished. In 1928 Sir Aston Webb's architectural practice had converted one of the committee rooms on the top floor into a small commemorative chapel for the use of the staff.[5]

1. This was the subject of criticism in vol. 1 of the *Builder,* 1849, 437, 438. The design is discussed as No. 1 of 'Recent Public Buildings of London', and an alternative elevation was proposed on p. 446.
2. See Charles Welch, *Modern History of the City of London,* 1896, 184; Colvin, 464.
3. See *City Press,* 13 January 1904. The Methodists had bought the site for £15,000.
4. *City Press,* op. cit.
5. See *Builder,* 1929, 198, and accompanying photographs of the chapel interior, pp. 188, 191, 200. In Pevsner, *London 1,* 1957, 194 and also second edn. 1962, the incorrect impression is given that Sir Aston Webb & Son rebuilt the whole structure in 1928.

FROME, Somerset, **Holy Trinity, Sunday School Room** *1840*

**128a** *Obv.* View of Infant and Sunday School building.

*Rev.* Inscription: FROME TRINITY CHURCH INFANT AND SUNDAY SCHOOL ROOM OPENED CHRISTMAS DAY 1840.

Bronze, White Metal, 34 mm. 1840 (BM)

128a

This small building must have been an adjunct of the recently completed Holy Trinity Church (1837) by H. E. Goodridge (qv.). That also has stepped lancets and corner turrets.

LONDON, Tower Hamlets, **Philosophical Institution,** Beaumont Square, Mile End *1840*

129a

**129a** *Obv.* Portrait bust to right. BARBER BEAUMONT. Below, OBIIT 15 MAY 1841. Signed on truncation G.R. COLLIS F.

*Rev.* Façade of five bays beneath a pediment. PHILOSOPHICAL INSTITUTION FOUNDED 1840.

Bronze, 56 mm. 1841 (BM)

Built in 1840 at the expense of the painter, author and philanthropist J. T. Barber Beaumont.[1] The building was designed to act as a literary and scientific institute for the working-class inhabitants of East London. It was endowed with £13,000 by Beaumont and this money was ultimately used to develop the nearby 'Peoples Palace' (see No. 213). The building became a club in 1880, and was demolished in 1937. (The medal is given by H. A. Grueber in *Num. Chron.*, 1887, 266, together with a biographical note on the remarkable Barber Beaumont.)

1. The *Illustrated London News,* 10 December 1852, 518 reported that Mr Barber Beaumont had 'designed and erected, at a cost £5,000, the noble building'. In the preface to W. Spencer Beaumont, *A Brief Account of the Beaumont Trust and its Founder J. T. Barber Beaumont,* London, 1887, it is stated that Barber Beaumont was present at the opening ceremony in November 1840.

SHEFFIELD, South Yorks., **Wesley College,** Glossop Road (now King Edward VII Grammar School) *1837–40*

**130a** *Obv.* Main elevation, with seven-bay central portico and flanking pavilion blocks pedimented. Below, WESLEY COLLEGE. Outside central panel, SHEFFIELD FOUNDED 1837 VIRTUS RELIGIO DOCTRINA. Signed on decorated frame to panel, J. MOORE BIRM.

*Rev.* Border forming wreath around. (Blank for inscription).

Silver, 64 mm. ?1840s (Watt Coll.)

(This copy presented 1877.)

Completed 1840, by William Flockton of Sheffield. With giant Corinthian columns to the centre portico and end pavilions, 'a quite exceptionally ambitious piece of school design for its date' (Pevsner).

See: Pevsner, *Yorks.*, *W Riding*, 461.

130a

WINDSOR, Berks., **Windsor Castle** (remodelling) *1824–40*

**131a** *Obv.* Portrait head, to right of King George IV. GEORGIUS IV DEI GRATIA BRITTANNIARUM REX. Signed on truncation, STOTHARD. F., and around below, RUNDELL BRIDGE & RUNDELL.

*Rev.* View of King George IV gateway and newly restored Round Tower to left. Around, WINDSOR CASTLE FOUNDED BY WILLIAM THE CONQUEROR. In exergue, below a phoenix, RESTORED BY GEORGE IV 1828. Signed on exergue bar, STOTHARD F.

Bronze, 72 mm. 1828 (BM)

**131b** *Obv.* Portrait head, to left of King George IV. HIS MOST GRACIOUS MAJESTY GEORGE IV.

*Rev.* View on axis to new King George IV gateway of Windsor Castle. In exergue, DIED AT WINDSOR CASTLE JUNE 26 1830. AGED 67.

Bronze, 51 mm. and White Metal, 50 mm. 1830 (BM)

When, in 1823, George IV decided to take up residence at Windsor, the palace was inconvenient to use and had been little improved since the time of Charles II. In 1824 £150,000 was voted by Parliament for its remodelling and Jeffry Wyatt was chosen to undertake the work.[1] In his initial, and very comprehensive drawings, Wyatt set out to 'Gothicise' the severe buildings of the Upper Ward with their round-headed windows, and to heighten and crown the great Round Tower. The medals show the result of these improvements together with the new main King George IV gateway which was created by a duplication of the existing York tower. Although the cost of the work rapidly grew, and was ultimately well over £1 million, Jeffry Wyatville's scheme was finally completed in 1840. The medal of 1828 marks the completion of the first stage of the works when, on 9 December, George IV officially moved into his new Private Apartments.[2]

See: D. Linstrum, *Sir Jeffry Wyatville,* 1972, chap. 7.

1. In a limited competition with Nash (qv.) and Sir Robert Smirke. After this appointment Wyatt was granted a Royal Warrant to change his name to Wyatville.
2. Wyatville was then knighted and granted a residence in the Winchester Tower.

131a

132a

LEEDS, West Yorks., **St Peter's Parish Church,** Kirkgate *1839–41*

**132a** *Obv.* Portrait bust, facing to right. Around, THE REV WALTER FARQUHAR HOOK D D VICAR OF LEEDS 1837.

*Rev.* Elevation, east–west, of church with fence and gates in foreground. Around, S$^{T}$ PETER'S CHURCH LEEDS, REBUILT 1841. Below, BY THE VOLUNTARY CONTRIBUTIONS OF THE INHABITANTS. CONSECRATED SEP 2. Signed, OTTLEY.

Bronze,* White Metal, 50 mm.
1841 (Leeds City Museum) (BM)*

**132b** *Obv.* View of church from west end. Below, LEEDS PARISH CHURCH.

*Rev.* Crossed keys. Around, JUBILEE OF THE RESTORATION ·1841–1891·

Bronze, White Metal, 39 mm. 1891 (Leeds City Museum)

**132c** *Obv.* Crowned bust, to left of Queen Victoria. VICTORIA QUEEN · AND · EMPRESS. At left, TO COMMEM-ORATE THE 60$^{TH}$ YEAR; at right, OF HER MAJESTY'S REIGN. Signed below bust, F. BOWCHER. F.

*Rev.* View of LEEDS PARISH CHURCH. In exergue, SUNDAY SCHOOLS 1897. Signed, SPINK & SON. LONDON.

White Metal, 38 mm. 1897 (BM)

An important, and original, gothic church design of the late 1830s; by R. D. Chantrell for Dean Hook, vicar of Leeds from 1837 to 1859. Built in a transitional style, between Decorated and Perpendicular; it has an unusual axial plan form with the tower and entrance placed in the middle of the north side.

See: Pevsner, *Yorks., W Riding,* 310; D. Linstrum, *Historic Architecture of Leeds,* 1969, 41.

133a

LONDON, Islington, **South Islington and Pentonville Schools,** Denmark Terrace *1841*

**133a** *Obv.* End elevation of school building. SOUTH ISLINGTON AND PENTONVILLE BRITISH SCHOOLS. Below, ERECTED MDCCCXLI. Signed, DAVIS BIRM.

*Rev.* Inscription: TO IMPART USEFUL LEARNING, TO INCULCATE RIGHT PRINCIPLES, TO DISSEMINATE DIVINE TRUTH, THE ISLINGTON & PENTONVILLE BRITISH SCHOOLS HAVE BEEN ESTABLISHED, AND ARE OPEN TO CHILDREN OF ALL RELIGIOUS DENOMINATIONS.

White Metal, 43 mm. 1841 (Watt Coll.)

The medal shows the end elevation of an apparently 'basilican' plan (i.e. nave and side 'aisles') with suitably neo-Romanesque windows. The architects are reputed to have been Gough (qv.) and Roumieu (who were to 'modernise' Barry's St Peter, Islington in 1843).[1] The building existed as a school until 1901 when it was converted to commercial use.

1. See H.-R. Hitchcock, *Early Victorian Architecture,* 125.

LONDON, Wandsworth, **Christ Church,** Christchurch Road, Streatham *1840–41*

134a

**134a** *Obv.* View of west end of church in neo-Romanesque style, with campanile to right. Around, CHRIST CHURCH STREATHAM. Below, CONSECRATED 19$^{TH}$ NOV$^{R}$ 1841. Signed, J. TAYLOR LONDON.

*Rev.* Inscription: Around, NATIONAL SCHOOLS INSTITUTED 19$^{TH}$ NOV$^{R}$ 1844. In centre, surrounded by wreath, FOR GOOD CONDUCT AND PROFICIENCY.

Silver, 49 mm. 1844 (Watt Coll.)

A large, and comparatively inexpensive, brick church by J. Wild.[1] The design is an outstanding example of 'Rundbogenstil' which suddenly became popular in the 1840s (cf. Wilton Church No. 154) and which used Italian Romanesque and Early Christian forms, e.g. the round-headed openings and campanile. The brick chosen is of a rich yellow; this is combined at the arches and the cornice with red and white bricks to give an early example of Victorian polychromy.

See: H.-R. Hitchcock, *Early Victorian Architecture,* 105, 106, pl. iv, 10; Pevsner, *London 2*, 442.

1. 1,200 sittings, cost £6,000 (cf. Wilton smaller at £20,000). See H.-R. Hitchcock, op. cit., 104, 105.

MACCLESFIELD, Cheshire, **Christ Church School,** Pinfold Street *1840–41*

135a

**135a** *Obv.* School building on corner site. Signed, A. FENWICK, F. BIRM.

*Rev.* Inscription around: JUBILEE CELEBRATION OF CHRIST CHURCH SCHOOL. MACCLESFIELD. In centre, OPENED MAY 3 $^{RD}$ 1841 CELEBRATED MAY 3 $^{RD}$ 1891.

White Metal, 38 mm. 1891 (BM)

The street front is an 'Italian Villa' composition of the sort that was appearing in housebuilder's pattern books of the early 1840s.[1] The school shared the Free Grammar School endowment. It is now used as a church centre.

1. E.g. Charles Parker's *Villa Rustica.* The third book of 1841 had various designs for National Schools in the 'Italian Villa' style.

BIRMINGHAM, West Midlands, **St Philip's National School,** Lichfield Street *1842*

136a

**136a** *Obv.* Façade of school. S$^{T}$ PHILIP'S SCHOOLS, below, BIRMINGHAM IN UNION WITH THE NATIONAL SOCIETY — ERECTED — 1842. Signed, D. & R. FEC.

*Rev.* Christ blessing children surrounded by his disciples. Below, MATTHEW CHAP. 19. VER. 13.14.15. Signed, DAVIS BIRM.

Bronze, 52 mm. 1842 (BM)

The School had three main schoolrooms and could house 512 (Boys, Girls plus Infants).[1] The building and site were sold, and demolished, in the 1880s.

1. *VCH, Warwicks.*, vol. 7, 536.

DUDLEY, West Midlands, **St James' School** *1842*

137a

**137a** *Obv.* View of school building. Above, ST JAMES' SCHOOL DUDLEY. Below, W. BOURNE ARCHITECT. ERECTED A.D. 1842.

*Rev.* The Saviour blessing little children. TRAIN UP A CHILD IN THE WAY HE SHOULD GO AND WHEN HE IS OLD HE WILL NOT DEPART FROM IT. Below, SUFFER LITTLE CHILDREN TO COME UNTO ME.

White Metal, 47 mm. 1842 (Eidlitz 110, pl. 7) (BM)

The medal gives W. Bourne as architect. Bourne was also the architect of St James and St John churches — both of 1840 in St James Road, Dudley.

GREAT AYTON, North Yorks., **Ayton School** *c. 1817 and 1842 on*

138a

**138a** *Obv.* View of three-storey school building and house; in foreground landscaped gardens and bridge. AYTON SCHOOL JUBILEE 1891.

*Rev.* Within a wreath, JON. BACKHOUSE EDWARD PEASE THOS RICHARDSON FOUNDERS 1841.

Bronze, 39 mm. 1891 (BM)

The medal shows the school grounds with the River Leven in the foreground. This is a Friends' School and was formed in 1841 with the purchase of an existing house of *c.* 1817 (in centre of view).[1] The tall block (to left) was designed in 1842 under the direction of William Holmes of Newcastle, but was not erected until 1846 – then under the supervision of a Darlington architect John Middleton. A small eighteenth-century building (to the right) is the Meeting House; the bridge in the foreground was a gift in 1841 of the School's chief benefactor Thomas Richardson.

1. This house, bought from Philip Heselton, had its original mortgage conveyed in May 1817; it replaced two cottages related to the tanneries formerly on the site. I am grateful to the Principal and Archivist of the School for details of the building history.

BIRMINGHAM, West Midlands, **Hebrew National School,** Hurst Street *1843*

**139a** *Obv.* Elevation of five bay, three-storey façade.[1] Around, STRUCK TO COMMEMORATE LAYING THE FOUNDATION STONE THE HEBREW NATIONAL SCHOOL BIRMINGHAM. At top, BY SIR MOSES MONTEFIORE F.R.S. ASSISTED BY BARON DE ROTHSCHILD A. A. GOLDSMID ESQ. I. COHEN ESQ. D. SALOMONS ESQ. AND OTHER DISTINGUISHED INDIVIDUALS. Signed, G. R. COLLIS F.

139a

*Rev.* Biblical scene described on border around, JOSEPH INTRODUCING HIS FATHER JACOB TO PHARAOH KING OF EGYPT.

Bronze, White Metal, 73 mm. 1843 (BM)

See R. D. Barnett, *Catalogue of the Jewish Museum*. London, 1974, No. 1148.

**139b** *Obv.* Elevation of building. HEBREW NATIONAL SCHOOL BIRMINGHAM. Signed on exergue, T.H.F.

*Rev.* Inscription: THE FOUNDATION STONE LAID BY SIR MOSES MONTEFIORE F.R.S. AUG. 9 A.M. 5603* — Around in border Hebrew inscription,[2] and, PUBLISHED BY MYER MYERS. BIRMINGHAM.

Bronze, 45 mm. *1843 (BM)

Built 1843 in Hurst Street, and following the example of the Jewish Free School in London. Standard subjects, plus Hebrew Language and Literature were taught to approximately eighty-five boys. The school moved to Ellis Street in 1856, and the building was demolished.

See: *VCH, Warwicks.*, vol. 7, 483.

1. There are slight variations shown in the elevation when compared to the medal below, e.g. no hood mould to central door, or surround mouldings to upper windows.

2. Taken from Proverbs 22, v. 6: 'Train up a child in the way he should go and even when he is old he will not depart from it' (Revised version).

CHELTENHAM, Gloucs., **Cheltenham Proprietary College,** *1842–43*

**140a** *Obv.* View of 'Elizabethan' style buildings with tower and pinnacles. In foreground, driveway and fence. Around, CHELTENHAM PROPRIETARY COLLEGE. In exergue, THE BUILDING WAS COMMENCED 1842 AND OPENED IN AUGUST 1843. Signed in script, OTTLEY.

*Rev.* Imperial crown and sceptre rest on the HOLY BIBLE. A wreath around of oak leaves and acorns.

White Metal, 53 mm. 1843

140a

**140b** *Obv.* Corner view of whole range of college buildings. Below, CHELTENHAM COLLEGE – – – Signed, MARTIN + C° CHELTENHAM. On exergue bar, J. MOORE. F.

*Rev.* Wreath (Blank for inscription).

Silver, 44 mm. ?1860s[1] (Watt Coll.)

(This copy presented 1911)

A symmetrically planned building in the Perpendicular style, by James Wilson of Bath, was put up 1842–43. This arranged the classical and modern departments either side of a central tower (see view No. 140a). In 1853 north and south wings were added to this block (as shown on No. 140b), and the resultant quadrangle enclosed by a chapel 1858. Further additions to the south, still Perpendicular, were made in the 1860s.

See: Pevsner, ed., D. Verey, *Gloucs., Vale*, 134; M. Seaborne, *The English School*, 249.

1. Medal shows later additions forming a quadrangle behind the original building.

141a

LIVERPOOL, Merseyside, **Collegiate Institution**, Everton, Shaw Street (now Liverpool Collegiate High School) *1840–43*

**141a** *Obv.* Elevation of building. COLLEGIATE INSTITUTION LIVERPOOL. Below, ESTABLISHED M.DCCC.XLIII FOR SOUND LEARNING & RELIGIOUS EDUCATION. Signed, THOMAS OTTLEY MEDALLIST BIRMINGHAM.

*Rev.* Inscription, with Mitre and Shield: THE FOUNDATION STONE OF THIS INSTITUTION WAS LAID BY THE RIGHT HON$^{\text{LE}}$ LORD STANLEY M.P. THE PATRON OCTOBER 22$^{\text{ND}}$ 1840 IT WAS OPENED JANU$^{\text{RY}}$ 6$^{\text{TH}}$ 1843 IN THE 6$^{\text{TH}}$ YEAR OF THE REIGN OF HER MAJESTY QUEEN VICTORIA.

White Metal, 53 mm. 1843 (BM)

**141b** *Obv.* Elevation of building. COLLEGIATE INSTITUTION LIVERPOOL. Below, ESTABLISHED M.DCCC.XLIII FOR SOUND LEARNING & RELIGIOUS EDUCATION. Signed THO$^{\text{S}}$ OTTLEY BIRM$^{\text{M}}$.

*Rev.* Shield and inscription: PRIZE MEDAL.

Bronze, 31 mm. ?1840s (BM)

Built to a design by H. L. Elmes although, after a quarrel with the committee of this proprietary school, he was not allowed to supervise its construction (1840–43). Elmes, who had already won the competition for St George's Hall (No. 170), designed the Institution in the Perpendicular style then expected for educational buildings.[1] The main elevation (see medal) is closely modelled on Barry's Birmingham Grammar School (see No. 116) but has a more emphatic central entrance. This led through the main block to a linked octagonal building containing a large horse-shoe plan assembly hall—an innovation in school design seen in the Liverpool Mechanics Institution (No. 119) and the City of London School (No. 120).

See: Pevsner, *N Lancs.* 223; M. Seaborne, *The English School,* 247, 248 (plan).

1. Second in competition with Elmes were Scott and Moffat (qv.).

142a

LONDON, Redbridge, **Infant Orphan Asylum,** Holly Bush Hill, Wanstead (later the Royal Wanstead School) *1841–43*

**142a** *Obv.* View of building. THE INFANT ORPHAN ASYLUM AT WANSTEAD FOR 400 CHILDREN — G. G. SCOTT & W. B. MOFFATT ARCHITECTS. Signed, TAYLOR BIRM:

*Rev.* Coats of arms of England, Ireland, Scotland, and Wales and four crowns. THE INFANT ORPHAN ASYLUM WAS INSTITUTED A.D. 1827. INCORPORATED A.D. 1843 THE FIRST STONE OF THE NEW BUILDING WAS LAID BY H.R.H. PRINCE ALBERT JULY 24. 1841 & THE BUILDING OPENED BY HIS MAJESTY THE KING OF THE BELGIANS JUNE 27. 1843.

Bronze, Brass, 49 mm. 1843 (Eidlitz 941, pl. 108) (BM)

The medal view shows the extensive, symmetrical, range of buildings in the design by Scott and Moffatt. They are built of grey stone, with buff dressings, in a Jacobean style complete with mullioned windows and strapwork decoration. Converted 1974 for use as Crown Courts.

See: Pevsner, *Essex,* 413; *Builder,* vol. 1, 1849, 458–60; *Building,* 6 June 1975, 79–82.

LONDON, Westminster, **The Nelson Monument,** Trafalgar Square *1840–43*

**143a** *Obv.* Bust of Nelson, to left. Around on garter ENGLAND EXPECTS EVERY MAN WILL DO HIS DUTY. Signed below bust, J. DAVIS BIRM.

*Rev.* View of Trafalgar Square, with column in foreground. THE NELSON COLUMN LONDON, ERECTED 1843. On exergue bar, W. RAILTON ESQ ARCH.

Bronze, 43 mm. 1843 (*British Naval Medals*, no. 532) (BM)

**143b** *Obv.* Bust of Nelson, half left. ADM$^{L}$ LORD NELSON. Signed, W. GRIFFIN LONDON.

*Rev.* View of Trafalgar Square, with National Gallery and St Martin-in-the-Fields in the background. In the foreground: THE NELSON COLUMN TRAFALGAR SQU$^{R}$ LONDON. TENERIFFE. COPENHAGEN NILE. TRAFALGAR. In exergue, W RAILTON ESQ: ARCH: 1843. Signed on bar, J. TAYLOR BIRM.

White Metal, 44 mm. 1843 (*British Naval Medals,* no. 530) (BM)

143b

**143c** *Obv.* Bust of Nelson, to left. ADM$^{L}$ LORD NELSON.

*Rev.* View of the Nelson Monument. NELSON COLUMN ERECTED 1843. TENERIFFE. COPENHAGEN. NILE. TRAFALGAR.

Bronze, White Metal, 26 mm.
1843 (*British Naval Medals,* no. 533) (BM)

The Nelson Monument is a column of granite with a Corinthian capital cast from gun-metal. It was the competition winning design of the architect William Railton and was erected 1840–43. The statue is by E. H. Baily. Trafalgar Square itself was formed in the 1820s as part of John Nash's Metropolitan Improvements; he planned to link it with a straight road to the British Museum. The medal view also shows, in the background, the National Gallery (1834–38) by William Wilkins (qv.), and St Martin-in-the-Fields (1722–26) by James Gibbs (qv.).

BROWN EDGE, STOKE-ON-TRENT, Staffs., **St Anne's Church** *1844*

**144a** *Obv.* View of simple pitched roofed church with belfry. Around, + SAINT ANNE'S CHURCH + BROWN EDGE. Signed, ALLEN & MOORE BIRM$^{M}$

*Rev.* Man and woman with two children, all kneeling in prayer. Legend: REMEMBER THY CREATOR IN THE DAYS OF THY YOUTH.

Silver, 39 mm. ?1844 (Watt Coll.)

144a

The medal shows the south side of the church as built and consecrated in 1844. By J. & C. Trubshaw in a Norman style, with short chancel and three round-headed 'lancets' for the east window. A north-east tower and spire were added 1851–54 by the local benefactor H. H. Williamson; this covered an elaborate Norman-style arch originally the main entrance.

See: Pevsner, *Staffs.* 82.

GLOUCESTER, Gloucs., **St James's Parochial Schools,** Upton Street
*1844*

145a

**145a** *Obv.* View of school buildings with steeply pitched roofs and decorated bargeboards. SAINT JAMES' PAROCHIAL SCHOOLS, GLOUCESTER. Below, 1844. Signed, DAVIS BIRM.

*Rev.* Inscription: NOW THEREFORE HEARKEN UNTO ME, O YE CHILDREN : FOR BLESSED BE THEY THAT KEEP MY WAYS. HEAR INSTRUCTION AND BE WISE, PROV: VIII. 32.

White Metal, 41 mm. 1844 (BM)

The related church of St James (1841) is also in Upton Street; it is by Sampson Kempthorne.[1] This school building, with its mixture of curved bargeboards and Tudor windows, perhaps derives from a contemporary pattern book; it was built and endowed by the vicar of the parish, the Revd T. A. Hedley, and opened 25 July 1844. Additions were made in 1911, and the school is still in use.

1. Scott worked in his office and helped with the design of workhouses. Kempthorne emigrated to New Zealand in 1841.

LONDON, City, **Royal Exchange,** Threadneedle Street and Cornhill
*1842–44*

FOUNDATION STONE LAYING IN 1842:

146a

**146a** *Obv.* Conjoint heads of Victoria and Albert to left. VICTORIA BORN MAY $24^{TH}$ 1819. ALBERT BORN $AUG^{T}$ $26^{TH}$ 1819*.

*Rev.* View of the portico of NEW ROYAL EXCHANGE LONDON. In exergue, FIRST STONE LAID BY H.R.H. PRINCE ALBERT IN THE $5^{TH}$ YEAR OF THE REIGN OF H.M.G.M. VICTORIA $JAN.^{Y}$ 17.1842 W. TITE $ESQ^{R}$ F.R.S. F.G.S. $\&^{C}$ ARCHITECT. Signed, DAVIS BIRM.

Bronze, White Metal, 54 mm. 1842 (BM)

**146b** *Obv.* Heads of Victoria and Albert jugate to left. VICTORIA BRITAN: REGINA, ET ALBERT SAX COBURG GOTHA PRINCEPS. Signed on truncation, HALLIDAY.

*Rev.* View of the Royal Exchange. NEW ROYAL EXCHANGE. In exergue, THE FOUNDATION STONE LAID BY H.R.H. PRINCE ALBERT JANUARY 17 1842 — PUBLISHED BY HYAM HYAMS. CORNHILL.

Bronze, 62 mm. 1842 (Eidlitz 994, pl. 114) (BM)

**146c** *Obv.* View of the new Royal Exchange (as No. 146b).

*Rev.* Queen Elizabeth surrounded by courtiers. In exergue legend in five lines: QUEEN · ELIZABETH · PROCLAIMING THE · BURSE · TO · BE · CALLED THE · ROYAL · EXCHANGE · FOR · EVER. 1570.

White Metal, 61 mm. 1842 (BM)

The reverse of this is as No. 36a, the Old Royal Exchange.

**146d** *Obv.* View of the new Royal Exchange as reverse of No. 146b, but signed T.H.

*Rev.* View of the Old Building (but not the same as obverse of No. 36a). ROYAL EXCHANGE. Below, BUILT BY $S^{R}$ $THO^{S}$ GRESHAM

1566 DESTROYED BY THE FIRE OF LONDON REBUILT 1669 . AGAIN BURNT JAN$^{Y}$. 10 1838 — Signed, HALLIDAY. F: PUBLISHED BY HYAM HYAMS CORNHILL.

White Metal, 61 mm. 1842 (BM)

**146e** *Obv.* Head of Albert, to right. ALBERTVS VBIQVE HONORATVS · Signed below truncation, A. I. STOTHARD. F.

*Rev.* Elevation of portico to the Royal Exchange. SVB AVSPICIO PRINCIPIS. In exergue, RESTAVRATIO IANVAR : XVII MDCCCXLII.

Silver, Bronze, 44 mm. 1842 (BM)

OPENING IN 1844:

***a. Medals by Allen & Moore***

**146f** *Obv.* Busts of Victoria and Albert, jugate to left. QUEEN VICTORIA AND PRINCE ALBERT. Signed on truncation, A & M (Allen & Moore).

*Rev.* The Royal Exchange. ROYAL EXCHANGE LONDON. In exergue, FIRST STONE LAID 1842 BY P: ALBERT OPENED BY QUEEN VICTORIA 1844.

Brass, 22 mm. 1844 (Eidlitz 995, pl. 114) (BM)

**146g** *Obv.* View of the new Royal Exchange, as reverse of No. 146f.

*Rev.* Wellington, on horseback, to right. WELLINGTON STATUE LONDON ERECTED 1844. Below, COST L9000 RAISED BY SUBSCRIPTION.

Brass, 22 mm. 1844 (BM)

**146h** *Obv.* View of the ROYAL EXCHANGE LONDON. Below, FIRST STONE LAID JAN · 19 · 1842 BY H.R.H. PRINCE ALBERT OPENED BY H.M.G.M. VICTORIA 1844. Signed ALLEN & MOORE BIRM.

*Rev.* Wellington, on horseback, to right. THE WELLINGTON STATUE LONDON ERECTED 1844. Below, RAISED BY PUBLIC SUBSCRIPTION TOTAL VALUE L10500.[1]

White Metal, 26 mm. 1844 (BM)

1. This included the value of metal given by the Government (see No. 146i).

**146i** *Obv.* View of the Royal Exchange. ROYAL EXCHANGE LONDON. In exergue, FIRST STONE LAID JAN: 19.1842 BY H.R.H. PRINCE ALBERT. OPENED BY H.M.G.M. VICTORIA 1844. At left, W$^{M}$ TITE ESQ:ARCH: Signed, ALLEN & MOORE. BIRM.

*Rev.* Statue of Wellington on horseback. THE WELLINGTON STATUE LONDON ERECTED JUNE 18. 1844. At left, SIR F. CHANTRY. (*sic*) SC: In exergue, COST £9000 RAISED BY PUBLIC SUBSCRIPTION. THE METAL WORTH £1500 GIVEN BY GOVERNMENT.

White Metal, 38 mm. 1844 (Eidlitz 991, pl. 114) (BM)

**146j** *Obv.* Busts, jugate to left of QUEEN VICTORIA AND PRINCE ALBERT. Signed ALLEN & MOORE BIRM$^{M}$.

*Rev.* View of the ROYAL EXCHANGE LONDON. Below, FIRST STONE LAID JAN 19 1842 BY HRH PRINCE ALBERT OPENED BY H·M·G·M·VICTORIA 1844. Signed, WM TITE ESQ ARC. . . RE BI. . . (imperfect striking).

White Metal, 39 mm. 1844 (BM)

**146k** *Obv.* Conjoint heads to left; around, QUEEN VICTORIA and PR : ALBERT. On a raised border (8 mm): Oak leaves, Shamrock; Crown and Trophies (at top); Trident, Aesculapian symbol, Rose and Thistle (below).

*Rev.* View of building; around, NEW ROYAL EXCHANGE LONDON. In exergue, FIRST STONE LAID JAN. 19 1842 BY H.R.H. PRINCE ALBERT OPENED BY H.M.G.M.VICTORIA OCT$^{R}$ 23 1844. Signed on exergue bar, W. TITE ESQ ARCH: ALLEN & MOORE BIRM$^{M}$ On a raised border (8 mm): Standing figures on pedestals left and right representing (?) Mathematics and the Arts. On top section: FOUNDED BY SIR THOMAS GRESHAM KNT : 1566, OPENED IN STATE AND PROCLAIMED 'ROYAL EXCHANGE' BY Q: ELIZABETH 1570, DESTROYED BY THE GREAT FIRE 1666. On lower section: FIRST STONE OF THE SECOND BUILDING LAID BY KING CHARLES THE SECOND 1667 WHICH WAS ALSO DESTROYED BY FIRE JAN$^{Y}$ 10 1838.

Bronze, White Metal, 51 mm. 1844 (BM)

### *b. Medals by J. Davis*

**146l** *Obv.* Head of Queen Victoria to left. VICTORIA. BORN MAY 24, 1819 CROW. JUNE 28 1838 MARR. FEB 10 1840.

*Rev.* View of the NEW ROYAL EXCHANGE. Below, THE FIRST STONE LAID BY H.R.H. PRINCE ALBERT 1842. COMPLETED 1844. Signed, DAVIS.

White Metal, 24 mm. 1844 (BM)

**146m** *Obv.* Head, to right of PRINCE ALBERT BORN AUGUST 26 1810.

*Rev.* View of the new Royal Exchange as obverse of No. 146n.

Bronze, 24 mm. 1844 (BM)

**146n** *Obv.* View of the NEW ROYAL EXCHANGE. Below, THE FIRST STONE LAID BY H.R.H. PRINCE ALBERT 1842 COMPLETED 1844. Signed, D.

*Rev.* Equestrian statue, to right. THE WELLINGTON STATUE LONDON. ERECTED JUNE 18. 1844. Below, WATERLOO.

Bronze, 24 mm. 1844 (BM)

**146o** *Obv.* Heads, jugate to left of QUEEN VICTORIA & PRINCE ALBERT.

*Rev.* View of the NEW ROYAL EXCHANGE. Below, THE FIRST STONE LAID BY H.R.H. 1842 COMPLETED 1844. Signed, DAVIS BIRM.

Bronze, 29 mm. 1844 (BM)

**146p** *Obv.* View of the Royal Exchange. NEW ROYAL EXCHANGE LONDON. In exergue FIRST STONE LAID JAN. 19. 1842 BY H·R·H· PRINCE ALBERT. OPENED BY H.M.G.M. VICTORIA. 1844. Signed, DAVIS BIRM.

*Rev.* Equestrian statue of Wellington. THE WELLINGTON STATUE IN FRONT OF THE ROYAL EXCHANGE LONDON. On a pedestal, SERINGAPATAM ASSYE TALAVERA BADAJOZ SALAMANCA VITTORIA TOULOUSE WATERLOO. In exergue, ERECTED JUNE 18. 1844.

Bronze, White Metal, 43 mm. 1844 (Eidlitz 992, pl. 114) (BM)

**146q** *Obv.* Jugate heads to left of QUEEN VICTORIA & PRINCE ALBERT. Signed, J. DAVIS BIRM$^{M}$· under busts.

*Rev.* View of the new Royal Exchange, as obverse of No. 146p.

White Metal, 44 mm. 1844 (BM)

**146r** *Obv.* Queen Victoria, seated on a throne, receiving members of the City. Below, PRESENTATION OF THE ADDRESS.

*Rev.* View of the NEW ROYAL EXCHANGE LONDON. Below, FIRST STONE LAID JAN.19.1842 BY H.R.H. PRINCE ALBERT OPENED BY H.M.G.M. VICTORIA OCT. 28. 1844. Signed, DAVIS BIRM.

Bronze, 44 mm. 1844 (BM)

**146s** *Obv.* Presenting the city address to the Queen. Coats of arms above. In exergue, PRESENTATION OF THE CITY ADDRESS.

*Rev.* View of the Royal Exchange. Above, coat of arms, and on a band, ROYAL EXCHANGE LONDON. Below, OPENED BY H.M.G. MAJESTY VICTORIA OCT: 28: 1844. In exergue, FOUNDED BY SIR THOMAS GRESHAM, A.D. 1566. PROCLAIMED ROYAL EXCHANGE 1570. DESTROYED IN THE GREAT FIRE 1666 RESTORED, 1667. AGAIN DESTROYED BY FIRE, 1838 FIRST STONE OF PRESENT EDIFICE LAID BY H·R·H· PRINCE ALBERT JANUARY 17. 1842. Signed, J. DAVIS MEDALLIST BY COMMAND TO H.R.H. PRINCE ALBERT.

Bronze, White Metal, 51 mm. 1844 (Eidlitz 990, pl. 114) (BM)

**146t** *Obv.* View of the Royal Exchange as reverse of No. 146s.

*Rev.* Equestrian statue, to left. THE WELLINGTON STATUE IN FRONT OF THE ROYAL EXCHANGE LONDON ERECTED JUNE 18 1844 COST £9000 RAISED BY PUBLIC SUBSCRIPTION. On plinth, SERINGAPATAM ASSYE TALAVERA BADAJOZ SALAMANCA VITTORIA TOULOUSE WATERLOO.

White Metal, 51 mm. 1844 (BM)

**146u** *Obv.* The Royal Exchange. ROYAL EXCHANGE LONDON 1844. In exergue, FOUNDED BY SIR THOMAS GRESHAM A.D. 1566, VISITED IN STATE BY QUEEN ELIZABETH AND PROCLAIMED "ROYAL EXCHANGE" 1570. DESTROYED BY THE GREAT FIRE 1666. FIRST STONE OF SECOND BUILDING LAID BY KING CHARLES II. 1667, WHICH WAS ALSO DESTROYED BY FIRE JAN. 10. 1838. Signed, J. DAVIS. MEDALLIST TO H.R.H. PRINCE ALBERT.

*Rev.* Another view of the building. ROYAL EXCHANGE LONDON NORTH EAST. In exergue, FIRST STONE OF THE PRESENT EDIFICE, LAID BY H.R.H. PRINCE ALBERT. JAN 17. 1842. OPENED BY H.M.G. MAJESTY VICTORIA OCT. 28. 1844. — W. TITE ESQ$^{R}$ ARCH$^{T}$

Bronze, White Metal, 60 mm. 1844 (Eidlitz 996, pl. 114) (BM)

### *c. Other Medallists*

**146v** *Obv.* View of the Royal Exchange as reverse of No. 146b.

*Rev.* Equestrian statue of Wellington, to right. On plinth, WELLINGTON — ERECTED JUNE 18 1844. Signed around rim, PUB. BY. H. HYAMS.

White Metal, 62 mm. 1844 (BM)

**146w** *Obv.* Equestrian statue of Wellington. THE WELLINGTON STATUE LONDON ERECTED JUNE 18. 1844.

*Rev.* View of the Royal Exchange. ROYAL EXCHANGE LONDON. In exergue, FIRST STONE LAID BY H.R.H. PRINCE ALBERT JAN. 17. 1842 OPENED BY THE QUEEN OCT. 28. 1844. Signed, J. TAYLOR BIRM.

Bronze, 38 mm. 1844 (Eidlitz 993, pl. 114)

**146x** *Obv.* Bust of Thomas Gresham to left in court attire with cap. EMPORIVM REGIVM A. THOMA GRESHAM EQ. AVR. CIVE LONDINENSI CONDITVM A.S. MDLXXI. Signed on truncation, W. WYON R.A.

*Rev.* Courtyard of the Royal Exchange, with statue of Queen Victoria in foreground. REST. ET. APERT. AVSP. VICTORIA REG. On the base of the statue, A: S. MDCCCXLIV XXVIII OCT. In exergue, W. TITE F.R.S. ARCH$^{T}$ Signed, W. WYON R.A. FECIT.

Silver, Bronze, 72 mm. 1844 (Eidlitz 989, pl. 114) (BM)

Wyon's wax model for this portrait of Thomas Gresham (1519–79) is in the Fitzwilliam Museum, Cambridge. For the reverse, see also Plate 13.

146x

**146y** *Obv.* View of building. ROYAL EXCHANGE. Below, LONDON.

*Rev.* Inscription: WILLIAM TITE ARCHITECT 1844.

Bronze, 31 mm. 1844 (Eidlitz 988, pl. 114)

LONDON, **Royal Exchange,** Threadneedle Street and Cornhill

*1842–44*

After Edward Jarman's Royal Exchange (No. 36) had burnt down in 1838 a new and enlarged building was put up (1842–44) to the design of William Tite. His solution followed one of the typically muddled architectural competitions of the nineteenth century; in this prizes had been awarded to Grellier, de Chateauneuf, and Sydney Smirke, together with a commendation for the best design study to T. L. Donaldson (qv.).[1] However, all these were set aside and Tite and C. R. Cockerell (qv.) were asked to submit drawings for a final selection. Cockerell's submission was a magnificent project,[2] and the failure to build it has since been much regretted; it was however Tite's inoffensive design that was selected in 1840. As Goodhart-Rendel noted 'Sir William has supplied the goods ordered and has done so with strict commercial integrity and none of the unpredictability that might have been feared in a transaction with an artist'.[3] The medal views concentrate on the Corinthian portico to the main west front of Tite's design. They also indicate the continuous range of giant Corinthian pilasters which modulate the sides of the building and provide for shop fronts within rusticated arches between them. Some views show in the background the tower situated over the centre of the east front; this was built as a reference to the earlier tower, with its symbolic grasshopper, of the seventeenth-century building. In the centre of the Royal Exchange was a large open courtyard surrounded by arcades; the only medal to show this (No. 146x) also shows the statue of Queen Victoria by J. G. Lough set up in 1845.[4] This courtyard was covered in with a glazed roof in 1880.[5] Many of the medals, which celebrate the opening of the Royal Exchange by Queen Victoria in October 1844, also take the opportunity to commemorate the setting up of a bronze equestrian statue to the Duke of Wellington on the forecourt outside. This was unveiled in 1844, on the anniversary of Waterloo, and was one of the last works of Sir Francis Chantrey (it was completed by Weekes). Its location on such an important site was a recognition by the City of London of their debt to the Duke for his assistance in getting the new London Bridge (see No. 102) through the various Parliamentary procedures.[6]

See: Pevsner, *London 1,* 179; H.-R. Hitchcock, *Early Victorian Architecture,* 305–309, pl. x, 1 to 4.

1. Illustrated N. Taylor, *Monuments of Commerce,* RIBA, 1968, p. 7.
2. Illustrated N. Taylor, op. cit., pp. 8, 9; D. Watkin, *C. R. Cockerell,* London, 1974.
3. In P. Ferriday, ed., *Victorian Architecture,* p. 92.
4. See Gunnis, p. 243, for contemporary comments on this. There is a companion statue of Prince Albert.
5. Sir Joseph Paxton (qv.) had prepared a design for covering it with a glazed roof in 1851. See H.-R. Hitchcock, op. cit., pl. xvi 17.
6. See C. Welch, *History of Tower Bridge,* 1894, 133. Additionally, the City were grateful for his absence from the opening of London Bridge, as his presence might have sparked off reform riots.

LONDON, Southwark, **St Giles's Church,** Camberwell Church Street
*1842–44*

147a

**147a** *Obv.* View of church. Around, THE CHURCH OF S$^{T}$ GILES CAMBERWELL. In exergue, SCOTT & MOFFAT ARCHITECTS — J. TAYLOR MEDALIST BIRM.

*Rev.* Inscription; on border: · THE ANCIENT CHURCH WAS DESTROYED BY FIRE FEBRUARY 7. 1841 . + In centre panel: THE FIRST STONE OF THE NEW CHURCH WAS LAID SEPTEMBER 23. 1842 CONSECRATED NOV. 21. 1844 THE REV$^{D}$ J.G. STORIE, M.A. VICAR & PATRON.

White Metal, 48 mm. 1844 (BM)

When completed, in 1842, this was an influential and admired building that was to be a model for a new generation of church designers. Particularly commended was its liturgical correctness (e.g. its long chancel) and its purity of style. By the young Gilbert Scott, with W. B. Moffatt, it was an early essay in the thirteenth-century 'Middle Pointed' Gothic that was to become Scott's favourite. It is built of Kentish rubble stone, with lighter Caen stone trim; the decorative contrast of these are seen clearly on the 200-ft high spire.[1]

See: Pevsner, *London 2,* 74, 75.

1. The church cost £14,500 and held 1,500 (H.-R. Hitchcock op. cit., p. 120).

LIVERPOOL, Merseyside, **Royal Infirmary Medical School,** Dover Street *c. 1844–45*

148a

**148a** *Obv.* Elevation of one-storey, three-bay, neo-classical building. Around on border, THE ROYAL INFIRMARY MEDICAL SCHOOL LIVERPOOL In exergue, ESTABLISHED ANN:DOM: 1834.

*Rev.* Wreath (blank for inscription). Signed, & JACOB LIVERPOOL.

Bronze, 49 mm. 1844 (BM)

A small, severe, Greek revival design that could be the work of John Foster Jnr, the architect of the Royal Infirmary (see No. 82). The original Medical School had been opened 1834 in an existing building; the new building for the school, shown on the medal, was erected *c.* 1844–45.[1] The site, in Dover Street, is now occupied by the University's Thompson–Yates Laboratories; the Medical School was demolished to make way for these in the 1950s.[2]

1. The building, with its ground plan, is shown on the 1850 OS map. See also H. A. Ormerod, *The Early History of the Liverpool Medical School from 1834–1877, c.* 1953, pp. 26–30.

2. The façade of an addition to the east end of the building remains adjacent to the University's Department of Orthopaedic Surgery, near Brownlow Street. I am grateful to Mr. A. R. Allen of the University Archives Department for this information.

LIVERPOOL, Merseyside, **St Mary's Church** (Roman Catholic), Highfield Street *1844–45*

**149a** *Obv.* View towards screen. INTERIOR VIEW OF S$^{T}$ MARY'S CATHOLIC CHURCH LIVERPOOL. Signed below top rim, DAVIS BIRM.

*Rev.* Inscription around: CHURCH OPENED 19 AUGUST 1845 SCHOOLS OPENED 12. FEBR$^{Y}$ 1844. In centre, PRESENTED BY THE SOCIETY FOR ERECTING THE CATHOLIC CHURCH AND SCHOOLS OF S$^{T}$ MARY LIVERPOOL TO (blank) IN GRATITUDE FOR HIS SERVICES AS A COLLECTOR — A.D. 1845.

Silver, 46 mm. 1845 (BM)

149a

The medal shows the interior of this town church by A. W. N. Pugin. The chancel has been stressed and unified as a space with the rest of the church, only the ceiling changes to a system of panelled arches rather than the wooden trusses over the nave. The church was moved and rebuilt in the 1880s, then demolished in the 1940s. The exterior is illustrated in P. Stanton, *Pugin*, p. 132.

See: H.-R. Hitchcock, *Early Victorian Architecture,* 88.

LONDON, Camden, **Lincoln's Inn, New Hall and Library** *1843–45*

**150a** *Obv.* Conjoint heads to left of QUEEN VICTORIA & PRINCE ALBERT.

*Rev.* View of NEW HALL & LIBRARY. In exergue — LINCOLNS INN — OPENED BY H.M.G.M. VICTORIA OCT. 30. 1845. Signed, DAVIS BIRM.

White Metal, 24 mm. 1845 (BM)

**150b** *Obv.* Conjoint heads to left of VICTORIA and ALBERT on border of roses, thistles and shamrocks. Signed below truncation, J. DAVIS BIRM.

*Rev.* View of NEW HALL AND LIBRARY LINCOLN'S INN. In exergue, FIRST STONE LAID BY VICE-CHANCELLOR KNIGHT BRUCE APRIL 20. 1843 OPENED BY H.M.G. MAJESTY VICTORIA OCT$^{R}$ 30. 1845 P. HARDWICK ESQ. R.A. ARCH$^{T}$

White Metal, 44 mm. 1845 (BM)

150b

By Philip Hardwick, and completed with the help of his son P. C. Hardwick in 1845. The buildings are of red diapered brick in a Tudor Gothic style that made, for the critics of the 1840s, an enjoyable contrast to the restrained Palladian Stone Buildings[1] across the garden. The medal view shows the east front to this garden, with the library block to the right of the hall. The library was altered internally and extended further forward into the garden by Scott in 1873.

See: Pevsner, *London 1,* 278, 279; H.-R. Hitchcock, 313–15 and pl. x12, x13.

1. By Sir Robert Taylor (1714–88). His Lincoln's Inn buildings included the Six Clerks Office; this was shown on a medal by Kirk of 1776 (given by H. A. Grueber in *Num. Chron.* 1887, 263).

SHEFFIELD, South Yorks., **Mount St Mary's College,** Spinkhill
*1842–45*

151a

**151a** *Obv.* Madonna enthroned. Around on border · SEDES · SAPIENTIÆ · ORA · PRO · NOBIS.

*Rev.* South elevation of three-storey school building, with linking galleries on two floors and semi-octagonal ends to projecting wings. Around on border . . PRÆMIUM . . SANCTA · MARIA · AD · MONTÉM.

Silver, 53 mm. *c.* 1845–59 (Watt Coll.)

The medal shows the school (established in 1842) after alterations by J. A. Hansom were completed in 1845. He had been called in to improve on work of 1842–44 which had created the building by linking together a former Catholic chapel of 1790 (made into the west wing) and a brew house (east wing). Hansom added a third floor to the linking block, arched 'ambulatories' on first and second floors, semi-octagonal ends to the wings, and a clock tower.[1] Further wings were added 1859, and in 1890 the courtyard in front of the arches was roofed in.

1. I am indebted to Fr Francis Keegan SJ for an account of Hansom's work at the school.

BIRMINGHAM, West Midlands, **St Andrew's Church,** Bordesley
*1844–46*

152a

**152a** *Obv.* View of church. Legend: SUFFER LITTLE CHILDREN TO COME UNTO ME. In exergue, CONSECRATED 1846.

*Rev.* Inscription: ST. ANDREWS BORDESLEY 1850. Within a shield, CHURCH SUNDAY SCHOOLS.

Bronze, 24 mm. 1850 (BM)

By R. C. Carpenter. A red sandstone church, in which the architect has used correct fourteenth-century gothic details and the liturgical arrangements advocated by Pugin. This crude medal view shows the stone spire which was demolished after storm damage in 1894.

See: Pevsner, *Warwicks.* 130.

LONDON, Kensington and Chelsea, **Brompton Hospital,** Fulham Road *1844–46*

153a

**153a** *Obv.* Portrait heads, to left conjoint, Queen Victoria and Prince Albert. HIS ROYAL HIGHNESS THE PRINCE ALBERT LAID THE FOUNDATION STONE ON THE 11TH OF JUNE 1844.

*Rev.* Main view of entrance court, with projecting side wings. In exergue, THE NEW HOSPITAL FOR CONSUMPTION AND DISEASES OF THE CHEST. BROMPTON — · — PATRON THE QUEEN. Signed, J. DAVIS BIRMM.

Bronze, White Metal, 54 mm. 1844 (BM)

**153b** *Obv.* Conjoint heads to left of Queen Victoria, wearing tiara, and Prince Albert. PATRON HER MOST GRACIOUS MAJESTY QUEEN VICTORIA · XVIII JUNE MDCCCXLVI.

*Rev.* View of main front of hospital. HIS ROYAL HIGHNESS PRINCE ALBERT LAID THE FOUNDATION STONE ON THE 11$^{TH}$ OF JUNE 1844. In exergue, THE NEW HOSPITAL FOR CONSUMPTION AND DISEASES OF THE CHEST BROMPTON. Signed on bar, J. DAVIS BIRMINGHAM MEDALIST TO H.R.H. PRINCE ALBERT.

White Metal, 64 mm. 1846 (BM)

In the late sixteenth-century Tudor style that became popular for schools and hospitals at this period. Built in 1844–46 by Horace Francis; the medals show the symmetrical front with central gatehouse. Extensions of 1879–82 by T. H. Wyatt (qv.).

WILTON, Wilts., **St Mary and St Nicholas Church** *1843–46*

**154a** *Obv.* View of church. In exergue, WILTON CHURCH ERECTED BY THE HON$^{E}$ SIDNEY HERBERT A D 1846 GO THOU AND DO LIKEWISE. At right, WYATT & BRANDON · A. Signed, E. AVERN · F.

*Rev.* View of the interior. In exergue, INTERIOR OF WILTON CHURCH PUB BY F. T. PRICE CUTLER SARUM AUG 12 · 1846. Signed at left, E · AVERN · F. At right, TIFFIN · D.

White Metal, 54 mm.
1846 Private collection (Eidlitz 1080a, pl. 123)

One of the most sumptuous Anglican churches of the 1840s and the prime example in England of the round-arch style, the 'Rundbogenstil', then popular in Europe, and especially in Germany. Built (1843–46) in cream-coloured stonework to the designs of T. H. Wyatt and D. Brandon, it develops an Early Christian basilican theme with a west façade linked to a separate campanile (cf. Wild's Christchurch, Streatham, No. 134). This is enriched with expensive and correct archaeological detail, and the use of medieval glass. Cosmati work, and magnificent Renaissance fittings for the interior. The donor of the considerable cost, £20,000, was the Rt Hon. Sidney Herbert, Secretary of War, and his exhortation on the medal obverse was one that few patrons of the time would have been prepared to follow.

See: Pevsner, *Wilts.* 514; H.-R. Hitchcock, *Early Victorian Architecture*, pl. iv, 6–8.

154a

WORSLEY, Salford, Greater Manchester, **Worsley Hall** *1840–46*

**155a** *Obv.* Bust of Queen Victoria, crowned, to left. VICTORIA, QUEEN OF GREAT BRITAIN. Around on border: oak leaves, roses, thistle and shamrocks.

*Rev.* Distant view of Worsley Hall with, in the foreground, a royal barge being rowed on the lake. Around, on border, TO COMMEMORATE THE VISIT OF HER MOST GRACIOUS MAJESTY QUEEN VICTORIA & H.R.H. PRINCE ALBERT TO THE EARL OF ELLESMERE · In exergue, WORSLEY HALL OCT$^{R}$ 9 & 10 1851 — Signed, J. C. GRUNDY D. ALLEN & MOORE F.

Bronze, 51 mm. 1851 (BM)

An immense, essentially symmetrical, stone-built house in the late sixteenth-century 'Elizabethan' style by Edward Blore for Lord Francis

155a

Egerton, later 1st Earl of Ellesmere (see medal reverse). It was completed 1846 and demolished in the twentieth century. The medal gives a poor impression of the main front which had a keep-like tower set back to the left.

Illustrated, with plan, in H.-R. Hitchcock, *Early Victorian Architecture,* pl. viii, 7.

156a

BOOTLE, Merseyside, **St Mary's Church,** Irlam Road *1827 and 1847*

**156a** *Obv.* View from west end with tower and steeple. On scroll, S$^{T}$ MARY'S CHURCH BOOTLE.

*Rev.* Inscription: REWARD FOR REGULARITY PROFICIENCY & GOOD CONDUCT AT SCHOOL.

Silver, 32 mm. ?1850s (Watt Coll.)

A gothic design by the Liverpool surveyor Edward Eyes. As originally consecrated in July 1827 it had twin west towers; these were replaced by a single tower and spire (shown on the medal) after a fire in 1846. The church was destroyed by bombing in 1940.

157a

LONDON, Camden, **The Orphan Working School,** Haverstock Hill *c. 1847*

**157a** *Obv.* View of three-storey building in Italianate style. THE ORPHAN WORKING SCHOOL. Below, HAVERSTOCK HILL HAMPSTEAD ROAD FOR 240 CHILDREN.

*Rev.* Within wreath, inscription: FOR CHILDREN OF BOTH SEXES, OF EVERY DENOMINATION, AND FROM ALL PARTS OF THE KINGDOM. FOUNDED 1758 AT HOXTON, REBUILT 1773 IN CITY ROAD, AND REMOVED TO HAVERSTOCK HILL HAMPSTEAD ROAD 1847.

White Metal, 49 mm. 1847 (BM)

A large Italianate block, designed by an architect, Alfred Ainger, and built in the neighbourhood of Maitland Park. This area was developed to the east of Haverstock Hill, *c.* 1845–55, and was much favoured by charitable institutions[1] (cf. No. 160). The Orphan Working School, which moved here in 1847 from the East End, housed children aged seven to fourteen. The building was extended in 1860 by the addition of two wings. Demolished *c.* 1947 for the Maitland Park housing estate.

1. Pevsner, *London 2,* 374.

158a

BIRMINGHAM, West Midlands, **St Michael's Church,** Warstone Lane Cemetery *1847–48*

**158a** *Obv.* West view of the church and cemetery. In exergue, CHURCH OF ENGLAND CEMETERY BIRMINGHAM. Signed, HALLIDAY BIRM.

*Rev.* Inscription: CONSECRATED BY THE LORD BISHOP OF WORCESTER AUGUST 8$^{TH}$ 1848 — HAMILTON & MEDLAND ARCHITECTS.

White Metal, 38 mm. 1848 (Eidlitz 492) (BM)

Completed 1848 and consecrated as part of a new Church of England cemetery in Warstone Lane; this provided a further area of 9 acres near the older Key Hill Cemetery (see No. 112). The Perpendicular style design by Hamilton & Medland consisted of a west tower and spire, nave and chancel, plus ambulatories extending to either side of the west tower (as shown on the medal view). These north and south ambulatories were separated from the nave by stained glass doors, and that to the south had 21 catacombs below it.[1] The building was used as the church of St Michael between 1854 and 1878, and after that only for funeral services. Declared unsafe and demolished in 1954.

1. W. Wilson, ed., *History of the Church of England Cemetery,* Birmingham, 1900, 23, 24. The construction cost of the church and buildings was £9,467.

LIVERPOOL, Merseyside, **Sailors' Home,** Canning Place *1846–48*

**159a** *Obv.* Portrait head to left of H.R.H. PRINCE ALBERT. Signed below truncation, ALLEN & MOORE BIRM$^{M}$.

*Rev.* View of building. SAILORS HOME LIVERPOOL — Around on border, TO COMMEMORATE THE LAYING OF THE FIRST STONE BY HIS ROYAL HIGHNESS PRINCE ALBERT JULY 31 1846

White Metal, 44 mm. 1846 (BM)

**159b** *Obv.* Portrait head to right. Around, HIS ROYAL HIGHNESS PRINCE ALBERT. Signed, J. MAYER DIR.

*Rev.* Perspective view of Sailors' Home. Around, THE FIRST STONE LAID BY H.R.H. PRINCE ALBERT JULY 31 1846. Below, SAILORS HOME LIVERPOOL. Signed on exergual bar, DAVIS BIRM.

Silver, 43 mm. 1846

159b

**159c** *Obv.* Portrait head to right of HIS ROYAL HIGHNESS PRINCE ALBERT. Signed on truncation, J. HINKS F.

*Rev.* View of building. FOUNDATION STONE OF THE SAILORS HOME LAID BY H.R.H. PRINCE ALBERT. In exergue, JULY 31. 1846.—— PUBLISHED BY R. L. JOSEPH AT THE REPOSITORY 42 BOLD S$^{T}$ LIVERPOOL.

White Metal, 45 mm. 1846 (BM)

A seamen's lodging house with a 'Jacobethan' exterior rather loosely modelled on prototypes such as Woolaton or Hardwick. The immense decorated portal led into an inner covered court surrounded by five stories of galleries, all in cast-iron construction. The building, which was by the Liverpool architect John Cunningham, was burnt 1860, rebuilt 1862, and demolished in the 1970s. (Sectional drawing in H.-R. Hitchcock, *Early Victorian Architecture,* pl. xv 48; illus. in Q. Hughes, *Seaport*, 1964, 48, 49.)

160a

LONDON, Camden, **Governesses Benevolent Institution Asylum,** Grafton Street, Kentish Town *1848–49*

**160a** *Obv.* Head to right of H.R.H. ADOLPHUS FREDERICK DUKE OF CAMBRIDGE FIRST ROYAL PATRON. Signed, G. C. ADAMS. D.[1] ALLEN & MOORE F.

*Rev.* View of building. GOVERNESSES BENEVOLENT INSTITUTION FOUNDED 1843. In exergue, ASYLUM ERECTED A · D—1848. WYATT & BRANDON. ARCHITECTS. On the exergual bar, ALLEN & MOORE. F: BIRM.

White Metal, 64 mm. ?1849[2] (Eidlitz 1080b, pl. 123) (BM)

A branch of the Institution opened 1849 near the Maitland Park area (cf. No. 157). Designed by T. H. Wyatt and D. Brandon in a domestic Tudor style with steep pitched roofs and gables and leaded lights to the windows (see medal reverse). The 'asylum' was similar in programme to many twentieth-century old persons' homes and comprised: eighteen bed sitting rooms (seven ready furnished), dining room, common room, offices, etc.

1. This signature appears to be an error for G. G. Adams (qv.) who was at this time still comparatively unknown. G. G. Adams did a medal of Adolphus Frederick, Duke of Cambridge, from sittings (Forrer, vol. 1, 24).

2. *GM*, August 1849, 194, indicates a formal opening and 'fancy fair'—an occasion for which the medal is likely to have been struck; the address and building details are also given.

161a

LONDON, City, **Coal Exchange,** Lower Thames Street *1847–49*

**161a** *Obv.* Portrait bust of Queen Victoria, crowned, to left. Around, H:M:G:M:QUEEN VICTORIA. Around on border, BORN MAY 24 1819. CROWNED JUNE 28 1838. MARRIED FEB 10:1840. + Signed, A + M on truncation.

*Rev.* Exterior view of building, showing corner portico and cupola. Around, THE NEW COAL EXCHANGE, LONDON. Below, OPENED BY HER MAJESTY [*sic*] OCT$^{R}$ 30 1849. Signed, J. B. BUNNING ARCH. ALLEN & MOORE F. on exergual bar.

Bronze, White Metal, 38 mm. 1849 (BM)

**161b** *Obv.* Portrait bust, crowned, to left. Around, H.M.G.M. QUEEN VICTORIA. Around on border, BORN MAY 24 1819. CROWNED JUNE 28 1838. MARRIED FEB : 10 1840.

*Rev.* Exterior view of building, showing corner portico and cupola. Around, THE NEW COAL MARKET, LONDON. Below, OPENED BY HER MAJESTY [*sic*] OCT : 30 1849.

White Metal, 27 mm. 1849 (BM)

Both the portrait and building are identical to the medal above (No. 161a by Allen & Moore) but at a reduced size.

**161c** *Obv.* Head of Queen Victoria in centre, with heads of Prince Albert, the Prince of Wales, and the Princess Victoria in circular frames above and to sides. Scenes of welcome to the royal party in panels. NEW COAL EXCHANGE OPENED OCT. 30$^{TH}$

161c

1849. Below, ON BEHALF OF HER MAJESTY QUEEN VICTORIA BY H.R.H. PRINCE ALBERT. Signed on rim, B. WYON SC.

*Rev.* Interior of the Coal Exchange; a section showing galleries and dome in perspective. Heraldic ornaments at sides, shield of the City of London at bottom. THE R$^{T}$ HON$^{BLE}$ SIR JAMES DUKE LORD MAYOR — JOHN WOOD ESQ$^{RE}$ CHAIRMAN OF THE COMMITTEE — JAMES B. BUNNING ESQ$^{RE}$ ARCHITECT. Signed on rim, B. WYON SC.

Bronze, 89 mm. 1852[1] (Eidlitz 160, pl. 18) (BM)

One of the very finest of nineteenth-century commemorative medals. It forms one of the City of London Series (see pp. 214–15, and Plate 10).

A building which has been acclaimed as '... the prime City monument of the Early Victorian period',[2] and whose demolition in the 1960s has been called '... the great conservationist horror story'.[3] The Coal Exchange was designed by J. B. Bunning, the City Architect, and its opening by Prince Albert was a historic occasion in itself with a royal arrival by river (see obverse panels of No. 161c). The building was in two distinct parts: (i) An L-shaped exterior consisting of two blocks of characteristic City Commercial street architecture; these were set at an angle to each other with a circular tower and portico acting as the junction between them and as the entrance to the building (see view on medal No. 161a); (ii) The Exchange itself—a circular court 60 ft in diameter, surrounded by three floors of galleries whose vertical structure developed into a glazed dome over the court. This great circular space had its entire skeleton constructed of cast iron with an integral system of decoration, much of it based on a rope motif symbolic of the coal-miners and the colliers. (This motif is used by B. Wyon on both the obverse and reverse of No. 161c.) In addition there were painted panels by Francis

Sang depicting the mining industry and the tree ferns found in coal fossils (shown on the reverse of No. 161c).

See: Pevsner, *London 1*, 168, 169; H.-R. Hitchcock, *Early Victorian Architecture*, 320–24, pl. x 14–24.

1. Forrer, vol. 8, 295, gives this date which marks the exhibition of the medal at the Royal Academy Salon. In the end Queen Victoria was not able to come to the opening, and medal No. 161a was caught out by this.
2. Hitchcock, op. cit. 316.
3. H. Hobhouse, *Lost London*, 1972, 178.

London, Southwark, **Licensed Victuallers' Asylum, 'The Ladies Wing'**, Asylum Road, off Old Kent Road *1849*

162a

**162a** *Obv.* Portrait head to left of H.R.H. PRINCE ALBERT. Signed below truncation, ALLEN & MOORE BIRM$^{M}$ (as No. 159a Liverpool Sailor's Home).

*Rev.* View of portico, and range of buildings around entrance court. Above, "THE LADIES' WING" OF THE LICENSED VICTUALLERS' ASYLUM, OLD KENT ROAD. FIRST STONE LAID BY H.R.H. PRINCE ALBERT, 2$^{ND}$ JUNE 1849. — C. J. KEMP ARCH$^{T}$.

White Metal, 45 mm. 1849 (BM)

The 'Ladies Wing' (1849) comprised an extra twenty-five units to add to the original one hundred and one dwellings of the institution (erected in 1827–33). The main buildings, of brick, with a giant Ionic portico (see medal), are 'the only grand composition amongst the many almshouses of Camberwell' (Pevsner). Hitherto Henry Rose has been given as the architect of all stages of the buildings up to 1850.[1] The medal reverse, however, attributes the 'Ladies Wing' to C. J. Kemp. Since 1960 the building has been used an an old peoples' housing and day centre.[2]

See: Pevsner, *London 2*, 82.

1. See Colvin, 514.
2. Renamed Caroline Gardens, and owned by the Borough of Southwark.

RICHMOND, North Yorks., **School,** Station Road *1849*

163a

**163a** *Obv.* View of original school building from river front. LIBERÆ SCHOLÆ BURGENSIUM DE RICHMOND.

*Rev.* Within a wreath: DETUR DIGNIORI. Around, IN PIAM MEMORIAM JACOBI TATE A.M. ARCHIDIDASCALI.

Bronze, White Metal, 40 mm. ?1849 (BM)

The medal view shows the first part of the school, known as the 'Tate Testimonial' (see reverse). It was designed 1849 by George T. Andrews. Several buildings have since been added, including a hall in a Perpendicular style (1867 by Austin and Johnson) which was linked to the left of the building shown.

See: Pevsner, *Yorks: N Riding*, 294.

MENAI STRAIT, Gwynedd, **Britannia Tubular Bridge** *1846–50*

**164a** *Obv.* Profile head to right of ROBERT STEPHENSON. Signed, L. C. WYON.

*Rev.* View of bridge with sailing ships and steamer on the Menai Strait. Below, 1846–1850.

Bronze, 58 mm. 1850 (BM)

164a

**164b** *Obv.* View of Menai Strait with tubular bridge in foreground, and Thomas Telford's earlier suspension bridge in distance. THE MENAI SUSPENSION, AND BRITANNIA TUBULAR BRIDGES.

*Rev.* Inscription: DETAILS OF THE BRIDGES. To left: SUSPENSION TOTAL LENGTH 910 FT HEIGHT OF ROADWAY ABOVE HIGH WATER 100 FT HEIGHT OF THE TWO MAIN PILLARS 153 FT SUSPENDED WEIGHT OF IRON 489 TNS TOTAL WEIGHT OF IRON 2186 TNS EXTREME LENGTH OF CHAIN 1714 FT. To right: TUBULAR TOTAL LENGTH OF TUBES 1513 FT HEIGHT ABOVE HIGH WATER 102 FT HEIGHT OF THE TWO LAND TOWERS 203 FT DO CENTRE TOWERS 221 FT WEIGHT OF EACH OF THE FOUR LARGE TUBES 1800 TNS DO SMALL TUBES 700 TNS TOTAL WEIGHT 10,000 TNS. Signed, PUBLISHED BY J. ARONSON, BANGOR.

White Metal, 64 mm. 1850 (BM)

To commemorate the completion of the tubular bridge in 1850.

Medal No. 164a shows Robert Stephenson, the engineer of this fine early railway bridge (1846–50). In the project he was again collaborating with the architect to the line, Francis Thompson, and it was the latter who designed and detailed the rock-faced masonry work of the pylons and finalised their subtle flat-topped shape.

Illustrated in H.-R. Hitchcock, *Early Victorian Architecture*, pl. xv 34–38.

LONDON, Kensington and Chelsea, **Great Exhibition Building,** Hyde Park, 'The Crystal Palace' *1850–51*

***a. Medals by Allen & Moore***

**165a** *Obv.* The exhibition building. THE CRYSTAL PALACE. In exergue, FOR THE GREAT EXHIBITION IN LONDON OF 1851. Signed on the exergual bar, A & M.

*Rev.* Inscription: DIMENSIONS. LENGTH 1848 FEET, WIDTH 456 FEET; HEIGHT OF ROOF 66 FEET; HEIGHT OF TRANSEPT 108 FEET; GLAZED SURFACE 900,000 SUP. FEET. OCCUPIES 18 ACRES. Rim beaded on obverse and reverse.

Brass, 22.5 mm. (Eidlitz 762a, pl. 85)

**165b** *Obv.* Bust, to left. Around, H.R.H. PRINCE ALBERT., and on border, BORN AUGUST 26 1819. MARRIED FEBRUARY 10 1840. Signed A & M on truncation.

*Rev.* The exhibition building. THE CRYSTAL PALACE. In exergue, FOR THE GREAT EXHIBITION IN LONDON OF 1851. Signed, ALLEN & MOORE BIRM:

White Metal, 27 mm. (BM)

**165c** *Obv.* The exhibition building. THE BUILDING FOR THE INTERNATIONAL EXHIBITION. In exergue, LONDON 1851. Signed, A & M.

*Rev.* Inscription: THE CONSTRUCTION IS OF IRON AND GLASS; 1848 F$^{T}$ LONG ABOUT HALF IS 456 F$^{T}$ WIDE, THE REMAINDER 408 F$^{T}$ WIDE, AND 66 F$^{T}$ HIGH, WITH TRANSEPT 108 F$^{T}$ HIGH. SITE UPWARDS OF 20 ACRES. COST £150,000—JOS$^{H}$ PAXTON ESQ$^{R}$ ARC$^{T}$.

White Metal, 30 mm. (Eidlitz 764, pl. 83)

**165d** As No. 165c above, but White Metal, 27 mm. (BM)

**165e** *Obv.* The exhibition building. THE INDUSTRIAL EXHIBITION LONDON, 1851. In exergue, PROPOSED BY PRINCE ALBERT DESIGNED BY J. PAXTON ESQ ERECTED BY FOX, HENDERSON & C$^{O}$. Signed, ALLEN & MOORE BIRM$^{M}$.

*Rev.* Inscription: THE MATERIALS ARE IRON AND GLASS LENGTH 1848 FEET; WIDTH 456 FEET; HEIGHT OF ROOF 66 FEET; HEIGHT OF TRANSEPT 108 FEET; GLAZED SURFACE 900,000 SUP. FEET; OCCUPIES 18 ACRES OF GROUND VALUE £150,000. Rim beaded on obverse.

White Metal, 30 mm. (Eidlitz 760, pl. 83)

165f

**165f** *Obv.* The exhibition building. THE BUILDING AT LONDON, FOR THE INTERNATIONAL EXHIBITION 1851. In exergue, heads of Queen Victoria and Prince Albert, jugate to right, in ornamented frame flanked by genii. J. PAXTON ESQ. ARCHITECT. Signed, ALLEN & MOORE F.

*Rev.* Interior of the building. In exergue, EXPOSITION 1851. Signed, ALLEN & MOORE.

Bronze, White Metal, 39 mm. (Eidlitz 755, p. 83) (BM)

See also Plate 2.

**165g** *Obv.* The exhibition building. EXPOSITION INTERNATIONALE DE L'INDUSTRIE. LONDRES, 1851. In exergue, PROPOSE PAR SON A.R.LE PRINCE ALBERT. LE BATIMENT A ETE DESSINE PAR M$^{R}$ JOS$^{H}$ PAXTON M.S.R. ET ELEVE PAR MESSIEURS FOX, HENDERSON ET CIE. Signed, ALLEN ET MOORE BIRM$^{M}$.

*Rev.* Interior of the building, as reverse of No. 165f above.

White Metal, 39 mm. (Eidlitz 758, pl. 83)

**165h** *Obv.* Bust of Queen Victoria, crowned, to left. Around, H.M.G.M. QUEEN VICTORIA and on border + BORN MAY 24 1819. CROWNED JUNE 28 1838. MARRIED FEB 10 1840. Signed, A & M on truncation.

*Rev.* The exhibition building with cameo of Victoria and Albert, busts jugate, as obverse of No. 165f.

White Metal, 39 mm. (Eidlitz 759, pl. 83) (BM)

**165i** *Obv.* The exhibition building, as obverse of No. 165f above.

*Rev.* Inscription: THE MATERIALS ARE IRON AND GLASS, IN SHAPE A PARALLELOGRAM 1848 F$^{T}$ LONG BY 408 F$^{T}$ BROAD, AND 66 F$^{T}$

HIGH, IT IS CROSSED MIDWAY BY A TRANSEPT 108 F$^{T}$ HIGH, ON THE NORTH SIDE IS AN ADDITIONAL 936 F$^{T}$ IN LENGTH BY 48 F$^{T}$ IN BREADTH; TOTAL AREA OF SPACE 855,360 CUBIC F$^{T}$; OR NEARLY 21 ACRES; ESTIMATED VALUE £150,000.

White Metal, 39 mm. (Eidlitz 757, pl. 83) (BM)

**165j** *Obv.* The exhibition building, as obverse of No. 165f above.

*Rev.* Inscription: THE MATERIALS ARE IRON AND GLASS; IT IS IN SHAPE A PARALLELOGRAM, 1848 F$^{T}$ LONG BY 408 F$^{T}$ BROAD, AND 66 F$^{T}$ HIGH; IT IS CROSSED, MIDWAY BY A TRANSEPT 108 F$^{T}$ HIGH; ON THE NORTH SIDE IS AN ADDITION OF 936 F$^{T}$ IN LENGTH BY 48 F$^{T}$ IN BREADTH, TOTAL AREA OF SPACE, 855,360 CUBIC F$^{T}$ OR NEARLY 21 ACRES, ESTIMATED VALUE, £150,000. Legend: THERE ARE 2,244 IRON GIRDERS, 3,300 COLUMNS, 202 MILES OF SASH BARS, AND 900,000 SUP F$^{T}$ OF GLASS.

White Metal, 45 mm. (Eidlitz 756, pl. 82) (BM)

*Note.* Area given in 'cubic feet' is an error for square feet in this and the preceding medal.

**165k** *Obv.* Busts of Victoria and Albert, jugate to left in a wreath of laurel and oak and in an ornamented frame. QUEEN VICTORIA & PR: ALBERT.

*Rev.* The exhibition building. THE INTERNATIONAL INDUSTRIAL EXHIBITION, 1851. In exergue, PROPOSED BY H.R.H. PRINCE ALBERT, DESIGNED BY JOSEPH PAXTON ESQ. F.L.S., ERECTED BY FOX, HENDERSON & C$^{O}$ LENGTH 1848 FEET, WIDTH 456 FEET, HEIGHT OF PRINCIPAL ROOF 66 FEET, HEIGHT OF TRANSEPT 108 FEET, GLAZED SURFACE 900,000 SUP FEET OCCUPIES 18 ACRES OF GROUND. ESTIMATED VALUE £150,000. Signed, ALLEN & MOORE BIRM$^{M}$.

White Metal, 51 mm. (Eidlitz 748, pl. 82) (BM)

**165l** *Obv.* Crowned bust of Queen Victoria to left, in an open wreath of roses, thistle, shamrock and oak. VICTORIA, QUEEN OF GREAT BRITAIN, as obverse of No. 179h.

*Rev.* The exhibition building, as reverse of No. 165k.

Bronze, White Metal, 51 mm. (Eidlitz 749) (BM)

**165m** *Obv.* Head of Prince Consort to right. PRINCE ALBERT, CONSORT OF QUEEN VICTORIA. Signed, A & M. Rim ornamented.

*Rev.* The exhibition building, as reverse of No. 165k.

White Metal, 51 mm. (Eidlitz 750) (BM)

**165n** *Obv.* Portrait head of Prince Albert, as obverse of No. 165o below.

*Rev.* The exhibition building. THE INTERNATIONAL INDUSTRIAL EXHIBITION LONDON, 1851. In exergue, PROPOSED BY H.R.H. PRINCE ALBERT, DESIGNED BY JOSEPH PAXTON ESQ. F.L.S., ERECTED BY FOX, HENDERSON & C$^{O}$. LENGTH 1848 FEET, WIDTH 456 FEET, HEIGHT OF PRINCIPAL ROOF 66 FEET, HEIGHT OF TRANSEPT 108 FEET, GLAZED SURFACE 900,000 SUP FEET, OCCUPIES 18 ACRES OF GROUND, ESTIMATED VALUE £150,000. Signed, ALLEN & MOORE BIRM$^{M}$.

White Metal, 51 mm. (BM)

**165o** *Obv.* Portrait head to right, within a decorated border. Around, PRINCE ALBERT. CONSORT OF QUEEN VICTORIA. Signed, ALLEN & MOORE.

*Rev.* The exhibition building. THE INTERNATIONAL INDUSTRIAL EXHIBITION LONDON, 1851. In exergue, PROPOSED BY H.R.H. PRINCE ALBERT THE BUILDING DESIGNED BY JOSEPH PAXTON ESQ$^{R}$ F.L.S. ERECTED BY FOX HENDERSON & C$^{O}$ THE MATERIALS ARE IRON AND GLASS: LENGTH 1848 FEET: WIDTH 456 FEET; HEIGHT OF PRINCIPAL ROOF 66 FEET · HEIGHT OF TRANSEPT 108 FEET; GLAZED SURFACE 900,000 SUP. FEET; OCCUPIES 18 ACRES OF GROUND: ESTIMATED VALUE £150,000 · Signed, ALLEN & MOORE F. ET D. BIRM$^{M}$ ·

White Metal, 64 mm. (BM)

## *b. Other Medallists*

**165p** *Obv.* Head to right of HIS ROYAL HIGHNESS PRINCE ALBERT.

*Rev.* The exhibition building. THE GREAT PALACE FOR THE EXHIBITION OF THE INDUSTRY OF ALL NATIONS, ORIGINATED BY, H.R.H. PRINCE ALBERT. LONDON 1851. In exergue, LENGTH 1848 F, WIDTH 456 F, HEIGHT 64 F EXHIBITION SURFACE 21 ACRES, CONTRACT FOR USE £79 800 IF RETAINED £150 000 DESIGNED BY JOS PAXTON ESQ FLS. Signed, DAVIS BIRM.

White Metal, 44 mm. (BM)

**165q** *Obv.* Heads of the Prince Consort and Queen, jugate to left. TO COMMEMORATE THE EXHIBITION OF THE INDUSTRY OF ALL NATIONS. PROPOSED BY H.R.H. PRINCE ALBERT & PATRONISED BY H.M.G. MAJESTY THE QUEEN. Signed, DAVIS, BIRM.

*Rev.* View of the exhibition building. In exergue figures representing four quarters of the globe. LENGTH OF THE BUILDING 1848 F$^{T}$ WIDTH 456 F$^{T}$ HEIGHT 66 F$^{T}$ TRANSEPT 108 F$^{T}$ GLAZED SURFACE 900,000 F$^{T}$ OCCUPIES NEARLY 21 AC$^{S}$ OF GROUND 3300 IRON COLUMNS, 2224 GIRDERS, 1128 GALL$^{Y}$ BEARERS 205 MILES OF SASH BAR, VALUE £150000. OPENED BY H.M.G. MAJESTY VICTORIA MAY 1. 1851. On bar forming the exergue, DESIGNED BY J PAXTON ESQ ERECTED BY FOX HENDERSON & CO.

White Metal, 49 mm. (Eidlitz 752, pl. 82) (BM)

**165r** *Obv.* Head of the Prince Consort to left. H.R.H. PRINCE ALBERT. Signed, G.DEE. F. Ornamented border.

*Rev.* View of the exhibition building. THE CRYSTAL PALACE LONDON 1851. In exergue, COVERING AN AREA 18 ACRES LENGTH 1848 F$^{T}$ BREADTH 408 F$^{T}$ HEIGHT 66 F$^{T}$ TRANSEPT 108 F$^{T}$ HIGH COST £150,000.

White Metal, 30 mm. (Eidlitz 763, pl. 83) (BM)

**165s** *Obv.* The exhibition building. THE CRYSTAL PALACE. In exergue, FOR THE WORLD'S SHOW IN LONDON 1851. Signed, HEATON.BIRM.

*Rev.* Inscription: DIMENSIONS — LENGTH 1848 FT WIDTH 408 FT HEIGHT OF ROOF 66 FT HEIGHT OF TRANSEPT 108 FT GLAZED SURFACE 900,000 SQ FT AND OCCUPIES 18 ACRES.

White Metal, 30 mm. (Eidlitz 761, pl. 83) (BM)

**165t** *Obv.* View of the exhibition building. THE CRYSTAL PALACE DESIGNED BY MR PAXTON. In exergue, FOR THE GREAT EXHIBITION IN LONDON OF 1851. Signed, HEATON BIRM.

*Rev.* Inscription: DIMENSIONS LENGTH 1848 FEET WIDTH 408 FEET HEIGHT OF ROOF 66 FEET HEIGHT OF TRANSEPT 108 FT GLAZED SURFACE 900,000 FEET AND OCCUPIES 18 ACRES.

White Metal, 34 mm. (BM)

**165u** *Obv.* View of exhibition building. THE GREAT EXHIBITION PALACE LONDON 1851. In exergue, PROPOSED BY H.R.H. PRINCE ALBERT DESIGNED BY JOSH PAXTON. F.L.S. ERECTED BY FOX HENDERSON & CO OCCUPIES 18 ACRES. Signed, HEATON. BIRM.

*Rev.* Inscription: LENGTH 1848 FEET 408 FT WIDE ROOF 66 FT HIGH HEIGHT OF TRANSEPT 108 FT 900,000 SQ FT GLAZED SURFACE 3320 CAST IRON COLUMNS 358 WROT IRON TRUSSES 202 MILES OF SASH BARS 400 TONS OF GLASS VALUE £150,000.

White metal, 38 mm. (BM)

**165v** *Obv.* Head of the Prince Consort to right. HIS ROYAL HIGHNESS PRINCE ALBERT.

*Rev.* The exhibition building. THE BUILDING FOR THE GREAT EXHIBITION IN LONDON, 1851. In exergue, PROPOSED BY H.R.H. PRINCE ALBERT. DESIGNED BY JOSEPH PAXTON ESQ. F.L.S. BY FOX, HENDERSON & CO 1848 FEET. WIDTH 456 FEET. HEIGHT OF PRINCIPAL ROOF 66 FEET. HEIGHT OF TRANSEPT 108 FEET. GLAZED SURFACE 900000 FEET OCCUPIES 18 ACRES OF GROUND.

White Metal, 53 mm. (Eidlitz 753, pl. 82) (BM)

**165w** *Obv.* The exhibition building, as reverse of No. 165v above.

*Rev.* Four figures, one with olive branch, one with a sheaf of wheat, one with a hammer; the fourth holds a wreath aloft. Signed, OTTLEY, MEDALLIST, BIRMM. Rim milled.

White Metal, 53 mm. (cf. Eidlitz 754, and pl. 82) (BM)

*Note.* Eidlitz entry 754 (given as BM) is in error; the obverse should read 'Same as *Reverse* to No. 753'.

**165x** *Obv.* Head of the Prince Consort to left in a wreath of laurel and oak. HIS ROYAL HIGHNESS PRINCE ALBERT. Signed, OTTLEY. BIRMM.

*Rev.* The exhibition building. THE BUILDING FOR THE GREAT EXHIBITION IN LONDON. 1851. In exergue, PROPOSED BY H.R.H. PRINCE ALBERT. DESIGNED BY JOSEPH PAXTON ESQ. F.L.S. ERECTED BY FOX, HENDERSON, & CO — DIMENSIONS — LENGTH 1848 FEET, WIDTH 456 FEET, HEIGHT OF PRINCIPAL ROOF 66 FEET, HEIGHT OF TRANSEPT 108 FEET, GLAZED SURFACE 900000 FEET, OCCUPIES 18 ACRES OF GROUND.

White Metal, 53 mm. (BM)

**165y** Similar to No. 165x above, but the reverse legend is differently spaced.

White Metal, 74 mm. (Eidlitz 747, pl. 83) (BM)

**165z** *Obv.* The exhibition building in a wreath of roses, thistle and shamrock. Above, heads of Queen Victoria and Prince Albert each in an oval frame: between them the coat of arms of Great Britain. PROPOSED BY H.R.H. PRINCE ALBERT. DESIGNED BY JOSEPH PAXTON ESQ$^{RE}$ F.L.S. ERECTED BY FOX, HENDERSON C$^{O}$. Legend: EXHIBITION OF INDUSTRY, OF ALL NATIONS. LONDON. 1851. Signed, OTTLEY BIRM.

*Rev.* Britannia standing, holding laurel branch and surrounded by symbols of industry, art, thrift and transportation.

White Metal, 74 mm. (Eidlitz 746, pl. 83) (BM)

**165aa** *Obv.* Head of Prince Albert to left. H.R.H. PRINCE ALBERT. Below, STRUCK IN THE BUILDING OF THE EXHIBITION. Signed W. J. TAYLOR MEDALLIST LONDON.

*Rev.* Royal coat of arms. GREAT EXHIBITION OF THE INDUSTRY OF ALL NATIONS. Below · LONDON 1851 ·

Bronze, White Metal, 38 mm. (Eidlitz 751, pl. 82) (BM)

**165bb** *Obv.* The exhibition building. EXHIBITION PALACE In exergue, LONDON 1851. Rim beaded.

*Rev.* Similar to obverse but signed in exergue; one letter at left illegible, at right the letter B. The rim is not beaded.

Bronze, 22 mm. (Eidlitz 764a, pl. 85)

*Note.* Eidlitz records a variant with head of Queen Victoria on the reverse.

**165cc** *Obv.* The exhibition building. THE CRYSTAL PALACE LONDON 1851. Below, PROPOSED BY PRINCE ALBERT.

*Rev.* Inscription: DIMENSIONS — · — LENGTH 1848 F$^{T}$ WIDTH 408 F$^{T}$ HEIGHT OF ROOF 66 F$^{T}$ HEIGHT OF TRANSEPT 108 FEET GLAZED SURFACE 900,000 S$^{Q}$ F$^{T}$ AND OCCUPIES 18 ACRES.

White Metal, 26 mm. (BM)

**166dd** *Obv.* Head, to left, of VICTORIA REGINA.

*Rev.* The exhibition building. THE CRYSTAL PALACE LONDON 1851. In exergue, PROPOSED BY H.R.H. PRINCE ALBERT — COST L.150000.

Brass, 27 mm. (BM)

**165ee** *Obv.* Crowned head to left of VICTORIA QUEEN OF GREAT BRITAIN.

*Rev.* The exhibition building. THE CRYSTAL PALACE LONDON 1851. In exergue, COVERING AN AREA OF 18 ACRES LENGTH 1848 F$^{T}$ BREADTH 408 F$^{T}$ HEIGHT 66 F$^{T}$ TRANSEPT 108 F$^{T}$ HIGH COST £150,000.

White Metal, 29 mm. (BM)

**165ff** *Obv.* View from within the transept, showing Colonel Sibthorp's elm tree. INTERIOR VIEW OF THE CRYSTAL PALACE LONDON 1851.

*Rev.* Inscription: THIS UNIQUE STRUCTURE HAS 3320 CAST IRON COLUMNS 358 WROUGHT-IRON TRUSSES 8 MILES OF EXHIB$^{N}$ TABLES 34 MILES OF GUTTERS 202 MILES OF SASH BARS 400 TONS OF GLASS AND COST £150.000.

White Metal, 30 mm. (BM)

**165gg** *Obv.* Head, to left, of VICTORIA REGINA.

*Rev.* The exhibition building. THE CRYSTAL PALACE, FOR THE EXHIBITION OF ALL NATIONS LONDON 1851. In exergue, COVERING AN AREA OF 18 ACRES. LENGTH 1848 F$^{T}$, BREADTH 408 F$^{T}$, HEIGHT 66 F$^{T}$, TRANSEPTS 108 F$^{T}$ HIGH. COST £150.000.

Bronze, 35 mm. (BM)

LONDON, Kensington and Chelsea, **Great Exhibition Building**, Hyde Park, 'The Crystal Palace' *1850–51*

The range of medals issued for the 'Great Exhibition of the Industry of All Nations' forms the largest single group depicting any nineteenth-century building—and ironically in this case one not designed by a trained architect.

(i) *Inscriptions*: These provide an immediate reference to the amazing statistics of size, area, materials and cost, as well as noting the main protagonists in the building's design: Joseph Paxton[1] and the contractors Fox and Henderson. But these statistics only reflect the astounding production process involved—the unprecedented application, on such a scale, of prefabrication techniques which would enable the 'Crystal Palace' to be designed, manufactured, assembled, glazed and occupied within the space of nine months between 1 August 1850 and 1 May 1851.

(ii) *Exterior Views*: These show the building in its fine Hyde Park landscape and the rectangular profile of its stepped section, broken only by a skyline of flags and the great arched roof to the transverse transept. The latter, not shown in Paxton's original design published in the *Illustrated London News*[2] (nor on No. 165v), was an inspired late addition to the design, both in accommodating Colonel Sibthorp's elm tree within it, and creating the most significant space and a focus for the whole building.[3] The exterior views also emphasise the unbroken repetition of the basic glazed walling unit; this realisation of Paxton's original blotting paper sketch, around the concept of standard modular structural bays and infill units, was even to be extended to provide a separate little boiler house, to the north-west of the main building, in the same system (cf. p. 206 and the 'Brompton Boilers').

(iii) *Interior views*: The extraordinary perspective down the interior of the main 'nave', with its galleries for exhibitors and the continuous 'ridge and furrow' roof glazing (e.g. as shown in No. 165f) was modified by an important system of decoration. This was the application by Owen Jones of his 'science of colour' in painting the metalwork. Jones's scheme made use of a pale blue as the principal colour, with a strong red for the underside of girders, behind galleries, and for screens, together with yellow for diagonal faces of columns. The critics were quick to note affinities with the paintings of Turner, and a contemporary essay in the *Art Journal* remarked, 'For practical purposes the effect of the interior of the building resembles that of the open air . . . To a spectator seated in the gallery . . . the more distant part of the building appears to be enveloped in a blue haze . . .'[4]

(iv) *Portraits*: These are of the Queen, who opened the Crystal Palace,[5] and Prince Albert, whose key role in organising the Royal Commission, and effecting a grand idea, was widely recognised. It was not until the rebuilding at Sydenham (see No. 171) that Paxton's portrait appears as designer. One name that receives no medallic reference is that of Sir Henry Cole, the dynamic secretary to the 1851 Exhibition; his was the original idea presented to Albert, and he it was who ran the campaign for an international exhibition and obtained money and exhibitors. After 1851 Cole's life was centred on the development of the South Kensington cultural centre and he was closely involved with the creation of the Victoria and Albert Museum, the 1862 Exhibition (No. 182), and the Albert Hall (No. 189).

See: H.-R. Hitchcock, *Early Victorian Architecture*, 530–46; pl. xvi 1–16; G. F. Chadwick, *The Works of Sir Joseph Paxton*, 1961; P. Beaver, *The Crystal Palace*, 1970.

1. Even at this stage labelled 'architect' on some medals—a source of potential discomfort to a profession awarding its Gold Medal in 1851 to T. L. Donaldson (qv.).
2. 6 July 1850. This was an approach to the public for support.
3. The idea of the flags, and the arched transept roof, are credited to the architect Sir Charles Barry (qv.) who was on the building committee. The construction of the arch ribs was of laminated timber.
4. Art Journal, *Illustrated Catalogue*, appended essay 'The Harmony of Colours', p. 11.
5. A name originally coined by Jerrold in *Punch*, after Paxton's initial proposal. It was not to become commonly used until autumn 1851 and hence its scarcity on medal inscriptions.

LONDON, Tower Hamlets, **Victoria Park Hospital**, Approach Road, Bethnal Green (now the London Chest Hospital) *1851 on*

166a

**166a** *Obv.* View of main entrance to buildings. VICTORIA PARK HOSPITAL LONDON.

*Rev.* Inscription: MATRON'S MEDAL KNOWLEDGE IS POWER. In centre, PRESENTED TO, space for name.

White Metal, 39 mm. ? 1850s (Watt Coll.)

Prince Albert laid the foundation stone of the City of London Hospital for Diseases of the Chest in 1851.[1] The architect for this large red-brick building was F. W. Ordish,[2] and the medal view shows how he employed a simple late Stuart manner, with small window panes, that was soon to be called 'Queen Anne' revival. The hospital had also approached Sir Joseph Paxton (qv.) for advice on designing a glass and iron 'exercise room'; Paxton's scheme (unbuilt) for a 200 ft by 75 ft space is illustrated in H.-R. Hitchcock, *Early Victorian Architecture*, pl. xvi 21.

1. I am indebted to Mr K. Howes of the British Museum for confirming this, and for visiting the building. A drawing of the hospital is in *Illustrated London News*, 28 June 1851.
2. H.-R. Hitchcock, op. cit. 333.

BIRMINGHAM, West Midlands, **General Institution for the Blind,** Carpenter Road (now Royal Institution for the Blind) *1851–52*

**167a** *Obv.* Perspective view of building. In exergue, GENERAL INSTITUTION FOR THE BLIND BIRMINGHAM, COMMENCED BY PRIVATE BENEVOLENCE 1846 ESTABLISHED AS A PUBLIC INSTITUTION 1848. Signed on exergue bar, ALLEN & MOORE F.

*Rev.* Inscription: THE CORNER STONE OF THIS BUILDING WAS LAID BY THOMAS GOODMAN ESQ$^{R}$, TREASURER, 28. APRIL. 1851. — XLII ISAIAH, 16. Around on border, THE RIGHT HONB$^{LE}$ EARL HOWE, PRESIDENT.

White Metal, 51 mm. 1851 (BM)

The obverse of this medal was used again for the opening in the next year.

167a

**167b** *Obv.* Perspective view of building. As obverse of No. 167a above.

*Rev.* Inscription: THIS BUILDING WAS COMMENCED 23$^{RD}$ APRIL 1851 AND COMPLETED 22$^{ND}$ JULY 1852. — ISAIAH XLII, 16. On border, around. THE LORD BISHOP OF WORCESTER, PRESIDENT ⁖ THO$^{S}$ GOODMAN ESQ$^{E}$, TREASURER.

White Metal, 51 mm. 1852 (BM)

The medal shows this Jacobean style building by Samuel Hemming with its symmetrical plan form, gables, and oriel windows; in red brick with stone trim.

See: Pevsner, *Warwick*. 168–69.

LONDON, Richmond on Thames, **Metropolitan & City Police Orphanage,** Wellesley House, Hampton Road, Twickenham *1852–53*

**168a** *Obv.* Within a border of oak leaves, roses, thistles, etc., 'young' head of Queen Victoria, to the left. HER MAJESTY THE QUEEN PATRON.

*Rev.* View of three-storey building, with trees and grounds. METROPOLITAN & CITY POLICE ORPHANAGE. In exergue, TWICKENHAM 1870.

White Metal, 41 mm. ?1874 (BM)

168a

The medal shows the symmetrical Italianate centre block of Wellesley House, built in 1852–53 as a school and known as 'T.J. Scale's Academy'. There are two-storey wings to the sides of four bays each. The Police Orphanage was founded in 1870[1] and, in 1871, given Royal Patronage (see medal obverse). In 1874 Wellesley House, Hampton Road, Twickenham, was purchased and the orphanage moved there, with accommodation for 200. Demolished in 1971.

1. Initially at Fortescue House, Twickenham (eighteenth century), which had already been 'long devoted to charitable purposes'. See E. Walford, *Greater London*, 1, 77.

169a

WOLVERHAMPTON, West Midlands, **Orphan Asylum,** Penn Road. (now Royal Wolverhampton School) *1853*

**169a** *Obv.* View of buildings, with flêche over main gateway. WOLVERHAMPTON ORPHAN ASYLUM. In exergue, FOUNDED 1850.

*Rev.* Blank for inscription.

Silver, 34 mm. ?1850s (Watt Coll.)[1]

By Joseph Manning 1853. A brick and stone range with a tower in the middle. Wings added in 1863.

See: Pevsner, *Staffs.* 323.

1. This copy presented 1892.

170a

LIVERPOOL, Merseyside, **St George's Hall** *1842–54*

**170a** *Obv.* Allegorical scene[1] set before the south front of St George's Hall. The bust of ELMES on a plinth, is crowned with a wreath by the central seated figure of Liverpool. To the left Architecture, standing, shows a drawing of St George's Hall to History, seated opposite; behind her are Justice and Music for whose use the building was designed. Signed in exergue, J. MAYER. D and on rim, ALLEN & MOORE. F.

*Rev.* Inscription, within a wreath of laurel: — · — SAINT GEORGE'S HALL LIVERPOOL. H.LONSDALE ELMES ARCH$^{T}$. — · — Above, THE FOUNDATION STONE LAID JUNE 28$^{TH}$ 1838, BY WILLIAM RATHBONE, MAYOR. Below, OPENED FOR PUBLIC USE SEPTEMBER 18$^{TH}$ 1854. JOHN BUCK LLOYD, MAYOR.

Bronze, White Metal, 44 mm. 1854 (BM)

In 1839 Harvey Lonsdale Elmes, at the age of twenty-five, won the competition for a proposed St George's Hall—a building to provide a large concert hall for Liverpool of the sort J. A. Hansom had designed for Birmingham (see No. 108). In 1840 Elmes won a second competition, that for the new Assize Courts. It was the decision to combine the two designs, that provided Elmes with the programme for the single immense neo-classical building which still dominates the centre of Liverpool, and which even before its completion was recognised as one of the great nineteenth-century monuments. The medal indicates only the south portico; behind it, along the central axis of the building, lies the main concert hall, flanked at either end by the two court-rooms, and a smaller elliptical concert room at the north end. The sheer scale of the project and the combining of the two earlier schemes broke Elmes's health, and, in 1843, he died abroad. C. R. Cockerell (qv.) ultimately completed the design (1851–54) and provided the interiors with their rich materials and polychromy.[2]

See: *Marble Halls,* 79, 80; H.-R. Hitchcock, *Early Victorian Architecture,* 309–12, pl. x 6, 7, 8; Pevsner, *S Lancs.* 155–57; Q. Hughes, *Seaport,* 1964, 95–104.

1. Described in *GM,* January 1855, pp. 51, 52.
2. The completion of the structural shell, and the 80-ft span of the central hall roof, was carried through by the engineer Sir Robert Rawlinson.

LONDON, Sydenham, **'The Crystal Palace'** *1852–54*

**171a** *Obv.* Framed bust to left in wreath of laurel. Below, SIR JOSEPH PAXTON.

*Rev.* The Crystal Palace. THE PEOPLE'S CRYSTAL PALACE SYDENHAM. BEING A VAST REPOSITORY OF INSTRUCTION AND AMUSEMENT. OPENED JUNE 1854. In exergue, DESIGNED BY SIR JOSEPH PAXTON F.L.S. ERECTED BY FOX, HENDERSON & C$^{O}$ THE BUILDING AND GROUNDS OCCUPY 300 ACRES LENGTH 1608 F$^{T}$, NAVE 110 F$^{T}$ HIGH, CENTRE TRANSEPT 194 F$^{T}$ HIGH, AND 120 WIDE SIDE TRANSEPTS 110 F$^{T}$ HIGH, AND 72 F$^{T}$ WIDE. Signed on exergue bar, ALLEN & MOORE.

White Metal, 51 mm. 1854 (Eidlitz 770, pl. 82) (BM)

**171b** *Obv.* Allegorical group, Britannia in centre with the symbols of industry and peace. Signed, DOWLER BIRM.

*Rev.* View of the Crystal Palace. THE MIGHT OF INDUSTRY, THE GLORY OF PEACE. Signed, DOWLER BIRM$^{M}$. In exergue, THE CRYSTAL PALACE SYDENHAM ERECTED MDCCCLIII FOX, HENDERSON & CO. CONTRACTORS.

White Metal, 74 mm. ?1854 (Eidlitz 771)

The obverse of this medal was later used, at same size, for the obverse of medal No. 182i of the 1862 Exhibition Building.

**171c** *Obv.* Head to left of SIR JOSEPH PAXTON. Signed on truncation, L. C. WYON.

*Rev.* The Crystal Palace. DESIGNED BY SIR JOSEPH PAXTON. In exergue, THE FIRST COLUMN ERECTED BY SAM$^{L}$ LAING ESQ$^{RE}$ M.P. AUG$^{T}$ 5$^{TH}$ 1852 OPENED JUNE 10$^{TH}$ 1854. Signed, T. R. PINCHES LONDON.

White Metal, 41 mm. 1854 (Eidlitz 769, pl. 84) (BM)

**171d** *Obv.* Banner with horns and trumpets, crowns above. JUNGIMUS HOSPITIO DEXTRAS. Signed, PINCHES, LONDON.

*Rev.* Façade of the Crystal Palace. TO COMMEMORATE THE VISIT OF THE BAND OF THE IMP: REG: OF GUIDES. In exergue, TO THE CRYSTAL PALACE SYDENHAM OCTOBER 28. 1854.

White Metal, 41 mm. 1854 (Eidlitz 776, pl. 84)

**171e** *Obv.* Coat of arms with an eye above. THE ANCIENT ORDER OF FORESTERS. In exergue, VISITED THE CRYSTAL PALACE SYDENHAM OCTOBER 28. 1854.

*Rev.* The Crystal Palace. As reverse of No. 171c above.

White Metal, 41 mm. 1854 (Eidlitz 777, pl. 84)

**171f** *Obv.* Head to left of PAXTON. Signed L. C. WYON.

*Rev.* Inscription: THE CRYSTAL PALACE — DESIGNED BY SIR JOSEPH PAXTON OPENED JUNE. 10. 1854. Below, crossed branches of laurel.

White Metal, 63 mm. 1854 (Eidlitz 765, pl. 84)

Eidlitz notes a variant of this in bronze, with the reverse blank for inscription.

171g

**171g** *Obv.* Head of Paxton to left, as obverse of No. 171f above.
*Rev.* View of the Crystal Palace. Above, CRYSTAL PALACE. Below, OPENED. MDCCCLIV. Signed, PINCHES LONDON.
Bronze, 63 mm. 1854 (Eidlitz 766, pl. 84) (BM)

**171h** *Obv.* Female figure with emblems of peace and war, a lamb and a helmet at her feet, opens the doors INDUSTRY SCIENCE to the exhibition. Signed in exergue, PINCHES.
*Rev.* View of the Crystal Palace. As reverse of No. 171g above.
Bronze, White Metal, 63 mm. 1854 (Eidlitz 767, pl. 84) (BM)

**171i** As No. 171h above.
White Metal, 41 mm. 1854 (Eidlitz 768, pl. 84) (BM)

**171j** *Obv.* View of the Crystal Palace. Above, DESIGNED BY SIR JOSEPH PAXTON. In exergue, ERECTED BY MESS$^{RS}$ FOX & HENDERSON. Signed, W. J. TAYLOR LONDON.
*Rev.* Inscription: THE FIRST COLUMN OF THE CRYSTAL PALACE AT SYDENHAM DESTINED FOR THE RECREATION AND INSTRUCTION OF THE MILLION WAS ERECTED ON THE 5 DAY OF AUGUST 1852 BY SAMUEL LAING ESQ. M.P. CHAIRMAN OF THE CRYSTAL PALACE COMP. IN COMMEMORATION OF WHICH EVENT THIS MEDAL IS PRESENTED TO THE SUBSCRIBERS OF THE AGE WEEKLY NEWSPAPER.
White Metal, gilt, 44 mm. 1852 (Eidlitz 773, pl. 84)

**171k** *Obv.* View of the Crystal Palace. CRYSTAL PALACE SYDENHAM BEING THE GREAT EXHIBITION OF 1851 REMOVED FROM HYDE PARK. In exergue, FIRST COLUMN ERECTED AUG 5. 1852 THE PALACE OF THE PEOPLE OPENED JUNE 10. 1854. Signed, on bar forming exergue, W. J. TAYLOR LONDON.
*Rev.* Inscription: STRUCK IN THE CRYSTAL PALACE · BY W. J. TAYLOR — VISITORS TO THE 30 APRIL 1866 18,607,852 — In ten panels radiating from centre, WIDTH OF THE BUILDING 324 FEET — LENGTH OF NAVE 1602 F$^{T}$ HEIGHT 104 F$^{T}$ — HEIGHT OF CENTRE TRANSEPT 174 FEET IRON USED IN WATER TOWERS 1600 TONS WATER TOWERS 284 F$^{T}$ ABOVE CROSS OF S$^{T}$ PAULS PALACE AND

GROUNDS COVER 200 ACRES HANDEL ORCHESTRA SEATS 5000 PERSONS — GLASS USED IN BUILDING 25 ACRES — IRON USED IN BUILDING 9641 TONS — LENGTH OF HOT WATER PIPES 50 MILES —

White Metal, 42 mm. 1866 (Eidlitz 774, pl. 84)

171l *Obv.* View of the Crystal Palace. CRYSTAL PALACE SYDENHAM. In exergue, FIRST COLUMN ERECTED AUG 5. 1852 OPENED JUNE 10. 1854. Signed on exergue bar, W. J. TAYLOR LONDON.

*Rev.* Inscription, as reverse of No. 171k above.

White Metal, 42 mm. 1866 (Eidlitz 775, pl. 84)

LONDON, Sydenham, '**The Crystal Palace**' *1852–54*

After the success of the 1851 exhibition there was a move to retain it at Hyde Park, as a Winter Garden, and for this Sir Joseph Paxton prepared a first design for its enlargement. (It was at this stage that Paxton was also producing a flurry of designs for 'Crystal Palaces' and structures in glass and iron, e.g. a roof for the Royal Exchange No. 146; an exercise room for Victoria Park Hospital No. 166.) When Parliament insisted that the Hyde Park site be cleared, the 'Crystal Palace Company' was formed to buy the materials and re-erect them at Sydenham. This was done in 1852–54 and the successful dismantling and re-erection of Paxton's original structure, albeit in an expanded form, finalised the technological triumph of the concept. The new building at Sydenham was the work of the same 1851 team, i.e. Paxton (of whom there are portraits on Nos. 171a, c, f, g), with Fox and Henderson as contractors and Owen Jones as consultant for decoration. The medals record the size of the much enlarged structure (e.g. No. 171k, Eidlitz 774) and show the new exterior (surprisingly, there appear to be no interior views). As completed Paxton's Sydenham rebuilding had the 'nave' surmounted by an arched transparent roof throughout its length; instead of the one main 'transept' of the 1851 Exhibition there are now subsidiary north and south transepts as well (cf. Paxton's finest glass and iron project, possibly for a site at St Cloud, near Paris, where he proposed three great domed pavilions attached to the front of the structure[1]). The familiar silhouette of the water towers at either end of the building resulted from designs by the engineer I. K. Brunel (these are not shown on the medals; but an early alternative appears on No. 171a, Eidlitz 770). The medal inscriptions indicate the new functional role of the rebuilt Crystal Palace, e.g. 'Vast repository of Instruction and Amusement'; 'Designed for the recreation and instruction of the million'; 'The Palace of the People'.[2] The building continued in this pattern of use until 1936, when it was totally destroyed by fire.[3]

See: P. Beaver, *The Crystal Palace*, 1970; G. F. Chadwick, *The Works of Sir Joseph Paxton*, 1961.

1. H.-R. Hitchcock, *Early Victorian Architecture*, pl. xvi, 20; and Chadwick, op. cit. 183.
2. The 'instruction' included a series of courts representing the architecture, sculpture, and ornament of different countries and periods. The architect for these was Sir Matthew Digby Wyatt (1820–77).
3. The north transept shown on the medals had already been burnt down by fire in 1866, and that end of the building never rebuilt.

LANCASTER, Lancs., **Royal Grammar School,** Quernmore Road *1851–55*

172a

**172a** *Obv.* View of Lancaster Royal Grammar School. Below, LANCASTER. Signed, B. WYON SC.

*Rev.* Emblazoned shield with motto. EIN DOE AND SPAIR NOT.

Bronze, 35 mm. 1856[G] (BM)

The obverse view shows the castellated Tudor-style buildings put up in 1851–55 for the Lancaster Royal Grammar School; the architects were the local firm of Sharpe and Paley. The design, which picturesquely suggests by its tower and gateway the feudal castle and baronial hall, followed the firm's earlier work of remodelling the medieval Hornby Castle in Lancashire (cf. the image of Wyatville's work at Windsor Castle, No. 131). The school, which is a fifteenth-century foundation, has used this die for its Greg Gold Medal for mathematics.[1]

1. Information by courtesy of the Lancaster City Museum.

MANCHESTER, Greater Manchester, **Art Treasures Exhibition Building,** Old Trafford *1856–57*

173a

**173a** *Obv.* In a central roundel of 42 mm: View of exterior of exhibition buildings, showing three glass-roofed sections. Around, EXHIBITION OF ART TREASURES. In exergue, OPENED AT MANCHESTER BY HIS ROYAL HIGHNESS PRINCE ALBERT MAY 5TH 1857. On a 10 mm border: coats of arms of England, Wales, the Sovereign, and City of Manchester. Between these, garlands bearing artists' names: MURILLO FLAXMAN VANDYKE RUBENS CELLINI RAPHAEL M.ANGELO TURNER.

*Rev.* An allegorical scene representing the Arts. In exergue, MDCCCLVII. Signed, PINCHES F. LONDON.

White Metal, 62 mm. 1857 (BM)

**173b** *Obv.* View of exterior of exhibition buildings as central roundel of No. 173a above.

*Rev.* Allegorical scene: a group of the Arts. In exergue, MDCCCLVII. Signed, PINCHES LONDON.

Bronze, White Metal, 41 mm. (BM)

**173c** *Obv.* Portrait bust, to left, of Queen VICTORIA REGINA. Signed, PINCHES. LONDON.

*Rev.* View of exterior of exhibition buildings as central roundel of No. 173a above.

Bronze, 41 mm. (BM)

Following the success of Paxton's building, a committee was formed in Manchester to 'erect a Crystal Palace in an eligible situation'. The aim was to accommodate treasures of art—not works of industry—and the resultant design was opened at Old Trafford in 1857.[1] The main cast iron structure (656 ft by 200 ft wide) was by the engineering firm C. D. Young & Co.[2] and the ornamental brick front attached to one end (shown on medal obverse) was by the local architect Edward Salomons.

1. Competition entrants included Owen Jones. See *Marble Halls*, 117.
2. Illustrated in C. Stewart, *The Stones of Manchester*, 1956, 66.

DERBY, Derbyshire, **St. Michael's Church,** Queen Street *1858*

**174a** *Obv.* View of church. ST MICHAEL'S CHURCH DERBY. In exergue, RE-OPENED APRIL 8 1858. Signed, OTTLEY BIRM.

*Rev.* Within a cartouche, St Michael standing facing, with hands resting on shoulders of small child. Around cartouche, SAINT MICHAEL'S + CHURCH + AND + SCHOOLS + DERBY. Legend, FOR REGULAR ATTENDANCE — AT THE SUNDAY SCHOOL.

White Metal, 46 mm. 1858 (BM)

In a thirteenth-century style, stone faced; by H. J. Stevens, 1858. The medal is the same format as that of St Peter, Stoke-on-Trent (No. 98a).

See: Pevsner, *Derbs.* 115.

174a

LEEDS, West Yorks., **Town Hall**, The Headrow *1853–58*

**175a** *Obv.* Conjoint heads of Queen Victoria and Prince Albert to left. Around on a border, H.M.G.M. QUEEN VICTORIA & H.R.H THE PRINCE CONSORT.

*Rev.* View of the Town Hall. Around, LEEDS TOWN HALL. In exergue, OPENED BY HER M.G. MAJESTY QUEEN VICTORIA SEPT: 7. 1858 PETER FAIRBAIRN ESQ. MAYOR. Signed on exergue bar, OTTLEY. BIRM.

Bronze or White Metal, 46 mm. 1858 (Leeds City Museum)

175a

**175b** *Obv.* View of the Town Hall as reverse of No. 175a above.

*Rev.* Inscription, around within border: VISIT OF JOHN BRIGHT TO LEEDS. In central panel, GREAT WEST RIDING REFORM DEMONSTRATION OCT $8^{\text{TH}}$ 1866.

White Metal, 46 mm. 1866 (Leeds City Museum)

A good example of a die being reused for another, and very different, occasion several years later.

As with Birmingham (No. 108) and Liverpool (No. 170), the competition for a new town hall led to the emergence of a young, talented, but virtually unknown architect. At Leeds, Cuthbert Brodrick produced for the rapidly developing city 'one of the most convincing buildings of its date in the country, and of the classical buildings of its date no doubt the most successful' (Pevsner). The obvious exemplar for the design, with its single giant order of Corinthian columns and pilasters, was the partially completed St George's Hall by Elmes. However, it was to be Brodrick's addition of the superb 225 ft high tower, so symbolic of civic pride, that was to make the building very much his own—and one that was widely copied for town halls during the rest of the century.[1]

See: Pevsner, *Yorks., W Riding*, 314, 315: *Marble Halls*, 83; D. Linstrum, *Historic Architecture of Leeds*, 54–57.

1. It has been suggested that Sir Charles Barry (qv.), who judged the competition in 1852, encouraged the addition of a tower to Brodrick's scheme.

176a

WALSALL, West Midlands, **St John's Church,** Pleck Road *1857–58*

**176a** *Obv.* View of church. S$^{NT}$ JOHN'S PLECK & BESCOT CHURCH. Below, WALSALL — GRIFFIN & WELLER. ARCHTS. Signed, J. MOORE. FECIT.

*Rev.* Emblem of an eagle; below, the legend: SCHOOL OPENED OCT$^{R}$ 14$^{TH}$ 1855 CHURCH CONSECRATED JULY 27$^{TH}$ 1858 — "I WAS GLAD WHEN THEY SAID UNTO ME, LET US GO INTO THE HOUSE OF THE LORD."

White Metal, 39 mm. 1858 (BM)

1857–58 by Griffin & Weller. Built of local limestone, with dressings of red sandstone from Codsall. Closed for demolition in 1976.

See: Pevsner, *Staffs*. 297.

177a

OXFORD, **The Oxford University Gymnasium,** Alfred Street *1858–59*

**177a** *Obv.* View of the gymnasium building. Around, on a border designed to look like a belt, MENS SANA IN CORPORE SANO.

*Rev.* Inscription on border, OXFORD GYMNASIUM. In centre, surrounded by wreath, space for inscription.

Silver, 49 mm. 1858 (Watt Coll.)[1]

Built in 1858–59 for Archibald Maclaren (died 1884). Maclaren was a progressive figure in the case for physical education and author of several books on the subject. The architect was William Wilkinson, who was to make such an impression on north Oxford domestic architecture during the 1860s and 1870s with his gothic vernacular style. The main block was extended in 1861, to complete Wilkinson's design, by the addition of a single-storey children's gymnasium (demolished in 1965). The building as shown is now used as a printer's works and offices.

1. This copy inscribed DREWETT ORMONDE BROWN LENT TERM 1858 EXETER COLL.

178a

BIRMINGHAM, West Midlands, **The Mint,** Icknield Street, Birmingham Heath *c. 1860*

**178a** *Obv.* View of manufacturing buildings. Around, RALPH HEATON AND SONS COINERS THE MINT BIRMINGHAM. Below, TO THE BRITISH FRENCH ITALIAN & OTHER GOVERNMENTS.

*Rev.* Coat of arms, with laurel and oak sprays. Below, TO COMMEMORATE THE VISIT OF THEIR ROYAL HIGHNESSES THE PRINCE & PRINCESS OF WALES. Around, BIRMINGHAM 3 NOV. 1874 J. CHAMBERLAIN ESQ. MAYOR.

Bronze, 38 mm. 1874 (BM)

The medal shows Heaton's Mint at Icknield Street. Heaton's were makers of tubes, and brass founders, as well as coiners. Their building, in the newly developing Birmingham Heath industrial area, was described as 'new, light and airy' by the Children's Employment Commission in 1863.[1]

1. See *VCH, Warwicks.*, vol. 7, 133.

LONDON, Westminster, **The Houses of Parliament** *1840–60*

**179a** *Obv.* Head of Queen Victoria to left. VICTORIA REGINA. Below, 1846. Signed on truncation, A & M.

*Rev.* View of the Houses of Parliament and the Thames. NEW HOUSES OF PARLIAMENT. In exergue, OPENED NOV: 1847 — H. HYAMS LONDON. Rim beaded.

Bronze, Brass, 22 mm. 1847 (Eidlitz 54, pl. 5) (BM)

**179b** *Obv.* Busts of Queen Victoria and Prince Albert, jugate to left. H · M · G · M· QUEEN VICTORIA. AND H · R · H · PRINCE ALBERT. Signed, A & M.

*Rev.* The Houses of Parliament and the Thames. NEW HOUSES OF PARLIAMENT. In exergue, C. BARRY ESQ$^{RE}$ ARCHT. — Signed, ALLEN & MOORE BIRM · . Rim milled on obverse and reverse.

Bronze, 27 mm. ?1847 (Eidlitz 55, pl. 5) (BM)

**179c** *Obv.* View of the Houses of Parliament and the Thames. NEW HOUSES OF PARLIAMENT. In exergue, LONDON — C. BARRY ESQ. ARCHITECT — Signed, DAVIS BIRM.

*Rev.* Interior of the House of Lords. INTERIOR OF THE HOUSE OF LORDS.

Bronze, White Metal, 44 mm. 1847 (Eidlitz 53, pl. 5) (BM)

179c

**179d** *Obv.* Head of Queen Victoria to left. Legend: VICTORIA D: G: BRITANNIAR: REGINA F:D:. Signed on truncation, DAVIS.

*Rev.* The Houses of Parliament and the Thames; above radiated, KING — LORDS COMMONS. In exergue, NEW HOUSES OF PARLIAMENT C. BARRY ESQ: ARCHT: — Signed, J. DAVIS BIRM: MEDALLIST BY COMMAND TO H:R:H: PRINCE ALBERT.

Bronze, White Metal, 64 mm. ?1847 (Eidlitz 56, pl. 5) (BM)

**179e** *Obv.* British officers making peace with Chinese mandarins. Angel of peace above. In exergue, THE TRIUMPH OF THE BRITISH ARMS 1842. Signed, DAVIS. BIRM.

*Rev.* The Houses of Parliament and the Thames. As reverse of No. 179d above.

Bronze, 64 mm. ?1847 (Eidlitz 57)

**179f** *Obv.* View of Houses of Parliament. In exergue, PARLIAMENT HOUSE DESTROYED BY FIRE OCT 16 1835 REBUILT 1844–5. Signed, PUBLISHED BY HYAM HYAMS. CORNHILL.

*Rev.* View of the new Royal Exchange. As reverse of No. 146b, but signed TH.

White Metal, 61 mm. ?1847 (BM)

**179g** *Obv.* Crowned bust of Queen Victoria to left, in an open wreath of roses, thistle, shamrock and oak. VICTORIA, QUEEN OF GREAT BRITAIN.

*Rev.* View of the Houses of Parliament and the Thames. Three female figures and symbols. HOUSES OF PARLIAMENT. Above in centre, a triangle, QUEEN LORDS COMMONS, and scrolls inscribed, MAGNA CHARTER and REFORM BILL. Edge milled on obverse and reverse.

Bronze, 51 mm. ?1847 (Eidlitz 52, pl. 5)

**179h** *Obv.* Conjoint heads to left, Queen Victoria and Prince Albert. Around centre panel, QUEEN VICTORIA & PR : ALBERT. Border and wreath of shamrock, oak, etc. Crown and trophies on border at top. (As No. 165k.)

*Rev.* View as above (No. 179g reverse).

White Metal, 51 mm. ?1847 (BM)

**179i** *Obv.* Bust to right of SIR C. BARRY. R. A. ARCHITECT. Signed, LEOPOLD WIENER. ART-UNION OF LONDON 1862.

*Rev.* River front of Houses of Parliament with Victoria Tower behind. In exergue, · COMMENCED 1837 · INAUGURATED 1847 · Signed, J. WIENER.

Bronze, 59 mm. 1862 (Eidlitz 58, pl. 5) (BM)

One of the Art-Union Series (see pp. 213 and 225); published in 1862, two years after the architect's death. (See also Plate 7.)

179i

LONDON, **The Houses of Parliament** *1840–60*

In October 1834 the complex of buildings which formed the old Palace of Westminster burned down; only the medieval Westminster Hall was saved to be incorporated into a new building. In 1835 an architectural competition was held, with the required condition that the 'style of the building be either Gothic or Elizabethan'.[1] The winner was Charles Barry, with drawing assistance from the young A. W. N. Pugin; a collaboration already established for the King Edward VI School at Birmingham (see No. 116). The basic building history after this was: Foundation Stone of superstructure laid, 1840; Opening of House of Lords, 1847; Opening of House of Commons, 1852; completion of main fabric by the time of Barry's death in 1860.[2] After assisting with the competition drawings, Pugin was not involved again until 1844, when he worked on the scheme until his death in 1852. The medals showing the exterior of the building were, in the majority of cases, apparently struck for the formal opening of the House of Lords in 1847 by Queen Victoria (e.g. Nos. 179a, Eidlitz 53; 179c, Eidlitz 56). At that date only the river façade was completed, as a result the medallists have chosen to interpret Barry's final competition design, *not* that as built, e.g. the clock tower (later 'Big Ben') is smaller and of different profile, the central octagon does not have its final form, the Victoria Tower is much lower, and the river façade has a system of stepped buttresses and arched window openings (as at the Birmingham School). The differences in the final scheme are in part demonstrated by J. Wiener's view of 1862 (No. 179g) where the over-all grid of windows, the higher roofs[3] and the great size of the Victoria Tower with its two stages of tall windows (*c.* 1849 and *c.* 1855) are correctly shown. Only the crown of the Victoria Tower in Wiener's view is slightly wrong; this was to be finished off in the mid-1860s by Barry's son, E. M. Barry (1830–80), who then remained as executive architect. Within the building, the all-important chamber of the House of Commons was completed in 1850, but Barry was immediately made to lower the ceiling height, in the face of opinions from Members that this would produce better acoustics; the resulting chamber was finally opened in 1852.[4] The chamber of the House of Lords (see interior on No. 179c) had, however, been well received when it was opened in 1847; it remains an outstanding example of the contribution made by Pugin in the detailing and decoration of the Houses of Parliament, and one of the definitive interiors of the gothic revival.

See: H.-R. Hitchcock, *Early Victorian Architecture*, 43–51, 268–93, pl. ii 20–25, ix 7–25; *Marble Halls*, 1–5; M. H. Port, *The Houses of Parliament*, Yale, 1976.

1. A condition which was to exacerbate the so-called 'battle of the styles' between Classic and Gothic supporters.
2. At a cost at that date of over £2 million.
3. These now show behind the pinnacles; they were made with sheets of iron to be part of Barry's fireproof structural design.
4. Destroyed by fire in the 1940s.

LONDON, Kensington and Chelsea, **Buildings of the Horticultural Society**, near Prince Consort Road *1861*

**180a** *Obv.* Profile portrait in high relief of ALBERT EDWARD PRINCE OF WALES PRESIDENT. Signed, G. MORGAN SC. below bust.

*Rev.* View of the Horticultural Society's arcades and conservatory; in a composition including the Albert Hall and Memorial. LONDON ANNUAL INTERNATIONAL EXHIBITION OF ALL FINE ARTS INDUSTRIES AND INVENTIONS MDCCCLXXIII. Signed, J. GAMBLE DES. G. MORGAN SC.

Gilt Bronze, 71 mm. 1873 (BM)

Inscribed around edge C. HOLMES CATALOGUE NO. 4015.

**180b** *Obv.* Profile portrait head of ALBERT EDWARD PRINCE OF WALES PRESIDENT. Signed below head, G. MORGAN SC. and on truncation, BOEHM.

*Rev.* View of Horticultural Society's arcades (as No. 180a above). Around, LONDON · ANNUAL · INTERNATIONAL · EXHIBITION · OF · ALL · FINE · ARTS · INDUSTRIES · AND · INVENTIONS · On exergue panel, MDCCCLXXIV.

Bronze, 51 mm. 1874 (BM)

The edge of this specimen reads: A. W. FRANKS, M.A. F.S.A., CATALOGUE Nº 6580 AND FOR SERVICES.

180b

This medal was prepared by the Commissioners to be presented to every exhibitor whose name appeared in the official Exhibition Catalogue, and to those who had rendered services.

The medal view shows, in the foreground, the arcades and conservatory which were built on land leased to the Horticultural Society by the 1851 Exhibition Commissioners. This site was next to the future Albert Hall, and the conservatory, designed by Captain Fowke RE, was later to form the southern entrance to the Hall. The northern (crescent) arcades and the central side arcades enclosing the Society's garden were the work of the architect Sydney Smirke.[1] The buildings were opened by the Prince Consort in 1861; the majority were demolished *c.* 1889 (see Imperial

Institute, No. 221), but some related galleries remained[2] until the Imperial redevelopment of the 1960s.

See: *Marble Halls*, 140; *Survey of London*, xxxviii, 124–32, pls. 26–9.

1. 1797–1877. Younger brother of Sir Robert Smirke, and best known for his design of the Reading Room at the British Museum.

2. Pevsner, *London* 2, 257. These had been put up for the International Exhibition of 1871.

LONDON, Redbridge, **Merchant Seamen's Orphan Asylum,** Hermon Hill (Now the Wanstead Hospital) *1861*

181a

**181a** *Obv.* Portrait bust to front, in naval uniform. IN MEMORIAM · ROBERT · C · HALPIN · D.L · J.P · R.N.R.

*Rev.* View, from driveway and grounds, of extensive range of buildings, beneath, SNARESBROOK. Around on border, MERCHANT · SEAMEN'S · ORPHAN · ASYLUM · SWIMMING · CHAMPIONSHIP · MEDAL. Signed, on lower edge of view, VAUGHTON BIRM.

Bronze, 51 mm. ?1860s to 1880s (BM)

The medal view fails to show that this building, by G. S. Clarke, is a design in the Venetian gothic so highly commended by Ruskin. It is of red brick with stone elements, windows, etc., all correctly detailed in the Venetian manner.

See: Pevsner, *Essex,* 413 and illus. 62a.

LONDON, Kensington and Chelsea, **International Exhibition Building,** Cromwell Road *1861–62*

***a. Medals by G. Dowler***

**182a** *Obv.* View of the exhibition building. THE EXHIBITION BUILDING (WEST FRONT VIEW) OPENED MAY 1 1862. In exergue, LENGTH 1200 F: WIDTH 700 F: HEIGHT 100 F: NAVE 85 F: WIDE: COST £300'000.

*Rev.* The date 1862 on a band encircling the globe (as No. 182b below)

White Metal, 26 mm. 1862 (Eidlitz 430, pl. 50) (BM)

**182b** *Obv.* View of the exhibition building. THE INTERNATIONAL EXHIBITION BUILDING. (WEST FRONT VIEW) OPENED MAY 1ST 1862. In exergue, LENGTH 1200 FT, WIDTH 700 FT, HEIGHT 100 FT, NAVE 85 FT WIDE, HEIGHT OF DOMES 250 FT, DIAMR AT BASE 160 FT, COST £300'000. Signed, G. DOWLER BIRMM.

*Rev.* The date 1862 on a band encircling the globe, in a closed laurel wreath. Above, TO COMMEMORATE THE EXHIBITION. Below, OF THE ARTS AND INDUSTRY OF ALL NATIONS. Palm branch at sides.

White Metal, 36 mm. 1862 (Eidlitz 429, pl. 50) (BM)

**182c** *Obv.* View of the exhibition building. THE INTERNATIONAL EXHIBITION. In exergue, AT KENSINGTON OPENED 1. MAY 1862. SOUTH FRONT VIEW. Signed, G. DOWLER.

*Rev.* Inscription: THE INTERNATIONAL EXHIBITION 1862 COVERS A SPACE OF 26 ACRES. LENGTH 1200 FT WIDTH 700 FT HEIGHT 100 FT NAVE 85 FT WIDE. HEIGHT OF DOMES 250 FT AND 100 FT DIAM: AT BASE DESIGNED BY CAPT. FOWKE R.E. CONTRACTORS MESSRS KELK & LUCAS.
White Metal, 38 mm. 1862 (Eidlitz 432, pl. 50)

**182d** *Obv.* Bust to left of H.M.G. MAJESTY QUEEN VICTORIA.
*Rev.* View of THE BUILDING FOR THE INTERNATIONAL EXHIBITION (SOUTH FRONT VIEW) OPENED MAY 1 ST 1862. Below, COVERS A SPACE OF 26 ACRES. LENGTH 1200 FT. WIDTH 700 FT. HEIGHT 100 FT. NAVE 85 FT. WIDE. THE BUILDING IS OF BRICK. THE DOMES ARE OF IRON AND GLASS, HEIGHT 250 FT AND 160 FT DIAM: AT BASE, (THE LARGEST DOMES EVER ERECTED) COST £300,000. Signed, G. DOWLER BIRMM
White Metal, 51 mm. 1862 (BM)

**182e** *Obv.* Head, to right. Around, PRINCE ALBERT CONSORT OF QUEEN VICTORIA BORN AUGT 26 1819. DIED DECR 14 1861.
*Rev.* View of the exhibition building (as reverse of No. 182d).
White Metal, 52 mm. 1862 (BM)

**182f** *Obv.* View of the exhibition building (as reverse of No. 182d).
*Rev.* Inscription, within wreath: EXHIBITION OF THE ARTS AND INDUSTRY OF ALL THE WORLD.
White Metal, 52 mm. 1862 (BM)

**182g** *Obv.* View of 1862 exhibition building (as reverse of No. 182h).
*Rev.* The Crystal Palace Building. THE MIGHT OF INDUSTRY THE GLORY OF PEACE. In exergue, THE CRYSTAL PALACE SYDENHAM. Signed, DOWLER BIRMM.
White Metal, 52 mm.
1862 (Eidlitz 772, pl. 82, and Eidlitz 427) (BM)

**182h** *Obv.* Crowned portrait bust, three-quarters to left of HER MOST GRACIOUS MAJESTY VICTORIA QUEEN OF GREAT BRITAIN.
*Rev.* View of THE BUILDING FOR THE INTERNATIONAL EXHIBITION (SOUTH FRONT VIEW) OPENED MAY 1ST 1862. In exergue, COVERS A SPACE OF 26 ACRES, LENGTH 1200 FT WIDTH 700 FT, HEIGHT 100 FT, NAVE 85 FT WIDE THE BUILDING IS OF BRICK, THE DOMES ARE OF IRON AND GLASS, HEIGHT 250 FT AND 160 FT DIAM: AT BASE (THE LARGEST DOMES EVER ERECTED) COST £300,000. Signed on exergue bar, G. DOWLER BIRM:.
White Metal, 73 mm. 1862 (BM)

**182i** *Obv.* Allegorical group, Britannia in centre with the symbols of industry and peace. Signed, DOWLER BIRM:. Rim milled on obverse and reverse.
*Rev.* View of the building (as reverse of No. 182h above).
White Metal, 74 mm. 1862 (Eidlitz 422, pl. 50)

The obverse is as used for No. 171b of Crystal Palace, Sydenham.

***b. Other Medallists***

**182j** *Obv.* Cameo portraits of Emperor Napoleon III and Queen Victoria. Within cameos, NAPOLEON VICTORIA. Signed, ALLEN & MOORE BIRMINGHAM.

*Rev.* View of INTERNATIONAL EXHIBITION OPENED MAY $1^{ST}$ 1862. In exergue, WEST FRONT VIEW. COVERS A SPACE OF 26 ACRES 1200 $F^{T}$ LONG. 700 $F^{T}$ WIDE DOMES 250 $F^{T}$ HIGH COST £300,000.

White Metal, 39 mm. 1862 (BM)

**182k** *Obv.* Head of Queen Victoria to left. VICTORIA QUEEN OF ENGLAND. Signed, A. BOVY.

*Rev.* West front of the exhibition building. In exergue, UNIVERSAL EXHIBITION OF LONDON 1862 MASSONNET EDITOR.

Bronze, White Metal, 50 mm. (Eidlitz 433, pl. 50) (BM)

A variant of this exists (Eidlitz 434) with inscriptions in French.

182l

**182l** *Obv.* Portrait cameo of Prince Albert, with around, emblems and figures of arts and industry and a mourning angel. In exergue, BORN 26TH AUG. 1819 DIED 14 TH DEC. 1861. Signed, G L REGISTERED 26TH APRIL 1862 LONDON.

*Rev.* View of the exhibition building. Above, IN MEMORY OF HIS ROYÁL HIGHNESS ALBERT PRINCE CONSORT FOUNDER OF THE EXHIBITION OF 1851 & PROJECTOR OF THE EXHIBITION OF 1862. Below, THE INTERNATIONAL EXHIBITION BUILDING (WEST FRONT VIEW) OPENED MAY $1^{ST}$ 1862 LENGTH 1200 FT. WIDTH 700 FT. HEIGHT 100 FT. NAVE 85 FT. WIDE HEIGHT OF DOMES 250 FT. DIAMR. AT BASE 160 FT. COST £300,000. On exergue bar, LONDON.

White Metal, 69 mm. 1862 (BM)

**182m** *Obv.* View of the exhibition building; above it, a flying angel. THE INTERNATIONAL EXHIBITION IN THE $25^{TH}$ YEAR OF THE REIGN OF QUEEN VICTORIA. In exergue, OPENED $1^{ST}$ MAY 1862. DESIGNED BY CAPTAIN FOWKE R.E. — ERECTED BY $MESS^{RS}$ KELK AND LUCAS. Signed OTTLEY $BIRM^{M}$.

*Rev.* Britannia standing, holding laurel branch and surrounded by symbols of industry, art, thrift and transportation (cf. No. 165z).

White Metal, 41 mm. 1862 (Eidlitz 426)

**182n** *Obv.* Crowned bust of the Queen to left. H.M.G. MAJESTY QUEEN VICTORIA. Signed, OTTLEY $BIRM^{M}$. Rim beaded.

*Rev.* View of the exhibition building (as obverse of No. 182m).

White Metal, 41 mm. 1862 (BM)

**182o** *Obv.* Crowned bust of the Queen to left. H.M.G. MAJESTY QUEEN VICTORIA. Signed, OTTLEY $BIRM^{M}$. Rim beaded.

*Rev.* View of the exhibition building; above it, a flying angel. Above, THE INTERNATIONAL EXHIBITION OF 1862. Below, * OPENED $1^{ST}$ MAY 1862 * DESIGNED BY CAPTAIN FOWKE R.E. ERECTED BY $MESS^{RS}$ KELK AND LUCAS. Signed, OTTLEY $BIRM^{M}$.

White Metal, 53 mm. (Eidlitz 424, pl. 50) (BM)

**182p** *Obv.* The exhibition building. Above, INTERNATIONAL EXHIBITION. Below, WEST FRONT. In exergue, OPENED MAY 1ST MDCCCLXII.
*Rev.* Two figures, one with the British flag, the other with a flag inscribed: EUROPE ASIA AFRICA AMERICA AUSTRALASIA. Signed, PINCHES LONDON.
White Metal, 42 mm. (Eidlitz 428, pl. 50) (BM)

**182q** As above (No. 182p) but *without* words WEST FRONT on the obverse inscription.
White Metal, 42 mm. (BM)

**182r** As No. 182p above, but enlarged.
Bronze, White Metal, Aluminium, 51 mm. (BM)

**182s** *Obv.* Head of Prince Albert to left. TO THE COMMEMORATION OF HIS LATE R.H. THE PRINCE CONSORT ALBERT. Signed, SCHNITZPAHN F. Rim beaded.
*Rev.* Interior view of the exhibition building. In exergue, INTERNATIONAL EXHIBITION 1862. STAMPED IN THE BUILDING. At sides, BY H. UHLHORN OF GREVENBROICH PRUSSIA. Signed J. WIENER.
Bronze, 41 mm. (Eidlitz 435, pl. 50) (BM)

**182t** *Obv.* View of west front of the exhibition building. INTERNATIONAL EXHIBITION 1862. In exergue, STAMPED IN THE BUILDING BY H. UHLHORN OF GREVENBROICH PRUSSIA. Signed, J. WIENER.
*Rev.* Interior view (as No. 182s, reverse) of the exhibition building. Signed J. WIENER.
Silver, Bronze, Brass, 41 mm. (Eidlitz 436, pl. 50) (BM)

**182u** *Obv.* Head of Prince Albert to left (as obverse of No. 182s).
*Rev.* View of west front of exhibition building (as obverse of No. 182t).
Silver,* Bronze gilt,* Bronze,* Brass, 41 mm. (BM)*

**182v** *Obv.* Head, to left, of VICTORIA REGINA.
*Rev.* View of INTERNATIONAL EXHIBITION OPENED 1 MAY 1862. In exergue, 1200 F. LONG. 700 F. WIDE DOMES 250 F.HIGH. COVERS A SPACE OF 26 ACRES.
Brass, 22 mm. (BM)

**182w** *Obv.* Head to left of H.M.G.M. QUEEN VICTORIA in a circle of beads.
*Rev.* View of the exhibition building. THE EXHIBITION BUILDING OPENED MAY 1 1862. In exergue, LENGTH 1200 F: WIDTH 700 F: HEIGHT 100 F: NAVE 85 F: WIDE. COST £300'000. Edge milled. Rim beaded on obverse and reverse.
Brass, 23 mm. (Eidlitz 431, pl. 50) (BM)

LONDON, **International Exhibition Building** *1861–62*

After the close of the Great Exhibition of 1851, and with the proceeds from it, the Exhibition Commissioners acquired the whole Kensington Gore estate, between Hyde Park and the Cromwell Road to the south, for development as a national cultural centre. The building for the 1862 International Exhibition was on a site facing the Cromwell Road, now occupied by the Natural History Museum. Designed by Captain Francis Fowke RE[1] for Sir Henry Cole, who hoped that it might be turned into one of the permanent buildings of the development. Certainly the building's outward expression reflected this with heavy masonry walls and pavilion roofs; within (see No. 182s) a fairly traditional 'basilican' section had solid roofs and was lit by clerestorey and aisle windows only (cf. the over-all roof glazing of Paxton's interior, No. 165f). The building also boasted two immense domes; the decoration for these and the rest of the interior, was by J. G. Crace, who, in contrast to Owen Jones, relied heavily on stencilled and other ornamental effects.[2] Francis Fowke's building was demolished after the exhibition and some of the materials ultimately reused on building the Alexandra Palace in north London at Wood Green, Haringey (see No. 196). The site was then bought by the Government to house the Natural History collections of the British Museum. A competition for this building was held in 1864 and out of thirty entrants (and to the horror of the architectural profession) Francis Fowke was declared the winner. Following Fowke's death the next year, Alfred Waterhouse (qv.) was asked to take the design over and finally produced the building we know today.

1. Appointed direct by Cole, and fuel to the architects v. engineers controversy raging at that time. See *Survey of London*, xxxviii, 137–47, pls 30–7.
2. See, *Marble Halls*, 118, where the scheme for a dome is illustrated.

183a

BLACKPOOL, Lancs., **The North Pier** *1862–63*

**183a** *Obv.* Within a scalloped edged frame a view of the pier. BLACKPOOL PIER 1863.

*Rev.* Inscription: THE FIRST PILE WAS SCREWED JUNE 27TH 1862 ...... OPENED TO THE PUBLIC MAY 21ST 1863 LENGTH 1350 FEET · BREADTH 21 FEET.

White Metal, 31 mm. 1863 (BM)

Two other medals with seaside structures are: the Brighton Chain Pier (No. 79a) and, at the end of the century, the Blackpool Tower (No. 222a). This pier was designed by the civil engineer Eugenius Birch and, as built, was 1,405 ft long. In 1874 an 'Indian Pavilion' was added.

184a

LANCASTER, Lancs., **Ripley Hospital,** Ashton Road (now St Thomas's Secondary School) *1856–64*

**184a** *Obv.* View of three linked blocks, forming Orphanage. Below, RIPLEY HOSPITAL LANCASTER.

*Rev.* Inscription: BUILT AND ENDOWED FOR THE EDUCATION & SUPPORT OF ORPHAN CHILDREN BY JULIA RIPLEY OF SPRINGFIELD HALL LANCASTER IN ACCORDANCE WITH THE BENEVOLENT WISHES OF HER LATE HUSBAND THOMAS RIPLEY. INAUGURATED NOV. 3. 1864. Signed, A. SEWARD LANCASTER.

Bronze, 51 mm. 1864 (BM)

Built as an orphanage (see medal reverse) by John Cunningham, the designer of the seamen's lodging house at Liverpool (No. 159). The gothic grimness of the original composition (and its gothic thrill) has now been lost by the removal in the twentieth century of the top storeys with their dormers, pinnacles and chimneys. The remaining, essentially two-storey, school building, has standard pitched slate roofs, a lower flat-topped tower, and a shortened left-hand wing.[1]

See: Pevsner, *N Lancs.*, 162.

1. I am grateful to Mr E. H. Lowe, the District Librarian at Lancaster, for notes and sketches describing this.

LONDON, City, **Guildhall, Hall Interior** *1864–65*

**185a** *Obv.* Royal Coat of Arms on shield with crown, radiated; three other emblazoned shields linked with banners and drapery behind. Motto below, PEACE UNITY CONCORD. Around, · TO COMMEMORATE THE COLONIAL & INDIAN RECEPTION AT THE GUILDHALL · LONDON 1886. Signed, ELKINGTON & C° LONDON.

*Rev.* View of interior of Guildhall rebuilt in 1865. To right, City Sword. To left, Mace. In exergue, City of London shield with motto, DOMINE DIRIGE NOS.

Bronze, 76 mm. 1886 (BM)

One of the City of London series (see p. 215).

This interior view records an interesting phase in the history of roofing John Croxton's great hall (of *c.*1411–*c.*1440). The original roof, possibly of stone arches, was destroyed in the Great Fire of 1666. Sir Christopher Wren replaced this with a flat plaster ceiling in the classical manner. This was in turn replaced in 1864 by the City Architect, Horace Jones, with a pseudo-hammer-beam roof shown on the medal.[1] Jones's roof was destroyed in the fire of 1940 (along with the Guildhall Council Chamber, see No. 206); it has now been replaced by Sir Giles Scott's design of stone arches.

See: J. E. Price, *A Descriptive account of the Guildhall of the City of London*, 1886, 65 ff. with plates; *RIBAJ, Sessional papers*, 26 June 1865, 177–85; Christopher Wilson, 'The Original Design of the City of London Guildhall', *Journal of the British Archaeological Association*, cxxix, 1976, 1–14, pls. 1–6.

1. Designed to resemble a timber prototype; a report to the Corporation in 1864, by the architects M. Digby Wyatt and Edward Roberts, set out to establish the correct form for this. The new roof was illustrated by H. Jones in a paper read to the RIBA, op. cit.

185a

BEWDLEY, Hereford and Worcester, **Wyre Hill Schools** *1868*

186a

**186a** *Obv.* View of small pitch-roofed school building. WYRE HILL HOME MISSION. Below, SCHOOLS BEWDLEY FOUNDED 1859 BY MISS POUNTNEY. Signed, SMITH F. BIRM.

*Rev.* Inscription: TO COMMEMORATE THE OPENING OF THE WYRE HILL SCHOOLS OCT. $9^{TH}$ 1868 SUGGESTED BY THE MAYOR OF BEWDLEY W. H. RYLAND ESQ AND ERECTED BY PUBLIC SUBSCRIPTION.

White Metal, 38 mm. 1868 (BM)

The *P.O. Directory,* 1892, gives this as an infants' school, built for sixty children. The building has recently been in commercial use.

GRETTON GREEN, Near WINCHCOMBE, Gloucs., **Christ Church** *1867–68*

187a

**187a** *Obv.* View of church. CHRIST CHURCH GRETTON.

*Rev.* Inscription: THE FIRST STONE OF THIS CHURCH WAS LAID ON THE $8^{TH}$ DAY OF APRIL 1867. IT WAS ERECTED TO REPLACE THE ORIGINAL CHURCH, WHICH, AFTER HAVING BEEN DEDICATED TO THE SERVICE OF GOD FOR NEARLY 600 YEARS, HAD FALLEN INTO DECAY. $REV^{D}$ J. HARVEY, VICAR OF WINCHCOMBE. $REV^{D}$ R. NOBLE JACKSON, R.N. CURATE OF GRETTON. & OF ST MARY'S, SUDELEY MANOR, $W^{M}$ WARDER, CHURCHWARDEN J. DRAYTON WYATT. ARCHITECT, LONDON COLLINS & CULLIS, BUILDERS, TEWKESBURY. CONSECRATED THE $4^{TH}$ DAY OF JUNE 1868, BY THE RIGHT $REV^{D}$ C. J. ELLICOTT, D.D. LORD BISHOP OF GLOUCESTER AND BRISTOL. Signed, OTTLEY MEDALIST $BIRM^{GM}$.

White Metal, 60 mm. 1868 (Gloucester Museum Cat.N.1635)

By J. Drayton Wyatt, in a thirteenth-century gothic style—as befitting Sir Gilbert Scott's chief draughtsman.

See: Pevsner ed., D. Verey, *Gloucs., The Vale,* 258.

CHESTER, Cheshire, **Town Hall,** Northgate Street *1864–69*

188a

**188a** *Obv.* Conjoint heads to right of ALBERT EDWARD PRINCE OF WALES * PRINCESS ALEXANDRA OF DENMARK. Signed on truncation, J. MOORE.

*Rev.* View of building. Around CHESTER TOWN HALL. Below, T. G. FROST MAYOR 1869.

Copper, 38 mm. 1869

1864–69 by W. H. Lynn. Its style is thirteenth-century gothic, and Lynn was no doubt well aware of E. W. Godwin's influential town hall for nearby Congleton (1861–64) in a similar Gothic and with a central tower. Other sources for the scheme would include continental town halls[1] and the gothic of north Italian cities.

See: Pevsner, *Cheshire,* 158.

1. Cf. the series of medals of public buildings by J. Wiener (qv).

LONDON, Kensington and Chelsea, **The Albert Hall** *1867–71*

**189a** *Obv.* Head to left H.R.H. THE PRINCE OF WALES K.G. · PRESIDENT OF ROYAL COMMISSION · . Signed below truncation, J. S. & A. B. WYON SC.

*Rev.* View of the Albert Hall. In panel, in exergue, STRUCK IN EXHIBITION M.D.CCC.LXXII.

White Metal, 30 mm. 1872 (BM)

189a

**189b** *Obv.* Portrait bust of the Queen. VICTORIA REGINA. Signed, J.S. + A. B. WYON SC.

*Rev.* Elevation of the Albert Hall. STRUCK IN EXHIBITION MDCCCLXXIII.

White Metal, 30 mm. 1873

These medals relate to the London Annual Exhibitions of 1872–74 (see Nos. 180a, b). They show the large hall, which Sir Henry Cole had been striving to establish on the South Kensington cultural site ever since the 1851 Exhibition. The hall as built (1867–71, circular and inspired by the form of a Roman amphitheatre) was based on an initial model of 1864 by Captain Francis Fowke RE.[1] This design was then developed by his successor, Major-General Henry Scott, and was finished in the same combination of red-purple brick and terracotta decoration as Fowke's other buildings. The external facing also includes a bold mosaic frieze which represents 'The Triumph of Art and Letters'. The Commissioners of the 1851 exhibition donated the land, and the building was financed by the sale, on long leases, of individual seats and boxes.

See: Pevsner, *London 2*, 255; *Survey of London*, xxxviii, 177–95, pls 48–54.

1. Illus: *Marble Halls,* 142.

SALTAIRE, West Yorks., **The Institute** *1867–71*

**190a** *Obv.* Head of Queen Victoria, to left. Around on border, VICTORIA REG: JUBILEE YEAR· 1887 ·. Signed below head, HEATON.

*Rev.* View of Saltaire Institute. Around on border, THE ROYAL YORKSHIRE JUBILEE EXHIBITION · 1887 ·. In exergue, SALTAIRE.

White Metal, 32 mm. 1887 (Leeds City Museum)

190a

Saltaire is named after Sir Titus Salt (1803–76), who in 1853 moved his textile mills to a single new structure on a country site by the River Aire outside Shipley. Around this mill he laid out a workers' housing estate, built to high standards for that time, and planned it to incorporate a number of community buildings. The architects for the estate generally, and the Institute of 1867–71 shown on the medal above,[1] were the Bradford firm of Lockwood and Mawson.

See: Pevsner, *Yorks., W Riding,* 427–28; *Sir Titus Salt, baronet* by Robert Balgarnie, 1877 (reprint 1970, Settle, Brenton).

1. The accommodation provided in the Institute 'for the moral and physical welfare of the community' included lecture halls for 800 and 200, library, reading room, laboratory, classrooms, and gymnasium. See Balgarnie, op. cit. 228–32.

191a

TUNBRIDGE WELLS, Kent, **St John's Church,** St John's Road
*1858 and 1871*

**191a** *Obv.* Bust to left of H.R.H. PRINCESS MARY ADELAIDE · DUCHESS OF TECK · Signed on truncation, SALE BIRM.
*Rev.* View of church. VISITED TUNBRIDGE WELLS · WEDNESDAY MAY 20 1896 ·.
Aluminium, 39 mm. 1896 (BM)

The medal shows the church as it was in 1896, prior to major alterations; to help meet the cost of these a Royal Bazaar was opened by the Duchess of Teck (see obverse). The original church was designed by A. D. Gough of London in 1858. The north transept was added in 1864 and a north aisle in 1871. The further alterations of 1896–97 included the building of a south aisle, removal of the spire, and rebuilding of the tower at the west end with entrance lobbies to either side.[1] The architects for all the works of 1864, 1871, and 1897 were the local firm of H. H. & E. Cronk, and the original design only survives in the eastern parts.

See: Pevsner, ed., and J. Newman, *W Kent and The Weald,* 555.

1. When reconsecrated in June 1897, the medal illustrated was deposited as part of a memorial in one of the top stones of the new Victoria Tower.

192a

GODALMING, Surrey, **Charterhouse School** *1870–72*

**192a** *Obv.* Charterhouse School building. FLOREAT ÆTERNVM 1811. 1872. 1897.
*Rev.* Arms of school · IN . MEM . CARTH . DOM . COLL . TRANSLATI . ANNOS XXV.
Silver, 23 mm. 1897 (Watt Coll.)

This small medal, with suspension loop, celebrates the twenty-fifth anniversary of the new buildings at Godalming for Charterhouse School. They had been designed by P. C. Hardwick,[1] and were completed 1872 to house the school when it moved from Finsbury (cf. No. 59a). Stone built, gothic, in a picturesque and essentially asymmetrical composition.

See: Pevsner, ed., and Ian Nairn, *Surrey,* 121, 122; *Builder,* xxviii, 1870, 566, 567.

1. Hardwick's perspective of the scheme (*c.* 1869) inscribed 'First Sketch' is reproduced in *RIBAJ* xli, 1934, 726.

193a

MANCHESTER, **St Thomas's Girls' School,** Niven Street, Ardwick
*1872*

**193a** *Obv.* View of ST THOMAS'S GIRLS' SCHOOL ARDWICK.
*Rev.* Inscription, around: DEDICATION STONE LAID BY HUGH BIRLEY ESQ. M.P. NOV 30. 1872. In centre, THE FEAR OF THE LORD IS THE BEGINNING OF WISDOM.
White Metal, 45 mm. 1872 (BM)

The medal shows the Girls' School block of 1872 facing Niven (formerly North) Street, and opposite St Thomas's Church, Ardwick Green North. The architects may well have been Royle and Bennett, who had designed the very similar Boys' School block of 1870 at the other end of the site, i.e.

facing Paddock Street.[1] The buildings still stand in the midst of a twentieth-century urban renewal area.[2]

1. An unattributed nineteenth-century illustration in Manchester Central Library shows the Boys' block and is signed 'Royle & Bennett. Archts.' It is stylistically similar to the Girls' block, and is also of six bays with gabled first floor windows.

2. Both blocks have dated dedication stones at first floor level; that for the Girls' School carries the same biblical text as the medal reverse. I am grateful to Mr L. Sutton for his notes on Ardwick, and to Mr P. H. K. Smith for visiting the site.

### WINCHESTER, Hants, **The Guildhall** *1871–73*

**194a** *Obv.* View of main façade of building with central tower. THE NEW GUILDHALL WINCHESTER.

*Rev.* Coat of arms of city. Above, FOUNDATION STONE LAID BY THE R$^{T}$ HON. LORD VISCOUNT EVERSLEY DEC$^{R}$ 22$^{ND}$ 1871. Below, OPENED MAY 14 $^{TH}$ 1873 BY THE R$^{T}$ HON. LORD SELBORNE LORD HIGH CHANCELLOR OF GREAT BRITAIN.

White Metal, 45 mm. 1873 (BM)

194a

Won in a competition by Jeffery & Skiller. Built in 1871–73 in a thirteenth-century gothic, with a dominant central tower and steep French pavilion roofs to emphasize the end bays. Cf. the earlier Chester Town Hall (No. 188).

See: Pevsner, *Hants,* 697.

### BLACKBURN, Lancs., **Library and Museum** *1872–74*

**195a** *Obv.* View of building. FREE LIBRARY AND MUSEUM. In exergue, BLACKBURN — · — OPENED JUNE 11$^{TH}$ 1874. Signed, OTTLEY BIRM$^{M}$.

*Rev.* Coat of arms with crest and motto. Around, ART AND GENERAL EXHIBITION 1874 JOHN PICKOP E$^{SQ}$ MAYOR.

Bronze, White Metal, 45 mm. 1874 (BM)

195a

In a simple thirteenth-century gothic manner. It is an early work of T. E. Collcutt, then in the partnership of Woodgate and Collcutt.

See: Pevsner *N Lancs.,* 64.

### LONDON, Haringey, **Alexandra Palace,** Wood Green *1874–75*

**196a** *Obv.* View of building and grounds. THE ALEXANDRA PALACE. In exergue, THE GROUND PLAN OF THIS BUILDING OCCUPIES AN AREA OF $7\frac{1}{2}$ ACRES. DIMENSIONS OF GRAND CENTRAL HALL 386 F$^{T}$ BY 184 F$^{T}$.

*Rev.* Inscription within a wreath. THE ALEXANDRA PALACE OPENED TO THE PUBLIC MAY DAY 1875.

White Metal, 51 mm. 1875 (BM)

196a

Following the success of the re-erected and enlarged Crystal Palace at Sydenham in south London (see No. 171), it was decided to provide a similar entertainment area for north London. After the close of the 1862 International Exhibition (see No. 182) much of the building materials were purchased and used to construct the 'first' Alexandra Palace;

dominating the design was one of the original large domes placed over the central transept. This building opened in May 1873, but was destroyed by fire the next month. The medal view commemorates the opening of a 'second', rebuilt, Alexandra Palace in 1875. The architect of both first and second buildings was John Johnson; he incorporated in the rebuilt version a main hall, concert hall, theatre, exhibition spaces, picture galleries, and restaurants. The building has been considerably altered in the twentieth century.

MANCHESTER, **Manchester Town Hall,** Albert Square *1868–77*

197a

**197a** *Obv.* View of main front to Albert Square. Around, TOWN HALL MANCHESTER. In exergue, city arms and motto. Signed, PINCHES MAN$^{B}$.

*Rev.* Inscription: TO COMMEMORATE THE OPENING OF THE MANCHESTER NEW TOWN HALL BY THE MAYOR ABEL HEYWOOD ESQ. SEP$^{TR}$ 13$^{TH}$ 1877. Surrounded by a wreath.

White Metal, 40 mm. 1877 (BM)

Alfred Waterhouse was the ultimate winner of the open competition in 1867, and his proposal was built 1868–77. This immense work, which was to replace an earlier, smaller, town hall by Francis Goodwin (qv.), has been described as the 'highest manifestation' of the use of the nineteenth-century gothic idiom in any Victorian public building.[1] It also reflected one of Waterhouse's great strengths as an architect (and the one which gained him the commission): his masterly grasp of complex planning problems. In this building the accommodation is organised around the perimeter of a triangular site to serve a central Great Hall (cf. the programme at earlier city halls at Liverpool and Leeds). This hall is richly finished with Early English gothic details, and a hammerbeam roof, to act as a suitable climax to the whole design; for this Waterhouse would have had Horace Jones's recently re-roofed Guildhall interior (see No. 185) as an interesting analogy in the fourteenth-century style.

See: Pevsner, *S Lancs.* 281–282; F. Jenkins, in *Country Life,* 16 February 1967, 336–39; *Marble Halls,* 87—hall interior.

1. Goodhart-Rendel, in *Victorian Architecture,* 1963, 98.

DERBY, Derbyshire, **Free Library and Museum,** Wardwick *1878–79*

198a

**198a** *Obv.* View of buildings. Around, DERBY FREE LIBRARY & MUSEUM JUNE . 28 . 1879.

*Rev.* Inscription TO COMMEMORATE THE OPENING JUNE 28$^{TH}$ 1879 OF THE LIBRARY & MUSEUM BY M.T. BASS ESQ.M.P. THE DONOR.

Brass, 32 mm. 1879 (Leeds City Museum)

This small, unsigned, and crudely executed design represents the Victorian architectural medal at its worst. The buildings, by Richard Knill Freeman of Bolton, are of brick in a gothic style 'with a Franco-Flemish central tower', and with moulded tile decoration.[1]

See: Pevsner, *Derbs.* 118.

1. It was specially illustrated in *Builder,* 17 July 1879 as No. VIII in the series 'The architecture of our large Provincial Towns'.

BIRMINGHAM, West Midlands, **The Mason Science College,** Edmund Street *1875–80*

**199a** *Obv.* Bust to right of SIR JOSIAH MASON BORN FEB: XXIII MDCCXCV. THE FOUNDER OF THE ALMSHOUSES & ORPHANAGE AT ERDINGTON & SCIENCE COLLEGE BIRMINGHAM. Signed on truncation, J. MOORE. F.

*Rev.* Elevation of entrance front in gothic style, emphasised by central dormer and oriel windows. In exergue, THE MASON SCIENCE COLLEGE J. A. COSSINS ARCHITECT. Around on border FIRST STONE LAID FEB. XXIII MDCCCLXXV AND OPENED OCT. 1. MDCCCLXXX BY SIR JOSIAH MASON.

Bronze, 51 mm. 1880 (BM)

199a

The elevation shows an example of red-brick gothic which was considered appropriate for an educational building of 1880. Designed by J. A. Cossins, the building opened in 1880 with four science professors, five demonstrators, and ninety-five day students. It rapidly became the nucleus of the new University of Birmingham which, after its charter in 1900, was rehoused at Edgbaston on the campus designed by Sir Aston Webb (qv). The Mason College building continued in use until the early 1960s, when it was demolished to make way for the new civic centre.

BIRMINGHAM, West Midlands, **Birmingham and Midland Institute,** Extension in Paradise Street *1881*

**200a** *Obv.* Bust, half left, of SIR WILLIAM SIEMENS, D.C.L., LL.D., F.R.S., PRESIDENT. Signed on truncation, JOS$^{H}$ MOORE F.

*Rev.* Elevation of four-bay, four-storey, gothic façade of the extension building. In left panel, BIRMINGHAM & MIDLAND INSTITUTE. In right panel, BIRMINGHAM — INCORPORATED 1854.

Bronze, 63 mm. *c.* 1881[1] (BM)

This very fine medal shows the exuberant gothic design which was used to extend E. M. Barry's original Italianate building of 1857 (cf. the nearby Mason College, No. 199). Designed by J. H. Chamberlain in 1881, each floor is given a markedly different outward expression and only the entrance doors break the pattern. Demolished in the 1960s.

See: *VCH, Warwicks.*, vol. 7, 230, 231, describe the function of the Institute.

1. Grant gives 1854 as date for this medal, apparently from the inscription only, whereas the building is of 1881.

200a

BRADFORD, West Yorks., **Technical College,** Great Horton Road
*1880–82*

201a

**201a** *Obv.* View of main front of BRADFORD TECHNICAL COLLEGE * LABOR OMNIA VINCIT *. Signed on exergue bar, FATTORINI + SONS BRADFORD.

*Rev.* Allegorical scene with the lamp of learning being offered to a workman. Around, BRADFORD FINE ART AND INDUSTRIAL EXHIBITION * 1882 *.

Silver, 43 mm. 1882 (Watt Coll.)

Designed by T. C. Hope, of Hope & Jardine, following a competition, and opened in 1882 by the Prince of Wales. The medal shows the almost symmetrical Italianate façade with giant Corinthian half-columns to the right of the centre, and similar pilasters to the left.

See: J. Ayers, *Architecture in Bradford,* 1972, 25, illus. 44.

LONDON, City, **City of London School for Boys,** Victoria Embankment
*1881–82*

**202a** *Obv.* Conjoint portraits of Prince and Princess of Wales, to right. ALBERT EDWARD ALEXANDRA. Signed, J. S. & A. B. WYON.

*Rev.* Elevation of main façade. CITY OF LONDON SCHOOL NEW BUILDINGS OPENED BY HIS ROYAL HIGHNESS THE PRINCE OF WALES 12 DEC. 1882. Signed, J. S. & A. B. WYON.

Bronze, 78 mm. 1882 (BM)

Struck as one of the City of London series (see p. 215), to mark the occasion of the opening.

The original City of London School (see No. 120) had proved very successful, but suffered from a cramped site and too few small classrooms, i.e. those for classes of thirty to forty. A competition was held, and a replacement building to the design of Davis & Emmanuel was put up, 1881–82, on a site at the Victoria Embankment. The medal shows the

202a

main block facing the river, of which a new 'Great Hall' occupies the entire first floor and roof volume. The completed façade was of Portland stone, with polished red granite shafts to the windows; the roof had green slates and a copper flêche, Statues of Bacon, More, Shakespeare, Milton and Newton stand in niches of the spandrels. The *Builder* described it at the time as 'in the style of the Italian Renaissance', while Pevsner refers to it as 'an amazingly unscholastic façade rather like a permanent Exhibition Palace'.

See: *Builder,* 15 May 1880, illus. and plans, 602–5, and 16 December 1882, 789, 790; Pevsner, *London 1*, 273.

WORCESTER, Hereford and Worcester, **Exhibition Building,** Shrub Hill Road *1864 on and 1882*

**203a** *Obv.* Elevation of entrance façade. WORCESTERSHIRE EXHIBITION OPENED JULY 18TH 1882.

*Rev.* The arms of the County, impaling those of the City of Worcester. Around on border, FLOREAT SEMPER FIDELIS CIVITAS.

Silver, Bronze, White Metal,* 38 mm. 1882 (BM)*

203a

The die was by Henry Smith, of Birmingham. About two thousand medals were struck in White Metal, some of which were bronzed and others gilt. Six were struck in silver and twelve in bronze.[1]

The building had originally been put up as part of the premises of the Worcester Engine Works Company, founded in 1864. The design was prepared that year by Thomas Dickson, then assistant to the Engineer of the West Midland Railway. The Company proved a financial disaster, and the works, covering most of the Shrub Hill Estate, were closed and sold in 1871. Following this a variety of industries were housed until, in 1882, the buildings were adapted for the Worcestershire Exhibition;[2] the latter was highly successful and helped to provide funds for a local Technical and Commercial Institute. Since 1903 the whole complex (which represents an interesting example of Victorian industrial architecture) has been in continuous use as engineering workshops. The main frontage shown on the medal is of brick with stone facings.[3]

1. William A. Cotton, *Coins, Tokens and Medals of Worcestershire,* 1885, 146.
2. This exhibition aimed to give the best possible illustration of the progress at that date in the industries of the county. *VCH, Worcs.,* vol. 2, 299.
3. I am grateful to Mr John Algie for his notes on the history of this building.

204a

HUDDERSFIELD, West Yorks., **Technical School and Mechanics Institution,** Queensgate *1881–83*

**204a** *Obv.* Bust of Duke of Albany, facing to right. Around on border, BEAUMONT PARK OPENED BY H.R.H. THE DUKE OF ALBANY · OCT $13^{TH}$ 1883.

*Rev.* View of three-storey, turreted, building. Around, TECHNICAL SCHOOL & MECHANICS INSTITUTION. Below, HUDDERSFIELD. Signed on exergue bar, PEARCE + SONS.

Brass, 38 mm. 1883 (Leeds City Museum)

By Edward Hughes. The building, which now forms part of Huddersfield Polytechnic, was opened in July 1883 by the Duke of Somerset. It had originally been planned that the Duke of Albany would officiate; he did not however visit Huddersfield until he opened a public park donated by H. F. Beaumont (see medal obverse).

205a

OLDHAM, Greater Manchester, **Library and Art Gallery,** Union Street *1881–83*

**205a** *Obv.* Civic arms, wreath and inscription: FINE ART AND INDUSTRIAL EXHIBITION OPENED BY SIR JOHN LUBBOCK BART F.R.S. D.C.L. M.P. AUG $1^{ST}$ 1883. Signed, G.F. + S.

*Rev.* View of building. FREE REFERENCE LIBRARY & MUSEUM. Below, OLDHAM. Signed, HINTON & ARMISTEAD.

White Metal, 39 mm. 1883 (BM)

Built in 1881–83. The medal commemorates the opening by Sir John Lubbock. The architect was Thomas Mitchell.

19a

COVENTRY, West Midlands, **St John's Schools,** Gloucester Street/Percy Street *1884*

See the reverse of No. 19a which shows St John's church reopened after restoration in 1877. The medal was struck in 1884 upon the opening of the School.

Designed by the architect N. W. Vickers; completed by C. Haywood Jnr, in 1884. This building replaced an earlier St John's Schools, Holyhead Road and Bangor Street, of 1839. Red brick with Bath stone dressings; accommodation for 550 boys and girls. It was demolished in 1964.

LONDON, City, **Guildhall, New Council Chamber** *1883–84*

**206a** *Obv.* Allegorical scene: crowned figure of the City of London, at a throne supported by Commerce and Magistracy, addressing Liberty, Liberality and Learning.[1] A riband inscribed with city motto, DOMINE DIRIGE NOS, and mace and sword. Signed on exergue bar, J. S. & A. B. WYON.

*Rev.* View of interior of the Chamber showing an almost complete half section of the polygonal space. On the frame to the view: THE NEW COUNCIL CHAMBER GUILDHALL LONDON OPENED 2ND OCTOBER 1884. Signed, J. S. & A. B. WYON SC. H. JONES ARCHITECT.

Bronze, 76 mm. (BM)

One of the City of London series (see p. 215). (See also Plate 11.)

Designed by the City Architect, Horace Jones, and built 1883–84 to the north side of the Guildhall. This superbly detailed medal shows the interior of the twelve-sided space, 54 ft in diameter and 61 ft high. The columns and arches were of Hopton Wood stone, the roof structure and lantern of oak. The Chamber seated 206 members with a dais for the Lord Mayor and Aldermen; the statue shown behind the dais is that of George III, brought from the previous domed and top lit Council Chamber designed by George Dance (qv.).[2] The canopied screens, separating the space from a surrounding corridor, are carved with the arms of City Companies; in the spandrel panels above the windows are frescos representing the trades and crafts of the Livery Companies. The building was destroyed, together with Horace Jones's Guildhall roof (No. 185), in the fire of 1940.

See: J. E. Price, *A Descriptive Account of the Guildhall of the City of London,* 1886, 176–77.

1. C. Welch, *Numismata Londinensia,* 1894, 129.
2. Demolished 1908. It foreshadowed the work of Dance's pupil John Soane. See D. Stroud, *George Dance,* 1971, 113–16, pl. 36.

206a

LONDON, Camden, **Holborn Restaurant,** Holborn *1883–85 and 1894*

**207a** *Obv.* Group of figures in evening dress against an elaborate architectural interior, with columns and lower flights of a staircase. HOLBORN RESTAURANT. ESTD 1874.

*Rev.* View of ballroom interior PRESENTED BY THE PROPRIETORS to (with scroll for name and date to be engraved).[1]

Lead, 70 mm. 1895[G] (BM)

The Holborn Restaurant was established 1874, in a property near the corner of Little Queen Street and Holborn. The gradual acquisition and redevelopment of this whole corner site by the Restaurant included the construction of two new blocks, one to Holborn (1883) and one to Little Queen Street (1885); both these were designed by Archer and Green. A final rounded corner block linking these two was designed by T. E. Collcutt (1894). The whole group was demolished in 1955.

See: *Builder,* 31 January 1885, 164 ff. for illustration of blocks by Archer and Green.

1. Example illustrated has 'J. H. Brown Esq., Jan 16th 1897.'

207a

LONDON, Wandsworth, **The Albert Palace,** Battersea Park *1885*

208a

**208a** *Obv.* View of pleasure grounds, with building in background.

*Rev.* Inscription: ALBERT PALACE · BATTERSEA · OPEN JUNE 1885.

White Metal, 18 mm. 1885 (BM)

Opened 1885, it provided picture galleries (with paintings for sale), entertainment and restaurant areas. The building, which stood on land at the south-east end of Battersea Park, had followed on from encouragement given by Prince Albert to plans for developing a south London recreation park. Only the central transept and one wing of the structure were ever completed; as it did not prove a financial success it was closed in 1888 and soon afterwards demolished to make way for Albert Palace Mansions and Battersea College of Technology.[1]

1. See: *Historic Views of Battersea 1752–1885,* Wandsworth Libraries Department, pl. 6.

WOLVERHAMPTON, West Midlands, **Art Gallery,** Lichfield Street
*1883–85*

**209a** *Obv.* Corner view of Italianate building. HONOUR TO ART, TO INDUSTRY SUCCESS — 30 MAY 1884. In exergue, ART GALLERY.

*Rev.* Coats of arms, with supporting shields, in a quatrefoil frame. Around, WOLVERHAMPTON STAFFORDSHIRE · FINE ARTS & INDUSTRIAL EXHIBITION ·.

White Metal, 45 mm. 1884 (BM)

209a

By J. A. Chatwin in a functional Italianate style. There are windows to the ground floor, but the main first floor galleries are top lit. The blank walls have long relief panels related to the building's use.

See: Pevsner, *Staffs.* 317.

BURNLEY, Lancs., **Burnley and District Hospital,** Thursby Road (now the Victoria Hospital) *1884–86*

**210a** *Obv.* Within ornamented frame an elevation of main building with circular domed wing blocks. Above, BURNLEY & DISTRICT HOSPITAL. Below J. BUTTERWORTH ESQ. J.P. CHAIRMAN.

*Rev.* Inscription, within decorated border: FOUNDATION STONE LAID BY COL. THURSBY MAY 24 TH 1884.

Bronze, 38 mm. 1884 (BM)

210a

Opened by Prince Albert Victor on 13 October 1886. The architects were W. Waddington & Sons, Burnley; they designed the two surgical wards as circular wings, each of 60 ft diameter for thirty-six patients.[1] The original buildings shown have been considerably added to, and now constitute the Victoria Hospital.

1. Barrett's *Directory of Burnley and District,* 1937.

HINDLEY, Greater Manchester, **Library and Museum,** Market Street
*1887*

**211a** *Obv.* Profile head of Queen Victoria, crowned, to left. Around on border, A · VICTORIA · D · G · BRITANNIARUM · REGINA · F · D · INDIAE · IMPERATRIX · 1887 ·. Signed on truncation, ELKINGTON & CO.

*Rev.* Elevation of Hindley Library building. Below, LEYLAND FREE LIBRARY & MUSEUM. Around on border, HINDLEY JUBILEE CELEBRATION ✠ 1837 · 1887 ✠ .

Silver, 51 mm. 1887 (Watt Coll.)

211a

The Hindley Library, built 1887, houses the Leyland collection. The architect for the building was Thomas Worthington, with John Elgood.

See: Pevsner, *S Lancs.* 123.

LONDON, Camden, **New College,** Finchley Road *1887*

**212a** *Obv.* Elevation of buildings, with central gate tower. Above two shields, left and right, and legend: NEW COLLEGE. LONDON FOUNDED A.D. 1850. Below, in a panel, FORMED BY THE FEDERATION OF HOMERTON COLLEGE FOUNDED 1696 — COWARD COLLEGE FOUNDED 1738 — HIGHBURY COLLEGE FOUNDED 1778. Signed, ALLAN WYON SC.

*Rev.* In three panels: (*left*) Seated figure studying, above, SEARCH THE SCRIPTURES JOHN · V · · 39; (*centre*) A preacher at the pulpit, above, PREACH CHRIST CRUCIFIED 1 · COR · 1 · 23 (*right*) Widow and child with visitor, above, VISIT THE FATHERLESS JAMES · 1 · 27. Below the left and right panels, PRINCIPALS OF NEW COLLEGE J. HARRIS D.D. 1850 R. HALLEY D.D. 1857 S. NEWTH D.D. 1872 R.V. PRYCE D.D. 1889. Signed in centre panel, ALLAN WYON SC.

Bronze plaquette, 84 × 54 mm (rectangular). 1889^G (BM)

Brick buildings, with majolica trim and Tudor type windows, by M. P. Manning.

See: Pevsner, *London 2*, 189.

212a

LONDON, Tower Hamlets, **'The Peoples Palace'**, Mile End Road *1885–87*

**213a** *Obv.* Elevation of building, with tower to left-hand side. Surrounded by a wreath of floral and gardening emblems. Around, THE PEOPLES PALACE AND EAST LONDON HORTICULTURAL SOCIETY. 1894. Signed, RESTALL BIRM.

*Rev.* Wreath of fruit and flowers. (Blank for inscription.) On edge, J. A. R.

Silver, 38 mm. 1894 (Watt Coll.)[1]

213a

An attempt to provide for the cultural, intellectual and recreational needs of the East End of London. Built in 1885–87, from the altered plans of the London School Board architect E. R. Robson,[2] it was developed with the aid of money, and ideals, established by Barber Beaumont for his earlier Philosophical Institution (see No. 129). The accommodation included concert hall, library, sports centre with swimming baths, technical school and workshops.[2] An isolated clock tower was added in 1890 and a new auditorium to the west in 1936.

See: Pevsner, *London 2*, 420–21.

1. Three copies presented 1911, 1912, 1913.
2. 'Grecian gone gaudy', Pevsner, op. cit.
3. Wheatly, *London Past and Present,* 1891, vol. 2, 542.

LONDON, Westminster, **National Liberal Club,** Whitehall Place *1884–87*

**214a** *Obv.* Portrait bust of Gladstone. Around, IN COMMEMORATION OF THE FOUNDATION STONE OF THE NATIONAL LIBERAL CLUB BEING LAID BY THE RT : HON : W. E. GLADSTONE M.P. OCT[R] 1884.

*Rev.* Perspective view of building, from corner tower. Signed, KENNING LONDON.

Bronze, 77 mm. 1884

Designed by Alfred Waterhouse to adjoin the exuberant Whitehall Court block of flats (1884) by Archer and Green (qv.), and to maintain the same height. The medal shows an exaggerated perspective view of the gothic corner tower of the Waterhouse building.

See: Pevsner, *London 1*, 585.

214a

215a

MANCHESTER, **Jubilee Exhibition Buildings**, Trafford Park *1886–87*

**215a** *Obv.* Veiled head, to left, of Queen Victoria. Around, ROYAL JUBILEE EXHIBITION MANCHESTER 1887. Signed, HEATON.

*Rev.* View of buildings. Below, OPENED BY T.R.H. THE PRINCE & PRINCESS OF WALES MAY 3$^{RD}$ 1887.

Bronze, White Metal, 45 mm. 1887 (BM)

Portrait head as No. 22a, St Giles Cripplegate, also published in the Jubilee year.

Designed by the local firm of Maxwell and Tuke; now demolished. The view of the exhibition buildings given on the reverse of this medal demonstrates how the medallic portrayal of architecture in the nineteenth century might mean poor delineation and perspective; poor detailing; a superficial indication of finishes.

216a

TRURO, Cornwall, **The Cathedral (Choir and Transepts)** *1880–87*

**216a** *Obv.* View of cathedral from south. In exergue, TRURO CATHEDRAL.

*Rev.* Shield with arms of Bishopric surmounted by a mitre; around, a laurel wreath. Inscription in centre: FOUNDATION STONE LAID BY H.R.H. PRINCE OF WALES MAY 20$^{TH}$ 1880 CONSECRATED BY THE LORD BISHOP OF TRURO NOV 3$^{RD}$ 1887.

White Metal, 44 mm. 1887 (BM)

The Act establishing a new diocese at Truro was passed in 1876, and in 1878 J. L. Pearson was commissioned as architect for the new cathedral. The view shows his Early English gothic design, which was not to be finally completed until 1910; it also shows the aisle of the old St Mary's Church (to the right of the south transept) which was incorporated into the new building as a third south choir aisle. At the 1887 consecration, for which the medal was struck, only the choir and transepts were complete; the nave and central towers were built 1898–1903, and the west towers 1903–10.[1] The three spires are a characteristic Pearson feature, and are one in a fine series of designs (e.g. St Michael, Croydon) based on the gothic church towers of northern France.

See: Pevsner, *Cornwall,* 233; B. Clarke, *Church Builders,* 203–5.

1. The later parts were completed to the original design, after Pearson's death, by his son, F. L. Pearson.

217a

HARROGATE, North Yorks., **Royal Bath Hospital,** Cornwall Road *1888–89*

**217a** *Obv.* Municipal coat of arms. Below, HARROGATE BATH HOSPITAL & RAWSON CONVALESCENT HOME OPENED JULY 18$^{TH}$ 1889 BY H.R.H. PRINCE ALBERT VICTOR OF WALES K.G.

*Rev.* View of hospital buildings. Signed on exergue bar, A. FATTORINI HARROGATE.

White Metal, 38 mm. 1889 (Leeds City Museum)

Built in 1888–89 in a Tudor style by Worthington and Elgood of Manchester.

See: Pevsner, *Yorks. & W Riding,* 249.

BIRMINGHAM, West Midlands, **Victoria Law Courts,** Corporation Street *1887–1891*

**218a** *Obv.* Head of Queen Victoria to left, crowned and with veil. IN COMMEMORATION OF QUEEN VICTORIA'S JUBILEE. 1887. ✠.

*Rev.* View of buildings. BIRMINGHAM LAW COURTS. Below, FOUNDATION STONE LAID BY QUEEN VICTORIA MARCH 23 RD 1887.

Bronze, 38 mm. 1887 (BM)

218a

Built 1887–91 to the competition-winning design of Aston Webb & Ingress Bell. For Birmingham this was a landmark in its nineteenth-century architectural history, and the Law Courts' consistent use of red ornamental terracotta with red brick gave impetus to a new, and popular, local idiom.[1] The style chosen by Webb and Bell was French domestic gothic of *c.*1500, i.e. 'early Tudor' in England, and the buildings group informally around a great hall with hammer-beam roof. Another poor medal for a major work of architecture.

See: Pevsner, *Warwicks.* 117, 118; *Building News,* 13 July 1886, 24 July 1891.

1. The competition assessor was Alfred Waterhouse (qv.), already a great enthusiast for the use of terracotta and brick.

KETTERING, Northants, **School,** Montagu Street *1892*

**219a** *Obv.* View of school buildings. On scrolls, KETTERING EDUCATION AUTHORITY. Signed, VAUGHTON · BIRM.

*Rev.* Inscription: AWARDED TO (blank panel) FOR PUNCTUAL ATTENDANCE EVERY TIME THE SCHOOL WAS OPENED DURING THE —— SCHOOL YEARS ENDED (blank panel).

Silver, 39 mm. ?1890s (Watt Coll.)[1]

219a

The building shown is the present Kettering Secondary School for Boys, formerly known as the Stamford Road School. Opened in 1892; the design of J. A. Gotch and his partner Charles Saunders.

1. This copy for 1904–9.

BRISTOL, Avon, **Exhibition Building,** Colston Avenue *1893*

**220a** *Obv.* View of exhibition building, 1893.

*Rev.* Inscription, above spray of oak leaves: BRISTOL INDUSTRIAL AND FINE ART EXHIBITION 1893.

Pewter, 38 mm. 1893 (BM)

220a

The medal shows the temporary wooden building opened 28 August 1893 and closed 31 January 1894. Designed by the civil engineer E. S. Sinnott of Clifton,[1] construction was started in the spring of 1893 at a cost of £11,000. The 520 ft by 120 ft structure was dismantled immediately after the exhibition.[2]

1. According to the *Clifton Chronicle* for 30 August 1893, p. 5.
2. Details are given in *The annals of Bristol in the nineteenth century (concluded) 1887–1900,* by John Latimer, 1902, p. 35. Photographs of the building appear in Reece Winstone, *Bristol in 1840s,* 1960.

LONDON, Kensington and Chelsea, **Imperial Institute**, Prince Consort Road *1887–93*

**221a** *Obv.* Portrait bust of Queen Victoria to left, crowned and veiled. Around, VICTORIA · DEI GRA · BRITT · REG ·.

*Rev.* View of main façade. THE IMPERIAL INSTITUTE OF THE UNITED KINGDOM THE COLONIES AND INDIA. Signed on exergue bar, JENKINS BIRM.

White Metal, 38 mm. ?1893 (BM)

The portrait of the Queen is after T. Brock's 'Old Head' type, e.g. as the coinage struck 1893–1900.

221b

**221b** *Obv.* Portrait bust of Queen Victoria to left, with Jubilee crown. Around, VICTORIA REGINA ET IMPERATRIX. Signed on truncation, TB.

*Rev.* View of Institute building with 'Colcutt' Tower. Ribbed border to medal. On banner in background, THE IMPERIAL INSTITUTE TO COMMEMORATE THE JUBILEE OF VICTORIA R ET I 1887. In exergue, ALBERT EDWARD P. PRESIDENT. Signed, J P, at side of exergue panel.

Silver, 38 mm. 1893 (BM)

This medal is illustrated in Forrer, vol. 6, 388, under 'Waterlow & Sons Ltd', who are credited with its issue. Forrer, vol. 4, 548, indicates that the medal was engraved by John H. Pinches (see reverse) and De Saulles (see obverse); in the latter case the head is from a rejected obverse design by T. Brock for the coinage of 1892, hence the initials on the truncation.

The concept of an 'Imperial Institute' resulted from the Colonial Exhibition in London of 1886 (for which medal No. 185a was produced). The site finally selected lay in Kensington, behind the Albert Hall and then part occupied by the Horticultural Society Gardens and Arcades (see No. 180a, b); the latter were accordingly demolished in 1889. Following a limited competition, the scheme by T. E. Collcutt was begun in 1887, and provided for a rather vague programme including reception hall, library, conference rooms and exhibition galleries. The symbolic function[1] was, however, well served by Collcutt's great, brick-banded, stone building with its main 280-ft tower and copper domes. The style was a singular blend, described by the contemporary *Building News* as 'a phase of Renaissance in which the English details have been combined with Flemish characteristics'. Queen Victoria laid the foundation stone in July 1887 and opened the building in May 1893. The whole of the Imperial Institute, other than the main tower, was demolished by the 1960s to make way for a new Imperial College.

See: Pevsner, *London 2*, 257; *Marble Halls*, 141; *Survey of London*, xxxviii, 220–7, pls 68–9.

1. Originally to commemorate the Golden Jubilee and to represent 'Arts, Manufactures and Commerce of the Queen's Colonial and Indian Empires'.

BLACKPOOL, Lancs., **The Tower** *1891–94*

**222a** *Obv.* View, in trefoil, of the Tower. In left panel, TOWER BLACKPOOL. In right panel, HEIGHT 450 FEET. Below, MAXWELL & TUKE ARCHITECTS.

*Rev.* Coat of arms with motto, PROGRESS. Below, FOUNDATION STONE LAID SEPT. $25^{TH}$ 1891 BY SIR MATTHEW WHITE RIDLEY BART. M.P. JOHN BICKERSTAFFE MAYOR.

White Metal, 38 mm. 1891 (Leeds City Museum)

Completed height is 518 ft, to compare with the Eiffel Tower (1889) of 984 ft. By Maxwell & Tuke, with R. J. J. Read. (B. Jones, *Follies and Grottoes,* London, 1974, 209.)

222a

COLNE, Lancs., **Town Hall,** Albert Street *1894*

**223a** *Obv.* View of building. On border, CHARTER DAY CELEBRATIONS · $14^{TH}$ $SEP^{T}$ 1895.

*Rev.* Coat of arms. On border, BOROUGH OF COLNE · INCORPORATED $17^{TH}$ JULY 1895 · Signed, BUSFIELD COLNE.

Silver, Bronze, White Metal, 39 mm. 1895 (BM)

**223b** *Obv.* View of building. On border, CHARTER DAY CELEBRATIONS · $14^{TH}$ $SEP^{T}$ 1895. Signed in exergue, EASTWOOD COLNE.

*Rev.* Coat of arms. On border, BOROUGH OF COLNE · INCORPORATED $17^{TH}$ JULY 1895.

Silver, Bronze, 32 mm. 1895 (BM)

By J. W. and R. F. Beaumont in 1894. Gothic windows set within a rather rectilinear structural frame. Central front tower in the tradition of Chester (No. 188) and Congleton. Pevsner calls it 'really entirely undistinguished'.

See: Pevsner, *N Lancs.* 106.

223a

LONDON, City, **Bishopsgate Institute,** Bishopsgate *1893–94*

**224a** *Obv.* Elevation of entrance gate tower. BISHOPSGATE FOUNDATION. Signed in exergue, NEAL.

*Rev.* Inscription: BISHOPSGATE INSTITUTE FOUNDATION STONE LAID BY REV. W. ROGERS MAY $13^{TH}$ 1893.

Silver, 39 mm. 1893 (BM)

The medal shows the broad arched entrance to Harrison Townsend's design of 1894. It departed from the more usual gothic or classical formats, and used instead an original combination of ideas derived from the Arts and Crafts movement, and from the work of H. H. Richardson in America. The frieze of stylized trees, the oddly detailed parapets and the dominant arch were all to be reworked, and much improved, in Townsend's next and most important building, the Whitechapel Art Gallery.

See: Pevsner, *London 1*, 195.

224a

LONDON, City, **Tower Bridge** *1886–94*

**225a** *Obv.* Conjoint busts to left: Queen Victoria with, on either side, the Prince and Princess of Wales.

*Rev.* View of the bridge from downstream on the South Bank. In the background are the Tower of London, the Monument, and the Dome of St Paul's. The bascules of the bridge are raised and a steam yacht is passing through. Around, TOWER BRIDGE OPENED 30TH JUNE 1894. Below, ON BEHALF OF HER MAJESTY QUEEN VICTORIA BY HRH THE PRINCE OF WALES. The City of London shield is in the centre at bottom. Signed on top of exergue bar, F BOWCHER FECIT.

Bronze, 76 mm. 1894 (BM)

A City of London series medal (see p. 215).

Designed (1885)[1] by the City Architect, Horace Jones, in association with the civil engineer John Wolfe Barry. It provided a low-level bascule bridge that would allow ocean-going ships access to the Pool of London; the original studies for this suggested to Jones 'a feudal style of architecture, and that the bridge should be raised and lowered by chains somewhat like the drawbridge of a Crusaders castle'.[2] The medal view shows how this 'feudal style' was to be maintained (after the architect's death in 1887) and was used to clad the steel framework of the two towers. The view also indicates in the background the Tower of London, and its proximity to the completely different scale of this uniquely nineteenth-century creation.

See: Charles Welch, *History of the Tower Bridge,* 1894.

1. The City of London had been discussing alternatives since 1875. See *Marble Halls,* 120–22; 121 shows Jones's early bascule design of 1878.

2. *History of Tower Bridge,* op. cit. 203.

225a

HALIFAX, West Yorks., **Municipal Technical School,** Francis Street (now Percival Whitley College) *1893–95*

**226a** *Obv.* View of college building. In exergue, on shields, 1893 and coat of arms. Around on border, MUNICIPAL · TECHNICAL · SCHOOL HALIFAX · YORKSHIRE.

*Rev.* Engineering and technical instruments. Above, the sun radiant. Around, ENGINEERING · EMPLOYERS · FEDERATION * HALIFAX DISTRICT * Within, MECHANICAL ENGINEERING FIFTH YEAR'S COURSE.

Bronze, 45 mm. ?1890s (BM)[1]

226a

The foundation stone was laid 24 May 1893 and the building completed 1895. The original stone faced buildings, by Jackson and Fox, have since been extended.

See: Pevsner, *W. Riding*, 235.

1. This copy presented 1917.

LONDON, City, **Cripplegate Institute,** Golden Lane *1894–96*

**227a** *Obv.* View of building from corner; radiated. In foreground seated figures of learning and the arts. On scrolls CRIPPLEGATE INSTITUTE · FOUNDED · 1896 ·

*Rev.* Wreath (blank for inscription).

Silver, 50 mm. 1890s (Watt Coll.)[1]

227a

Of red brick, by Smith and Hammond. Opened by the Lord Mayor in 1896, it contained a concert hall, library and reading rooms. The Institute vacated the building in 1969, and it has since been used by the Arts Educational Schools.

1. This copy presented 1904.

BILSTON, West Midlands,
**Technical, Science and Art Schools,** Mount Pleasant *1897*
**Waterworks,** Bratch, Womburne *1897*

**228a** *Obv.* View of Waterworks building. BILSTON WATERWORKS. Around on border, SUPPLY BEGAN JULY 2ND 1896 COMPLETED DIAMOND JUBILEE YEAR 1897 ★ GOD SAVE THE QUEEN ★ .

*Rev.* View of schools building. Around on border, BILSTON TECHNICAL SCIENCE & ART SCHOOLS OPENED A.D. 1897 ★ LET BILSTON FLOURISH ★ Signed, S.

Bronze, White Metal, 54 mm. 1897 (BM)

228a

The Technical Schools were designed by the Town Engineer, C. L. N. Wilson. They now form an annexe to Bilston College of Further Education.

The Waterworks were architect designed by Baldwin Latham, of Westminster, with C. L. N. Wilson as site engineer. They are still in use as a pumping station.

LONDON, Westminster, **St Gabriel's Church,** Warwick Square

*1854 and 1897*

**229a** *Obv.* Bust of Queen Victoria to left, crowned and with veil. VICTORIA REGINA.

*Rev.* View of church. Above, S$^{\text{T}}$ GABRIEL'S CHURCH, PIMLICO REV. RUPERT H. MORRIS VICAR. In exergue, TO COMMEMORATE THE 60$^{\text{TH}}$ YEAR OF HER MAJESTYS REIGN 1837–1897 "FEAR GOD — HONOUR THE KING".

Lead, bronzed, 78 mm. 1897 (BM)

The obverse of this medal is identical to No. 90a (St Peter's, Eaton Square), and therefore after T. Brock (see Grant); size, material and format are also identical.

The main body of the church, with south-west tower and spire, is in a decorated style of Thomas Cundy Jnr, 1854. The outer aisles were added by Arthur Baker in 1897—the year of the Jubilee which the medal celebrates.

See: Pevsner, *London 1*, 427.

229a

NORTHWICH, Cheshire, **Verdin Technical School,** London Road *1897*

**230a** *Obv.* Head of Queen Victoria to left, with tiara and veil. Around on border, VICTORIA QUEEN OF GREAT BRITAIN AND IRELAND : EMPRESS OF INDIA · ASCENDED THE THRONE 1837 · COMPLETED 60 TH YEAR OF REIGN 1897.

*Rev.* View of buildings with coat of arms above. Around, on scrolls, VERDIN TECHNICAL SCHOOL & GYMNASIUM DISTRICT OF NORTHWICH G. B. CLIFF CHAIRMAN.

White Metal, 38 mm. 1897 (BM)

Built of brick and red terracotta, 1897 by Joseph Cawley.

See: Pevsner, *Cheshire,* 296.

230a

BRISTOL, Avon, **Cabot Memorial Tower,** Brandon Hill *1897–98*

**231a** *Obv.* Aerial view of the tower. Above symbolic crown and bird. THE CABOT TOWER.

*Rev.* Inscription: THE CABOT TOWER BRISTOL OPENED 6 SEP 1898 BY THE MARQUESS OF DUFFERIN.

Silver, 37 mm. 1898 (BM)

By the architect W. V. Gough. The tower is rock-faced, with canopied balconies, and has unconventional gothic details.

See: Pevsner, *N Som. and Bristol,* 423.

231a

# ARCHITECTS AND DESIGNERS 4

These entries relate to individuals and firms responsible for designing buildings listed in the medallic catalogue (Section 3 and Index, Section 2). Where a building shown had already been the subject of major rebuilding or addition, and the architect is referred to in the architectural notes, a relevant biographical entry is also provided.

Below each biographical entry are listed all the buildings in the medallic index by that architect, together with their completion dates and the key reference numbers.

Each biography is intended to provide the basic dates and major works of the architect, and also to offer a brief context for reading the building notes given with the medallic entry. Emphasis has been placed on providing information about less well-known names, particularly local firms of architects not usually indexed in the main architectural histories. For the more important designers reference is made to suitable key publications with their specialist biographies, e.g. *The Imagination of Vanbrugh* by Laurence Whistler, or *Hawksmoor* by Kerry Downes.

In compiling this section individual architects and designers have been quoted for buildings and works of the seventeenth century and later. Prior to that, for the question of the role of the architect or master mason, initial reference should be made to *The Mediaeval Architect* by John Harvey; in addition a discussion of what constitutes 'an architect' is set out in the preface to the invaluable *Biographical Dictionary of English Architects 1661–1840* by H. M. Colvin. For further information on architects and designers of the second half of the nineteenth century, reference should be made to obituary notices in the *Builder* and the *RIBAJ*, and also to the individual entries in *Marble Halls* and the *Catalogue of the RIBA Drawings Collection (RIBA Dwgs Coll.).*

Where architectural medals show portraits of the architect (e.g. as in the Art-Union series) this is noted, either as a reference to the medallic index if the medal also portrays a building, or by providing separate medallic details below the biographical entry.

AINGER, Alfred (1797–1859). Entered the RA Schools 1816, and later ran a small London practice. He designed the North London Hospital, 1833 (rebuilt 1897–1906, and now University College Hospital).

*See*: Colvin.

**157 London, The Orphan Working School** (*c.* 1847)

ANDREWS, George Townsend (1805–55). Trained at the RA Schools, and as an assistant to the country house architect, P. F. Robinson; he worked with Robinson on the rebuilding of York County Gaol (1826–*c.* 1836). Andrews then set up his own York practice and is best known for his railway buildings, e.g. stations at York (1840–41), Scarborough, Whitby (1847), Hull (1847–48), and Richmond (1848). In 1852–53 he added a hotel block across the end of the York platforms—an early example of the traditional railway terminus layout.[1] Andrews's works also include two churches in Yorkshire, and St John's College, York (1845).

*See*: Colvin; *RIBA Dwgs Coll.* (A); *Marble Halls*, 69, 103, 106.

**163 Richmond,** North Yorks., **School** (1849)

1. Details of this hotel building are given in RCHM, *City of York,* vol. iii, 1972, 54–56.

ARCHER, Thomas (*c.* 1668–1743). After education at Trinity College, Oxford, and travel abroad, he obtained a court appointment in 1705 which he maintained during the reigns of Anne, George I, and George II. He was made one of the Commissioners for building fifty new churches under the Act of 1711. Archer's houses and churches bear the stamp of the late Roman baroque—a taste rare in England at the time—and reflect the design approach of Italian architects such as Borromini. His first big church commission was at Birmingham (1709–15, see below); taken together with his London churches of St Paul, Deptford (1712–30) and St John, Smith Square (1714–28), this group shows Archer's original approach to design and planning problems and his development of the English baroque style.

*See*: Colvin; *RIBA Dwgs Coll.* (A); Marcus Whiffen, *Thomas Archer,* Art & Technics, London, 1950.

**41 St Philip, Birmingham** (now the Cathedral) (1715)

ARCHER & GREEN. A London architectural partnership of the 1870s and 1880s, formed by Thomas Archer, who had been chief assistant to Samuel Dawkes,[1] and Green, one of Dawkes's pupils. The partnership was responsible for Cambridge Gate (1875); two parts of the Holborn Restaurant site (completed by T. E. Collcutt (qv.) in 1894); the Café Royal; Tooths' Picture Galleries; Whitehall Court flats, and the Hyde Park Hotel. The latter two were completed by Thomas Archer (in association with Francis Hooper) after the partnership was dissolved in 1889.

*See*: *The Builder's Journal*, 5 November 1895, pp. 200, 201 for an interview with Thomas Archer; Pevsner, *London 1 and 2.*

**207 London, Holborn Restaurant** (1885)

1. S. W. Dawkes (1811–80) formerly of Gloucester, cf. entry on Hamilton and Medland.

AUSTIN, George (*c.* 1786–1848). Appointed *c.* 1820 Surveyor to Canterbury Cathedral. He found it in a dangerous state and set about a programme of extensive repairs and conservation. The decayed north-west tower was taken down and Austin prepared a new design to correspond with that at the south-west angle; this was built 1832 to 1841. He was succeeded as surveyor to the cathedral by his son H. G. Austin.

*See*: Colvin; *Builder*, vii, 1849, 205.

**1 Canterbury Cathedral:** North-west tower (1841)

BAKER, Arthur (1841–96). A pupil of Scott's. His design for St Paul, Vicarage Gate, Kensington, 1887 is described by Pevsner (*London 2*, 245) as a serious study in brick in the Early English style. In the Pimlico church (below) he added outer aisles to the building by Cundy Jnr (qv.).

**229 London, St Gabriel,** Warwick Square (1897)

BARRY, Sir Charles (1795–1860). One of the nineteenth century's most influential architects, he helped to inaugurate the use of the 'Italianate' style that became so popular for both public and domestic buildings. In the Traveller's Club (1830) and Reform Club (1837) he showed how the prototype of the Italian palazzo of Florence or Rome could provide a viable alternative to the familiar tradition of Graeco–Roman buildings. This theme was developed further in his Bridgewater House (1849) and Halifax Town Hall (design 1859). Barry was articled to a firm of London surveyors and, after an extensive 'Grand Tour', set up in practice on his return in 1820. His first works were churches and all were in the gothic style. The Brighton church (below) resulted from a competition, as did the King Edward VI Grammar School in Birmingham; the latter was his earliest major building in the gothic style and he was assisted by A. W. N. Pugin (qv.) and the stonecarver J. Thomas. This school at Birmingham was to form a prelude to his *magnum opus*—the Houses of Parliament, for which he won the competition in 1836 and where he was again assisted by Pugin and Thomas. As well as his many public buildings, which included the Royal Institution (now City Art Gallery) Manchester (1835) and the Board of Trade Building, Whitehall (1845), he was also responsible for a great output of domestic architecture, e.g. Bowood (1834), Highclere (1837), Harewood (1843–50), Clivedon (1851), Clumber (1857). Elected RA 1844. Knighted 1852. Was an FRS. Vice President of the RIBA, and received their Gold Medal 1850. Two years after his death he was commemorated by the Art Union of London (qv.) with a medal in their series. His son E. M. Barry became a prominent architect and completed his father's work at Westminster.

*See*: Revd A. Barry, *The Life and Works of Sir Charles Barry*, 1867; *Builder*, xviii, 1860, 305–7, 321, 322–24, 342–44; H.-R. Hitchcock, *Early Victorian Architecture*, 162–219; 'Sir Charles Barry' in P. Ferriday ed., *Victorian Architecture*, 1963; *Marble Halls*, 1–5, 16, 38, 96; Colvin; *RIBA Dwgs Coll.* (B). His portrait is on the obverse of the Art-Union medal (No. 179i).

**91 Brighton, St Peter's Church** (1828)
**111 Manchester, Royal Institution** (1835)
**116 Birmingham, King Edward VI Grammar School** (1837)
**179 Westminster, Houses of Parliament** (1860)

BEAUMONT, J. W. (1848–1931). Articled to Sir James Picton of Liverpool; set up in practice in Manchester 1872. Designed town halls at Hyde and Colne; Whitworth Art Galleries, Manchester; Whitworth Hospital, Matlock; also banks, libraries and newspaper offices. In 1900 and 1919 took his sons into partnership. President, Manchester Society of Architects, 1903–4.

*See*: *RIBAJ*, v, 38, 10 September 1931, 739.

**223 Colne,** Lancs., **Town Hall** (1894)

BEDFORD, Francis (1784–1858). Between 1811 and 1813 travelled in Greece and made drawings and notes for publication by the Society of Dilettanti. Exhibited at RA 1814–32. Designed a number of London churches in the 1820s and Christ Church, Tunstall, Staffs., 1830–31.

*See*: Colvin; *RIBA Dwgs Coll.* (B) itemises his travel sketches with J. P. Gandy-Deering (qv.).

**83 London, Southwark, St George's Church,** Wells Way (1824)

BLORE, Edward (1787–1879). Initially a skilled architectural draughtsman with an enthusiasm for gothic works. Provided illustrations for John Britton in his *English Cathedrals*. In 1816 introduced to Sir Walter Scott, who took him up and employed him to design his house Abbotsford. This began a prosperous career for Blore as a country house architect—with all his works in the gothic, Tudor or Elizabethan styles of which he was keen to promote a revival. Appointed 'special architect' to King William IV, and initially to Queen Victoria; for them he carried out works at Windsor Castle (after Wyatville's death) and Buckingham Palace (after dismissal of Nash). From 1827 to 1849 he was surveyor to Westminster Abbey. His works include the rebuilding of much of Lambeth Palace (1824–28) and the building for the Pitt Press, Cambridge (1831–32). He left forty-eight volumes of architectural drawings now in the BM (Add. MSS. 42000–42047).

*See*: Colvin; *RIBA Dwgs Coll.* (B).

**155 Worsley Hall** (1846)

BOURNE, William (*fl.* 1840–60). Given in Goodhart-Rendel's index (RIBA) as 'of Dudley'. This index lists six churches by Bourne in the Dudley and Birmingham area. These include St James, Eve Hill, Dudley (1840) to which the school below relates.

**137 Dudley, St James School** (1842)

BRANDON, David (1813–97). RA student 1830. From 1831 to 1851 in partnership with T. H. Wyatt (qv.) as Wyatt and Brandon. After 1851 his main works included: The Junior Carlton Club, Pall Mall, London (1866–69); Sidbury Manor, Devon (1853); Eagle Life Office, Pall Mall. (For joint works see: Wyatt, T. H.)

*See*: *RIBAJ* iv, 1897, 144; *RIBA Dwgs Coll.* (B).

BRODRICK, Cuthbert (1822–1905). Articled to Henry Lockwood of Hull in 1837 and stayed with him as assistant until 1844. Went on a study tour of England, France and Italy and returned to open his own practice in Hull 1845. Brodrick designed the Royal Institution, Hull (1852), and on winning the competition (1853) for Leeds Town Hall opened an office there. His major works include Leeds Corn Exchange (1860–63); Hull Town Hall (1861–66); Grand Hotel Scarborough (1862–67); Institute of Science, Art and Literature, Leeds (1865–68). He entered, unsuccessfully, several major competitions, then gave up practice abruptly in 1869 and retired to France.

*See*: D. Linstrum, 'Cuthbert Brodrick' in *Journal of the Royal Society of Arts,* cxix (1971), 72–87; *Builder,* lxxxviii (1905), 272; *Marble Halls,* 57, 83, 86, 128; *RIBA Dwgs Coll.* (B).

**175 Leeds Town Hall** (1858)

BROOKES, William McIntosh (*fl.* 1822–44). Practised in London; exhibited RA 1829 to 1838. His buildings include churches in Surrey at Albury (1840 and 1841): Epsom (1844); Dorking (see below); Thames Ditton (additions 1826).

*See*: Colvin.

**117 Dorking,** Surrey, **St Martin's Church** (1837)

BROOKS, William (1787–1867). Entered the Royal Academy Schools, 1808; exhibited RA 1803 to 1815. His London buildings include: The London Institution, Finsbury Circus (1819); Islington, College of the Church Missionary Society; Finsbury, Unitarian Chapel (both illus.: Elmes, *Metropolitan Improvements*, 1831).

*See*: Colvin.

**69 Dudley, St Thomas's Church** (1818)

BUNNING, James Bunstone (1802–63). Articled to George Smith, who was Surveyor to the Mercers' and Coopers' Company in the City of London. Set up in private practice and *c.* 1826 became Borough Surveyor of Bethnal Green; to this he soon added six other Surveyorships (including those to the Thames Tunnel and the Foundling Hospital). His first major new building was the City of London School (1835–37); he was later I. K. Brunel's architect for the Hungerford Suspension Bridge (1837–45). In 1843 Bunning was elected 'Clerk of the City's Works' (title changed to 'Architect' to the Corporation in 1847), and in this capacity his designs for London included: Holloway Prison (1852), Billingsgate Market (1852), Caledonian Market (1855), and the Coal Exchange (1847–49). It was the last building, with its cast-iron rotunda, which was

Bunning's masterpiece, and is now seen as one of the significant monuments of the early Victorian era. His many responsibilities for the City of London also included planning 'improvements', and he prepared the layout for the New Cannon Street opened in 1854.

*See*: H.-R. Hitchcock, *Early Victorian Architecture*, 317–20, for an account of Bunning's role as City Architect; *Marble Halls*, 50, 52, 53, 70, 77, 78, 92, which illustrate all the City works referred to above; *RIBA Dwgs Coll.* (B); obituary, *Builder*, xxi, 1863, 782–83.

**120 City of London School** (1837)
**161 London, The Coal Exchange** (1849)

BURTON, Decimus (1800–81). Son of the successful London builder, and architect, James Burton.[1] Started in practice 1821 and was one of the foundation members of the IBA. Initially involved with public buildings, he later devoted himself to domestic and garden architecture; he also carried out several planning schemes, e.g. at Folkestone, at Bournemouth, and the Calverley Estate, Tunbridge Wells (1828–52). In his many buildings, public and domestic, he remained a supporter of the classical traditions of the Regency period; only a few churches, e.g. Holy Trinity, Tunbridge Wells, are in a gothic idiom. Burton's works include: The Colosseum, Regent's Park (1823–27); Hyde Park, Ionic Screen and Arch, Constitution Hill (1828); Athenaeum Club (1827–30); Palm House, Kew (1844–48, with Richard Turner); Grimston Park, Yorks. (1840–50).

*See*: Colvin; *RIBA Dwgs Coll.* (B).

**109 London, Charing Cross Hospital** (1834)

1. James Burton built many of Nash's terraces in Regent's Park and was prepared to take sites to make the Regent Street scheme a success. In return Nash was able to help his son at the start of his architectural career.

CARPENTER, Richard Cromwell (1812–55). Practised in London. Had a central interest in the correct use of gothic for new buildings and church restorations; by the age of twenty he had designed a gothic church for Islington (unbuilt). Was a friend of Pugin (qv.); associated with the Cambridge Camden Society; became one of the Incorporated Church Building Society's two model architects (the other was Butterfield). In 1840–41 helped to restore Old Shoreham, Sussex; this led to a meeting with Canon Woodard who became the client for Carpenter's two masterpieces: Hurstpierpoint College (1851–53) and Lancing College (1854 onwards).

*See*: B. Clarke, *Church Builders of the Nineteenth Century*, 116–17; *RIBA Dwgs Coll.* (C–F); obituary, *Builder*, xiii, 1855, 165.

**152 Birmingham, St Andrew, Bordesley** (1846)

CAWLEY, Joseph (*fl.* 1890s).

**230 Northwich,** Cheshire, **Verdin Technical School** (1897)

CHAMBERLAIN, John Henry (1831–83). An important local architect during the rapid expansion of Birmingham in the second half of the nineteenth century. He was educated in Leicester, then went to practise in Birmingham from 1858—first on his own, later in partnership with W. Martin. Responsible for the detailed drawings and design for the 1870s redecoration of the Town Hall. Works include Municipal School of Art (1885), in an exuberant Gothic style, cf. the medal below; 'Highbury' (1879–80)—a house for the politician Joseph Chamberlain (no relation).

*See*: *Builder*, 1883 (11), 570, Pevsner, *Warwicks.*

**200 Birmingham and Midland Institute**, extension (1881)

CHAMBERS, Sir William (1723–96). Born in Sweden, and had an initial education in England, at Ripon. 1740–49 voyaging with the Swedish East India Company, but on his travels studying architecture. After a formal training in Paris and in Rome 1749–55, he returned to London to build up a practice largely involved with country houses. In 1761 appointed, jointly with Robert Adam, as 'Architect of the Works' by the King. Due to his influence with George III (to whom he had been architectural tutor) he became a driving force in setting up the Royal Academy, and its first Treasurer. Knighted by the King of Sweden in 1770, Chambers was allowed to assume the title in England.

From 1776 until his death he was chiefly involved with designing and organising the new public offices at Somerset House. He published three influential books: *Treatise on Civil Architecture* (1759), which became the standard English treatise on the use of the Orders; *Designs for Chinese Buildings* (1757); and *Dissertation on Oriental Gardening* (1772). His theories on gardening were put into practice at Kew Palace where he planned the grounds and designed orangery, temples and pagoda.

*See*: Colvin; *RIBA Dwgs Coll.* (C-F); J. Harris, *Sir William Chambers*, 1970. His portrait is on the obverse of the Art-Union medal below.[1]

**52 London, Somerset House** (1786)

1. This medal, together with a note on Chambers, is given in H. A. Grueber's 'English Personal Medals from 1760', *Num. Chron.* 1888, 281,282. He has Chambers's date of birth incorrect.

CHANTRELL, Robert Dennis (*fl.* 1807–68). Pupil of Sir John Soane, 1807–14. In practice in Leeds from 1819 to 1846. His major work was Leeds parish church (see below). He designed over twenty other churches in Yorkshire as well as the Public Baths (1820) and the Literary and Philosophical Institution (1821) in Leeds.

*See*: Colvin; *RIBA Dwgs Coll.* (C-F).

**132 Leeds, Parish Church of St Peter** (1841)

CHATWIN, Julius Alfred (1829–1907). Educated at King Edward VI's School, Birmingham, and London University; in 1851 articled to Sir Charles Barry (qv.) and assisted with drawings for the House of Lords. Then returned to Birmingham and built up a large practice. Work in the city included eight churches (and many restorations); also Lloyds Bank, Temple Row (1864), Grand Hotel (1875).

*See*: Ware, 62; B. Clarke, *Church Builders of the Nineteenth Century*, 252.

**209 Wolverhampton, Art Gallery** (1885)

CLARKE, George Somers (1825–82). Trained in the office of Sir Charles Barry (qv.). He later illustrated *The New Palace of Westminster* together with J. Johnson and J. Thomas. He was among the architects selected to compete for the Foreign Office, St Pancras Station, and Law Courts competitions. He built up a large private practice and was an exponent of the 'Ruskinian' gothic. Works in this style included the Wanstead Hospital (see below); Bank of Australasia, Lothbury (1866); Wyford Court, Oxon. (1872). His son Somers Clarke (1841–1926) was a well-known church architect and antiquary.

*See*: *Builder*, xlviii, 1882, 60, 94, 160; *RIBA Dwgs Coll.* (C-F).

**181 London, Merchant Seamen's Orphan Asylum,** Wanstead (1861)

COCKERELL, Charles Robert (1788–1863). Second son of S. P. Cockerell, in whose office he began his training. Between 1810 and 1817 he travelled abroad in Greece, Asia Minor and Italy. On his return he prepared drawings of antiquities seen, and lectured on Greek and Roman architecture. In 1819 Cockerell succeeded his father as Surveyor to St Paul's Cathedral and became fully involved with architectural practice. His first independent work was the enlargement of the Old Schools at Harrow (see medal below); although for this he selected a Tudor style, most of his public buildings reflect his admiration for the works of classical antiquity together with an interest in the use of applied sculpture. His rejected design (1839) for the Royal Exchange is now recognised as by far the finest that was submitted (illus: Ferriday, xxxvi; Watkin, pl. 121, 123, 124); major executed works include: the Ashmolean Museum and Taylor Institute, Oxford (1841–45); Westminster Fire Office (1829–30, dem.); Cambridge University Library (1837–40); completion of Fitzwilliam Museum (1845–63) and of St George's Hall, Liverpool (after the death of Elmes, qv.). To these must be added the various branch offices which he designed for the Bank of England, after being appointed their architect in 1833. He was President of the RIBA 1860–61 and first recipient in 1848 of the Royal Gold Medal. He was elected RA in 1836, and between 1840 and 1857 he was Professor of Architecture of the RA Schools.

*See*: Colvin; *RIBA Dwgs Coll.* (C-F); P. Ferriday, ed., *Victorian Architecture*—essay by E. M. Dodd on C. R. Cockerell; *Marble Halls*, 49, 79–81; D. Watkin, *C. R. Cockerell*, London, 1974.

**73 Harrow School,** new wing (1820)
**120 Liverpool, St George's Hall,** completion (1854)

COLLCUTT, Thomas Edward (1840–1924). Having trained in the office of G. E. Street, who was then working on the Law Courts, Collcutt developed a large and successful practice. An early work at Blackburn (on the medal below), was apparently in association with Woodgate;[1] from *c.* 1908 he was in partnership with Stanley Hamp. His main work was the Imperial Institute (1887–93) won in a limited competition; it displayed his characteristic striping of brick on stone. Other works included Wakefield Town Hall (1877–80); Savoy Hotel, London (1887 and 1903–4); Wigmore Hall, London (1890); Midland Bank, Ludgate Hill (1890). RIBA Gold Medal 1902. President RIBA 1906–8.

*See*: *RIBAJ*, 18 October 1924, 666–68; *RIBA Dwgs Coll.* (C-F); *Marble Halls*, 141.

**195 Blackburn, Free Library and Museum** (1874)
**221 London, Imperial Institute** (1893)
**207 London, Holborn Restaurant**—final phase (1894)

1. Blackburn Free Library is given as by T. E. Collcutt in the *RIBAJ*, 8 November 1924, 24; Pevsner, *N Lancs.* gives Woodgate and Collcutt.

COSSINS, J. A. One of a group of Birmingham architects who were responsible for the main public and commercial buildings of the Victorian city centre.[1] His works included the former Liberal Club (1885) in a gothic format, and the Birmingham and Midland Ear, Nose and Throat Hospital (1891).

**199 Birmingham, The Mason Science College** (1880)

1. E.g. J. H. Chamberlain (qv.), Yeoville Thomason, W. H. Ward. See *VCH, Warwicks.*, vol. 7, 45.

CRONK, Henry Hickman (*c.* 1838–1902). Senior partner in the Tunbridge Wells practice of H. H. & E. Cronk. They were architects for St Peter's Church; St John's Church (1897); rebuilding of the General Hospital (1870); and new houses in the town.

*See*: *Builder*, 1902, (11), 611.

**191 Tunbridge Wells, St John**—additions (1871)

CUNDY, Thomas, Jnr (1790–1867). Eldest son of Thomas Cundy, who in 1821 became Surveyor to Lord Grosvenor's London estates. Thomas Junior succeeded to his father's practice and position as Surveyor. He designed a number of gothic churches in London.

*See*: Colvin.

**229 Pimlico, St Gabriel's Church,** Warwick Square (1854)

CUNNINGHAM, John (1799–1873). Studied at Edinburgh to be an architectural draughtsman. After a short visit to New York returned to England 1834 and set up a practice in Liverpool. He built churches, institutions and mansions in the area; for a while he was in partnership with Arthur Holme, a former pupil of Thomas Rickman (qv.).

*See*: Ware.

**159 Liverpool, The Sailor's Home** (1848)
**184 Lancaster, Ripley Hospital** (1864)

DANCE, George, Jnr. (1741–1825). The youngest son of George Dance (d. 1768) whom he succeeded as Clerk of the City (of London) Works in 1768. This was a position which occupied most of his time[1] and which he held until 1815. His most famous work for the City was Newgate Prison (1770–78) with its overtones of Piranesi.[2] In 1777 he designed the Common Council Chamber at the Guildhall and in 1788–89 rebuilt the south front in gothic style. As a town planner Dance was responsible for a variety of schemes in London, including Finsbury Circus (1777); he also proposed imaginative improvements for the Port of London. In 1768 he became one of the earliest members of the RA and its Professor of Architecture in

1. Cf. a later holder of this appointment J. B. Bunning (qv.).
2. During Dance's studies in Italy, 1758–63, he had met Piranesi in Rome.

1798. His most famous pupil was Sir John Soane.

*See*: Colvin; *RIBA Dwgs Coll.*; D. Stroud, *George Dance*, 1971.

**53 London, Guildhall,** south entrance front (1789)

DAVIS and EMMANUEL. A London architectural practice with offices at Finsbury Circus, where they built the south-west quadrant, Salisbury House. Winners of the competition for a new City of London School to replace that of 1837 by J. B. Bunning (qv.). Other London works include The Mastersingers' Club, 63 St James's Street (*c.* 1887); Synagogue, Upper Berkeley Street (1870).

*See*: Pevsner, *London 1* and *2*.

**202 City of London School for Boys,** Victoria Embankment (1882)

DONALDSON, Thomas Leverton (1795–1885). Son of an architect; student at RA under Sir John Soane. Grand Tour 1818–23. His achievements lay in his influence as a teacher, as a writer, and as a founder member of the (R)IBA, where he was one of its first Honorary Secretaries in 1835, President, 1863–64, and the Royal Gold Medallist, 1851. From 1842 to 1865 he was Professor of Architecture at University College. Widely respected by colleagues and students he was referred to in 1879, by the Prince of Wales, as the 'father of the Institute and of the Profession'. He suggested to the IBA its motto *Usui Civium Decori Urbium*[1] and incorporated this into his design for the Institute's first medal, executed by Benjamin Wyon (see below). Among his publications was *Architectura Numismatica*, 1859, which examines the architectural medals of classical antiquity and the buildings they portrayed. Donaldson was on the committee of the Art Union of London (qv.).

*See*: Sandra Blutman in *RIBAJ*, December 1967, 542–44; *RIBA Dwgs Coll.* (C–F), the original wash drawings for *Architectura Numismatica* are in the collection; obituary, *RIBA Trans.*, 1885, vol. 2, 89–95.

**24 Temple** (Allegorical: IBA Medal) (as fifth century BC)

1. 'For the use of citizens, for the beauty of towns.' He also evolved the Institute symbol of a column flanked by lions from the Lion gateway at Mycenae.

The following portrait of Donaldson is on a prize medal founded at University College London, to mark his retirement from the Chair of Architecture:

**232a** *Obv.* Head to right: · THOMAS · LEVERTON DONALDSON · PH: D: EMERITUS · PROF: UNIV: COLL: LOND: Below, 1865. Signed J. S. & A. B. WYON SC.
*Rev.* Inscription, within a wreath of laurel: TO COMMEMORATE LONG & ZEALOUS SERVICES IN PROMOTING THE STUDY OF ARCHITECTURE.
Bronze, 57 mm.
1865 (Eidlitz 304, pl. 40) (BM)

232a

EDGE, Charles. Architect, of Birmingham. *c.* 1831 he rebuilt St Peter, Dale End, by Rickman (qv.) after it was damaged by fire. Completed the Town Hall (1835 onwards) after the bankruptcy of Hansom (qv.). His Market Hall (1833–35) was destroyed in 1940.

*See*: Colvin.

**112 Birmingham, Key Hill Cemetery Chapel** (1836)
**108 Birmingham Town Hall,** completed (1835 onwards)

EDMONDS, Christopher W. C. Son of a Southwark architect and surveyor. Exhibited at RA between 1834 and 1839. He designed the church of St Peter, Sumner Street, Southwark (1839, gothic, destroyed in 1940).

**126 London, Southwark, St Saviour's School** (1839)

ELMES, Harvey Lonsdale (1814–47). Son of architect James Elmes (1782–1862—best known as the editor of Shepherd's *Metropolitan Improvements*). Studied under his father, then at the RA Schools and was assistant (1831–34) to H. E. Goodridge of Bath (qv.). In 1839 he won the competition for the design of St George's Hall, Liverpool, and the next year won the competition for the Assize Courts. These two he amalgamated into one single design, but the task of preparing the working drawings for this great building destroyed his health and he died, abroad, aged only thirty-four. St George's Hall was completed by C. R. Cockerell (qv.).

*See*: Colvin; *RIBA Dwgs Coll.*; *Marble Halls*, 68, 76, 79–81.

**141 Liverpool, Everton, The Collegiate Institution** (1843)
**170 Liverpool, St George's Hall** (1854)

EMLYN, Henry (*c.* 1729–1815). One of a family of builders at Maidenhead, Berks. The restoration of St George's Chapel, Windsor (in 1787–90) was carried out under his direction. In 1781 he published *A Proposition for a new Order of Architecture, with rules for drawing the several parts.* Emlyn used this 'British' Order for the portico of Beaumont Lodge, and it is shown on the medal below.

*See*: Colvin.

**55 Old Windsor,** Berks., **Beaumont Lodge** (1790)

EYES, Edward. One of a family of surveyors, who carried on their profession at Liverpool from *c.* 1700 until the death of Edward Eyes Jnr, in 1850.

*See*: Colvin, 202.

**156 Bootle, St Mary's Church** (1827)

FLOCKTON, William (1804–64). Architect, of Sheffield. His works include: the complete rebuilding of Bakewell Church, Derbyshire (1841) in accordance with the original design; Holy Trinity, Wicker near Sheffield (1848); an estate layout at Rotherham (*c.* 1840).

*See*: Colvin; and see Ware for his son T. J. Flockton (1824–99).

**130 Sheffield, Wesley Proprietary College** (1840)

FOSTER, John, Jnr (*c.* 1786–1846). Second son of John Foster (d. 1824, architect of Liverpool and surveyor to the Corporation). Pupil of Jeffry Wyatt (qv.). Abroad, on Grand Tour, 1809 to 1816 and was in the party with C. R. Cockerell when they discovered the Aegina marbles. Returned to Liverpool and, in 1824, succeeded his father as Architect and Surveyor to the Corporation. He designed many of Liverpool's public buildings, often in a correct Grecian style. Works include St John's Market (1820–24); Royal Infirmary (1822–24); The Custom House (1828–39).

*See*: Colvin.

**82 Liverpool, Infirmary** (1824)
**113 Liverpool, Railway Station,** entrance screen (1836)

FOWKE, Francis (1823–65). Commissioned in the Royal Engineers, 1842. Made Inspector for Science and Art at South Kensington in 1857, then in 1862 Superintendent for the construction of the Museum there. His architectural works include the original proposals for the Albert Hall (completed by Major-General H. D. Scott (qv.) 1871); the South Kensington Museum galleries (the major part of this is still in existence, incorporated into the Victoria and Albert Museum); and the galleries of the Horticultural Society (1861) in Prince Consort Road. In 1864 his design won the competititon for the nearby Natural History Museum, but he died before it could be executed.

*See*: *RIBA Dwgs Coll.* (C–F); *Marble Halls*, 140, 142, 143.

**180 London, Buildings of the Horticultural Society** (1861)
**182 London, International Exhibition Building** (1862)
**189 London, Albert Hall** (first design) (1871)

The following portrait of Fowke is on a prize medal of the School of Military Engineering, Chatham. First awarded in 1872, it was given annually to the Officer, and NCO or Sapper, who distinguished himself in Construction (see Hocking, vol. ii, 211).

**233a** *Obv.* Bust of Fowke, to left, in military uniform. Around, FRANCIS FOWKE. Signed on rim below bust, G. MORGAN SC.

*Rev.* Inscription, surrounded by a raised and decorated border: MEMORIAL MEDAL ESTABLISHED BY THE OFFICERS OF ROYAL ENGINEERS AS AN ARCHITECTURAL PRIZE IN THE CORPS.

Bronze, 58 mm. 1872 (BM)

233a

FOWLER, Charles (1792–1867). Born in Devon; apprenticed to John Powning of Exeter. In 1814 went as assistant to David Laing's office in London, and in 1818 set up his own practice there. Fowler is mainly remembered as an architect of market buildings, e.g. Covent Garden (1830); Hungerford (1833; courtyard roof 1835); Tavistock Cornmarket (1835); Exeter Lower Market (1837). Other works include: the Conservatory, Syon House (1830) and Honiton Church, Devon (1838). He entered for a variety of competitions, and won that for London Bridge in 1822, only to have the award set aside in favour of the design by John Rennie (qv.). He was a founder member of the IBA and co-secretary with T. L. Donaldson (qv.).

*See*: Colvin; Jeremy Taylor in *AR*, cxxxv, 1964, 174–82 and *Architectural History*, 11, 1968, 57–74; *RIBA Dwgs Coll.* (C–F).

**118 Exeter, Lower Market** (1837)

FRANCIS, Horace (1821–94). A London architect in practice with his brother, Frederick J. Francis, (1818–96), as F. &. H. Francis. Their work included Christ Church, Lancaster Gate (1855); St Mary, Priory Road, Kilburn (1862) and, with J. E. Saunders, the Grand Hotel (1880) and Hotel Metropole, both in Northumberland Avenue.

*See*: *RIBA Dwgs Coll.* (C–F); B. Clarke, *Church Builders*, 254.

**153 London, Brompton Hospital,** Fulham Road (1846)

FREEMAN, Richard Knill (1838–1904). Began his architectural career in Derby (cf. the medal below), but moved to Bolton where he established in the 1880s and 1890s one of the leading Lancashire practices. His main works (several of which were illustrated in the *Builder*) included churches in various parts of Lancashire; houses at Windermere; schools, homes, and a museum at Bolton; the municipal buildings at West Hartlepool (1889).

*See*: *Builder*, 9 July 1904, 46, 47.

**198 Derby, Library and Museum** (1879)

GANDY-DEERING, John Peter (1787–1850). John Gandy was a pupil of James Wyatt (qv.) and studied at the RA Schools. In 1811–13 he joined an expedition to Greece to study Greek antiquities for the Society of Dilettanti. His drawings and sketches were used in the resultant *Unedited Antiquities of Athica*, 1817, and *Pompeiana*, 1817–19. Most of his building work was done in the next ten years, when he had a considerable reputation as an authority on Greek architecture. In 1828 he assumed the name Deering (after inheriting an estate from his friend Henry Deering) and gradually gave up his professional life.

*See*: Colvin; *RIBA Dwgs. Coll.* (*vide* Bedford, F. O.).

**97 London, University College,** Gower Street (as an associate of W. Wilkins, qv.) (1829)

**99 London, Pimlico Grammar School** (1830)

GIBBS, James (1682–1754). Studied architecture in Italy and was a pupil of Carlo Fontana. In 1713 Edward Harley, Earl of Oxford, secured him a post in London as one of the Surveyors to the Commissioners for Building Fifty New Churches. In this capacity Gibbs designed St Mary-le-Strand (1714–17) and this brought him immediate fame. He developed his private practice, and Tory patronage gave him many country house commissions. In 1728 he published *A Book of Architecture* and, in 1732, *Rules for Drawing the Several Parts of Architecture.* These were much used by master builders and had great influence as pattern books in England and America. His most famous buildings include: London, St Martin in the Fields (1722–26); Cambridge, King's College, Fellows' Building (1724–49); Oxford, The Radcliffe Library (Camera) (1737–49).

*See*: Colvin; *RIBA Dwgs Coll.* (G–K); B. Little, *James Gibbs*, 1955.

**45 Cambridge, Senate House** (1730)
**48 Warrington, Bank Hall** (1750)

GOODRIDGE, Henry Edmund (*c.* 1800–63). Had an architectural practice in Bath with commissions in the south-west of England. Earliest work in the Greek revival manner, but also built gothic churches.

*See*: Colvin.

**71 Bath, Bathwick Hill House** (1820)
**74 Bath, Bathwick, Argyle Chapel** (1821)
**47 Bath, Prior Park**, staircase and terracing (1834)

GOODWIN, Francis (1784–1835). The author of *Rural Architecture*, 1835, he had a considerable London practice dealing with the industrial towns of the Midlands and north of England. For a short time *c.* 1830 he was in partnership with Richard Lane of Manchester. His works include: Commissioners' churches around Manchester and Birmingham (see below);[1] town halls at Manchester (1822), Macclesfield (1824), and Salford (1827). He entered for many architectural competitions and in 1833 his plans for a new House of Commons were judged the best submitted.

*See*: Colvin; M. H. Port in *Architectural History,* 1, 1958, 60–71, also *Six Hundred New Churches*, 1961, 69ff.

1. Goodwin's thrusting campaign to be chosen as an architect for Commissioners' churches is discussed in Port (op. cit). He might well have encouraged the striking of these medals to aid his own publicity; they all date from 1820 to 1822 and are inscribed Francis Goodwin Architect London.

**78 Birmingham, Holy Trinity, Bordesley** (1823)
**80 Ashton-under-Lyne, St Peter's Church** (1824)
**81 Kidderminster, St George's Church** (1824)
**92 West Bromwich, Christ Church** (1828)

GOTCH, John Alfred (1852–1942). The author of *Architecture of the Renaissance in England,* 1894, and *Early Renaissance Architecture in England,* 1901, as well as works on the English house, the buildings of Sir Thomas Tresham, and the architecture of Inigo Jones. Although best known as an architectural historian, Gotch was in practice at Kettering from 1879, and in partnership with Charles Saunders. They designed many schools, banks, and country houses in the Midlands area. Gotch was an FSA and President RIBA, 1923–25.

*See*: Obituary, *RIBAJ,* xlix, 1942, 66–67; *RIBA Dwgs Coll.* (G–K).

**219 Kettering, Northants., Stamford Road School** (1892)
**32 Rothwell, Market House** (completion) (1895)

GOUGH, Alexander Dick (1804–71). A pupil, and later assistant, in the office of Benjamin Wyatt during the years 1823 to 1836; he then set up in partnership with Robert Lewis Roumieu (1814–77). Their joint practice included much work in Islington, e.g. The Literary Institute, Almeida Street (1837); Milner Square Terraces (*c.* 1841);[1] alterations to Charles Barry's recent church of St Peter (*c.* 1843).[2] Later works by Gough included the Islington churches of St Matthew, Essex Road (1850); St Mark, Tollington Park (1854); St Anne, Poole's Park (1871); and at Lambeth, Holy Saviour, Herne Hill Road (1866–67).[3] His sons Charles and Hugh Roumieu Gough (1843–1904), became architects and assisted in the practice.

*See*: Ware, 107.

**191 Tunbridge Wells, St John's Church** (1858)

1. See Hitchcock, 420, pl. xiii 2; Pevsner, *London 2,* 236.
2. See Hitchcock, 125.
3. Pevsner, op. cit. 272, 'Hearty, robust and revolting'.

GOUGH, W. V. (1841–1918). Senior partner of W. V. & A. R. Gough of Bristol. The firm's works include several local churches, e.g. Knowle (1870–83); schools; public libraries; offices at Bristol for the Docks Board and for the Gas Company; an Institute at Newport, Isle of Wight.

*See*: *Builder*, 20 December 1918, 422.

**231 Bristol, Cabot Memorial Tower** (1898)

GRIFFIN and WELLER. Goodhart-Rendel's index (RIBA) gives eight churches in Staffs. between 1854 and 1858 by Griffin W. O., of Griffin and Weller, or by the partnership.

**176 Walsall, St John's Church,** Pleck Road (1858)

HAKEWILL, Henry (1771–1830). Eldest son of John Hakewill, painter and decorator. Architect to the trustees of Rugby School, the Radcliffe trustees, and to the Benchers of the Middle Temple. His work included: Rugby School Buildings and Chapel (1809); alterations at Oxford to the Radcliffe Camera, and to the Provost's Lodge of Oriel College. His sons, J. H. and E. C. Hakewill, both practised as architects.

*See*: Colvin.

**90 London, St Peter's Church,** Eaton Square (1827)

HAMILTON and MEDLAND. Hamilton was in partnership with Samuel Dawkes (b. 1811)[1] in Gloucester in the 1840s and James Medland joined them as chief assistant. When Dawkes went to London the firm became Hamilton and Medland; this must have been by 1848 when their name appears on the Birmingham Cemetery medal (see below). In 1850 they completed the Gloucester Savings Bank, and 1852 Medland altered Tibberton Court, Gloucs. By 1862 the firm was Medland, Maberley, and Medland,[2] designers of the Corn Hall, Cirencester.

*See*: Pevsner, ed. and Verey, D., *Gloucestershire and the Cotswolds*, 36, 61, 172.

**158 Birmingham, St. Michael's Church and Cemetery** (1848)

1. Cf. entry for Archer and Green.
2. James Medland's son, M. H. Medland, designed Nailsworth Church, Gloucs. (1898–1900).

HANSOM, Joseph Aloysius (1803–82). Born in York and apprenticed there to an architect named Philips. In 1828 went into partnership with Edward Welch at Halifax. With Welch he won the 1830 competition for Birmingham Town Hall. Essentially finished by 1834, and to considerable acclaim, the building process nevertheless forced the architects into bankruptcy. In an effort to retrieve his finances Hansom at this stage invented, perfected, and patented the 'Safety Cab' which bears his name. In 1842, seeing the need for communication among the building trades, he founded *The Builder*. In the 1850s and 1860s he was in partnership with his brother and with E. W. Pugin, and designed a number of churches for Roman Catholic use.

*See*: Ware; R. Williamson in *AR*, lxxx, 1936, 117–19.

**108 Birmingham, Town Hall** (1834)
**151 Sheffield, Mount St Mary's College** (1845)

HARDWICK, Philip (1792–1870). Son of the architect and surveyor Thomas Hardwick (d. 1829). Visited France and Italy 1815–19 and on his return set up independently in private practice. He held a wide variety of appointments including those of architect to the St Catherine's Dock Company and to the Goldsmiths' Company (whose Hall he built in 1829–35). As an architect, he is best known for his Greek revival Propylaeum, or Arch, to Euston Station (see below). Elsewhere, as at Lincoln's Inn, he experimented in Tudor or Elizabethan gothic styles. He was a founder member of the IBA and received its Royal Gold Medal in 1854. Elected FRS 1831, and RA 1841. His health failed in 1847 and his son P. C. Hardwick (1822–92) took over the practice.

*See*: Colvin; *Marble Halls*, 101.

**125 London, Euston Station, 'Euston Arch'** (1838)
**150 London, Lincoln's Inn, Hall and Library**[1] (1845)

1. Design only 1842; built by P. C. Hardwick.

HARDWICK, Philip Charles (1822–92). The son of Philip Hardwick (see above); he trained under Edward Blore (qv.) and then joined his father's practice in 1842. His major works included the Great Hall, Euston Station (1846–49); Aldermaston Court,

Berks. (1848–51); GWR Hotel, Paddington Station (1850–52); Bank of England, Leeds (1862–64).

*See*: *RIBA Dwgs Coll.* (G-K); *RIBAJ*, 1892, 174–75.

**192 Godalming, Charterhouse School** (1872)

HAWKSMOOR, Nicholas (1661–1736). Having heard of his 'early skill and genius for architecture' Sir Christopher Wren (qv.) took Hawksmoor into his service about 1679. He became Wren's chief assistant for nearly all of his works from 1684 onwards. After 1702 he was also employed by another great figure in the history of English architecture, Sir John Vanbrugh (qv.) and acted as assistant to him at Greenwich Hospital, Castle Howard and Blenheim Palace. At the same time Hawksmoor emerged as a figure of genius in his own right and is seen to have made an outstanding contribution to the English Baroque (a contribution which is also apparent in his many drawings for unbuilt schemes). The works for which he was personally responsible include: the London churches of St Alfege, Greenwich (1712–18), St Anne, Limehouse (1714–30), St George-in-the-East, Wapping (1714–19), Christ Church, Spitalfields (1714–29), St George, Bloomsbury (1716–31), St Mary Woolnoth, City (1716–24); the mausoleum at Castle Howard (1729–42); the old Clarendon Press, Oxford (1712–13). Early in the 1700s Hawksmoor was being consulted about new buildings for All Souls' College Oxford; his report to the college is perhaps the first time an English architect set out a case for preserving old buildings because they were sound and *useful*.[1] At Beverley Minster he proposed restoration work involving the amazing technical feat of screwing back to the vertical the whole north transept front, while his conservation abilities were finally exercised to the full in his design, in a very personal gothic, of new west towers to complete Westminster Abbey.

*See*: Colvin; *RIBA Dwgs Coll.* (G–K); Kerry Downes, *Hawksmoor*, 1969.

**8 London, Westminster Abbey,** west towers (1734 onwards)

1. I am indebted to Dr Derek Linstrum for this point in a paper 'English attitudes to historic buildings 1600–1725'.

HEMMING, Samuel. A Samuel Hemming 'of Birmingham' compiled a pattern book for the cheaper housing market of the 1850s entitled *Designs for Villa, Parsonages and Other Houses . . . from £200 to £5000.* (See H.-R. Hitchcock, *Early Victorian Architecture*, 427–30.)

**167 Birmingham, General Institution for the Blind** (1852)

HICKS, John (*fl.* 1860s). Of South Street, Dorchester. Following his work at Bridport Parish Church he is recorded as the designer of St Stephen's Church, Bettiscombe (1862); St Martin, Shipton George (1862); St John, East Holme (1866); All Saints, Stower Row (1867–); his other churches in the Dorset area include designs at North Poorton, Tornworth, West Lulworth, and Swanage.

*See*: Goodhart-Rendel index (RIBA, unpubl.).

**17 Bridport, St Mary's Church,** additions (1860)

HIGHWAY, Isaac. St Peter's Church, Walsall (1841) is a work of this little-known architect.

**122 Walsall Wood, St John's Church** (1837)

HOLME, Arthur Hill (1814–57). Son of a Liverpool builder. Articled to Thomas Rickman (qv.) in Birmingham. He then returned to Liverpool to set up an architectural practice; one of his first executed schemes was the Mechanics Institution (see below) which he won in an open competition while still apprenticed to Rickman.[1] Soon after this he went into partnership with John Cunningham (qv.). Holme was a founder member and first treasurer (in 1848) of the Liverpool Architectural Society. He designed eight churches in Liverpool, as well as the Asylum for the Blind, Hardman Street; additions to the Southern Hospital; Music Hall, Bold Street.[2]

*See*: *Building News*, 11 December 1857, 1302; Clarke, 256.

**119 Liverpool, Mechanics Institution** (1837)

1. J. A. Picton was the executive architect for the building; cf. p.107.

2. From 1851 to 1855 Holme withdrew from architectural practice to help with the family contracting business; this work included the construction of the military camp at the Curragh.

HOPE and JARDINE (*fl.* 1870s). A Bradford practice whose partner Thomas Campbell Hope (d. 1916) won the competition for the Technical College, Horton Street (see below). Their local works also included: Store for George Thorpe & Co., Tyrrel Street (1871); Board School, Lilycroft (1873). Later Hope was in partnership with G. Roberts.

*See*: *Builder*, 20 October 1916, 243.

**201 Bradford, Technical College** (1882)

HUGHES, Edward (d. 1886). Awarded RIBA silver medal 1859; elected Associate in 1863. In practice in Pimlico, London, 1863–70, and at Huddersfield, 1871–84, where he was Architect to the Corporation. He was the architect of Huddersfield Market Hall (1878–80, dem.)

**204 Huddersfield, Technical School** (1883)

INMAN, William Southcote (1798–1879). Attended RA Schools 1818. Entered the King's College, Cambridge, competition 1823. Surveyor of Works and Buildings, at the Office of Works, 1851–56. Vice-president RIBA.

*See*: Colvin.

**77 London Orphan Asylum, Hackney** (*c.* 1823)

JACKSON and FOX. Architects of George Street, Halifax. Goodhart-Rendel's index (RIBA) attributes to them: St George's Church, Ovenden, Halifax (1876); St Thomas, Charlestown, Halifax (alterations 1912).

**226 Halifax, Municipal Technical School** (1895)

JARMAN, Edward (d. 1668). One of the three surveyors appointed by the Corporation to control the rebuilding of the City of London after the Great Fire. They worked in conjunction with Wren (qv.), May and Pratt. Jarman prepared the designs for the rebuilding of the Royal Exchange, which was completed after his death. He also prepared designs for rebuilding the Drapers', the Vintners', and the Mercers' Company halls.

*See*: Colvin.

**36 London, Royal Exchange** (1671)

JEFFERY and SKILLER. Designed Emmanuel Church Blacklands, Hastings (1874–75). In 1889–92 Jeffery was joint architect for the extension of E. W. Godwin's town hall at Northampton—a building which had evidently influenced their Winchester design.

*See*: Pevsner, *Hants.*, 697.

**194 Winchester, Guildhall** (1873)

JOHNSON, John (1732–1814). Established in London in the 1770s, and exhibiting architectural designs. In 1782 appointed Surveyor to the County of Essex, for whom he designed his major work, the Shire Hall, Chelmsford (see below). Had a considerable country house practice. He designed several buildings in Leicester where he was born; these included the Town Gaol (1793), the County Rooms (1800), Theatre (1800), and the 'Consanguinitarium' (*c.* 1795)—a block of five small houses endowed for his poor relatives.

*See*: Colvin.

**56 Chelmsford, Shire Hall** (1791)

JOHNSON, John (1807–78). Author of *Johnson's Churches of Northampton.* Travelled in Italy after starting his career with the Gold Medallion of the Royal Society of Arts, 1833, and RA Medals, 1834 and 1835. His London work includes several churches; the first Alexandra Palace (destroyed 1873), and the rebuilt version (see below); and terraced housing in Bayswater (1865).

*See*: *Builder*, xxxvii, 1879, 53; *RIBA Dwgs Coll.* (G–K).

**196 London, Alexandra Palace** (1875)

JONES, Sir Horace (1819–87). Followed J. B. Bunning (qv.) as Architect to the City of London from 1864 to 1887. He had already established, in 1846, a private practice and the work from this and his City appointment included designs for many major public buildings, offices, and shops for London, e.g. Smithfield Market (1866); Marshall & Snelgrove, Oxford Street (1870, completed by Octavius Hansard); Guildhall Free Library and Museum (1873); Leadenhall Market

(1881); Tower Bridge (with the engineer J. Wolfe Barry, built 1886–94). President of the RIBA 1882–83. Knighted 1886.

*See*: *RIBA Dwgs Coll.* (G–K); *Marble Halls*, 121.

**185 London, Guildhall,** new roof (1865)
**206 London, Guildhall, Council Chamber** (1884)
**225 London, Tower Bridge** (1894)

JONES, Inigo (1573–1652). Famous as England's first Classical Architect—a position supported by his experience on two visits to Italy *c.* 1600 and again in 1613. Less well known has been his role as a designer of complex Masques for the Stuart Court. Following the second Italian journey[1] he was in 1615 appointed Surveyor of the King's Works. In 1628 John Webb (1611–72) became a pupil and the close associate of Jones, and later helped to link the period to the time of Wren. Many of the extant drawings for Jones's schemes are in Webb's hand, or were developed by him from sketches, e.g. the several proposals for a new Whitehall Palace in St James's Park of *c.* 1637–39. Jones's buildings included: The Prince's Lodging, Newmarket (*c.* 1619); Church of St Paul, and houses, Covent Garden (1631); Queen's House, Greenwich (1630–38, but work first started 1616); Winchester Cathedral, the Screen (*c.* 1638); new west front and portico St Paul's Cathedral (1635–42). Out of forty-five recorded works by Inigo Jones, only seven survive. There is a portrait of Jones on the obverse of the medal below.[2]

*See*: John Summerson, *Inigo Jones*, 1966; Catalogue, *The Kings Arcadia: Inigo Jones and the Stuart Court*, Arts Council 1973; *RIBA Dwgs Coll.* (Inigo Jones).

**34 London, The Banqueting House, Whitehall** (1622)

1. It was on this journey that Jones acquired Andrea Palladio's *I Quattro Libri dell'Architettura* of 1601—a vital source for his future work.

2. Eidlitz Nos. 608–10 gives three earlier portrait medals of Jones, one by Kirk. Nos. 608, 609 are also given in *Med. Ill.*, pp. 397, 398. They appear to be based on Van Dyck's drawing of *c.* 1640.

LANE, Richard (*fl.* 1815–58). A prominent Manchester architect. Exhibited at RA 1815. He was associated with Francis Goodwin (qv.) about 1830, and then practised with P. D. Alley. Founder and first President of the Manchester Architectural Society, 1837. Alfred Waterhouse (qv.) was one of his pupils. Works include Oldham, St Mary (1823–27); Salford, Town Hall (1825–27 with Goodwin) and at Manchester: Friends Meeting House (1828–30), Corn Exchange (1837), Royal Infirmary enlarged (1848–53).

*See*: Colvin; C. Stewart, *The Architecture of Manchester*, pamphlet, 1956, p. 51.

**110 Oldham, The Blue Coat School** (1834)

LATHAM, Baldwin. A Westminster, London, architect responsible for:

**228 Bilston, Waterworks** (1897)

LOCKWOOD and MAWSON (*fl.* 1849–78). A Bradford firm of architects created in 1849 by the partnership of Henry Francis Lockwood (1811–78) with William Mawson. Prior to this Lockwood had been in practice in Hull, where his most notable pupil and assistant was Cuthbert Brodrick (qv.). Lockwood and Mawson were selected by Sir Titus Salt for the design and planning of Saltaire, Yorks.;[1] their individual buildings for the development included the Mill (1851–53 in conjunction with the engineer Sir William Fairbairn) and the Congregational Church (1858–59). They were also responsible for many buildings in Bradford, e.g. St George's Hall (1851–53); Town Hall (1873); Exchange (1864–67); and the Kirkgate Markets (1877). In 1874 Lockwood moved to London, where the City Temple, Holborn Viaduct (1873–74), was built to his design.

*See*: Ware, 152; J. Ayers, *Architecture in Bradford*, Bradford Civic Society, 1972.

**190 Saltaire,** West Yorks., **The Institute** (1871)

1. An account of the client's initial interviews with Lockwood is given in *Sir Titus Salt, baronet*, by Robert Balgarnie, 1877 (reprint 1970, Settle, Brenton), 117–19.

LYNN, William Henry (1829–1915). Born near Larne, Ireland. Apprenticed to the County Surveyor of Antrim, Sir Charles Lanyon, and entered partnership with him. They designed the Custom House, Belfast

(1857) and won competitions to design the Town Halls at Chester (1864) and Barrow in Furness (1879). Another winning entry, for the Houses of Parliament, Sydney, Australia, was not built, but in 1910, aged eighty-one, Lynn won first prize for new buildings at Queen's College, Belfast. Other works include churches, commercial buildings, and library (1888) in the Belfast area. President RIAI 1885–89.

*See*: *RIBAJ*, xxii, 1915, 506; *RIBA Dwgs Coll.* (L–N).

**188 Chester, Town Hall** (1869)

MAINWARING, Boulton. Surveyor to the London Hospital and designer of its new buildings 1752–57. He retired from the Surveyorship 1771.

*See*: Colvin.

**49 London Hospital,** Whitechapel Road (1757)

MANNERS, George Philip (*fl.* 1829–49). City Architect of Bath. In 1835 he took down the classical St Michael, Broad Street, of 1742 (see No. 46a) to replace it with a gothic design (see below). He built other churches in Bath and Somerset; restored the Abbey (1835) and added a new Tepid Swimming Bath to the design of Decimus Burton (qv.).

*See*: Colvin.

**115 Bath, St Michael's Church** (1837)

MANNING, Joseph

**169 Wolverhampton, Orphan Asylum** (1853)

MANNING, Michael Prendergast (*fl.* 1866–1902). Architect in practice 1867 at Temple, London, EC. Built the church of St Mary, King Henry's Road, Hampstead, 1873 and, in the same area, New College (the former Hackney College). Resigned RIBA 1902.[1]

**212 London, New College,** Finchley Road (1887)

1. His initials are given as M. P., *corrected* from W. P., in the RIBA.

MAXWELL and TUKE. A large Manchester practice, formed in 1867 by the partnership of James Maxwell (d. 1893) and William Charles Tuke (d. 1894). Their work in the North of England included many banks in Lancashire; technical and infants' schools at Bury; the layout of the new town of St Annes-on-Sea, together with the design of its hotel and initial houses. As well as the buildings on the medals below, they designed the Ulster Reform Club, Belfast, and submitted schemes for public buildings in Japan and Ecuador.[1]

*See*: *RIBAJ*, 1894, p. 116.

**215 Manchester, Jubilee Exhibition Buildings** (1887)
**222 Blackpool, Tower Buildings** (1894)

1. They were among the nine firms of architects selected in 1884 to go through to the second stage of the competition for a new Admiralty and War Office Building, Whitehall.

MITCHELL, Thomas.

**205 Oldham, Library and Art Gallery** (1883)

MOFFATT, William Bonython (1812–87). A fellow pupil with Gilbert Scott (qv.). They set up in practice in 1834, and the medals below are signed Scott & Moffatt. In 1844 Scott, realising that Moffatt's unconventional character was hindering him, dissolved the partnership. Moffatt continued to do much work in the 1850s, but after imprisonment for debt in 1860, drifted into obscurity.

*See*: *RIBA Dwgs Coll.* (L–N).

**142 London, Infant Orphan Asylum,** Wanstead (1843)
**147 London, Camberwell, St Giles's Church** (1844)

MORGAN, James. In 1806 became assistant to John Nash, and was his draughtsman during the preparation of the great Regent Street/Regent's Park scheme. Appointed engineer to the Regent's Canal Company 1812. Built No. 326 Regent Street *c.* 1825.

*See*: Colvin, *RIBA Dwgs Coll.* (L–N).

**101 Wolverhampton, St George's Church** (1830)

NASH, John (1752–1835). Worked for nearly ten years for the architect Sir Robert Taylor. After an initial failure, set up a practice in London in 1796 with the landscape gardener

Humphrey Repton. A very extensive country house practice developed from this. With the patronage of the Prince Regent, Nash became in 1815 one of the three 'attached architects' to the Office of Works ((Sir) Robert Smirke, 1780-1867, and (Sir) John Soane (qv.) were the others). Between 1815 and 1821 he completely remodelled the Royal Pavilion at Brighton. Already in progress was his great town planning work: the creation, for the Crown, of the Regent Street route from Carlton House Palace to a new development in the (then) Marylebone Park. The plan was published in 1812 and the main line of Regent Street was built between 1817 and 1823. Nash's London works include; All Souls Church, Langham Place (1822–29, an important visual element in the Regent Street plan); Royal Opera Arcade, Haymarket (1816 with G. S. Repton); Buckingham Palace (1825–30); Carlton House Terrace (1827–33).

*See*: John Summerson, *John Nash, Architect to King George IV,* 1935; T. Davis, *The Architecture of John Nash,* 1960, and *John Nash, The Prince Regents' Architect,* 1966; Colvin; *RIBA Dwgs Coll.* (L–N).

**75 Brighton, The Royal Pavilion** (1821)

NORTON, Charles. A Birmingham builder and surveyor. Employed to rebuild the Theatre Royal there in 1793–94. After the results of the 1804 competition for Christ Church were set aside, Norton was appointed designer and directed the building.

*See*: Colvin.

**65 Birmingham, Christ Church** (1814)

ORDISH, F. W. His building for the Victoria Park Hospital (1851) was an early example of a reawakening of interest in the architecture of the late Stuart period, i.e. around 1700.[1]

**166 London, Hackney, Victoria Park Hospital** (1851)

1. Two years later, in 1853, a proposal to demolish twenty-three Wren churches was halted by a strong preservation lobby. In discussing John Shaw's Wellington College, Sandhurst (1856–59) the *Builder*, 12, 406, made a first reference to 'the style of Queen Anne, perhaps it may be called'. See H.-R. Hitchcock, *Early Victorian Architecture*, 331–33.

OWEN, Jacob. The architect of two Commissioners' churches in the Portsmouth area: All Saints, Portsea (1825–27); St John, Forton (1829–30). For the latter he was co-designer with his son T. E. Owen (1804–62).[1]

*See*: Port, pp. 72, 134, 145.

**86 Southsea,** Hants, **St Paul's School** (1826)

1. See T. Preedy and I. Stewart, 'Thomas Ellis Owen, Southsea Architect', unpubl., Portsmouth Polytechnic, 1972.

PAINE, John Davis. Born *c.* 1807. Gold medal at RA Schools 1833. Exhibited RA 1828–43. His works included two railway terminuses (one at what is now Waterloo, the other at St Petersburg, (now Leningrad) Russia) and lighthouse on the Goodwin Sands (1842).

*See*: Colvin.

**114 Newark, Christ Church** (1836)

PARSONS, William (d. *c.* 1860). Practised in Leicester. By the 1840s was in partnership with one of his pupils Abraham Gill. At Leicester he designed the County Gaol (1825–28) and the Theatre (1836).

*See*: Colvin.

**89 Leicester, St George's Church** (1827)

PAXTON, Sir Joseph (1801–65). Went to Chatsworth in 1826 and became the Superintendent of gardens for the Duke of Devonshire. In collaboration with Decimus Burton (qv.) he built the Great Conservatory there (1836–40). The experience gained from this, and its 'ridge and furrow' glazing, enabled him to submit his famous sketch design for the 1851 Exhibition Building, Hyde Park. This was accepted by the Commissioners at the last minute, and the rapid construction of the building, and its prefabricated format, constituted one of the technological triumphs of the Victorian Age. In 1852 this 'Crystal Palace' was dismantled and re-erected at a permanent exhibition site at Sydenham (with Paxton supervising a major increase in floor area and volume). Knighted in 1851, Paxton was soon providing schemes for a wide variety of glass and iron structures, e.g. for the Victoria Park Hospital, 1851 (No. 166a). Later he was responsible for laying out several parks as well as the new Edensor Village, Chatsworth. His portrait is on the obverse of medal 171g.

*See*: *Marble Halls*, 113–17; G. F. Chadwick, *The Works of Sir Joseph Paxton*, 1961.

**165 London, Great Exhibition Building** (1851)
**171 London, Sydenham, Crystal Palace** (1854)

PEARSON, John Loughborough (1817–97). Studied under the Durham architect Ignatius Bonomi, then worked in the London Offices of Anthony Salvin and Philip Hardwick (qv.). Set up in private practice 1843 and concentrated on design and restoration of churches, together with church furniture and fittings. He became one of the group of later Victorian church architects who tackled the design problem of the unified 'town church', e.g. in London: St Peter's, Vauxhall (1860); St Augustine's, Kilburn (1871); and St John, Red Lion Square (1878). Pearson's style was centred around the gothic of the thirteenth century, and of France, as demonstrated by the towers and spires of his Truro Cathedral (1880 onwards; completed 1910 by his son F. L. Pearson). RA and RIBA Royal Gold Medal 1880.

*See*: *RIBAJ*, 1898, 113–21; B. Clarke, *Church Builders*, 196–209.

**216 Truro Cathedral, Cornwall** (1887)

PILKINGTON, William (1758–1848). A pupil and later assistant of the architect Sir Robert Taylor. Appointed Surveyor to the Board of Customs (1782), and also Surveyor to the Sun Fire Assurance Office (1792) and to the Charterhouse (1792). His son Redmond William Pilkington (1789–1844) succeeded him later in the latter posts, and completed alterations begun by his father at the Charterhouse. William Pilkington's buildings included: Custom House, Portsmouth (1785); Chilton Lodge, near Hungerford (1800); works for the Earl of Radnor, and designs and improvements for several London and country houses.

*See*: Colvin.

**59 London, Charterhouse School** (1803)

POCOCK, William Fuller (1779–1849). Studied at the RA Schools, and was an early member of the IBA. His buildings include several works for City of London Companies, e.g. the Leathersellers' Company's Hall, Bishopsgate, and also a variety of commissions abroad.

*See*: Colvin.

**127 London, Wesleyan Centenary Hall** (1840)

POTTER, Joseph, Jnr (*c.* 1797–1875). Architect of Lichfield, with a practice in the Staffordshire area. Son of the Joseph Potter Snr, who between 1788 and 1795 supervised extensive restoration works at Lichfield Cathedral (see medal No. 6a) for James Wyatt. 'Joseph Potter' is given as the architect for the rebuilding of Grendon Hall, the home of the numismatist Sir George Chetwynd.[1] Potter was summarily dismissed from Oscott College when the prodigious Pugin (qv.) appeared upon the scene. Later in life he was defending Wyatt's restoration work at Lichfield against criticism.

*See*: Colvin.

**84 Grendon Hall, near Atherstone,** Warwicks. (*c.* 1825)
**100 Sheffield, St Mary's Church** (1830)
**124 Birmingham, Oscott College** (1838)

1. The role of Joseph, senior, in these earlier works is not clear. Colvin lists the work of father and son together.

PUGIN, Augustus Welby Northmore (1811–52). Son of the talented architectural illustrator and draughtsman Augustus Charles Pugin, in whose drawing school he studied. His short, and overcrowded, architectural career began when he set up his own practice in 1835 and was the same year converted to Roman Catholicism. Thereafter his aim was to represent 'those Glorious Catholic architects who lived in antient days' and he became the mainspring for the coming gothic revival. His greatest influence was through the writing of *Contrasts* (1836) and *The True Principles of Pointed or Christian Architecture* (1841). The latter grew out of the lectures he gave at Oscott College (see below) where he designed the influential chapel interior. For Sir Charles Barry (qv.)

he prepared the gothic detail for the Houses of Parliament (see below) together with much of the interior fitting, e.g. for the House of Lords. Their earlier collaboration at the gothic King Edward VI's School (see below) had been a rehearsal for this. But these works must be seen in conjunction with his prodigious output of churches, monasteries, and schools which were all telescoped into the years 1837–52. By 1843 the frontispiece to his *An Apology for the Revival of Christian Architecture in England* was already able to illustrate twenty-three of his churches completed, or building. Important secular commissions included Scarisbrook Hall (1837–45) and Alton Towers (1837–52).

*See*: *Marble Halls*, 1–5, 18; Phoebe Stanton, *Pugin*, 1971; B. Clarke, *Church Builders*, 45–71.

**116 Birmingham, King Edward VI's Grammar School** (1837)
**124 Birmingham, Oscott College,** chapel interior (1838)
**149 Liverpool, St Mary's Roman Catholic Church** (1845)
**179 London, Houses of Parliament** (1860)

RAILTON, William (*c.* 1801–77). Studied under the architect William Inwood. Visited Greece 1825–27, and then practised in London. His works are primarily churches and houses in the 1830s and 1840s.

*See*: Colvin.

**143 London, Nelson Monument, Trafalgar Square** (1843)

RAWSTHORNE, John. A pupil of James Wyatt (qv.), he set up as an architect in Birmingham. He designed the Royal Infirmary, Sheffield (1793–97); the Blue Coat School (1792–94) (see below); the Crescent, Birmingham (1790—part of a larger speculative housing scheme).

*See*: Colvin.

**57 Birmingham, Blue Coat School** (1794)

RENNIE, John (1761–1821). Scottish engineer whose designs for Waterloo Bridge, London (1811–17) and London Bridge (1821–31) must be seen as major nineteenth-century works in architecture. His reputation had been established when he assisted Boulton and Watt to design the machinery for the Albion Flour Mills, Southwark, 1784; but his ultimate fame rests on his civil engineering works, e.g. docks (such as those at Sheerness), aqueducts, and bridges. Rennie submitted a design for a new London Bridge in 1821, rather than support plans for improving the existing one. After Rennie's death, and an abortive competition won by Charles Fowler (qv.), this 1821 design was accepted and built by his son, the engineer (Sir) John Rennie (1794–1874).

*See*: Colvin.

**67 London, Waterloo Bridge** (1817)
**102 London Bridge** (1831)

There is a portrait of the elder Rennie on the following medal:

**234a** *Obv.* Head to left, around, JOHN RENNIE. Signed on truncation, BAIN. F.
*Rev.* Inscription, within a wreath of laurel; a circlet of stars above and an ornament below: CRINAN & LANCASTER CANALS / LONDON LEITH & SHEERNESS DOCKS / WATERLOO & SOVTHWARK BRIDGES / PLYMOUTH HOWTH & DVNLEARY HARBOURS / &ᶜ &ᶜ &ᶜ
Bronze, 63 mm. 1821 (Eidlitz 826, pl. 95) (BM)

234a

There are three other medals of Rennie by Bain recorded in Eidlitz (Nos. 825, 827, 828). He also notes, p. 141, that there is a portrait bust (*c.* 1818) by Sir Francis Chantrey which is inscribed 'John Rennie, Architect'.

RICKMAN, Thomas (1776–1841). Initially qualified as a doctor, then, while working in Liverpool 1808–13 as an insurance clerk, studied medieval buildings and church architecture. He wrote a paper which was reprinted (1817) as *An Attempt to Discriminate the Styles of English Architecture from the Conquest to the Reformation.* This was the first systematic study of English gothic and established the familiar terminology 'Norman', 'Early English', 'Decorated', and 'Perpendicular'. He opened a practice in Liverpool in 1817, and in 1821 went into partnership with his pupil Henry Hutchinson (d. 1831). Between 1814 and 1839 over fifty churches were built to Rickman's designs of which all but three were Gothic; St Peter, Dale End (on the medal below) was one of these exceptions. Rickman & Hutchinson's best-known secular building is the New Court, St John's College, Cambridge (1827–31) with its attendant 'Bridge of Sighs'.

*See*: Colvin.

**88 Birmingham, St Peter's Church,** Dale End (1827)
**94 Darwen,** Lancs., **Holy Trinity Church** (1829)
**123 Birmingham, Bishop Ryder Memorial Church** (1838)

ROBSON, Edward Robert (1836–1917). A pupil of John Dobson, and then, 1857–60, worked for Sir Gilbert Scott (qv.). From 1870 to 1889 he was the first Architect to the School Board for London, and then 1889–1904 Consulting Architect to the Board of Education. Robson was responsible for the building of many hundreds of elementary schools, and published his influential *School Architecture* in 1874. Amongst his London buildings were: the Royal Institute of Painters in Water Colours (1881); Queen Anne Mansions, Broadway (1876–88);[1] New Gallery, Regent Street (1888).[2]

*See*: Ware; Pevsner, *London 1* and *2*.

**213 London, Peoples Palace,** Mile End Road (1887)

1. 'That irredeemable horror'—Pevsner.
2. Referred to in *British Sculpture*, p. 13.

ROSE, Henry (*fl.* 1827–54). Architect of the Licensed Victuallers' School, Kennington Road, London (1835–36) and, for the same charity, their Asylum and associated buildings in the Old Kent Road (1831–50). He also designed Borough Market, Southwark (1851).

*See*: Colvin.

**162 London, Licensed Victuallers' Asylum, the Ladies' Wing** (1849)

SALOMONS, Edward (1827–1906). Had a large Manchester practice and was President, Manchester Society of Architects 1871–73. Principal buildings in the City were: 'Crystal Palace', Trafford Park, the entrance front (this housed the Art Treasures Exhibition: see below); Prince's Theatre (1864): Queen's Theatre (1870); Theatre Royal, remodelled (1875). His designs included warehouses, synagogues, several houses abroad, and Messrs Agnew's Galleries, London.[1]

*See*: C. Stewart, *The Architecture of Manchester*, pamphlet, 1956, pp. 52, 53.

**173 Manchester, Art Treasures Exhibition building** (1856)

1. The *Builder*, 1868, 759, commented 'This gentleman seems to go in for a new style in every building he erects'.

SCOTT, Sir George Gilbert (1811–78). Between 1827 and 1834 he gained training and experience in the offices of James Edmeston, Henry Roberts, and Sampson Kempthorne. He then set up in practice with a fellow pupil W. B. Moffatt (qv.) until dissolving the partnership in 1844. During this period he was inspired by the writings of Pugin (qv.) and 'cared for nothing, as regarded my art, but the revival of Gothic architecture'. Soon after he designed the Martyrs' Memorial (1843); Infant Orphan Asylum, Wanstead (1843); and St Giles, Camberwell (1844); all these are depicted on medals (Nos. 9b, 142a, 147a). There then followed the development of his enormous, and highly successful practice; at his death he was said to have been concerned with over seven hundred and thirty buildings *since* 1847.[1] The primary aspect of this work was ecclesiastical buildings: gothic churches either rebuilt or new; St Mary's Episcopal Cathedral at Edinburgh (see below); major restorations of sixteen cathedrals.[2] His London works included the

Albert Memorial (1863–72); the Foreign Office (1868–72, with Matthew Digby Wyatt); the Midland Hotel and St Pancras Station (1868–73). He prepared designs for important competitions, e.g. the Town Hall, Hamburg; the Law Courts, London, and his astonishing self-confidence and talent was to influence a new generation of Victorian church architects. RA. Knighted 1872. President RIBA 1873.

*See*: *Marble Halls*, 9, 150; B. Clarke, *Church Builders*, 160–72; G. G. Scott, *Personal and Professional Recollections*, London, 1879.

**142 London, Infant Orphan Asylum, Wanstead** (1843)
**147 London, Camberwell, St Giles Church** (1844)
**14 Nantwich,** Cheshire, **St Mary's Church** restored (1861)
**19 Coventry,** Warwicks., **St John's Church** restored (1877)

The Art-Union has a portrait of Scott on the penultimate medal of their series.[3] The cathedral depicted, at Edinburgh, was completed by his son, J. Oldrid Scott (1841–1913), who took over his practice.

**235a** *Obv.* Profile head, to left of SIR G. GILBERT SCOTT. R.A. Below, 1811–1878. Signed on truncation, G. G. ADAMS. S$^{C}$
*Rev.* View of St Mary's Episcopal Cathedral, including the proposed western towers (completed 1917). Around, ART-UNION OF LONDON. Below, 1884, and beneath building, EDINBURGH.
Silver, Bronze, 56 mm.
1884 (Eidlitz 942, pl. 108) (BM)

235a

1. *Builder*, xxxvi, 360.
2. These earned him a reputation, like James Wyatt before, of a destroyer of previous periods or those which were not in his eyes 'correct'.
3. See Beulah in *BNJ*, xxxvi, 1967, 179–85.

SCOTT, Major-General Henry Young Darracott (*c.* 1822–83). Like Francis Fowke (qv.) an officer of the Royal Engineers. After Fowke's death he developed the initial design of the Albert Hall and saw it to completion. Scott retired from the Army in 1871 and was appointed Director of New Buildings to the South Kensington Museum. He was architect of the Science Schools, Kensington (1872); the Cast Courts and the Art Library (1882) of the Victoria and Albert Museum.

*See*: *Marble Halls*, 142A.

**189 London, The Albert Hall** (1871)

SHARPE and PALEY. A Lancaster firm, the partnership in the 1840s and 1850s of Edmund Sharpe (1809–77) and E. G. Paley (1813–95). Sharpe, who had been a pupil of Thomas Rickman (qv.), became well known for his church of St Steven, Lever Bridge, near Bolton, Yorks. (1842–45) which achieved its florid decorated detail with a novel, and cheap, use of terracotta.[1] He published a number of works on gothic architecture and, together with Paley, they were seen to be architects with a serious medieval interest, e.g. at their church of St Thomas, Coventry (1848–49). Domestic work included the remodelling of Hornby Castle, Lancs. (1848 on), and the Bishop's House, Lancaster (1859 by Paley). Sharpe was Mayor of Lancaster 1848, and from 1851 involved with railway engineering; Royal Gold Medallist 1875.

*See*: Ware.

**172 Lancaster, Royal Grammar School** (1855)

1. Immediately dubbed the 'Pot Church'. See H.-R. Hitchcock, *Early Victorian Architects*, 118, 123.

SHAW, John, Snr (1776–1832). Began practice 1798. In 1816 elected architect and surveyor to Christ's Hospital, London, for which he made extensive additions (see below). He specialised in valuation of property in London for street improvements. Shaw designed the octagonal St Dunstan's in the West, Fleet Street, London (1829–33) as well as houses, house alterations and lodges.

His son John Shaw Jnr (1803–70) succeeded him as architect to Christ's Hospital.

*See*: Colvin.

**96 London, Christ's Hospital, the Great Hall** (1829)

SMITH and HAMMOND.

**227 London, Cripplegate Institute** (1896)

SOANE, Sir John (1753–1837). In 1768 entered the office of George Dance Jnr (qv.), the City Surveyor of London. There followed training at the RA Schools, a period as assistant to Henry Holland, and a visit to Italy 1778. He was appointed Surveyor to the Bank of England in 1788. This gave him his most important commission—the rebuilding of the Bank between 1788 and 1833. The position also introduced him to many wealthy clients and he established an extensive practice for country and town houses. He developed a unique and personal style independent of the attractions of any Greek or gothic revivals; this can be seen not only in his designs for the Bank, and such houses as Tyringham (1793–1800), Pitzhanger, Ealing (1800–3), the Picture Gallery, Dulwich College (1812), but also at his own house in Lincoln's Inn Fields (now the Soane Museum). He was elected RA in 1802; became Professor of Architecture at the RA Schools 1806; knighted 1831. Although barred by the rules of the RA from accepting the post of President of the IBA on its foundation in 1834, the admiration of the profession for Soane was such that a special Gold Medal (see below) was presented to him by three hundred and fifty subscribers. This has W. Wyon's portrait of Soane on the obverse.

*See*: Colvin; Stroud, D., *The Architecture of Sir John Soane*, 1961.

**106 London, Bank of England** (1833)

STARTIN, William. Given by the 'Leamington Spa Courier', 1831, as architect for:

**103 Leamington, Beech Lawn House** (1832)

STEVENS, H. J. Goodhart-Rendel's index of churches (RIBA) gives H. J. Stevens 'of Derby'. He records twenty-eight churches in the Derbyshire, Notts., Staffs., area between 1831 and 1858 by H. I. or H. J. Stevens.

**174 Derby, St Michael,** Queen Street (1858)

TAYLOR, James. Architect, of Islington.

**60 St Edmund's College, Old Hall Green,** Herts. (1805)

THOMPSON, Francis. Appointed architect to the North Midland Railway 1836, and to the Chester and Holyhead Railway 1846, he became well known for his station designs and for his collaboration with the engineer Robert Stephenson (1803–59). This culminated in the building of the Tubular Bridge across the Menai Strait (see below).[1] Thompson handled the architectural aspects of this, and H.-R. Hitchcock refers to the bridge as 'an almost unqualified masterpiece of engineering–architecture'. Other works by Thompson (in conjunction with Stephenson) were Trijunct Station and Hotel, Derby (1839–41); General Station, Chester (1844–48); Tubular Bridge, Conway (1845–49); and all the stations along the Chester and Holyhead Line. In 1842 J. C. Loudon published some rural station designs of Thompson's 'revised to serve as cottage residences'.

*See*: *AR*, 1968, 314–15; H.-R. Hitchcock, *Early Victorian Architecture in Britain*, 502–4 and 518–21.

**164 Britannia Tubular Bridge, Menai Strait** (1850)

1. There is a portrait of Stephenson on this medal; he was also Engineer-in-Chief for the London and Birmingham Railway and his name appears on the Euston Arch medal (1838).

TITE, Sir William (1798–1873). Articled in 1812 to David Laing, the architect of the Custom House. Had set up his own practice by 1824; his first work was the Scottish Presbyterian Church, Regent Square, London (1824–27).[1] In the 1840s his financial and family connections brought him a series of railway station commissions in both England and France (e.g. along the Le Havre to Paris line). His one major building was however to be the new Royal Exchange

(1842–44), which Tite secured after an abortive and confused competition, and in the face of the much admired submission by C. R. Cockerell (qv.). Although twice President RIBA, and Royal Gold Medallist 1856, Tite effectively retired from architecture after 1855 to become prominent in banking and as an MP. Baronet 1869.

*See*: H.-R. Hitchcock, *Early Victorian Architecture in Britain*, 301–2, 305–9.

**146 London, Royal Exchange** (1844)

1. 'Two tower front modelled on the example of York Minster, but on a scale which makes the comparison between the two slightly ridiculous'. Pevsner, *London 2*, 208.

TOWNSEND, Charles Harrison (1850–1928). Practised as an architect in London, but was also involved with the design of textiles and wallpapers. Master of the Art Workers Guild. The Bishopsgate Institute (see below) was one of his early large architectural works. It showed an understanding of continental Art Nouveau, as well as of the designs of H. H. Richardson in America. These themes were developed further in his Whitechapel Art Gallery (1897–99) and the Horniman Museum, London (1900–2); Pevsner refers to them as 'without question the most remarkable example of a reckless repudiation of tradition among English architects of the time'. Townsend's church of St Mary the Virgin, Great Warley, Essex (1904) offered a suitable enclosure for the outstanding Art Nouveau decorations of Sir William Reynolds-Stephens (1862–1943).

*See*: Ware; N. Pevsner, *Pioneers of Modern Design*, 1960, 165; H.-R. Hitchcock, *Architecture Nineteenth and Twentieth Centuries*, 292–93.

**224 London, Bishopsgate Institute** (1894)

TRUBSHAW and JOHNSON. Apparently the partnership of James Trubshaw (the younger; 1777–1853) of Haywood, Staffs., with Thomas Johnson (1794–1865) of Lichfield.[1] Trubshaw, who came from a family of builders, was more distinguished for his engineering works and bridges (Chester 1833, Derby 1850) than for his buildings. Trubshaw and Johnson built St Mary, Uttoxeter, 1828, as well as the Stoke on Trent Church (below). J. and C. Trubshaw were architects of St Anne, Brown Edge, 1844 (see No. 144).

*See*: Colvin.

**98 Stoke on Trent, St Peter's Church** (1829)

1. But see note by Colvin, p. 626, of another James Trubshaw in Johnson's office.

VANBRUGH, Sir John (1664–1726). Vanbrugh's early life revolved around his career in the army and then the staging of his two plays—*The Relapse* in 1696 and *The Provok'd Wife* in 1697. All this was superseded by architecture when he made initial designs in 1699 for the Earl of Carlisle's house at Castle Howard (built by 1726) and when, in 1702, he was appointed Comptroller of the King's Works and the principal colleague of Sir Christopher Wren (qv.). In 1705 he secured his greatest architectural opportunity with the commission to design Blenheim Palace (Gateway and outworks completed *c.* 1722). He was working on Greenwich Palace from 1703, and in 1716 took Wren's place as surveyor in charge. In much of his work Nicholas Hawksmoor (qv.) acted as both assistant and associate designer, and the careers and architectural ideals of the two men are closely interwoven. However, unlike Hawksmoor, Vanbrugh was not a church builder and all of his works are for public or domestic buildings; the last great example of the latter was at Seaton Delaval, Northumberland (*c.* 1720–28). Knighted 1714. His portrait, after a contemporary painting, is on the obverse of the medal below.

*See*: Colvin; L. Whistler, *The Imagination of Vanbrugh*, 1954.

**42 Blenheim Palace, Oxfordshire** (1720)

WADDINGTON, W., and SONS. Architectural practice in the Manchester area. Their work includes: Brunswick Methodist Church, Whitby (1891); Wesleyan Church, Bury Old Road, Manchester (1894).

**210 Burnley and District Hospital,** Lancs. (1886)

WAINWRIGHT, C. The inscription on the medal gives Wainwright as architect for enlarging this fine Somerset church in 1837.

**15 Shepton Mallet**, Somerset, **St Peter and St Paul**, alterations (1837)

WATERHOUSE, Alfred (1830–1905). Articled to Richard Lane (qv.). After studies in France, Germany, and Italy started a Manchester practice in 1854. He won the Manchester Assize Courts competition with a solution in the Venetian Gothic style (built 1859–64). In 1865 moved to London, and prepared an entry for the Law Courts competition. He then developed an extremely large practice handling works such as the Manchester Town Hall (after another competition success, 1868); Caius College, Cambridge (1870); Natural History Museum, South Kensington (1873–81); Chapel, Tower, and remodelling at Eaton Hall, Cheshire (1875); Prudential head office, Holborn (1879 and 1899–1906);[1] St Paul's School, Hammersmith (1881–85). Many of his buildings stood out by their assertive use of colour and of his favourite material, terracotta. In 1891 he was joined in partnership by his son Paul Waterhouse (1861–1924). He was President RIBA 1888–91; Royal Gold Medallist 1878.

*See: RIBAJ*, 1905, 609–18; *Marble Halls*, 14, 31, 72, 87, 139; C. Stewart, *The Architecture of Manchester*, pamphlet, 1956, pp. 56, 57.

**197 Manchester, Town Hall** (1877)
**214 London, National Liberal Club,** Whitehall Place (1887)

1. He was architect to the Prudential Assurance Co. and built offices for them in many large provincial Towns.

WEBB, Sir Aston (1849–1930). Set up in practice in London 1873, and did much of his work in association with E. Ingress Bell (1837–1914). Major works included: Victoria Law Courts, Birmingham (1887–91); Victoria and Albert Museum, London (1899–1909); Birmingham University, Edgbaston (1900–9); Admiralty Arch, London (1911); refacing of Buckingham Palace, London (1913). Knighted 1904; President RIBA 1902–4; Royal Gold Medallist 1905.

*See*: *Builder*, 1930, 333; Ware.

**218 Birmingham, Victoria Law Courts** (1891)

WHITWELL, Thomas Stedman (d. *c.* 1840). In 1811 was employed in the architect's office at the London Docks. By 1819 he was living at Leamington Spa, and in the next two years designed Carrs Lane Chapel (see below); New Library, Temple Row, Birmingham; Brampton Park, Hunts.

*See*: Colvin.

**72 Birmingham, Carrs Lane Chapel** (1820)

WILD, James William (1814–92). Articled to the architect George Basevi in 1830. Started practice with two churches in the gothic style: Holy Trinity, Blackheath Hill, London (1838–39) and St Laurence, Southampton (1839). His next design, Christ Church, Streatham (1840–41, see below), was an impressive example of the 'Rundbogenstil',[1] which used Italian Romanesque or Early Christian forms; this became fashionable in the 1840s amongst a group of young architects including T. H. Wyatt (qv.), whose Wilton Church is on medal No. 154a. Wild was in Egypt and the Mediterranean area 1842–48 and prepared a design for St Mark, Alexandria. His later works include St Martin's Northern District School, near Endell Street, London (1844)[2] and the shell of the Bethnal Green Museum (1875); the latter encloses the rebuilt cast iron structure that was the first museum building (1856) on the Victoria and Albert site at Brompton.[3] From 1878 Wild was Curator of the Soane Museum.

*See*: H.-R. Hitchcock, *Early Victorian Architecture in Britain*, 100 ff. and 401; Ware.

**134 London, Streatham, Christ Church** (1841)

1. 'Round arch style'. Also referred to in England as the 'Lombardic' style.
2. An Italian gothic design praised by Ruskin and Street. Wild designed it with a roof playground for this town site.
3. Nicknamed the 'Brompton Boilers' by G. Godwin, editor of the *Builder*, for whom it was a reminder of the boilerhouse built adjacent to the 1851 'Crystal Palace'.

WILKINS, William (1778–1839). Entered Caius College, Cambridge, as a scholar in 1796, and was later elected a Fellow. During 1801–5 he travelled extensively through Italy, Greece, and Asia Minor, and on his return soon emerged as a leading architect of the 'Greek Revival'. In this his own scholarship was combined with the advantage of his academic appointment and the support of the artist patron Thomas Hope. He built up a large practice from Cambridge, and the works where he was able to apply his theories on Greek architecture included: Downing College, Cambridge (1807–20); Grange Park, Hants (1809); Freemasons' Hall, Bath, and University College, London (see below); York Philosophical Society Museum (1827–30); The National Gallery, London (1834–38). For much of his collegiate and domestic work he had, however, to accept the contemporary preference for Tudor Gothic, e.g. in his new college buildings at Cambridge for Trinity (1821–23); Corpus Christi (1823–27); and King's (1824–28). Wilkins published a variety of works on architectural history; he was elected RA in 1826 and, in 1827, Professor of Architecture in succession to Sir John Soane (qv.).

*See*: Colvin; A. Beresford Pite in *RIBAJ*, 24 December 1932.

**70 Bath, The Freemasons' Hall** (1819)
**97 London, University College** (1828)

WILKINSON, William (1819–1901). An Oxford architect who built up a considerable practice in the area as a designer of suburban and small country houses. As surveyor to the Norham Manor Estate in North Oxford, he developed in the 1860s a domestic gothic vernacular of tall brick houses, gabled and with stone gothic motifs. His most prominent Oxford work, the Randolph Hotel 1864, fiercely reinforced this allegiance to the gothic, as did many designs for parsonages and schools, e.g. St Edward's School, Woodstock Road, 1873. Wilkinson's works also include Holy Trinity Church, Lew (1841); extension to Oxford Union Society (1863); Shelswell Park (1871); and Warneford Hospital (1877).

*See*: Pevsner and J. Sherwood, *Oxfordshire*.

**177 Oxford University Gymnasium** (1859)

WILSON, James. In practice at Bath from the 1840s.[1] Exhibited RA 1841–55. His church designs in Somerset include Shipham (1843), Redhill (1844), Uphill (1844), and, in a classical format, the Moravian Chapel, Charlotte Street, Bath (1845). Wilson is best known for his Cheltenham College (1842–43) and he became a schools architect favoured by the Noncomformists, e.g. Wesleyan Collegiate Institution (Queen's College) Taunton (1843); Kingswood School, Lansdown, Bath (1851); Lansdown College (Royal School) Bath (1856–58). In 1856 he proposed a 'Crystal Palace' for the Royal Victoria Park, Bath.

*See*: RIBA Biographies Index.

**140 Cheltenham Proprietary College** (1843)

1. After 1872 the firm is given in the *Bath Directory* as Wilson, Willcox, and Wilson, with James Buckley Wilson joining it.

WOOD, John, the elder (1705–54). The names of Wood, and his son John Wood, the younger (1728–81) are synonymous with the planning and development of Georgian Bath. Their work started with the elder Wood's Queen's Square (1729–36) and reached its final phase with the Royal Crescent (1767–75). As Bath became a fashionable resort, and the fame of the elder Wood's Palladian façades grew, he was invited by Ralph Allen to design the country house at nearby Prior Park (see below). This was built between 1735 and *c.* 1750 (but finished by Allen's clerk of works Richard Jones), and allowed Wood to undertake an ambitious re-creation of one of Palladio's villas. Towards the end of his life Wood was reviving his early proposals of 1725 for a 'Royal Forum' and a 'Grand Circus' in Bath. These were partly realised with the building of The Circus (1754 onwards).

*See*: Colvin; W. Ison, *The Georgian Buildings of Bath*, 1948.

**47 Bath, Prior Park, Combe Down** (1750)

WOODHEAD and HURST. Architectural practice of Doncaster. Their work included several Commissioners' churches, e.g. St George, Sheffield (1821–25), as well as Christchurch, Thorne Road, Doncaster (1827–29). After John Woodhead died (*c.* 1835), William Hurst (1787–1844) entered partnership with W. L. Moffatt; they were architects for further churches in the Midlands and public buildings in Leeds, Sheffield, and Wakefield.

*See*: Colvin; Port.

**85 Doncaster, New Betting Rooms** (1826)

WORTHINGTON, Thomas (1826–1909). After a period working with Sir William Tite, he set up a practice and became 'the most eminent architect of Victorian Manchester'. He later went into partnership with John Elgood (see medal below). President, Manchester Society of Architects 1875–77. Works include: Albert Memorial (1862) and Memorial Hall (1865), Manchester; Manchester College, Oxford (1891–93).

*See*: Ware; C. Stewart, *The Architecture of Manchester*, 1956, pamphlet, pp. 57, 58.

**211 Hindley,** Lancs., **Library and Museum** (1887)
**217 Harrogate,** W. Yorks., **The Royal Bath Hospital** (1889)

WREN, Sir Christopher (1632–1723). Initially embarked on a scientific career, in 1653 he became a Fellow of All Souls, Oxford, and in 1661 Savilian Professor of Astronomy as well as a founder member of the Royal Society. His turn to architecture was marked by his designs for the Sheldonian Theatre, Oxford (1664–69) and Pembroke Chapel, Cambridge (1663–65), and confirmed by his appointment to the Commission for replanning and rebuilding London after the Great Fire. In 1669 Wren was appointed Surveyor General of the King's Works—a post he held until 1718; in this capacity he worked with Hawksmoor (qv.) and, from 1702, Vanbrugh (qv.). His main architectural achievements can be grouped as:

The City churches (rebuilt from 1670 onwards). Suprisingly none of these appear to have been the subject of an architectural medal, although many appear on the token coinage of the late eighteenth century.

The rebuilding of St Paul's Cathedral (1675–1710). The Cathedral has been an obvious topic for the medallist; its portrayal has varied from the bad (No. 39b) to the outstanding (No. 39h), with an excellent interior (No. 39i).

University schemes, e.g. Emmanuel College, Cambridge (1668–73); Trinity College Library, Cambridge (1676–84); Tom Tower, Christ Church, Oxford, which became a careful conservation exercise executed by Wren in 'Gothick to agree with the Founder's Worke . . .' (1681–82).

Large residential buildings comprising several related blocks, e.g. Chelsea Hospital, Hampton Court Palace, Kensington Palace, Greenwich Hospital (all in the period 1682–1702). Wren also prepared a scheme for the building of a great new Whitehall Palace after the fire of 1698; this was to incorporate Inigo Jones's Banqueting House (see No. 34) as its centrepiece.

In 1838 Professor C. R. Cockerell (qv.) produced his well-known tribute which placed in one drawing all Wren's buildings. Unfortunately Wren has been the victim of many imperfect attributions, and Cockerell's drawing includes Temple Bar (No. 37)—now considered only indirectly Wren's design.

Portrait medal of Wren by G. D. Gaab.

There is a portrait of Christopher Wren on the obverse of No. 39h, p. 22, derived from Edward Pierce's marble bust of the architect at the age of forty.[1]

*See*: Colvin; M. Whinney, *Wren*, 1971.

**39 London, St Paul's Cathedral** (1710)

1. As with Inigo Jones (qv.), Wren had been the subject of a portrait medal in the eighteenth century: the magnificent bronze by G. D. Gaab, with an elevation of St Paul's on the reverse (BM; *Med. Ill.* ii, p. 468); and see p. 25.

WYATT, James (1746–1813). Studied in Italy 1762–68 and returned to London to set up as an architect-builder. Wyatt's design for the Pantheon, Oxford Street, London (1770–72, built by his brother Samuel) brought instant acclaim and began his career as a fashionable architect of country houses and public buildings, e.g. additions to Chiswick House (1788); the magnificent interiors at Heveningham Hall, Suffolk (1789); the 'pleasure building in the shape of an abbey' at Fonthill (1796–1807); Ashridge Park, Herts. (1808–13, completed by Jeffry Wyatt (qv.) 1817). In 1776 Wyatt became Surveyor of Westminster Abbey, and in 1796 Comptroller of Works in succession to Sir William Chambers (qv.). However, it was for his restorations of cathedrals (e.g. at Salisbury, Lichfield, Hereford) that he achieved another sort of reputation—that of 'Wyatt the Destroyer'. This sprang from Wyatt's aim when restoring, or 'improving', to achieve a uniformity of style and appearance; for this he often removed screens, monuments, or any elements which he considered intrusive. By contrast, and less well known, his refacing of Henry VII's chapel at Westminster (1809–13) proved to be a model example of conservation technique. When, in 1813, James Wyatt was killed, following a carriage accident, his own fame was established and that of the whole Wyatt family was beginning to find its special place in architectural history.

*See*: Colvin; *RIBA Dwgs Coll.* (Wyatt Family).

WYATT, John Drayton (1820–91). Articled to H. W. Inwood. In 1841 became assistant draughtsman to Scott and Moffatt (qv.) and stayed with Scott until 1867. Known as 'Scott's Wyatt' to distinguish him from the members of the Wyatt dynasty. He was diocesan architect for Bath and Wells and undertook many restorations.

**187** Gloucs., **Christ Church, Gretton Green** (1868)

WYATT, Lewis William (1777–1853). Nephew of James Wyatt (qv.) in whose office he worked in the early 1800s. He set up practice in London and in 1818 was appointed Clerk of Works at Whitehall. He was responsible for several house designs in a familiar Wyatt manner, e.g. Willey Park, Shropshire (1812); Hackwood, Hampshire (1805–13); completion of Tatton Park, Cheshire (1811–12) begun by his uncle Samuel (d. 1807).

*See*: Colvin; *RIBA Dwgs Coll.* (Wyatt Family).

**68 Stockport, St Mary's Parish Church** rebuilt (1817)

WYATT, Thomas Henry (1807–80). Educated privately in Brussels, and originally destined for a career in commerce, he became a pupil of Philip Hardwick (qv.). In 1838 started a partnership in London with David Brandon (1813–97); their collaboration lasted thirteen years and included the widely published, and influential, 'Lombardic' style Wilton Church (see below). Wyatt's practice had an emphasis on church buildings and large country houses in a Tudor format; he was also consultant architect to organisations such as the Institute of Civil Engineers, the Athenaeum Club and the Governesses Benevolent Institution. His office became highly successful and he and his assistants produced an immense number of buildings even by Victorian standards; two later works were Knightsbridge Barracks, London (1878–79) and the extension of Brompton Hospital, London (1879–82; cf. Horace Francis). Wyatt was elected President RIBA and Royal Gold Medallist 1873.

*See*: *RIBA Dwgs Coll.* (Wyatt family); *Builder*, xxxix, 1880, 193; *Marble Halls*, 37, 82.

**154 Wilton Church**, Wilts. (1844)

**160 London, Governesses Benevolent Institution, Kentish Town** (1848)

WYATVILLE, Sir Jeffry (1766–1840). Born Jeffry Wyatt, he was a nephew of James and Samuel Wyatt, and worked in both their offices between 1784 and 1799. He then set up his own London practice and became well known for his country house designs, e.g. the rebuilding at Longleat House, Wilts. (1801–11); Endsleigh, Devon (1810); completion of Ashridge, Herts. (1817); additions to Chatsworth (1820–40); and (from 1824 on) his major work, the reconstruction of Windsor Castle as a Royal residence for George IV. When the first stone was laid at Windsor by the King, the architect was authorised to call himself Wyatville[1] and on the completion of the royal apartments in 1828 he was knighted. A lavish production describing the works at Windsor was prepared by Wyatville and published after his death as *Illustrations of Windsor Castle by the late Sir Jeffry Wyatville RA*. When the IBA came into being in 1834 he was elected an Honorary Fellow, and it was he who in 1835 made the presentation of William Wyon's gold medal to Sir John Soane (qv.) as a 'Tribute of Respect from the British Architects' (see No. 106a).

*See*: Colvin; D. Linstrum, *Sir Jeffry Wyatville: Architect to the King*, 1972; *RIBA Dwgs Coll.* (Wyatt family).

**131 Windsor**, Berks., **Windsor Castle** (1840)

1. The royal licence states this to be a 'Mark of Our Royal Favour and to distinguish himself from the numerous branches of his family of the same profession'.

# MEDALLISTS SCULPTORS PUBLISHERS

# 5

Entries are provided for individuals or firms named on the medal inscriptions (see Section 3). Below each biographical note are listed all the buildings in the medallic index which were the subject of a medal by them; these are given in order of *date of completion of the medal* (shown to the left of the entry). In some cases the date of completion or issue of the medal may be later than the date on the medal inscription, e.g. with the Art-Union series. After each medal subject listed under a biography, there is the *key reference number* to provide immediate access to the medallic catalogue.

Each biography is intended to establish basic dates, place, and type of work. As with the architectural biographies, emphasis has been placed on establishing some context for less well known names, especially those not appearing in the definitive *Biographical Dictionary of Medallists* by L. Forrer. For such major figures as William or Benjamin Wyon reference is made to the extensive material provided by Forrer, and the biography is intended to provide purely a summary context to the artists' architectural works; the selection of other medals quoted is limited accordingly.

ADAMS, George Gammon (1821–98). Articled at sixteen to William Wyon (qv.) at the Royal Mint and attended the Royal Academy schools in 1840 on Wyon's recommendation. After leaving the Mint, was given further instruction on cutting medal and coin dies by Pistrucci—then living in retirement. Adams studied in Rome in 1846, but returned to England in 1847 to win an RA Gold Medal for a sculptured group. His design of 'Industry seated on cornucopiae receiving from Britain the reward of Fame' was selected for the Jurors' Medal of the 1851 Exhibition. He achieved great success as a sculptor from then on, with a wide variety of public statues, busts, and monuments. Forrer considered that his best designs for medals were achieved in the period 1865–93; these included several in the City of London series (e.g. Opening of Blackfriars Bridge and Holborn Viaduct 1869) and five of the Art-Union series

(Lawrence, Dyce, Etty, Mulready, Scott). His many other medals include the funeral medal of the Duke of Wellington; the George Godwin Bursary Medal[1] presented as a prize by the RIBA.

*See*: Forrer, vol. 1, 22; Gunnis, 13; *British Sculpture 1850–1914;* Beulah, 183–85.

1848 Duke of Cambridge;[2] *Rev.* **Governesses Benevolent Institution, London** **(160a)**
1884 Sir G. Gilbert Scott; *Rev.* Edinburgh Cathedral (**235a**, p. 203)

1. Illustrated in *The Builder,* 16 May 1885, 705. George Godwin (portrait on the obverse) had been the magazine's editor; he himself endowed the bursary in 1881.

2. The signature G. C. Adams appears on the obverse of this medal issued and signed by Allen & Moore. It must be an error for the then comparatively unknown artist. Adams is known to have made a medal of Adolphus Frederick, Duke of Cambridge, from sittings (Forrer, vol. 1, 24).

ALLEN & MOORE. A Birmingham firm of medallists formed by the partnership, in the 1840s and 1850s,[1] of John Allen (whose role was that of designer) with the die-engraver Joseph Moore (qv.). Address in 1854 was Great Hampton Row. Taken together with Moore's individually signed works, they provide a good example of the traditions of the 'Birmingham school' of die sinkers; their example reflected a revival of medallic production in the town after a decline from the promise of the early years of the nineteenth century. Many of the architectural medals over this joint signature are of the cheaper, white metal, variety but the building representations provide straightforward, and useful, street views. Usually signed: Allen & Moore Birm. (or Birmingham); Allen & Moore; A & M.

*See*: Forrer, vol. 1, 41; Hawkins, pt i, 1960, 95.

?1844 **St Anne's Church, Brown Edge** **(144a)**
1844 **Royal Exchange** **(146f–k)**
1846 **Liverpool, Sailors' Home** **(159a)**
1846 **Macclesfield Sunday School** **(66a)**
1847 **Houses of Parliament** **(179a, b)**
1847 **Shakespeare's House, Stratford on Avon** **(28b)**
1848 **Governesses Benevolent Institution, London** **(160a)**
1849 **Licensed Victuallers' Asylum, London** **(162a)**
1849 **Sherborne Abbey Church** **(21a)**
1849 **Coal Exchange, London** **(161a)**
1851 **Great Exhibition, Hyde Park** **(165a–o)**
1851 **Worsley Hall** **(155a)**
1852 **Institution for the Blind, Birmingham** **(167a, b)**
1854 **St George's Hall, Liverpool** **(170a)**
1854 **Sydenham Crystal Palace** **(171a)**
1862 **London, International Exhibition building** **(182j)**

1. Hawkins gives the partnership as lasting from 1840 to 1858; by 1860 Jos. Moore was describing himself as 'late Allen & Moore'. Grant recorded, however, a medal of 1864 (Shakespeare Tercentary) as one final item in their joint name; could this be an expedient re-use of the earlier 1847 die?

ART UNION OF LONDON (founded 1837; disbanded 1912). A society founded to encourage public interest in the fine arts, and at the same time provide a stimulus for British manufacturers and artists making 'art objects' or reproductions. This dual aim was furthered by offering members an engraving worth at least the value of their one guinea per year subscription. Mass production allowed a financial surplus from the process which then went to commission British works of art, medals, paintings or reproductions; these were used as prizes 'of substantial value' in a lottery open to all members. The medallic series 'The History of British Art' was initiated in 1842 to act as prizes and also to encourage a revival amongst British medallists and die-engravers. William Wyon (qv.) was asked to advise the Society in the setting up of the series, and he produced the first medal, of the sculptor Sir Francis Chantrey.[1] The silver medals (restricted to thirty in number each year) were used as the actual prizes, and the bronze medals were available to any member in lieu of the engraving for that year. Although the preference for this option was small, some hundreds of bronze medals would be struck when, as in 1876, the membership was over 20,000.[2] There were thirty medals in the series, which ran between 1842 and 1887. The subject categories were: fifteen painters; seven sculptors, six architects (listed below); one die-engraver, W. Wyon (qv.); the final medal, by Alfred Gilbert, was for the 1887 Jubilee. The Society had had Thomas Hope among its founders; the architect T. L. Donaldson (qv.), author of *Architectura Numismatica* (1859), later served on its committee.[3] In 1879 a building was put up for the Art-Union headquarters at 112 Strand;[4] their architect for this was E. M. Barry, the son of Sir Charles Barry (qv.) who in 1862 had been honoured with a medal in the series.

*See*: Beulah, G. K., 'The medals of the Art Union of London', *BNJ*, xxxvi (1967), 179–85 plus plates; *British Sculpture 1850–1914,* 44, 45.

The following are the medals portraying architects and their buildings in the Art-Union series. Dates are as given on the medals, with actual year of distribution in brackets. (The artists signing obverse or reverse are given; for these, and the architects named, see individual entries.)

1846 (1850) Sir Christopher Wren (W. Wilson); *Rev.* **St Paul's Cathedral** (B. Wyon) **(39h)**
1849 (1852) Inigo Jones (C. F. Carter); *Rev.* **Banqueting House, Whitehall** **(34a)**
1855 (1856) Sir John Vanbrugh (B. Wyon); *Rev.* **Blenheim Palace** (B. Wyon) **(42a)**
1857 (1857) Sir William Chambers (B. Wyon);[5] *Rev.* **Somerset House** (B. Wyon) **(52a)**
1862 (1862) Sir Charles Barry (L. Wiener); *Rev.* **Houses of Parliament** (J. Wiener) **(179i)**
1884 (1884) Sir George Gilbert Scott (G. G. Adams); *Rev.* **St Mary's Cathedral, Edinburgh** **(235a**, p. 203)

1. Dated 1843 for issue to prizewinners of that year, but not issued until 1847.
2. By 1895 this had dropped to 5000. The Society was wound up by resolution in 1912.
3. *British Sculpture 1850–1914,* 40.
4. Illustrated in H. Hobhouse, *Lost London,* 172. It was demolished in the 1930s. Also see *The Building News,* 28 February 1879, 7, 14 March, 11, 25 April, and the obituary of E. M. Barry, 30 January 1880, 143.
5. This medal had been commissioned in 1855 from L. C. Wyon (qv.) but was passed on to his relative Benjamin Wyon (qv.).

AVERN, Edward. Engraver and die-sinker of medals, tickets. *Fl.* 1815–46. Lived first in London at 9 Stanhope Street, Clare Market. Moved to Birmingham in 1834. His few known medals include one of Izaac Walton in 1824; a poor design on the death of George IV in 1830; and one struck in 1844 to commemorate the inauguration of the Nelson monument in Trafalgar Square.

*See*: Forrer, vol. 1, 93; vol. 7, 35; Hawkins, pt i, 1960, 96; pt iii, 1968, 57.

1834 **Birmingham Town Hall** **(108a)**
1846 **Wilton Church** **(154a)**

BAIN, W. (*fl.* 1825–62). Born Edinburgh early nineteenth century. Exhibited works at Royal Academy 1823 to 1847. Emphasis in Scottish subjects, but his medals include one of the architect Sir John Soane (qv.) issued in the year of Soane's death in 1837. The famous Scottish engineer John Rennie (qv.), who produced the design for London Bridge (see No. 102), is portrayed by Bain on medals of 1821, 1822, and 1823 in connection with the completion of Sheerness docks, and following Rennie's death. When London Bridge was finally opened in 1831 Rennie again was portrayed posthumously by Bain on a further medal.

*See*: Forrer, vol. 1, 122; vol. 7, 41.

1821 John Rennie **(234a**, p. 201)

BARBER, J. Engraver of medals, e.g. Pacification of Europe 1814 (in conjunction with T. Wyon), George Walter the great Railway Champion 1838, Sir Charles Napier 1841. He also produced a portrait medallion of the Prince Regent in 1814.

*See*: Forrer, vol. 1, 122; vol. 7, 45.

1838 **The 'old' Royal Exchange** **(36a)**

BARBER, CATTLE & NORTH. Signed a medal following the destruction by fire of the choir of York Minster. A firm of plate and silver manufacturers of Coney Street, York. Cf. the Cattle, Harrison & Cattle who issued a similar style York Minster medal in 1796.

1829 **York Minster;** *Rev.* **Interior of Choir** **(13a, b)**

BARKER, I. This signature, with date, appears on obverse and reverse of:

1844 **Chichester Cathedral;** *Rev.* **Chichester Cross** **(2a)**

BENNETT. Organised two medals of major English cathedrals. Bennett signed Salisbury with 'direx' and that of Winchester with 'Sarum', i.e. Salisbury as his address. The Salisbury medal is executed, and signed, by T. Halliday (qv.).

1830 **Salisbury Cathedral** **(10a)**
18–? **Winchester Cathedral** **(11a)**

BOVY, (Jean François) Antoine (1795–1877). The Bovys were a celebrated family of Swiss medallists and coin engravers all of whom worked for the Geneva mint. Antoine was one of three brothers, all medallists. The prodigious list of his works includes the Swiss federal coinage of 1850 and 1873 and among his medals is one showing the market buildings of Les Halles Centrales, Paris (demolished 1973–74). (Forrer, vol. 1, 243.) Bovy signs the obverse of the following, with 'Massonet Editor' on reverse:

1862 Queen Victoria; *Rev.* **London, International Exhibition Building** **(182k)**

BOWCHER, Frank (1864–1938). Sculptor. Student at Royal College of Art; studied in the studio of the sculptor E. Onslow Ford and also under the French medallist L.-O. Roty. First medal dates from 1886 and his nineteenth-century medals include three for the City of London series: Visit of the King and Queen of Denmark; Opening of Tower Bridge; Queen Victoria's Diamond Jubilee. The Tower Bridge medal, when contrasted to the earlier works in the series of Benjamin or J. S. and A. B. Wyon, shows how the soft, low relief, approach of Bowcher represented his allegiance to the then new 'French School' of medallists. The latter was typified by the medallic work of Roty and Chaplain.

*See*: Forrer, vol. 1, 252.

1894 **Tower Bridge, London** **(225a)**
1897 **Leeds, St Peter's Church** **(132c)**

BROCK, Sir Thomas (1847–1922). Born and studied at Worcester, then in 1866 entered the studio of the much admired Victorian sculptor J. H. Foley. After Foley's death in 1874, Brock completed many of his works. Brock designed the 'Old Head' of Queen Victoria for the coinage of 1893, to replace the much criticised 1887 'Jubilee' design by Boehm. His portrait head of the Queen appears as the model for several 1897 Jubilee medals (e.g. as below, and see De Saulles). Major works include the Queen Victoria memorial in front of Buckingham Palace 1901–11; the equestrian statue of the Black Prince, Leeds 1912. He became RA 1891, KCB 1911.

*See*: *British Sculpture 1850–1914,* 21.

1897 Queen Victoria;[1] **St Peter's Church, Eaton Square, London** **(90a)**

1. Not signed, but Grant gives obverse 'after T. Brock'.

BROOKES & ADAMS. Thomas Brookes (b. 1831) set up in partnership with Thomas Adams in 1853 as a firm of Birmingham die-sinkers. Both men had been apprenticed to Allen & Moore (qv.). While with Joseph Moore (qv.) Thomas Brookes cut dies for 'Head of Robert Nelson, founder of the Bath Blue Coat School', and 'Sir Joseph Paxton', reverse of Sydenham Crystal Palace (see 171a). By 1900 the firm of Brookes & Adams had expanded as a family business and produce a wide variety of medals. Medal below signed B & A.

*See*: Forrer, vol. 1, 297; Hawkins, pt i, 1960, 96.

1887 **Evesham Tower** **(30a)**

BUSFIELD. Issued a medal signed 'Busfield Colne'.

1895 **Colne, Lancs., Town Hall** **(223a)**

CARTER, Charles Frederick (1805–?). A pupil of T. Halliday (qv.). Known for his Brisbane and Neill medals for the Royal Society. His medal of Inigo Jones (qv.) for the Art Union shows a portrait of the architect based on Michael Rysbrack's marble bust (*c.* 1725) in the Chatsworth collection.

*See*: Illustration 412 in catalogue: *The Kings Arcadia,* Arts Council Exhibition 1973; Forrer, vol. 1, 356.

1837 **Liverpool Mechanics Institution** **(119a)**
1839 **London, Wesleyan Centenary Hall** **(127a, b)**
1849 Inigo Jones; *Rev.* **The Banqueting House** **(34a)**

CITY OF LONDON, Corporation of. Although, in a literal sense, there is no distinction to be made between those medals issued by the City of London and those from any other city or town commemorating important municipal events, it is usual to refer to the publication of a 'City of London series'.[1] This relates to the steady output of medals (twenty-nine in all) issued by the Corporation between 1831 and 1902; these all marked historic occasions in the City's life. Those portraying works of architecture are listed for reference below, together with the names of medallists who are indexed separately.

*See*: Welch, C., *Numismata Londinensia,* 1894, and *History of the Tower Bridge,* London, 1894, 3–5; *British Sculpture 1850–1914,* 39–43.

1831 **Opening of London Bridge** by William IV (B. Wyon; **102a**)
1834 **Foundation of City of London School** (B. Wyon; **120a**)
1838 Visit of Queen Victoria to the **Guildhall** (W. Wyon; **53b**)
1852 Opening of the **Coal Exchange** by Prince Albert (B. Wyon; **161c**)
1872 Thanksgiving service in **St Paul's Cathedral** (J. S. & A. B. Wyon; **39k**)
1878 Removal of **Temple Bar** (C. H. & J. Mabey; **37a**)
1882 Opening of **City of London School for Boys** (J. S. & A. B. Wyon; **202a**)
1884 Opening of new **Guildhall Council Chamber** (J. S. & A. B. Wyon; **206a**)
1886 Colonial and Indian reception in **Guildhall** (Elkington & Co., **185a**)
1894 Opening of **Tower Bridge** by Prince of Wales (F. Bowcher; **225a**)

1. They are not signed by the City of London (as for instance the Art-Union (qv.) often sign their medals), however many carry the City shield and insignia. The majority have details of Lord Mayor, Aldermen, and Visitors, etc., on the presentation boxes in which the medals were issued.

CLINT, Scipio (1805–39). The son of George Clint ARA. Appointed medallist to William IV in 1831, and seal engraver to Queen Victoria in 1838. Worked chiefly in these capacities but also carved some marble busts. Exhibited at the Royal Academy in 1835 and 1837 and Liverpool Academy 1837.

*See*: Gunnis, 105; Forrer, vol. 1, 441; *Num. Chron.* 1890, 59, for portrait medal of Clint.

1837 William Roscoe; *Rev.* **Liverpool Mechanics Institution** (**119a**)

COLLIS, George Richmond. Medallist, electro-plater, gold- and silversmith. Witgrave & Collis (later G. R. Collis) bought Sir Edward Thomason's (qv.) manufactory at Colmore Row, Birmingham, in 1835. This had specialised in gold and silver plating which was then being superseded by the new electro-plating process. Collis kept this works going until 1868, and also took over Thomason's appointments as consul for various foreign governments. Forrer quotes the 'fine medal' by Collis for the accession of Queen Victoria in 1837, with the bust copied from one by William Wyon.

*See*: Forrer, vol. 1, 449; vol. 7, 189; Hawkins, pt i, 1960, 313.

1838 **The 'Euston Arch'** (**125a, b**)
1841 **London, Philosophical Institution** (**129a**)
1843 **Birmingham, Hebrew National School** (**139a**)

CROSS, E. Signs a silver medal to mark the laying of the foundation stone for one of the Commissioners' churches:

1822 **London, Southwark, St George's Church** (**83a**)

DAVIS, Joseph. A Birmingham medallist. Entered business 1828; died about 1857. A large number of architectural medals produced in the 1830s and 1840s over his signature 'Davis Birm.'; the best known and executed are his set of English cathedrals inscribed (except for York and St Paul's) 'Dedicated by permission to H.R.H. Prince Albert'.

*See*: Forrer, vol. 1, 536; vol. 7, 212; Hawkins, pt i, 1960, 142.

1835 **Bath, St Michael's Old Church** (**46a**)
1835 **Bath, St Michael's Church** (**115a**)
1836 **Birmingham, King Edward VI School** (**116a**)
1837 **Walsall Wood, St John's Church** (**122a**)
1837 **Birmingham, Town Hall** (**108e**)
1837 **Birmingham, Baptist Meeting House** (**61a**)
1841 **London, S. Islington and Pentonville Schools** (**133a**)
1842 **Birmingham, St Philip's Schools** (**136a**)
1842 **Kettering, Baptist Mission House** (**40a**)
1842 **London, Royal Exchange** (**146a**)
1843 **London, Nelson Monument** (**143a**)
1844 **London, Brompton Hospital** (**153a**)
1844 **London, Royal Exchange** (**146l–u**)
1844 **Gloucester, St James Schools** (**145a**)
1845 **Liverpool, St Mary's Roman Catholic Church** (**149a**)
1845 **London, Lincoln's Inn, New Hall and Library** (**150a, b**)
1846 **London, Brompton Hospital** (**153b**)
1846 **Liverpool, Sailors' Home** (**159b**)
1847 **London, Houses of Parliament** (**179c–e**)
1851 **London, Hyde Park, Great Exhibition** (**165p, q**)
?1840s **London, St Paul's Cathedral** (**39g**)

From 1835[1] English Cathedrals series:

**Canterbury** **(1a)**
**Ely** **(4a, b)**
**Gloucester** **(5a)**
**Lichfield** **(6a)**
**Lincoln** **(7a)**
**London — St Paul's*** **(39f)**
**London — Westminster Abbey** **(8a)**
**Oxford** **(9a, b)**
**Worcester** **(12a)**
**York*** **(13c)**

1. Given by Grant. Those without dedication (*) may date from the 1830s prior to the Queen's marriage with Prince Albert in 1840, and his official title. One variety of Ely Cathedral (No. 4a) is also without this dedication.

DEE, G. His signature appears for a head of the Prince Consort:

1851 Prince Consort; *Rev.* **Great Exhibition Building** **(165r)**

DE SAULLES, George William (1862–1903). Trained in Birmingham at the School of Art, then apprenticed to Wilcox, a die-sinker. To London in 1884 where he worked for several years as a writer. Returned to Birmingham in 1888 and employed by medallist Joseph Moore (qv.) until 1892; then appointed engraver to the Royal Mint on the death of L. C. Wyon (qv.). His medallic portraits of the 1890s reflect the influence of the contemporary continental approach to design. He engraved the 1897 Jubilee medal with 'Old' and 'Young Heads' of Queen Victoria after models by T. Brock (qv.) and William Wyon (qv.). He also worked for Pinches (qv.), and Forrer (vol. 4, 548) gives the medal below as engraved by De Saulles for J. H. Pinches.

*See*: Forrer, vol. 1, 563; *Num. Chron.* 1903, iii, 311–13.

1892 Queen Victoria; *Rev.* **Imperial Institute, London** **(221b)**

DOWLER, G. Signs a large medal for the reopening of the Crystal Palace on its new site; also several for the 1862 Exhibition.

*See*: Forrer, vol. 7, 232.

1854 **Sydenham, Crystal Palace** **(171b)**
1862 **London, International Exhibition Building** **(182a–i)**

DURNING, B., and Ryder, C. Die-sinkers and seal engravers; at 54 Bull Street, Birmingham in the 1830s and 1840s. Two medals of Birmingham buildings are signed 'D & R Fecit', and Grant's list attributes to the firm the 1838 medal.

*See also*: Hawkins, Suppl. ii to pt i, 1971, 247.

1838 **Birmingham, Oscott College** **(124a)**
1842 **Birmingham, St Philip's Schools** **(136a)**

EASTWOOD, Signature 'Eastwood, Colne' on:

1895 **Colne, Lancs., Town Hall** **(223b)**

EDUCATIONAL SUPPLY ASSOCIATION. Best known as suppliers of school furniture and equipment, their name appears on:

?1852[1] **Eton College, Bucks.** **(31a)**

1. Given by Grant.

ELKINGTON & Co. A firm of London and Sheffield silversmiths, who occasionally during the nineteenth century edited medals. In the 1850s their name appears on four of the five English cathedral medals produced by J. Wiener (qv.). The latter are signed Elkington & Co/C/Sc London. Beulah, p. 180, suggests that they may have struck the 1862 Art-Union medal of Sir Charles Barry by L. & J. Wiener (179i).

1850s Cathedrals **Lincoln** **(7b)**
**London, Westminster Abbey** **(8b)**
**Winchester** **(11b)**
**York** **(13d)**
1886 **London, Guildhall interior** **(185a)**
1887 **Hindley, Greater Manchester, Library and Museum** **(211a)**

FATTORINI. Signs the 1882 medal below 'Fattorini & Sons Bradford'. They were Bradford clock manufacturers & jewellers, etc., of 22 Kirkgate and 28 Westgate (*P.O. Dir.* West Riding 1881). The 1889 medal is signed 'A. Fattorini, Harrogate'.

1882 **Bradford Technical College** **(201a)**
1889 **Harrogate Royal Bath Hospital** **(217a)**

FAULKNER, B. Refered to as 'a die sinker' by Forrer. Medals bearing his signature appear between 1805 and 1830.

1805 **Stockport Sunday School** **(62a)**
1823 **Birmingham, 'Pantechnatheca', New Street** **(76a)**

FENWICK, A. Medallist and die-sinker of Birmingham; a pupil of Joseph Moore. Medals include Jubilee commemoratives of 1887 and 1897.

*See*: Forrer, vol. 2, 86.
1891 **Macclesfield, Christ Church School** **(135a)**

FOOT & TEBAY. Executed the fine uniface medal to commemorate the removal of Temple Bar from the Strand in 1878. It was struck in lead, taken from the roof, and engraved by C. H. & J. Mabey (qv.).

*See*: C. Welch: *Numismata Londinensia,* pl. viii, no. 15.
1878 **London, Temple Bar** **(37a)**

FRAMPTON, Sir George J. (1860–1928). Born London, studied at Lambeth School of Art and then 1881–87 at RA Schools. 1888 studied sculpture in Paris under Antonin Mercié and developed interest in French Symbolism. Exhibits sculptures at the RA in early 1890s which reflect contemporary French manner; becomes well known on the continent as a leader in the Arts and Crafts movement through his writings in *The Studio.* (These interests and influences can be seen in the design of the Winchester medal below.) 1894 made joint head of LCC Central School of Arts and Crafts with the architect W. R. Lethaby. Knighted 1908. RA 1912. His most popularly known work is the figure of Peter Pan in Kensington Gardens, 1911. Medals exhibited at RA include: an award in gold for Glasgow University 1895; a bronze medal 'Civic Architecture' designed for the RIBA 1908.

*See*: Forrer, vol. 2, 136; vol. 7, 317; *British Sculpture 1850–1914,* 12–15 and 23.
1893 **Winchester College** **(27a)**

GAMBLE, J. A composite view of the Albert Hall, Albert Memorial, and buildings for the 1873 London Annual Exhibition is signed 'J. Gamble Del.', with G. Morgan (qv.) as sculptor.

1873 and 1874 **Buildings of the Horticultural Society, Kensington** **(180a, b)**

HALLIDAY, Thomas (*c.* 1780–1855). Flourished in Birmingham as medallist and token engraver. Engraved and manufactured tokens and medals at his own works in Newhall Street for traders who wished to issue them, e.g. Edward Thomason (qv.). William Wyon (qv.) started to learn the art of die engraving with Halliday, as did C. F. Carter, Joseph Moore, and W. J. Taylor (qv.). Halliday's works are commended by Forrer as including 'some of the best commemorative medals of national and personal events, including Reform, Anti-Slavery and Public Institution medals'; these span the years 1797 to 1849. Signatures include Halliday F (or Fecit), T.H.F./T.H./H.

*See*: Forrer, vol. 2, 388; vol. 7, 412; Hawkins, pt i, 1960, 142.
1807 **London, St Paul's Cathedral** **(39b)**
1815 **Birmingham, St Philip's Church** **(41a)**
1816 **Dudley, St Thomas's Church** **(69a)**
1817 **Stockport, St Mary's Church** **(68a)**
1819 **Birmingham, Carr's Lane Chapel** **(72a, b)**
1822 **Birmingham, St Philip's Church** **(41b)**
1829 **Oldham, Blue Coat School** **(110a)**
1829 **Stonyhurst College, Lancs.** **(33a, b)**
1831 **Liverpool Infirmary** **(82a)**
1834 **Birmingham Town Hall** **(108b)**
1836 **Birmingham, King Edward VI Grammar School** **(116b–d)**
1837 **Birmingham Town Hall** **(108f)**
1837 **Liverpool Railway Station** **(113a, b)**
1839 **Bath, Prior Park** **(47a)**
1842 **London, Royal Exchange, 'new' and 'old'** **(146b, d)**
1843 **Birmingham, Hebrew National School** **(139b)**
1848[1] **Birmingham, St Michael's Church and Cemetery** **(158a)**
18–? **Salisbury Cathedral** **(10a)**
18–? **Nether Alderley, St Mary's Church** **(16a)**

1. The date of this medal does not agree with the suggestion in Norris, p. 74, that Halliday's death was in 1844.

HANCOCK, John Gregory (*c.* 1750–1805). Medallist and die-sinker of Birmingham, with a reputation as a skilful engraver of tokens. From 1787 undertook work for both

Matthew Boulton and Peter Kempson (qv.). For the latter he executed dies for several series of medals, e.g.: 'British victories over the French'; 'George III'; 'Statesmen of the Time'. Signature can be Hancock / I. G. Hancock / H.

*See*: Forrer, vol. 2, 410; Norris, 72, establishes his dates.

1802 **St Paul's Cathedral** **(39a)**

HEATON, RALPH, and Sons. A firm founded in 1819. As 'The Mint, Birmingham, Ltd.' they were major manufacturers of the coinage of England and her overseas territories in the nineteenth century. From 1860 Heaton's Mint was at Icknield Street (see medal 178a) and formed part of the new Birmingham Heath industrial area.[1] Two of the best-known medals issued at the Mint were those for the Jubilees of 1887 and 1897. It was Ralph Heaton who, with J. Hinks (qv.), first gave paying work and encouragement to the notable Birmingham medallist Joseph Moore (qv.). When Queen Victoria opened Aston Hall in 1858 Heaton paid for a gold impression of Moore's medal (35a) to be presented to the Queen. In discussing the firm's work Forrer wrote in 1904: 'As a result of the spread of the Arts and Crafts movement all over the world within recent years the Birmingham Mint has also had to break with the bonds of tradition and adopt modern principles and notions in connection with the medallic art. This is sufficiently shown by the employment of such artists as Mr. George Frampton, Mr. Emil Fuchs . . . Mr. Frank Bowcher who have made themselves the exponents in this country of the French and Austrian Schools'.

*See*: Forrer, vol. 2, 446; Hawkins, pt i, 1960, 142.

1851 **London, Hyde Park, Great Exhibition** **(165s–u)**
1874 **Birmingham Mint** **(178a)**
1887 **Manchester Jubilee Exhibition Buildings** **(215a)**
1887 **Saltaire, The Institute** **(190a)**

1. It should not be confused with the Soho Mint, which took its name from a neighbouring district of Birmingham, and which had been founded 1762 by Matthew Boulton. Under the name James Watt & Co. the Soho Mint closed in 1895.

HINKS, James. Ran a business at 69 Newhall Street, Birmingham, from *c.* 1846 to *c.* 1855. The firm is also listed in the 1840s as Smith & Hinks, at the same address, and described itself as 'late T. Halliday' (qv.). They acted as die-sinkers, medallists, stampers, button and counter manufacturers, etc. J. Hinks may have been senior partner in this firm and it was he who helped to find initial work for Joseph Moore (qv.). The medal below is signed J. Hinks and published by R. L. Joseph, Liverpool:

*See*: Forrer, vol. 4, 136; Hawkins, pt i, 1960, 180.

1846 **Liverpool, The Sailors' Home** **(159c)**

HINTON & ARMISTEAD. They sign the following, in connection with a Fine Art and Industrial Exhibition:

1883 **Oldham Library and Museum** **(205a)**

HOLLINS, Peter (1800–86). Born at 17 Great Hampton Street, Birmingham, in 1800. Son of W. Hollins—a self-taught artist, who did some architectural work and was also equally able to produce medallions and monuments. Trained in his father's studio as sculptor until *c.* 1822. Worked in London under Chantrey. First exhibition of his work 1833. Visited Italy 1835/36 and received important commissions on his return. In 1843 went back to Birmingham to take over the family business, which he ran until 1874. Gunnis, p. 205, considers that 'Hollins at his best was a very great artist and his monuments to Lady Bradford and to Sophia Thompson are as fine as anything executed by Chantrey'. Many busts and monuments by Hollins are in, and relate to, the Birmingham area. There is a statue by him of Dr Jephson at Leamington, 1846 (cf. medal 103b).

1822 Revd. Outram;[1] *Rev.* **St Philip's Church, Birmingham** **(41b)**
1838 Bishop Ryder;[2] *Rev.* **Memorial Church, Birmingham** **(123a)**

1. This date suggests that the commission may have been to his father W. Hollins. The portrait is signed 'Modeled by Hollins Thomason & Jones. D.'

2. Signed 'P. Hollins Inv. T. W. Ingram Sc.'

HYAMS, Hyam. Editor of medallets, jettons, etc., in the 1830s and 1840s. Addresses in City of London from 1813 to 1851. He issued a series of Model Crowns in 1848 with dies cut by Allen & Moore (qv.), and a portrait medal of Nathan Mayer Rothschild 1836.

*See*: Forrer, vol. 2, 584; Hawkins, pt iii, 1968, 129.

1842 **Royal Exchange, London, 'old'** **(36a)**
1842 and 1844 **Royal Exchange, London, 'new'** **(146b–d, v)**
1847 **London, Houses of Parliament** **(179a, f)**

INGRAM, Thomas Wells. Engraver and die-sinker employed at the Soho Mint, Birmingham. Later he had addresses at Birmingham in 1840s and 1850s. Contributed to Thomason's series of Great Men; medal of Canova 1823. Grant lists medals of his from 1806 to 1838.

*See*: Forrer, vol. 3, 26; vol. 7, 472; Hawkins, pt i, 1960, 182.

1826 **Doncaster, New Betting Rooms** **(85a)**
1828 **Birmingham, School of Medicine** **(93a)**
1837 **Shepton Mallet Church** **(15a)**
1838 **Birmingham, Bishop Ryder Church** **(123a)**

& JACOB. A part signature[1] with 'Liverpool' which appears on:

1844 **Liverpool, Royal Infirmary Medical School** **(148a)**

1. Hawkins, Pt ii, 1960/67, 196, notes Evans & Jacob*s* active in Liverpool 1850s and 1860s.

JENKINS, Henry, & Co. A firm of manufacturing jewellers in Birmingham. They made service medals and stars in the 1880s and 1890s.

*See*: Forrer, vol. 7, 478.

1893 **London, Imperial Institute** **(221a)**

JOSEPH, R. L. Published a medal with obverse signed by J. Hinks (qv.). Address given on medal 'The Repository, 42 Bold St., Liverpool'.

1846 **Liverpool, The Sailors' Home** **(159c)**

KELSEY, S. Grant gives this name for the initials S.K. on:

1841 **Bath, Argyle Chapel** **(74a)**

KEMPSON & KINDON. A partnership established in 1801 between the medallist Peter Kempson (active in Birmingham at the end of the eighteenth century) and Samuel Kindon.[1] Signatures K & K; P.K. FEC; P.K. Kempson produced several series of tokens including his 'Coventry Buildings' and 'Birmingham Buildings'. Peter and Thomas Wyon (qv.) both employed Kempson to engrave tokens, and J. G. Hancock (qv.) used him to cut commemorative medals (e.g. the 1802 medal below which is signed K & K and H.). Forrer (vol. 3, 141) notes other medals bearing Kempson's signature including: General Hospital, Birmingham; St Bartholomew's Hospital, Gloucester.

1802 and 1827 **St Paul's Cathedral** **(39a, c, d)**

1. Norris, p. 75, suggests the dates of this partnership as *c.* 1803 to 1829 at the latest. She also indicates the General Hospital, Birmingham 'attributed' to him (cf. Nos. 54a, b, c, dated 1823, 1826, and 1829).

KENNING, George. A London Masonic jeweller and publisher. Medals include items for railways, centenaries, and one for the installation of the Prince of Wales as Grand Master of the Masonic Order 1875.

*See*: Forrer, vol. 3, 144.

1884 **London, Whitehall Court, National Liberal Club** **(214a)**

LANGRIDGE, Joseph. Jeweller and silversmith of Brighton (see *Pigot's Commercial Directory: Sussex,* 1840). Published the following medals:

1830 **Brighton, St Peter's Church** **(91a)**
1837 **Brighton, Royal Pavilion** **(75a)**

MABEY, Charles Henry, & J. Engraved a uniface medal, also signed by Foot & Tebay who executed it, on the removal of Temple Bar from the Strand in 1878. This was struck from lead taken from the roof, and published by the City of London (qv.). C. H. Mabey exhibited at the RA: 'Mrs. J. Mabey', medallion 1863; 'portrait of a lady' 1880.

*See*: Forrer, vol. 3, 521; vol. 8, 1.

1878 **London, Temple Bar** **(37a)**

MAYER, J. Signs three Liverpool medals D or DIR(exit); these also name well-known die-sinkers: Allen & Moore (qv.); Carter (qv.); Davis (qv.).

1837 **Liverpool, Mechanics Institution** **(119a)**
1846 **Liverpool, Sailors' Home** **(159b)**
1854 **Liverpool, St George's Hall** **(170a)**

MOORE, Joseph (1817–92). The most eminent of the Birmingham medallists of the nineteenth century. He worked most of his life in the City and became 'so respected for his talents and general character' that his portrait was hung in the City Art Gallery. Moore entered the office of a silversmith at the age of ten, was apprenticed for eight and a half years with Thomas Halliday (qv.) and then started business for himself making dies for buttons—the 'Brummagem button' that was one of the chief industries of the town. Forrer indicates that at one stage he entered 'under advantageous conditions' the business of W. J. Taylor (qv.)—another pupil of Halliday's—and that he was encouraged in his medallic work by Ralph Heaton (qv.). Joseph Moore was a partner in Allen & Moore (qv.) and medals under the joint signature occur from the early 1840s to the late 1850s. From 1859 he was in business on his own. One of his finest architectural medals is that for the extension to the Birmingham and Midland Institute of 1881 (with obverse a portrait of Sir William Siemens) and this can be compared with contemporary work by J. S. & A. B. Wyon (qv.). The signature on medals under his name include J. Moore Sc / J. Moore F. / J. Moore Birm. / Joseph Moore / J.M.M. / Moore F. His son, also Joseph Moore, was an able medallist and helped with many of his father's later medals.

*See*: Forrer, vol. 4, 136; vol. 8, 74; Hawkins, pt i, 1960, 229.

?1840s **Sheffield, Wesley College** **(130a)**
?1850s **Cheltenham Proprietary College** **(140b)**
1858 **Birmingham, Aston Hall** **(35a, b)**
1858 **Walsall, St John's Church** **(176a)**
1869 **Chester, Town Hall** **(188a)**
1879 **Ackworth, Yorks., School** **(50a)**
1880 **Birmingham, Mason Science College** **(199a)**
1881 **Birmingham and Midland Institute, extension** **(200a)**

MORGAN, George T. (1845–*c.* 1920). Sculptor, medallist and die engraver. Born in Birmingham, studied at the Art School there, and then went to South Kensington on a scholarship for two years. Worked for Pinches (qv.) *c.* 1873–75. Grant gives a medal by him (of J. Dunbar) in 1870 and, following his medals of Francis Fowke (qv.) and of the 1873 Exhibition, he was commissioned by the Art Union (qv.) to produce their 1875 medal of David Roberts RA.[1] In 1879 he also made the David Cox medal in the Art-Union series. Morgan worked for a while as assistant engraver in the Mint at Philadelphia, USA, and is well known for the 'Bland' dollar of 1878 which he designed and executed.

*See*: Forrer, vol. 4, 148; *British Sculpture,* 41, 45.

1872 Captain Francis Fowke RE (**233a**, p. 192)
1873 and 1874 Prince of Wales; *Rev.* **Buildings of the Horticultural Society** **(180a, b)**

1. Well known for his paintings of Middle Eastern architectural and topographical subjects.

NEAL, Ralph. The business under the name of 'Ralph Neal' was active in London EC from 1866 to 1936; functions listed include die-sinker, medallist, heraldic and official seal engraver. Medals dated 1885, 1893, and 1896 are listed by Grant; no initial is shown. The firm was a leading producer in London of metallic checks.

*See*: Hawkins, Pt iii, 1968, 171.

1893 **London, Bishopsgate Institute** **(224a)**

OTTLEY, John. A medallist and engraver of tokens at Birmingham during the first half of the nineteenth century. He is known for a large series of tokens 'Ottley's Birmingham buildings' engraved in the early 1800s. Architectural medals noted under his full name by Forrer include Birmingham Hospital, 1826; Cholera Orphan School, 1833; Leeds Church, 1841. The many architectural medals listed below are only signed Ottley (sometimes in script) or Ottley Birm.; as none has an initial, see also Thomas Ottley (below).

*See*: Forrer, vol. 4, 337.

1824 **Birmingham, Blue Coat School** **(57a)**

1824 **Kidderminster, St George's Church**[1] **(81b)**
1826 **Birmingham, General Hospital** **(54b)**
1827 **Birmingham, St Peter's Church, Dale End** **(88a)**
1828 **Wolverhampton, St George's Church**[1] **(101a, b)**
?1829 **Doncaster, Prospect House Academy** **(95a)**
1833 **Bilston, Cholera Orphan School** **(104a)**
1833 **Birmingham, St John's Church, Perry Bar** **(105a)**
1835 Marquess of Camden; *Rev.* **Cambridge Senate House**[2] **(45a)**
1835 **Birmingham, Cemetery, Key Hill** **(112a)**
1836 **Newark, Christ Church** **(114a)**
1841 **Leeds Parish Church** **(132a)**
1842 Duke of Northumberland; *Rev.* **Cambridge Senate House**[2] **(45b, c)**
1843 **Cheltenham College** **(140a)**
1846 **Leamington, Beech Lawn House** **(103a, b)**
1847 Prince Consort; *Rev.* **Cambridge Senate House**[2] **(45d)**
1851 **London, Hyde Park, Great Exhibition** **(165v–z)**
1858 **Birmingham, Aston Hall** **(35c–e)**
1858 **Derby, St Michael's Church** **(174a)**
1858 **Leeds Town Hall** **(175a)**
?1850s **Stoke on Trent, St Peter's Church** **(98a)**
1862 Duke of Devonshire; *Rev.* **Cambridge Senate House**[2] **(45e)**
1862 **London, International Exhibition** **(182m–o)**
1868 **Gretton Green, Christ Church** **(187a)**
1874 **Blackburn, Library and Museum** **(195a)**
1884 **Stockport, Sunday Schools** **(62c)**

1. The design and size (64 mm.) of these Church medals is similar to three unsigned medals of churches in the Midlands by the architect Goodwin (Nos. 78a, 80a, 92a). They all date from the 1820s and appear to be Ottley.

2. Unsigned, but Grant gives the Cambridge Chancellors' series as probably struck by Ottley for Peters the Cambridge publisher; see also p. 70.

OTTLEY, Thomas. Given as a medallist of different Birmingham addresses in the following Directories: Pigot's: 1842—at 5 Newhall Street,; Slater's: 1850—at 121 Snowhill; Kelly's: 1854—at 59 Spencer Street. He signs the two medals below 'Birm.' and 'Birmingham'.

1843 **Liverpool Collegiate Institution** **(141a, b)**

PEARCE & SONS

1883 **Huddersfield Technical School** **(204a)**

PETERS, James. The Cambridge publisher for a series of medals commemorating the installation of University Chancellors. All have in common a view of the interior of the Senate House. (See John Ottley, as the likely medallist.)

1835, 1842, 1847, 1862 **Cambridge Senate House** **(45a–e)**

PHILLP, I. Coin engraver in employ of Matthew Boulton at Soho Mint, Birmingham in the early 1800s, and colleague of C. H. Kuchler. Only known medal as below (three variants).

*See*: Forrer, vol. 3, 494.

1808 **Cambridge, Christ College** **(29a–c)**

PINCHES. A family of London die-sinkers and medallists in the nineteenth century. Five brothers: Francis, Theophilus, William, John (died 1905), and Thomas R. The latter two are well known for their medallic work.

*See*: Forrer, vol. 4, 547.

PINCHES, Francis. First worked with his brothers in London, then later had a business in Manchester as a die-sinker. The following is signed 'Pinches Man[r]'.

*See*: Forrer, vol. 4, 547.

1877 **Manchester Town Hall** **(197a)**

PINCHES, John (1825–1905). Studied under W. J. Taylor (qv.) at Birmingham; worked for W. Wyon (qv.) at the Royal Mint *c.* 1846–51, and also at the Birmingham Mint.[1] Occasionally employed by Leonard Wyon (William's successor at the Mint) who executed the head of Paxton on an 1854 medal below. The following are all signed Pinches, London.

*See*: Forrer, vol. 4, 548.

1854 Sir Joseph Paxton (by L. C. Wyon); *Rev.* **Crystal Palace, Sydenham** **(171f–i)**
1856 **Chelmsford, Shire Hall** **(56b)**
1857 **Manchester, Art Treasures Exhibition** **(173a–c)**
1862 **London, International Exhibition** **(182p–r)**
1887 **Tintwistle Church, Cheshire** **(121a)**

1. There is a memorial medal to John Pinches with a portrait bust by G. W. de Saulles (see Hocking, ii, 240).

PINCHES, John H. (b. 1852). Entered his father's business *c.* 1867 and, 'this able medallist cut numerous dies from models supplied by sculptors'. These included:

*See*: Forrer, vol. 4, 548.

1893 **Imperial Institute, London** **(221b)**

PINCHES, Thomas Ryan. Cut many academic and private medals, including a memorial medal to Duke of Wellington 1852. Exhibited at RA in 1830s and 1840s. Following is signed T. R. Pinches:

*See*: Forrer, vol. 4, 550; vol. 8, 133.

1854 **Crystal Palace, Sydenham** **(171c, e)**

PROMOLI, W. B. Signs the medal below 'Published by W. B. Promoli, late Thos. Woolfield, Church St., Liverpool'.

1837 **Liverpool Railway Station** **(113b)**

RESTALL, James Andrew. Silversmith and medallist of 2 St Martin's Place, Birmingham (*Kelly's Directory,* 1892). A series of 21 Birmingham views were signed J.A.R. and published by Davis & McMillan in 1894.

*See*: Grant.

1894 **London, The Peoples Palace** **(213a)**

S. Signs:

1897 **Bilston, Waterworks, and Technical School** **(228a)**

SALE, Henry Bailey. The signature 'Sale, Birm.' on the medal below, suggests that this is Henry Bailey Sale, later, *c.* 1900, H. B. Sale Ltd. Grant lists the firm as makers of medals over the period 1881–1911. Their address from the mid-1860s was at Constitution Hill, Birmingham.

*See*: Hawkins, pt i, 1960, 311.

1896 **Tunbridge Wells, St John's Church** **(191a)**

SEWARD, A. Abram & Charles Seward were 'Whitesmiths' at 105 Market Street, Lancaster in 1851.

*See*: *Slater's Directory*: Lancashire.

1864 **Lancaster, Ripley Hospital** **(184a)**

SCHNITZPAHN, Christian (1829–77). German medallist and coin engraver. Worked in Berlin for medallist J. K. Fischer, then for one year (1856) in London as engraver under Benjamin Wyon. From 1858 on Court and Mint engraver at Darmstadt. His only medal related to England is the following, where he signs the head of Prince Albert and there is an alternative reverse (interior and exterior) by J. Wiener (qv.).

*See:* Forrer, vol. 5, 395.

1862 Prince Albert; *Rev.* **London, International Exhibition** **(182s, u)**

SMITH, Henry. In business at 17 Hampton Street, Snowhill, Birmingham, *c.* 1851–95. He described himself as die-sinker, seal engraver, maker of tokens etc. The 1868 medal, below, is signed 'Smith F. Birm.'

*See*: Hawkins, pt i, 1960, 312.

1868 **Bewdley, Wyre Hill Schools** **(186a)**
1882 **Worcester, Exhibition Building** **(203a)**

SPINK & SON LTD. Family firm established by John Spink in 1666. Jewellers, gold- and silversmiths, antiquities dealers, coin dealers, medallists, die-sinkers, etc. Earliest medals issued by Spink were in the 1880s. In an effort to set high standards in the medallic art at that time they employed top designers—including Frank Bowcher (qv.).

*See*: Forrer, vol. 5, 638; *Coins*, July 1973, no. 7, 18–21.

1897 **Leeds, St Peter's Church** **(132c)**
1890s **Rothwell Market House** **(32a)**

STOTHARD, Alfred Joseph (1793–1864). Son of the painter Thomas Stothard RA (1755–1824). Trained as a sculptor and was appointed medallist to George IV. Exhibited medallic portraits at the Royal Academy between 1821 and 1845; these included the fine portrait head of George IV commemorating the restoration of Windsor Castle. Other medals include: Sir Walter Scott (after Chantrey) 1827; John Flaxman 1826; Blundell's School *c.* 1834; Prince Albert 1842. Monuments to Charles Lane 1827 and Richard Collins 1831 both have medallion portraits. In 1828 he contracted to supply four bas-reliefs for Buckingham Palace from designs by his father—each relief to be 20 ft long.

*See*: Gunnis, 375; Forrer, vol. 5, 695; vol. 8, 224.

1828 George IV; *Rev.* **Windsor Castle** **(131a)**
1842 Prince Albert; *Rev.* **Royal Exchange** **(146e)**

TAYLOR, J. A number of medals, all but one of London subjects, are signed 'J. Taylor Birm.' or 'Taylor, Birm.', during the 1840s.[1] As there is no evidence that W. J. Taylor (qv.)

was in any way connected with Birmingham after his move to London in 1829, these medals are listed separately below.

*See*: Hawkins, pt i, 1960, 312, for a discussion of the possible identity of this medallist.)

1842 **Kettering, Baptist Missionary House** **(40b)**
1843 **Wanstead, Infant Orphan Asylum** **(142a)**
1843 **London, Nelson Monument** **(143b)**
1844 **Camberwell, St Giles' Church** **(147a)**
1844 **London, Royal Exchange** **(146w)**
?1840s **London Orphan Asylum, Clapton** **(77a)**

1. This may be the James Taylor who is listed in the Birmingham directories as a medallist between 1835 and 1856. By 1860 his last address, 71 Summer Lane, is in the name of Joseph Moore (qv.).

TAYLOR, William Joseph (1802–85). Medallist, die-sinker, and engraver. Born Birmingham. In 1818 became the first of several well-known die-sinkers to be trained under Thomas Halliday (qv.). He moved to London in 1829, and from 1845 to 1872 his name appears with addresses in the London Directories. In 1852 he organised the despatch of a complete coining press and plant to Melbourne; the dies for some Australian coins were made by Taylor. One of his best-known medals was struck 1842 (several variants) to commemorate the completion of Marc Isambard Brunel's Thames Tunnel (see Forrer, vol. 6, 41, and vol. 8, 233). There is a variety of signatures on the medals below, all apparently belonging to this medallist: W. J. Taylor / W. J. Taylor London / J. Taylor London. But: see also J. Taylor and discussion of the signature 'Taylor' in Hawkins, pt i, 1960, 312, and pt iii, 1968, 247.

1839 **London, St Saviour's School, Southwark** **(126a)**
1842 **Stratford upon Avon, Shakespeare's House** **(28a)**
1844 **London, Christ Church, Streatham** **(134a)**
1851 **London, Hyde Park, Great Exhibition** **(165aa)**
1852 and 1866 **Sydenham, Crystal Palace** **(171j, k, l)**
1872 **London, St Paul's Cathedral** **(39j)**

THOMASON, Sir Edward (1769–1849). A colourful figure on the Birmingham scene during the first part of the nineteenth century, he combined the roles of manufacturer, medallist, inventor, and diplomat. At sixteen he was apprenticed to Matthew Boulton at the Soho works, and by 1793 had started business on his own manufacturing buttons and, later, medals, tokens, bronzes, and reproductions of works of art. In 1796 he submitted to the Admiralty a 'model of a fire ship propelled by steam and steered automatically' and in 1798 patented a folding carriage door step. These two inventions were followed by a spate of ideas and 'improvements' during his lifetime. His principal medallic piece is probably the memorial to Matthew Boulton; the portrait for this was from a wax model by Rouw and it was published by Thomason in 1809. Forrer (vol. 6, 73) notes that 'after Boulton's death in 1809 Thomason produced the finest medals in Birmingham. He employed the best die-sinkers he could get hold of and we shall find the best known men working for him'. Amongst his many medallic issues were several large series, e.g. The Elgin Marbles (forty-eight medals) 1820; Mudie's national medals (forty-one types); The Kings and Queens of England, after Dassier; Bible Subjects, after famous paintings (sixty medals) 1830. In an inspired piece of advertising he presented sets of the latter series to all the sovereigns in Europe and received many honours in return; at one stage he was vice-consul in Birmingham representing eight different governments and eventually received the first knighthood awarded to a Birmingham industrialist in 1832. He retired in 1844.[1] Forrer gives London University foundation medal 1826 (97a unsigned) as Thomason; he also issued the portrait medal of George III by T. Halliday (qv.) with reverse St Paul's 1807 (39b).

*See*: Forrer, vol. 6, 73 ff; vol. 8, 235; Hawkins, pt i, 1960, 313.

The following is signed 'Modeled by Hollins Thomason & Jones ·D·':

1822 **Birmingham, St Philip's Church** **(41b)**

1. He sold his factory in 1835 to Witgrave & Collis, later G. R. Collis (qv.). The *VCH, Warwicks.*, vol. 7, 107, refers to the *Memoirs* which Thomason wrote as 'without doubt one of the most egotistical and snobbish productions ever published . . .'.

TIFFIN. Signs Tiffin. D (*Delineate*) for interior view on a medal by E. Avern (qv.). This was published by F. T. Price Cutler of Salisbury.

1846 **Wilton, St Mary and St Nicholas Church** **(154a)**

VAUGHTONS Ltd. Birmingham medallists specialising in sporting subjects. Medallists to Olympic Games 1908. There is a large oval advertisement panel by Vaughtons in the Birmingham City Art Gallery; this contains approximately two hundred and seventy medals and gives their address as Gothic Works, Livery Street, it dates from the reign of Edward VII.

?1880s **London, Merchant Seamen's Orphanage, Wanstead** **(181a)**
?1890s **Kettering, Northants., School** **(219a)**

WARD, Henry. Printer, 8 Mercery Lane, Canterbury. Publishes a medal by Davis (qv.) of the Cathedral with new north-west tower completed 1841.

*See*: *Pigot's Directory:* Kent, 1840.
*c.* 1841 **Canterbury Cathedral** **(1b)**

WATERLOW & SONS Ltd. A major firm of London printers, whose work includes stamps and banknotes. Forrer (vol. 6, 388) gives them as issuing the medal for the opening of the Imperial Institute (221b) engraved by J. H. Pinches (qv.).

WEBB, Thomas (*c.* 1760–1843). Birmingham medallist whose main work was in the years 1804–29.[1] Contributed several medals to Mudie's 'National Series', e.g. George III 1817 (the first of the series). Other medals include a number of Pitt Club medals for different cities, with a bust of Pitt. Webb's medal for the foundation stone laying by George III at Birmingham (below) is well known; *Gentlemen's Magazine* for October 1805, p. 915, describes why it was struck and comments on it as a medallic work.

*See:* building entry; also Forrer, vol. 6, 400.
1805 George III; *Rev.* **Birmingham, Christ Church, Colmore Row** **(65a)**

1. Norris, p. 73, establishes his dates, and notes that he had a Lichfield address when he died.

WIENER, Jacques (1815–99). Medallist and engraver. Studied drawing, modelling and engraving from 1828 with his uncle, an artist, at Aix-la-Chapelle. 1839 settled in Brussels; 1845 became a naturalised Belgian. His first medal of 1840: 'Surrender of the town of Venloo', immediately helped to attract official attention. In 1845 he had the idea of a series of medals showing the exterior and interior of notable buildings, to be engraved with great precision of detail. It is on this aspect of his work that his continuing fame as a medallist rests. His first development of the idea was a series of ten medals of famous Belgian churches; this was followed by other medals representing a selection of Belgian civic buildings, e.g. town halls, market halls, prisons. Encouraged by the success of these, he proposed a main series entitled 'Medals of the most remarkable Edifices of Europe' and aimed to issue one every two months to a total of fifty. Although this was not completed, Wiener achieved forty-one of these medals in the period 1849 to 1865. The monuments shown are, by countries: Germany, eleven; France, eight; Italy, seven; England, five; Spain and Portugal, four; Belgium, two; Russia, one; Holland, one; Norway, one; Turkey, one. The five cathedrals which form the English monuments are listed below, and all demonstrate the remarkable skill with which he could produce accurate interior views in perfect perspective.[1] This minute work was, however, to take its toll, and by 1872 he had almost completely lost his eyesight, and after 1874 produced no more medals. He trained his two brothers Charles (1832–88) and Leopold (qv.) who both became eminent engravers. Jacques Wiener also engraved a large number of portrait medals plus the first postage stamps for Belgium 1848; he headed a factory for the issue of Belgian stamps from 1848 to 1864. Together with the work of his brothers in the production of coins, the role of the Wiener family in Belgium can be compared to the Wyons in England.

For an extended list of works see Forrer, vol. 5, 484; there is a note on 'Jacques Wiener and his brothers' by A. Warner in *Coins,* July 1973, 15–17.

1849 **London, St Paul's Cathedral** **(39i)**
1854 **York Minster** **(13d)**
1856 **Lincoln Cathedral** **(7b)**
1856 **London, Westminster Abbey** **(8b)**
1856 **Winchester Cathedral** **(11b)**
1862 Sir Charles Barry (by Leopold Wiener); *Rev.* **Houses of Parliament** **(179i)**

1862 **London International Exhibition** **(182s–u)**

1. *The Builder*, 29 November, 1856, p. 649, noted enthusiastically his medals of St Paul's, Westminister Abbey, Lincoln, and York: 'These medals are exceedingly well executed: the effect given to the interior of St Paul's with the slight relief obtainable is very striking. --- It is to be regretted that medals are so little prized comparatively in Great Britain that the practice of medal die engraving is nearly confined to one family.'

WIENER, Leopold (1823–91). Studied under his brother Jacques (qv.) and at the Brussels Academy of Fine Arts. In 1845 became a pupil of the sculptor David d'Angers in Paris and also of J. J. Barre, the Chief Engraver of French coins. Returned to Brussels 1847, and to a competition success with the design for a new five franc piece. In 1864 appointed First Engraver to the Belgian Mint and was responsible for about one hundred and fifty pieces, including the currency of Leopold II from 1866 until 1891. His many medals include: Royal Society for the Encouragement of Fine Arts; Joseph Schadde, architect *c.* 1870; the bust of Barry (qv.) for the Art-Union medal below.

*See*: Forrer, vol. 6, 490; A. Warner, 'Jacques Wiener and his brothers', *Coins*, July 1973, 15–17.

1862 Sir Charles Barry; *Rev.* **Houses of Parliament** (by Jacques Wiener) **(179i)**

WILSON, W. Engraver and medallist, London. Exhibited at the Royal Academy in 1827, and was still active in 1863 when he was working on the dies for the Benjamin West medal in the Art-Union series. He had earlier been commissioned for two other medals in the series. One, of John Flaxman, which had been intended for issue in 1847 was handed over to W. Wyon (qv.) when Wilson failed to engrave anything after several years. For the other, Wilson produced the profile portrait of Sir Christopher Wren; this is based on the marble bust in the Ashmolean Museum, Oxford, of Wren in 1673 by Edward Pierce *(c.* 1635–95). However, after failing again to complete his commission, perhaps due to illness, the medal reverse was completed by B. Wyon (qv.) in 1848.

*See*: Forrer, vol. 6, 510; Beulah, 182.

1846 Sir Christopher Wren; *Rev.* **St Paul's Cathedral** (by Benjamin Wyon) **(39h)**

WYON. The name of a gifted family of medallists and die-sinkers who dominated the English medallic scene throughout the nineteenth century. They were descended from a German silver chaser and engraver who came to England in the reign of George II. The relationship of the medallists referred to individually in the separate biographies is shown on the simplified family tree on the next page. (For complete bibliographic and numismatic details of all the members of the Wyon family see Forrer, vol. 6, 571–690.)

WYON, Alfred Benjamin (1837–84). Second son of Benjamin Wyon (qv.). Born London; studied at RA School of painting; learned die engraving under his father. From 1865 associated with his brother Joseph Shepherd Wyon (qv.) as Chief Engraver of Seals; appointed to the title after his brother's death. A. B. Wyon was a partner with J. S. Wyon in a die-sinking business inherited from their father. After the death of J. S. Wyon, in 1873, new medals continued to be signed 'JS & AB Wyon' (from 1872 the younger brother Allan Wyon (qv.) worked with the firm). The Guildhall Council Chamber, for the City of London series, presents a fine interior view and stands comparison with his father's more famous Coal Exchange interior of 1849.

*See*: Forrer, vol. 6, 574.

1865 Professor T. L. Donaldson **(232a**, p. 190)
1872 **St Paul's Cathedral, interior** **(39k)**
1872 Prince of Wales; *Rev.* **Albert Hall** **(189a)**
1873 Queen Victoria; *Rev.* **Albert Hall** **(189b)**
1882 **City of London School for Boys** **(202a)**
1884 **Guildhall, New Council Chamber** **(206a)**

WYON, Allan (1843–1907). Medallist. Younger son of Benjamin Wyon (qv.). Entered his brothers' firm of J. S. & A. B. Wyon in 1872. Appointed Chief Engraver of Her Majesty's Seals on the death of his brother A. B. Wyon in 1884. His medals include Hampstead Hospital; Medical Department of Yorkshire College; National Gallery of Australia 1890s. He signs the plaquette listed below, Allan Wyon Sc.

*See*: Forrer, vol. 6, 579; vol. 8, 293.

*c.* 1889 **London, New College, Hampstead** **(212a)**

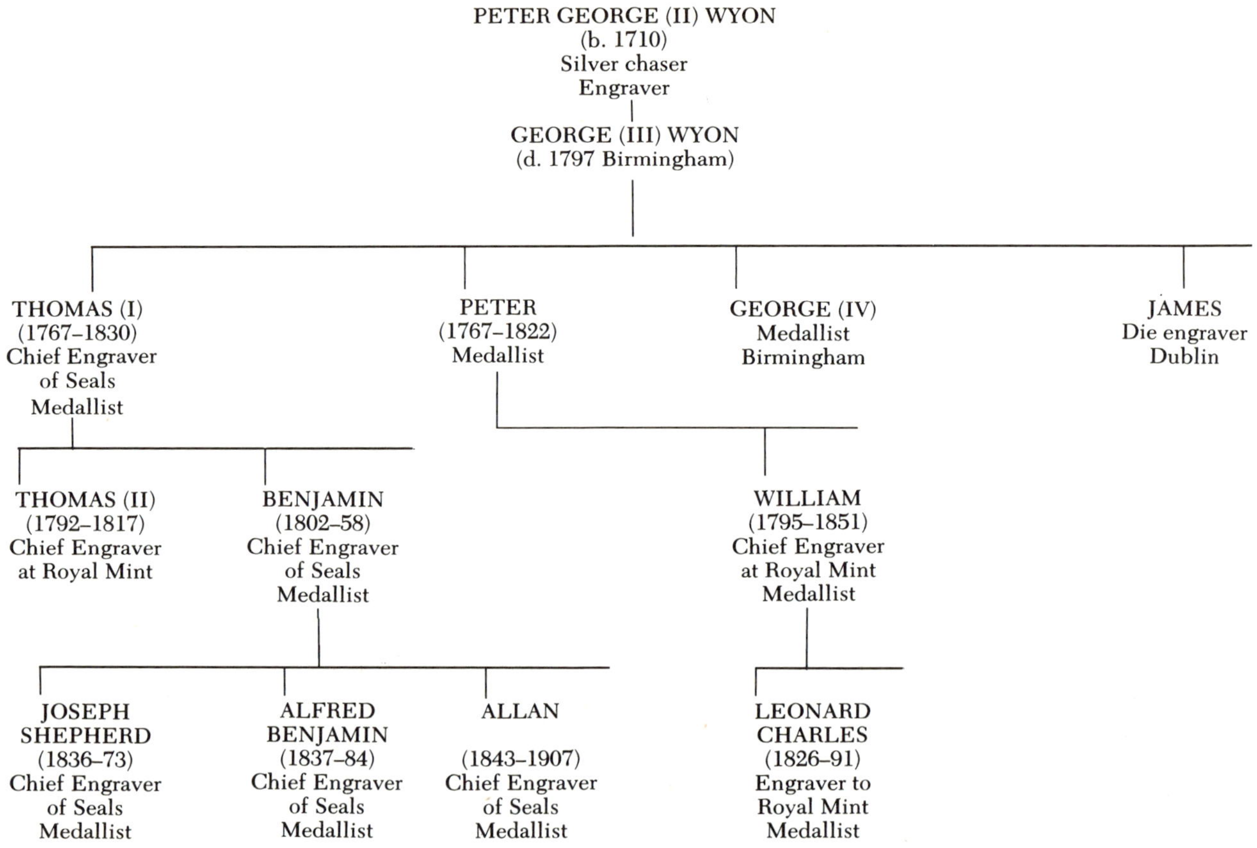


WYON, Benjamin (1802–58). The medallist of some of the finest English architectural pieces in the nineteenth century. His medal for the Coal Exchange opening is perhaps his best known; when in 1850 the Art Union of London (qv.) finally issued its medal of Sir Christopher Wren, with Benjamin Wyon's west elevation of St Paul's on the obverse, the *Art Journal*[1] wrote of it as 'one of the most successful medallic representations of a building ever executed'. Benjamin Wyon was the second son of Thomas Wyon the elder (qv.). He was born in London and received his tuition as a medallist from his elder brother Thomas Wyon the younger (1792–1817) who in 1815, at the age of twenty-three, had been appointed Chief Engraver to the Mint. In 1831 Benjamin succeded his father as Chief Engraver of His Majesty's Seals—a post which he held for the rest of his life, in parallel with running the die-sinking business that his father founded. His treatment of building subjects is very 'architectural' in that the majority of his medals show a selected façade of the building in true elevation—as from the drawing board—and modelled in high relief.[2] Only three of his building subjects[3] are low relief perspective 'views'; by contrast in the Coal Exchange and the IBA medal he develops and models section or elevation in one point perspective.

*See*: A full list of works in Forrer, vol. 6, 581 ff.

| | |
|---|---|
| 1823 **Brighton Pier** | **(79a)** |
| 1831 **London Bridge** | **(102a)** |
| 1833 **Grendon Hall, Warwicks.** | **(84a)** |
| 1836 **Temple** (Allegorical IBA medal) | **(24a)** |
| 1837 **City of London School** | **(120a)** |
| 1837 **Exeter, Lower Market** | **(118a)** |
| 1838 **Guildhall, City of London** | **(53c)** |
| 1839 **Dover Castle** | **(25a)** |
| 1839 **London, Christ's Hospital School, Great Hall** | **(96a)** |
| *c.* 1840 **London Hospital, Whitechapel Road** | **(49a)** |
| 1843 **London, Charing Cross Hospital** | **(109a)** |

(1846)[4] Sir Christopher Wren (by W. Wilson); *Rev.* **St Paul's Cathedral** **(39h)**
1852 **London, Coal Exchange** **(161c)**
1855 Sir John Vanbrugh; *Rev.* **Blenheim Palace** **(42a)**
1856 **Lancaster, Royal Grammar School** **(172a)**
1857 Sir William Chambers; *Rev.* **Somerset House** **(52a)**

1. *Art Journal,* 1850, 191.
2. See especially Blenheim Palace (1855) and, obverse, the fine portrait bust of its architect Sir John Vanbrugh (qv.). This was No. 8 in the Art-Union series.
3. Grendon Hall; Dover Castle; Lancaster School.
4. Reverse commissioned from B. Wyon 1848 (see Beulah, 182).

WYON, Joseph Shepherd (1836–73). Received his instruction as a medallist from his father Benjamin (qv.); studied at the RA Schools. He succeeded his father both as Chief Engraver of Her Majesty's Seals, and also as senior partner in the family die-sinking business which became J. S. & A. B. Wyon. His first important medal was of James Watt which, on the recommendation of Robert Stephenson, was adopted as the prize medal of the Institute of Civil Engineers. His medals include one in the Art-Union series (No. 21, John Gibson RA) and, with his younger brother A. B. Wyon (qv.), three in the City of London series. After J. S. Wyon's early death in 1873, medals still continued to be signed by the firm's name of J. S. & A. B. Wyon; for these see entry on A. B. Wyon.

*See*: Forrer, vol. 6, 588.

The following are signed J. S. & A. B. Wyon up to 1873:

1865 **Professor T. L. Donaldson PPRIBA (232a,** p. 190)
1872 **St Paul's Cathedral, interior** **(39k)**
1872 Prince of Wales; *Rev.* **Albert Hall** **(189a)**
1873 Queen Victoria; *Rev.* **Albert Hall** **(189b)**

WYON, Leonard Charles (1826–91). Studied art under his father William Wyon (qv.) and from him inherited a great skill in die engraving. Educated at Merchant Taylors' School. At the age of sixteen made his first medal and a year later appointed Second Engraver at the Royal Mint; in 1851 succeeded his father as Chief Engraver. His prolific output of coins and medals during the next forty years included the majority of British military and naval medals, as well as coins for countries throughout the British Empire. For the latter he not only engraved the dies but also prepared many of the designs. The large number of commemorative medals by L. C. Wyon include seven of the thirty forming the Art-Union series; for this series he produced the medal of his father William, commissioned in 1851 and issued 1855 (see Beulah, p. 183). In 1887 he engraved both sides of the Jubilee medal with: obverse, 'Queen Victoria' by J. E. Boehm; reverse, 'Allegory' by Frederick Leighton.

*See*: Forrer, vol. 6, 592 ff.

1850 Robert Stephenson; *Rev.* **Menai Tubular Bridge** **(164a)**
1854 Sir Joseph Paxton; *Rev.* **Crystal Palace** (by J. Pinches) **(171f, g)**

WYON, Peter (1767–1822). Brother of Thomas Wyon, the elder (qv.), with whom he went into business in Birmingham in 1796 as a die engraver. In 1800, when Thomas moved to London, Peter remained in Birmingham and subsequently worked for Matthew Boulton at the Soho Mint. He produced many tokens. Medals include items for Pitt Clubs at Dudley, Warrington, Wolverhampton, etc. 1814/15. Some later signed medals are thought to have been engraved by his son William Wyon (qv.).

*See*: Forrer, vol. 6, 632.

1805 **Old Hall, Green, Herts., St Edmund's College** **(60a)**

WYON, Thomas, the elder (1767–1830). After working in Birmingham with his brother Peter (qv.) as a die engraver, set up business in London in 1800. Appointed Chief Engraver of His Majesty's Seals in 1816. Two of his sons were distinguished as medallists: Benjamin (qv.) and Thomas, the younger (1792–1817), who died only two years after being appointed Chief Engraver to the Mint in 1815.[1] Medals by Thomas, the elder, include: Stonehenge 1796; Manchester Infirmary 1796; Turton's memorial of Nelson 1805; Liverpool Royal Institution, founded 1814.

*See*: Forrer, vol. 6, 635.

18–? **Sedgley Park School, Staffs.** **(44a)**

1. Richard Sainthill in *'Olla Podrida'* refers to the 'abilities which at so early an age place him at the

indisputed head of his profession in this country . . .'. Thomas, the younger, engraved coins for British Imperial and other currencies, also the dies for Maundy money 1817. Medals include: Pitt arousing the genius of Britain 1813; Waterloo medal 1815; opening of Waterloo Bridge 1817. (See Forrer, vol. 6, 641.)

WYON, William (1795–1851). The most famous member of this gifted family of medallists and die engravers. His qualities as an artist (given personal recognition by a medal in the Art-Union series)[1] were demonstrated by his skill as an engraver of medals, his modelling of extremely fine portrait pieces, and his production of a wide variety of coin designs for various parts of the British Empire during the reigns of George IV, William IV, and Queen Victoria.

William Wyon was born in Birmingham, the eldest son of Peter Wyon (qv.) to whom he was apprenticed in 1809. According to Forrer he was much influenced by the art of Flaxman. At the age of sixteen he produced a head of Hercules; this was praised by the gem engraver Nicholas Marchant, and William was encouraged to seek more exacting work. In 1812 he was invited to London by his uncle Thomas, the elder (qv.) and in 1813 he won the Society of Arts gold medal for a 'head of Ceres'. In 1815 he was again in London to help with engraving the new Great Seals, and next year was appointed Second Engraver to his cousin T. Wyon, the younger, at the Royal Mint. When in 1817 the latter died, Pistrucci was appointed Chief Engraver and there followed the well-known period of dispute. The core of this was that Pistrucci, although an outstanding artist, failed to work well at the Mint or to produce a satisfactory portrait for the coinage. As a result most of the responsibility devolved on W. Wyon.[2] This conflict was resolved in 1828 when William Wyon was made Chief Engraver (with back pay for services 1823–28) and a special post of Chief Medallist created for Pistrucci.

In 1830 Wyon started engraving the whole coinage series for the reign of William IV; the head for this was after the portrait by Sir Francis Chantrey (1781–1841).[3] Five years later he was invited to Portugal to model the head of Queen Donna Maria for the new coinage there. In 1837, following the visit of the young Queen Victoria to the Guildhall, the City of London commissioned a medal from William Wyon to mark the occasion (53b); it is this head of the Queen which became Wyon's best-known and admired medallic portrait, and it was used as a model for the 'Penny Black'—the first postage stamp of 1840.[4] Over two hundred medals by William Wyon are listed in Forrer; these include: Isaac Newton, with reverse the Hunterian Museum (demolished), Glasgow University 1827; University of London foundation 1827; Camden Medal, Cambridge University 1835;[5] Thomas Telford, engineer 1837; James Prinsep 1840; Prince Albert, as Cambridge Chancellor 1848; Prince Albert, on obverse of Council, Prize, Juror's, Service, and Exhibitor's medals of the Great Exhibition 1851. His medal for the Art-Union series (No. 1 issued 1847) is of the sculptor Chantrey, with reverse Chantrey's memorial to James Watt in Handsworth Church, Birmingham.[6]

*See*: Forrer, vol. 6, 650 ff.

| | |
|---|---|
| 1817 **Waterloo Bridge, London**[7] | **(67a)** |
| *c.* 1820 **Stockwell Park School** | **(43a)** |
| *c.* 1824 **Manchester Royal Institution** | **(111a)** |
| 1830 **Bodiam Castle** | **(26a)** |
| 1830 **Pimlico Grammar School**[8] | **(99a)** |
| 1834 Sir John Soane; *Rev.* **Bank of England** | **(106a)** |
| 1838 Queen Victoria; *Rev.* **Guildhall, South Front** | **(53a, b)** |
| 1844 **Royal Exchange** | **(146x)** |
| 1846 **Harrow School** | **(73a)** |
| 18–? **Coventry, St Michael's Church** | **(18a)** |

1. A series which W. Wyon was asked to advise on and initiate in 1843. See Beulah, p. 180.

2. An account of this controversy is given in Forrer, vol. 6, 651 ff.

3. A source used by his cousin Benjamin (qv.) for his London Bridge medal (No. 102a) of 1831.

4. The head of Queen Victoria, in profile, which was used for the penny and twopenny postage stamps printed 1840 up to 1879 was drawn by Henry Corbould from Wyon's portrait on the obverse of No. 53b.

5. Cf. Ottley (qv.) medals for publisher J. Peters of Cambridge. The Camden Medal by Wyon is Hocking, vol. ii, 254, No. 66.

6. Beulah, pp. 181, 182. For works of Chantrey see Gunnis, pp. 91–96.

7. Jointly with Thomas Wyon Jnr.

8. Mrs Joan Martin of the British Museum, attributes this medal to William Wyon.

# INDEX

This index is primarily a listing of persons, places and organisations.

Entries in ordinary type are PAGE numbers of material in the text.

Entries in **bold** type are CATALOGUE numbers of the medals; such entries indicate that the name, or the subject portrayed, appears on the medal listed. These references are grouped together after any standard page numbers.


Abercrombie, Hon. James, M.P., **97a**
Aberdeen, King's College, spire, 53
Ackworth School, West Yorks., 72, 220; **50a**
Adams, G. G., sculptor, 132n, 203, 211–12, 213; **160a, 235a**
*The Age* Weekly Newspaper, **171j**
Ainger, Alfred, architect, 130, 184
Albany, Duke of, **204a**
Albert, H.R.H. Prince, Prince Consort, 15, 23, 133, 142, 153, 170, 216, 222, 228; **1a, 4b, 5a, 6a, 7a, 8a, 9a, 12a, 35e, 45d, 142a, 146a–w, 150a, b, 153a, b, 155a, 159a–c, 161c, 162a, 165b, e, g, k, m–r, u–aa, cc, dd, 173a–c, 175a, 179b, d–f, h, 182e, l, s, u**
  Chancellor, Univ. of Cambridge, 221, 228
  medallic portraits of, **35e, 45d, 146a, e, f, j, k, m, o, q, 150a, b, 153a, b, 159a–c, 161c, 162a, 165b, k, m–r, v, x–z, aa, 175a, 179b, h, 182e, l, s, u**
Albert Victor, H.R.H. Prince, 171, **217a**
Alberti, L. B., 1
Allen, Ralph, 71, 207
Allen & Moore, medallists, 34, 212, 214, 219, 220; **21a, 28b, 66a, 144a, 146f–k, 155a, 159a, 160a, 161a, b, 162a, 165a–o, 167a, b, 170a, 171a, 179a, b, 182j**
Allom, Sir Charles, architect, 102
Alnwick Castle, 8n
Andrews, G. T., architect, 134, 184
Angell, John, 68
Anglesey, Marquess of, **54a**
Anson, Viscount, **54a**
Archer, Thomas, architect, 67, 184
Archer & Green, architects, 170, 173, 184
*Architectura Numismatica*, 2, 6, 19, 106, 190, 212
Architecture, prize medals, (R)IBA, 11, 54n, 99n, 212
  Royal Engineers, 191–2
  University College, 190
Arnold, John, **108d**
Arizona, U.S.A., 97
Aronson, J., **164b**
Art Union of London, 5, 13, 15, 24, 25, 31, 34, 59, 64, 67, 73, 152, 185, 190, 203, 212–13, 214, 220, 227, 228; **34a, 39h, 42a, 52a, 179i, 235a**
  architects, buildings, portrayed on medals, 213
  function of, 212
Artari, Giuseppe, 70
Ashton-under-Lyne, St Peter's Church, 85–6, 92, 193, 221n; **80a**
Athearn, Geo., **83a**
Auckland, Lord, **97a**
Audley End, Herts., 60
Austin, George, surveyor, 45, 184–5
Austin & Johnson, architects, 134
Avern, Edward, engraver, 213, 223; **108a, 154a**
Aylesford, Earl of, **54a, 108c**
Ayton, *see* Great Ayton

Backhouse, Jon., **138a**
Bacon, John, the elder, sculptor, 73, 76
Baddeley, John J., **22a**
Bagot, Lord, **54a**
Bagutti, Giovanni, 70
Baily, E. H., 119
Bain, W., medallist, 201, 213, **234a**

Baker, Arthur, architect, 180, 185
Baker, Sir Herbert, architect, 99
Baker, T. B., **17a**
Baldwin, Thomas, architect, 83
Bangs, builder, 77n
Baptist Missionary Society,
jubilee, **40a, b**
centenary, **40c**
Baptists, in Birmingham, 78
Barber, J., medallist, 213; **36a**
Barber, Cattle & North, 213; **13a, b**
Barclay, G. P., **125a**
Barff, Rev. Albert, **22a**
Baring, Alexander, M.P., **97a**
Barker, I., **2a**
Barker, Thos., **110a**
Barry, Sir Charles, architect, 20(Pl. 7), 21, 23, 27, 92, 102–3, 106, 114, 142n, 149n, 152–3, 185, 188, 200, 213, 224–5; **116a–d, 179b–e, i**
Barry, E. M., architect, 152, 165, 185, 213
Barry, Sir John Wolfe, engineer, 178, 197
Bass, M. T., **198a**
Bath, Argyle Chapel, 19, 83, 193, 219; **74a**
Bathwick new town, 81, 83
Bathwick Hill House, 81, 193; **71a**
Freemason's Hall, 19, 81, 207; **70a**
Prior Park, 71, 193, 207, 217; **47a**
Pulteney Bridge, 81
'Old' St Michael's Church (1742), 9, 70, 198, 215; **46a**
St Michael's Church, 104, 198, 215; **115a**
Beale, William, **108d**
Beauchamp, Earl, **54a**
Beaufort, Lady Margaret, 57
Beaumont, J. W. & R. F., architects, 177, 185
Beaumont, J. T. Barber, 112, 172; **129a**
Beaumont College, 75; **55a**. *See also* Windsor, Beaumont Lodge
Beaumont Park, Huddersfield, **204a**
Bedford, Francis, architect, 88, 185; **83a**
Belgians, King of the, **142a**
Bell, Ingress, architect, 175, 206
Bennett, 213; **10a, 11a**
Bentham, Jeremy, 94
Bernini, Giovanni Lorenzo, 67
Bewdley, Wyre Hill Schools, 160, 222; **186a**
Bickerstaffe, John, **222a**
Billiter, Richard, **83a**
Bilston, Cholera Orphan School, 19, 98, 221; **104a**
St Leonard's Church, 98
Technical, Science & Art School, 179–180; **228a**
Waterworks, 179–180; **228a**
Birch, Eugenius, engineer, 158
Birkbeck, George, **97a**
Bird, Francis, sculptor, 57, 66
Birley, Hugh, M.P., **193a**
Birmingham, Almshouses & Orphanage, Erdington, **199a**
Aston Hall, 31, 59–60, 218, 220, 221; **35a–e**
Baptist Meeting House, 78, 215; **61a**
Birmingham & Midland Institute, extension, 21, 165, 187, 220; **200a**
Bishop Ryder Church, 108, 202, 218, 219; **123a**
Blue Coat School, 76, 201, 220; **57a**
Carrs Lane Chapel, 82, 206, 217; **72a, b**
Cemetery Chapel, Key Hill, 103, 131, 190, 221; **112a**
first stone laid, **112a**
directors (listed), **112a**
Christ Church, Colmore Row, 8, 31, 79–80, 199, 224; **65a**
General Hospital, 9, 74–5, 101, 219, 221; **54a–c, 108d**
General Institution for The Blind, 143, 195, 212; **167a**
Hebrew National School, 116–17, 215, 217; **139a, b**
Holy Trinity Church, Bordesley, 84–5, 87, 92, 96, 193, 221n; **78a**
King Ed. VI Grammar School, 21, 93, 104–6, 118, 152, 185, 201, 215; **108f, 116a–d**
Queen's College, 93
Mason Science College, 165, 189, 220; **199a**
The Mint (R. Heaton & Sons), 34, 150, 218; **178a**
Old Meeting House, 76; **58a**
Oscott, St Mary's College, 27, 30(Pl. 12), 108–9, 200–1, 216; **124a**
'Pantechnatheca' (Repository of all the Arts), 13, 83–4, 217; **76a**
railway viaduct, **113a**
St Andrew's Church, Bordesley, 128, 187; **152a**
St John's Church, Deritend, 72; **51a**
St John's Church, Perry Bar, 99, 221; **105a**
St Michael's Church and Cemetery, Warstone Lane, 130–1, 194, 217; **158a**
St Peter's Church, Dale End, 90, 190, 202, 221; **88a, b**
St Philip's Church (later Cathedral), 67, 184, 217, 218, 223; **41a, b**
churchyard, 76
Rector of, **88b**
St Philip's National School, 115, 215, 216; **136a**
School of Medicine, Snow Hill, 92–3, 219; **93a**
Town Hall, 10(Pl. 1), 11, 21, 75, 90, 100–1, 144, 149, 187, 190, 194, 213, 215, 217; **108a–f**

building committee (listed), **108d**
Victoria Law Courts, 175, 206; **218a**
Birmingham centre for medal production, 34, 212
Soho Mint, Handsworth, 33n, 34, 218n, 219
The Mint (R. Heaton & Sons), 150, 218
Birmingham music festivals, 9, 75, 101; **54a–c, 108a–d, f**
concerts in Royal Hotel, 9, 75
presidents, **54a, b**
vice presidents, listed, **54a**
Birmingham, Soho Mint, Handsworth, 33n, 34, 218n, 219, 221, 223, 227
Birmingham, University of, 165, 206
Blackburn, Library & Museum, 163, 189, 221; **195a**
Blackpool, North Pier, 158; **183a**
The Tower, 158, 177, 198; **222a**
Blenheim Palace, 15, 17(Pl. 5), 67–8, 195, 205, 213, 227; **42a**
Blore, Edward, architect, 48, 129, 185–6, 194
Blomfield, Sir Arthur, architect, 91
Blue Coat Charity, **57a**
Bodley, G. F., architect, 66
Bodiam Castle, 55, 228; **26a**
Boehm, Sir J. Edgar, sculptor, **180b**
Boothby, I. B., **125a**
Bootle, St Mary's Church, 130, 191; **156a**
Boulton, Matthew, 33n, 34, 218, 221, 223, 227
Borromini, Francesco, 67
Bothwell, S., builder, **117a**
Bourne, William, architect, 116, 186; **137a**
Bovy, Antoine, medallist, 214; **182k**
Bowcher, Frank, sculptor, 33, 214, 215, 218, 222; **132c, 225a**
Bradford, Earl of, **54a**
Bradford, Technical College, 166, 196, 216; **201a**
Brandon, David, architect, 129, 132, 186, 209; **154a, 160a.** *See also* Wyatt & Brandon
Brett, John, **83a**
Bridges, John, 54
Bridport, St Mary's Church, 52, 195; **17a**
Bright, John, 10; **175b**
Brighton, Chain Pier, 85, 158, 226; **79a**
Royal Pavilion, 21, 83, 199, 219; **75a**
St Peter's Church, 21, 92, 185, 219; **91a**
Bristol, Cabot Memorial Tower, 181, 194; **231a**
Exhibition Building, 175; **220a**
'British Order of Architecture', 5, 191; **55a**
Britton, John, 4, 31, 185
Britton and Pugin, 61
Broadhead, William & George, masons, **80a**
Brock, Sir Thomas, sculptor, 91n, 176, 180, 214, 216; **221b**
Brodrick, Cuthbert, architect, 11, 149, 186, 197
'Brompton Boilers', the, 141, 206n
Bromsgrove, King Edward VI's Grammar School, 62; **38a**
Brookes, William McIntosh, architect, 106, 186
Brookes & Adams, medallists, 214; **30a**
Brooks, William, architect, 81, 186
Brougham, Henry, M.P. (later 1st Baron Brougham and Vaux), 94, 107n; **97a**
Brown, Commander Samuel, RN, **79a**
Brown Edge, St Anne's Church, 119, 212; **144a**
Bruce, Charles, **83a**
Bruce, Knight, **150b**
Brunel, Isambard Kingdom, engineer, 147, 186
Brunel, Marc Isambard, engineer, 223
*The Builder*, 194
Bunning, J. B., architect, 15, 23, 107, 133, 186–7, 190, 196; **120a, 161a, c**
Burges, William, architect, 23
Burlington, Lord, 59
Burnley & District Hospital, 171, 205; **210a**
Burse, proclaimed 'Royal Exchange' 1570, **36a, 146c, k, s, u**
Burton, Decimus, architect, 102, 187, 199
Busfield (Colne), **223a**
Bushnell, John, sculptor, 61, 62
Butterfield, William, architect, 23, 187
Butterworth, J., **210a**
Bygrave, Robert, **83a**

Calthorpe, Lord, **54a**
Calvert, E., **125a**
Cambridge, Chancellors of the University, medallic series, 15, 69, 221; **45a–e**
Cambridge, Adolphus Frederick, Duke of, 212; **160a**
Cambridge, Christ's College, 57, 221, **29a–c**
St. John's College, gateway, 57
Museum of Archaeology and Ethnology, 49n
Senate House, 15, 69–70, 193, 221; **45a–e**
Camden, Marquess of, 221; **45a**
Campbell, Thomas, **97a**
Canterbury Cathedral, 44–5, 184–5, 216, 224; **1a, b**
Carey, William, **40a–c**
Carlini, Augostino, 73
Caroe, W. D., architect, 91
Carpenter, John, 107; **120a**
Carpenter, R. C., architect, 53, 128, 187
Carter, C. F., medallist, 213, 214, 217, 220; **34a, 119a, 127a, b**
Castle Howard, Yorks., 67, 195, 205
Cawley, Joseph, architect, 181
Chamberlain, John H., architect, 23, 165, 187

Chamberlain, Joseph, 187; **178a**
Chambers, Sir William, architect, 5, 16(Pl. 4), 73, 187–8, 209, 213, 227; **52a**
Champ, P., publisher, 111
Chantrell, R. D., architect, 23, 114, 188
Chantrey, Sir Francis, 125, 201, 212, 218, 228
Chaplain, J. C., medallist, 33, 214
Charles I, King, 49, 61
Charles II, King, 61, 113; **146k, u**
Charterhouse School, *see* London, Charterhouse School; Godalming, Charterhouse School
Chateauneuf, Alexis de, architect, 125
Chatwin, J. A., architect, 67, 171, 188
Chelmsford, Shire Hall, 76, 196, 221; **56a, b**
Chelmsford Polytechnic Exhibition 1848, **56a**
Cheesman, J., **117a**
Cheltenham, Proprietary College, 117, 207, 220, 221; **140a, b**
Chester, George Henry Law, Bishop of, **68a, 78a, 80a**
Chester, Town Hall, 160, 163, 177, 198, 220; **188a**
Chetwynd, Sir George, 88, 200; **84a**
Chichester, Cathedral, 45, 213; **2a**
 Market Cross, 45, 213; **2a**
Cholera, 7, 19, 106; **104a**
 *Cholera in Bilston*, 98
Christ's Hospital School, 93–4
 Mathematical Prize, **96a**
Church Building Act (1818), 4
Church Commissioners, *see* Commissioners, The Church: Commissioners' Churches
Cibber, Caius Gabriel, 66
Cinque Ports Banquet 1839, **25a**
City of London, *see* London, Corporation of the City of
City of London Companies, 169
City of London Hospital for Diseases of the Chest, *see* London, Victoria Park Hospital
Clark, Thomas, **108d**
Clarke, Rev. A. J., **88a**
Clarke, George, **71a**
Clarke, George Somers, architect, 92, 154, 188
Clement XII, Pope, 1
Clements, of Liverpool, **119a**
Cliff, G. B., **230a**
Clint, Scipio, medallist, 215; **119a**
Clonmell, Earl, **54a**
Coal mining industry, 134
Cockerell, Professor Charles Robert, architect, 23, 82, 125, 144, 188–9, 191, 205, 208
Cohen, I., **139a**
Cole, Sir Henry, 142, 158, 161
Collcutt, Thomas Edward, architect, 163, 170, 176, 184, 189
Collis, G. R., medallist, 31, 215, 223n; **125a, b, 129a, 139a**
Collins & Cullis, builders, **187a**
Colne, Town Hall, 177, 185; **223a, b**
Colonial Exhibition, London 1886, 176
 Colonial & Indian reception, Guildhall, 215; **185a**
Commissioners' Churches, 15, 21, 85–7, 88, 90–2, 93, 95, 96, 193
Commissioners, The Church, 4; **78a, 88a, 89a**
 Local Commissioners, Birmingham (listed), **88a**
Commissioners for Building Fifty New Churches (Act of 1711), 184, 192
Congleton, Town Hall, 160, 177
Constitution, the, **39e**
*Contrasts*, 21, 74, 109, 200
Cooke, T., **125a**
Cope, John, **88a**
Copenhagen, Battle of, **143b,c**
Corbould, Henry, 228n
Cornwallis, Earl, **54a**
Corsini, Cardinal, 68
Cossins, J. A., architect, 165, 189; **199a**
Coventry, St John's Church, 53, 203; **19a**
 St John's Schools, 53, 168(illus.); **19a**
 St Michael's Church (later Cathedral), 52, 228; **18a**
Coward College, **212a**
Crace, J. G., 158
Crane, Rev. Samuel, **78a**
Craven, Earl of, **54a**
Creed, Richard, **125a**
Crompton, I. W., **108d**
Cronk, H. H., architect, 162, 189
Cropper, E., **125a**
Cross, E., 215; **83a**
Croxton, John, mason, 159
'Crystal Palace',
 Bath, Royal Victoria Park, 207
 Manchester, Trafford Park, 148, 202
Crystal Palace, The, 141–2, 147; *see also* London, Great Exhibition Building (1851); London, Crystal Palace (1854), Sydenham
Crystal Palace Company, 147
 Chairman, **171j**
Cubitt, Leonard W., **22a**
Cuffley & Starkey, architects, 52
Cundy, Thomas, jnr, architect, 180, 185, 189
Cunningham, John, architect, 104, 131, 158, 189, 195
Curtis, Robert, **83a**

D & R, *see* Durning & Ryder
Dalyngrig family, **26a**

Dance, George, jun., architect, 9, 18, 61, 74, 169, 189–190, 204
Dartmouth, Earl of, 8, 79; **54a, 92a**
Darwen, Holy Trinity Church, 93, 202; **94a**
Davey, Peter, **83a**
Davis, Joseph, medallist, 5, 8, 27, 34, 215–6, 220, 224; **1a, b, 4a, b, 5a, 6a, 7a, 8a, 9a, b, 12a, 13c, 39f, g, 40a, 46a, 61a, 108e, 115a, 116a, 122a, 133a, 136a, 143a, 145a, 146a, l–u, 149a, 150a, b, 153a, b, 159b, 165p, q, 179c–e**
Davis & Emmanuel, architects, 166, 190
Dawkes, Samuel, architect, 184, 194
Dee, G., **165r**
de Grey, second Earl, 54n
De Saulles, G. W., medallist, 176, 216, 221n
Denbigh, Earl of, **54a**
Derby, Library & Museum, 164, 192; **198a**
St Michael's Church, 95, 149, 204, 221; **174a**
Devonshire, Duke of, 221; **45e, 54a**
Dickson, Thomas, engineer, 167
Dodd, Charles, **83a**
Donaldson, Professor Thomas Leverton, architect, 2, 4, 6, 7, 54, 106, 125, 142n, 190, 192, 212; **24a**
portrait medal, 3, 16, 190, 225, 227; **232a**
Doncaster, New Betting Rooms, 88, 208, 219; **85a**
Prospect House, 93, 221; **95a**
St George's Church, Vicarage, 93
Dorking, St Martin's Church, 106, 186; **117a**
Douai, English College at, 77
Dover, Castle, 55, 226; **25a**
Dowler, G., 216; **171b, 182a–i**
Drury & Bateman, architects, 93
Dubois, E., medallist, 106n
Dudley, St James' Church, 116, 186
St James' School, 116, 186; **137a**
St John's Church, 116
St Thomas' Church, 81, 186, 217; **69a**
Dudley and Ward, Viscount, *see* Ward, John
Dufferin, Marquess of, **231a**
Dugdale, —, M.P., **54a**
Duke, Sir James, Lord Mayor of London, **161c**
Durand, J. N. L., architect, 106
Durham Cathedral, 45; **3a**
Durning & Ryder, engravers, 216; **124a, 136a**

Eastwood (Colne), **223b**
Edge, Charles, architect, 90, 101, 103, 190; **112a**
Edinburgh, St Giles Cathedral, spire, 53
St Mary's Episcopal Cathedral, 203, 212; **235a**
Edmonds, Christopher, jun., architect, 100, 190; **126a**
Education
National, **39n**
Salisbury Diocesan Board of, **10b**
Board of, 202; *see also* Schools
Educational Supply Association, **31a**
Edward II, King, 46
Edward VI, King, **38a, 116a–d**
Edward VII, King, *see* Prince of Wales
Edward the Confessor, St., 48
Elgood, John, architect, 171, 174, 208
Elizabeth I, Queen, **36a, 126a, 146c, k, u**
Elkington & Co., 215, 216; **7b, 8b, 11b, 13d, 185a, 211a**
Ellesmere, Francis Egerton, first Earl of, 129; **155a**
Elmes, Harvey Lonsdale, architect, 11, 23, 118, 144, 149, 188, 190–1; **170a**
Ely Cathedral, 45–6, 216; **4a, b**
Emlyn, Henry, 5, 75, 191
Engineering Employers Federation, **226a**
Essex, James, architect, 46, 47
Eton College, 57, 216; **31a**
Eversley, Viscount, **194a**
Evesham, Bell Tower, 57, 214; **30a**
Exeter, 19
Council, and Chamber, of, **118a**
Western, or Lower, Market, 5–7, 106, 192, 226; **118a**
Exhibitions (in date order)
Art, Manufacture & Science, Newcastle (1840), **20a**
Great Exhibition, London (1851), 141–2; **165a–gg**
Commissioners for, 142, 153, 157, 161
Medals for, 211, 228
Manchester Art Treasures (1857), 148; **173a–c**
International Exhibition, London (1862), 157–8; **182a–w**
London Annual Exhibition (1872–74), 153, 161; **180a, b, 189a, b**
Colonial Exhibition, London (1886), 176
Blackburn, Art & General (1874), **195a**
Bradford, Fine Art & Industrial (1882), **201a**
Worcestershire (1882), 167; **203a**
Oldham, Fine Art & Industrial (1883), **205a**
Wolverhampton, Fine Arts & Industrial (1884), **209a**
Manchester, Royal Jubilee (1887), 174; **215a**
Royal Yorkshire Jubilee (1887), **190a**
Bristol Industrial & Fine Art (1893), **220a**
Exhibition buildings, **165a–gg, 171a–l, 173a–c, 182a–w, 203a, 215a, 220a**
Eyes, Edward, surveyor, 130, 191

Fairbairn, Peter, **175a**

Fattorini & Sons, 216; **201a, 217a**
Faulkner, B., 217; **62a, 76a**
Fenwick, A., medallist, 217; **135a**
Filarete, Antonio, 1
Fire, commemoration of destruction by, **13b, 36a, 146d, k, s, u, 147a, 179f**
Fire, of London (1666), 159, 196, 208; **36a, 146d, k, s, u**
Fisher, James, **83a**
Foot & Tebay, 217; **37a**
Ford, E. Onslow, sculptor, 214
Foresters, Ancient Order of, **171e**
Fothergill, Dr John, **50a**
Fox, W. Sands, FRS, 93
Fidler, Jos[h], **83a**
Flockton, William, architect, 112, 191
Fontana, Carlo, 70, 192
Foster, John, jun., architect, 87, 103, 104, 110, 191
Fowke, Captain Francis, RE, 23, 153, 158, 161, 191–2; **182c, m–o**
portrait medal, 24, 191–2, 220; **233a**
Fowler, Charles, architect, 5–7, 23, 97, 106, 192, 201; **118a**
Fox, Henderson & Co., contractors, 141, 147; **165e, g, k–o, q, u–z, 171a, b, j**
Frampton, Sir George J., sculptor, 33, 217, 218; **27a**
Francis, Horace, architect, 129, 192, 209
Freeman, Richard Knill, architect, 164, 192
Freer, Rev. T. L., **105a**
Friends' School
Ackworth, 72
Great Ayton, 116
Frome, Holy Trinity, Church, 111
School Room, 111; **128a**
Frost, T. G., **188a**
Fry, William, **83a**
Fuller, Andrew, **40a, c**
Fuller, John ('Mad Jack'), 55n; **26a**

G. F. & S., **205a**
Gaab, G. D., medallist, 25, 209n
Galilei, Aless., architect, 1
Galton, S. T., **108d**
Gamble, J., 217; **180a**
Gandy-Deering, J. P., architect, 94n, 95, 185, 192
Gardner, Rev. Laurence, **54a, 88a, b**
Garnett, R., **125a**
Garratt, John, Lord Mayor, **102b, c**
Gedge, Rev. Sydney, **116a–d**
George III, King, 8, 11, 79, 80n, 187, 223, 224; **29a–c, 39a–d, 65a**
statue in Guildhall Council Chamber, 169
George IV, King, 8, 83, 113, 210, 222; **79a, 81a, b, 131a, b**
patron of Birmingham music festival, **54a, 54b**
Prince Regent, 80, 199; **67a**
Gibbons, Grinling, 66
Gibbs, James, architect, 15, 69–70, 71, 119, 192–3
Gieson, I., **119a**
Gilbert, Alfred, sculptor, 212
Gladstone, Rt Hon. W. E., M.P., **214a**
Gloucester, Cathedral, 46, 216; **5a**
Gloucester, St James' Church, 120
St James' Parochial School, 120, 215; **145a**
Gloucester and Bristol, Bishop of, **187a**
Glyn, G. C., **125a**
Godalming, Charterhouse School, 162, 195; **192a**. *See also* London, Charterhouse School
Godwin, E. W., architect, 23, 160, 196
Godwin, George, architect, 54n, 212
Goldsmid, A. A., **139a**
Goldsmid, Isaac Lyon, **97a**
Gooch, Henry, **83a**
Goodman, Thomas, **167a, b**
Goodwin, Francis, architect, 21, 23, 85–87, 89, 92, 96, 98n, 103, 164, 193, 197; **78a, 80a, 81a, 92a**
Goodwin, George, **112a**
Goodridge, H. E., architect, 19, 71, 81, 83, 111, 191, 193
Gotch, J. A., architect, 58, 175, 193
Gough, Alexander Dick, architect, 114, 162, 193
Gough, A. D. & Roumieu, R. L., architects, 114
Gough, John, of Perry Hall, **105a**
Gough, W. V., architect, 181, 194
Governesses Benevolent Institution, **160a**
Gower, Earl, **54a**
Grimshaw, Nicholas, **23a**
Graham, Robert, 93; **95a**
Grand Junction Railway, **113a, b**
Granville, Viscount, **54a**
Great Ayton, N. Yorks., Ayton School, 116; **138a**
Gregory, Richard (Gregory Medal), **73a**
Gregory, Olinthus G., **97a**
Grellier, William, architect, 125
Grendon Hall, Warwicks., 88, 200, 226; **84a**
Grenfell, P. St L., **125a**
Gresham, Sir Thomas, **36a, 146d, k, s, u, x**
medallic portrait, 33, 124; **146x**
Gretton Green, Christ Church, 160, 209, 221; **187a**
Griffin, W., **143b**
Griffin & Hyams, **36a**; *see also* Hyams, Hyam
Griffin & Weller, architects, 150, 194; **176a**
Grote, George, jun., **97a**
Grumbold, William, mason, 58

Grundy, J. C., **155a**
Guides, Imp. Reg. of, **171d**

H & L, **60a**
H & SS, **124a**
Haines, William, **108d**
Hakewill, J. H., architect, 91
Hakewill, Henry, architect, 91, 194
Halifax, Technical School, 179, 196, **226a**
Halley, Dr R., **212a**
Hallett, J[s]., **83a**
Halliday, Thomas, medallist, 34, 213, 214, 217, 218, 220, 223; **10a, 16a, 33a, b, 39b, 41a, b, 47a, 68a, 69a, 72a, 82a, 108b, f, 113a, b, 116b–d, 139b, 146b–d, 158a, 179f**
Halprin, Robert C., **181a**
Hamerani, O., medallist, 1
Hamilton & Medland, architects, 131, 194; **158**
Hammond, Rev. R. H., **100a**
Hancock, J. G., medallist, 217–18, 219; **39a**
Hansom, Joseph Aloysius, architect, 101, 128, 144, 190, 194; *see also* Hansom & Welch
Hansom & Welch, architects, 10, 11, 23, 101, 194; **108a–e**
Hardwick, Philip, architect, 110, 127, 194, 200, 209; **125a, b, 150b**
Hardwick, P. C., architect, 110, 127, 162, 194–5
Hardwick Hall, 131
Hardy, John Stockdale, **89a**
Harlech Castle, 55
Harris, Dr J., **212a**
Harrogate, Royal Bath Hospital, 174, 208, 216; **217a**
Harrow School, *see* London, Harrow School
Harrowby, Earl of, **54a**
Hartopp, Bt., **54a**
Harvey, Rev. J., **187a**
Harvey, John, mason, 70
Hasluck, Richard, **112a**
Hastings, Sea Bathing Infirmary, **26a**
Hatfield House, Herts., 60
Hawksmoor, Nicholas, architect, 48, 68, 195, 205, 208
Haywood, C., jun., architect, 168
Heaton, Ralph & Sons, coiners, 34, 150, 218, 220; **165s–u, 178a, 190a, 215a**
Hedge, John, builder, **92a**
Hedley, Rev. T. A., 120
Hemming, Samuel, 143, 195
Henry II, King, 55
Henry III, King, 48, 55
Henry VI, King, statue of, **31a**
Henry VII, King, 48, 57; **8b**
Henshaw, Thomas, **110a**
Henslowe, Rev. E. J. L. B., **17a**
Herbert, Rt Hon. Sidney, 129; **154a**
Heselton, Philip, 116n
Heywood, Abel, **197a**
Heywood, Sir Benjamin A., **111a**
Hicks, John, 52, 195
Highbury College, **212a**
Highway, Isaac, architect, 108, 195
Hindley, Library & Museum, 171, 208, 216; **211a**
Hinks, James, 218, 219; **159c**
Hinton & Armistead, **205a**
Hodges, William, artist, 74
Hodgson, D., **125a**
Hollins, Peter, sculptor, 218; **41b, 123a**
Holland, Henry, architect, 83, 204
Hollins, W., 218
Holme, Arthur Hill, architect, 107, 189, 195
Holmes, William, 116
Homerton College, **212a**
Hook, Rev. Walter Farquhar, **132a**
Hope, Henry Thomas, 212
Hope, Thomas, 207
Hope & Jardine, architects, 166, 196
Hornby Castle, Lancs., 148
Horticultural Society, The, Gardens & Arcades, S. Kensington, 153, 176
Horticultural Society, E. London, **213a**
Houldsworth, H., **125a**
Howe, Earl, **54a, b, 89a, 167a**
Howard, Robert, **83a**
Huddersfield, Technical School, 168, 196, 221; **204a**
Huddersfield Polytechnic, 168
Hudson, Benjamin, **112a**
Hughes, Edward, architect, 168, 196
Hume, Joseph, M.P., **97a**
Huntington, Rev. W., 79; **63a**
Hussey, R. C., architect, 108
Hutchinson, Henry, architect, 90, 202; **88a, b**
Hyams, Hyam, 219; **146b–d, v, 179f**

India, Bank of, 111
Inge, —, **54a**
Ingram, T. W., engraver, 218n, 219; **15a, 85a, 93a, 123a**
Inman, W. S., architect, 84, 196
Institute of British Architects (later Royal), 1–2, 6, 54, 106n, 187, 190, 192, 194, 204, 210, 226; **24a**
  prize medals, 11, 54n, 99n, 212
  emblem and motto, 54
Institute of Civil Engineers, prize medal, 227
Isaacson, Rev. S., **117a**

Jacks, James, **83a**
Jackson, Rev. R. Noble, **187a**
Jackson & Fox, architects, 179, 196
& Jacob (Liverpool), **148a**
James, John, architect, 48
James, Rev. J. A., **112a**
James, John Angel, **72a, b**
James, P. M., **108d, 112a**
Jarman, Edward, surveyor, 23, 61, 196
Jay, Rev. William, **74a**
Jeffery & Skiller, architects, 163, 196
Jenkins, Henry, & Co., 219; **221a**
Joseph, R. L., 218, 219; **159c**
Jephson, Dr Henry, 98, 218; **103a, b**
Jeune, Rev. Francis, **116a–d**
Johnson, John (1732–1814), architect, 76, 196
Johnson, John (1807–78), architect, 164, 196
Johnson, Owen, **61a**
Jones, Charles, 13, 83; **76a**
Jones, Sir Horace, architect, 23, 61, 159, 164, 169, 178, 196–7; **206a**
Jones, Inigo, architect, 14(Pl. 3), 31, 49, 59, 193, 197, 213; **34a**
Jones, Owen, 141, 147, 158
Jones, Richard, 71n, 207
Joyce, Rev. J., **117a**
Jubilees, 1887 and 1897, *see* Victoria, Queen

Kelk & Lucas, contractors, **182c, m–o**
Kelsey, S., 219; **74a**
Kemp, C. J., architect, **162a**
Kempson, Peter, medallist, 218, 219
Kempson & Kindon, medallists, 219; **39a, c, d**
Kempthorne, Sampson, architect, 120, 202
Kenning, George, 219; **214a**
Kettering, Baptist Mission House, 66–7, 215, 223; **40a–c**
School, 175, 193, 224; **219a**
Kettering Education Authority, **219a**
Kidderminster, St George's Church, 86–7, 92, 193, 221; **81a**
Kindon, Samuel, 219
Kirk, Rev. John, 68
Kirk, John, medallist, 8n, 127n, 197n
Kneller, Sir Godfrey, 67
Knight, Thomas, mason, 61

L. G., medallist, **1821**
Laing, Samuel, M.P., **171c, j**
Lancaster, Ripley Hospital, 158–9, 189, 222; **184a**
Royal Grammar School, 148, 203, 227; **172a**
Lane, Richard, architect, 102, 193, 197, 206; **110a**
Lanfranc, Archbishop, 45
Langridge, Joseph, silversmith, 219; **75a, 91a**
Lansdowne, Marquis of, **97a**
Latham, Baldwin, architect, 179, 197
Law, Rt Rev. George Henry, *see* Chester, Bishop of,
Lawley, —, Bt., **54a**
Lawley, —, M.P., **54a**
Leamington, Beech Lawn House, 97–8, 204, 221; **103a, b**
Jephson Gardens, 98
Ledsam, J. F., **125a**
Lee, Thomas, **108d**
Leeds, St Peter's Church, 114, 188, 214, 221, 222; **132a–c**
Jubilee of restoration (1891), **132b**
Town Hall, 11, 149, 164, 186; **175a, b**
Legge, —, **54a**
Leicester, St George's Church, 90–1, 199; **89a**
Leigh, Rev. William, 98; **104a**
Le Sueur, Hubert, 49
Lewis, Hayter, architect, 94
Leyland Free Library & Museum, *see* Hindley, Library & Museum
Lichfield, Abbott, 57
Lichfield Cathedral, 46–7, 200, 209, 216; **6a**
Lichfield & Coventry, Henry Ryder, Bishop of, 218; **54a, 88a, b, 105a, 123a**
Memorial Church, Birmingham, 108, 202, 218, 219; **123a**
Lilley, Samuel, **83a**
Lincoln, George Pelham, Bishop of, **89a**
Lincoln Cathedral, 47, 216, 224; **7a, b**
Liverpool,
Assize Courts, 144
Collegiate Institution, 118, 191, 221; **141a, b**
Infirmary, 87, 191, 217; **82a**
Railway Station, Lime Street, entrance screen, 103–4, 110, 191, 217, 222; **113a, b**
Mechanics Institution, 107, 118, 195, 214, 215, 220; **119a**
Royal Infirmary Medical School, 126, 219; **148a**
Sailors' Home, 131, 158, 189, 212, 215, 218, 219, 220; **159a–c**
St George's Hall, 11, 23, 118, 149, 164, 188–9, 191, 212, 220; **170a**
St Mary's Church, 127, 201, 215; **149a**
University buildings, 126
Liverpool, Manchester & Birmingham, Grand Junction Railway, **113a, b**
viaduct, at Birmingham, **113a**, over River Weaver, **113b**
Littleton, —, M.P., **54a**
Lloyd, John Buck, **170a**
Lockwood, Henry, architect, 186, 197

Lockwood & Mawson, architects, 161, 197
London, Porteus, Bishop of, **29a–c**
London, Corporation of the City of, 74, 97, 169, 178n, 196, 214–5; **39k, 53a–c, 120a, 146r,** s
  architect to, 9, 61, 133, 159, 169, 178, 186, 196; (*see also* Bunning, J. B.; Dance, G.; Jones, Sir Horace)
  medallic series, 9, 15, 31, 34, 211, 214–5, 219, 227, 228; **37a, 39k, 53b, 102a, 120a, 161c, 185a, 202a, 206a, 225a**; architectural subjects listed, 215
London Foundling Hospital, the Governors of, 72
London Hospital, Governors of, **49a**
London, School Board, architect to, 172, 202
London, Albert Hall, 24, 142, 153, 161, 176, 191, 203, 217, 225, 227; **180a, b, 189a, b**
  The Albert Palace, 170; **208a**
  Alexandra Palace, 158, 163–4, 196; **196a**
  Bank of England, *Frontis.*, 11, 24, 99, 188, 204, 228; **106a**
  Banqueting House, Whitehall, 14(Pl. 3), 59, 66, 197, 208, 213, 214; **34a**
  Battersea Park, 170
  Bethnal Green Museum, 206
  Bishopsgate Institute, 177, 205, 220; **224a**
  British Orphan Asylum, Clapham Rise, 89; **87a**
  British Museum, buildings, 23, 119
  Brompton Hospital, 128–9, 192, 209, 215; **153a, b**
  Charing Cross Hospital, 11, 102, 187, 226; **109a**
  Charterhouse School, 77, 200; **59a**
  Christ Church, Streatham, 115, 129, 206, 223; **134a**
  Christ's Hospital School, 93–4, 203–4, 226; **96a**
  City of London School, Milk Street, 107, 118, 166, 186–7, 215, 226; **120a**
  City of London School for Boys, 107, 166–7, 190, 215, 225; **202a**
  Coal Exchange, 15, 27, 28(Pl. 10), 132–4, 186–7, 212, 215, 227; **161a–c**
  Covent Garden Market, 5, 192
  Cripplegate Institute, 179; **227a**
  'Crystal Palace' (1854), Sydenham, 13, 23, 142, 145–7, 163, 199–200, 212, 216, 221, 222, 223, 227; **171a–l, 182g**. *See also* London, Great Exhibition Building (1851)
  Euston Propylaeum, or 'Arch', 21, 31, 109–10, 194, 215; **125a, b**
  Foreign Office, building, 2, 203
  Governesses Benevolent Institution Asylum, 132, 209, 212; **160a**
  Grays Inn Lane, Chapel, *see* London, Providence Chapel

London—*continued*
  Great Exhibition Building (1851), 3, 12(Pl. 2), 13, 19, 23, 135–42, 147, 148, 158, 199–200, 212, 215, 216, 218, 221, 223; **165a–gg**. *See also* London, 'Crystal Palace' (1854), Sydenham
  Guildhall, Colonial & Indian Reception, 215; **185a**
    Council Chamber, 27, 29(Pl. 11), 159, 169, 197, 215, 225; **206a**
    Hall interior, 159, 164, 169, 197, 215, 216; **185a**
    Queen Victoria's visit (1837), 9, 15, 74, 215, 228; **53a–c**
    South entrance facade, 9, 15, 18(Pl. 6), 73–4, 189–90, 215, 226, 228; **53a–c**
  Hackney Parochial Schools, 79; **64a**
  Harrow School, 82, 188–9, 228; **73a**
  Holborn Restaurant, 33, 170, 184, 189; **207a**
  Honey Lane Market, Cheapside, 107
  Horniman Museum, 205
  Horticultural Society Buildings, 153–4, 176, 191, 217, 220; **180a, b**
  Houses of Parliament, 8, 20(Pl. 7), 21, 27, 106, 151–3, 185, 201, 212, 213, 215, 219, 224, 225; **179a–i**
    House of Commons, interior, 152
    House of Lords, interior, 20(Pl. 7), 27, 153, 201; **179c**
  Hungerford Market, 7, 106, 192
  Imperial College, 154, 176
  Imperial Institute, 153, 176, 189, 216, 219, 221; **221a, b**
  Infant Orphan Asylum, Wanstead, 118, 198, 202–3, 223; **142a**
  International Exhibition Building 1862, S. Kensington, 13, 23, 24, 142, 154–8, 163, 191, 212, 214, 216, 221, 222, 225; **182a–w**
  Jewish Free School, 117
  Kings College, 73, 94n
  Law Courts, 23, 62, 189
  Licensed Victuallers' Asylum, 134, 202, 212; **162a**
  Lincoln's Inn, Hall & Library, 127, 194, 215; **150a, b**
  Lincoln's Inn, Stone Buildings, 127
  London Bridge, 3, 15, 85, 96–7, 125, 192, 201, 213, 215, 226, 228n; **102a–c**
  The London Hospital, 71–2, 198, 226; **49a**
  London Orphan Asylum, Clapton, 84, 196, 223; **77a**
  Merchant Seamen's Orphan Asylum, Snaresbrook, 154, 188, 224; **181a**
  Metropolitan & City Police Orphanage, Twickenham, 143; **168a**
  National Gallery, 119, 207
  National Liberal Club, 173, 206, 219; **214a**

London—*continued*
Natural History Museum, 158, 191, 206
Nelson Monument, 119, 201, 213, 215, 223; **143a–c**
New College, 172, 198, 225; **212a**
Orphan Working School, Hampstead, 130, 184; **157a**
'People's Palace', 112, 172–3, 202, 222; **213a**
Philosophical Institution, 112, 173, 215; **129a**
Pimlico Grammar School, 95, 192, 228; **99a**
Pimlico Literary Institute, 95
Providence Chapel, Grays Inn Lane, 31, 79; **63a**
Royal Exchange (1671), 9, 21–3, 61, 125, 196, 213, 217, 219; **36a, 146d**
Royal Exchange (1844), 3, 23, 32(Pl. 13), 33, 120–5, 147, 188, 204–5, 212, 215, 217, 219, 222, 223, 228; **146a–y**
St Gabriel's Church, Warwick Square, 180, 185, 189; **229a**
St George's Church, Wells Way, 87–8, 185, 215; **83a**
St Giles' Church, Camberwell, 21, 126, 198, 203, 223; **147a**
St Giles' Church, Cripplegate, 9, 54, 174; **22a**
St John's Church, Lambeth, 88
St Martin-in-the-Fields, 119, 193
St Paul's Cathedral, 11, 22(Pl. 8), 24, 25, 27, 62–6, 67, 188, 197, 208–9, 213, 215, 216, 217–18, 219, 223, 224, 225, 227; **39a–o, 102c**
St Peter's Church, Bankside, 110n
St Peter's Church, Eaton Square, 91, 180, 194, 214; **90a**
St Peter's Church, Islington, 114
St Philip's Church, Stepney, 85
St Saviour's School, Southwark, 110, 190, 223; **126a**
Sir John Soane's Museum, 24, 73, 99, 204, 206
Somerset House, 5, 16(Pl. 4), 72–3, 188, 213, 227; **52a**
South Islington & Pentonville Schools, 114, 215; **133a**
Stockwell Park School, 68, 228; **43a**
Strand Bridge, *see* London, Waterloo Bridge
Temple Bar, 9, 33, 61–2, 208, 215, 217, 219; **37a**
Thames Tunnel, 3, 186, 223
Tower Bridge, 21, 33, 178, 197, 214, 215; **39m, 225a**
University of,
Council members (1826), **97a**
Foundation medal, 94, 223
University (College) building, 19, 31, 94, 95, 192, 207; **97a**
University College, prize medal, 3, 190; **232a**

London—*continued*
Victoria & Albert Museum, 142, 191, 203, 206
Victoria Park Hospital, 142, 147, 199, 200; **166a**
Waterloo Bridge, 80, 201, 227; **67a**
Wesleyan Centenary Hall, 111, 200, 214; **127a, b**
Westminster Abbey, 47–8, 186, 195, 209, 216, 224; **8a, b, 39e**
Henry VII's chapel, 209; **8b**
Whitechapel Art Gallery, 177, 205
London & Birmingham Railway, **125a, b**
Directors (listed), **125a**
Loudon, John Claudius, 5, 204
Lough, J. G., 125
Lowe, T., **125a**
Lubbock, Sir John, **205a**
Lupton, Roger, 57
Lynn, W. H., architect, 160, 197–8

Mabey, C. H. & J., 215, 219; **37a**
Macauly, Zachary, **97a**
Macclesfield, Christ Church School, 115, 217; **135a**
Sunday School, 78, 80; **66a**
Mackintosh, Sir James, M.P., **97a**
Maclaren, Archibald, 150
Mainwaring, Boulton, surveyor, 71, 198
Malatesta, Sigismondo, 1
Manchester, Art Treasures Exhibition Building, 148, 202, 221; **173a**
Jubilee Exhibition Buildings, 174, 198, 218; **215a**
Royal Institution, 102–3, 185, 228; **111a**
St Thomas's Girls School, 162–3; **193a**
Town Hall, 11, 21, 164, 206, 221; **197a**
Manners, G. P., architect, 70, 104, 198
Manning, Joseph, architect, 144
Manning, Michael P., architect, 172, 198
Marlborough, Sarah, Duchess of, 68
Marshall, Joshua, mason, 61
Marshman, Joshua, **40c**
Marston, W. R., **112a**
Martin & Co. (Cheltenham), **140b**
Martyr, J., **117a**
Mason, Christopher, **83a**
Mason, Sir Josiah, **199a**
Mason, Oliver, **108d**
Massonet, —, 214; **182k**
Maxwell & Tuke, architects, 174, 177, 198; **222a**
Mayer, J., 220; **119a, 159b, 170a**

Medallic series:
Art Union, 213; *see also* Art Union of London
Cathedrals (J. Davis), 216

Chancellors of University of Cambridge, 69, 221n
City of London, 215; *see also* London, Corporation of the City of
'Most remarkable edifices of Europe' (J. Wiener), 224
Menai Strait, Britannia Tubular Bridge, 3, 135, 204, 227; **164a, b**
Methodist Missionary Society, 111
Meymott, W. G., **83a**
Middleton, John, architect, 116
Middleton, Lord, **54a**
Mill, James, **97a**
Millard, Thos., **15a**
Milton, Viscount, **99a**
Mitchell, Thomas, architect, 168
Moffatt, W. B., architect, 118, 126, 198, 202, 209; **142a, 147a**
Mole, Thomas, **57a, 78a**
Montefiore, Sir Moses, **139a, b**
Moore, Joseph, medallist, 21, 33, 34, 214, 216, 217, 218, 220; **35a, b, 50a, 130a, 140b, 176a, 188a, 199a, 200a**
Moore, Joseph, **108d**
Moorsom, Captain, C. R., RN, **125a**
Morgan, George T., medallist, 24, 191, 217, 220; **180a, b, 233a**
Morgan, James, architect, 96, 198; **101a, b**
Morgan, Rev. Thomas, **112a**
Morris, Rev. Rupert H., **229a**
Moss, Samuel, carpenter, **80a**
Myers, Myer (Birmingham), **139b**

Nantwich, St Mary's Church, 51, 203; **14a**
Napoleon III, Emperor, **182j**
Nash, John, architect, 21, 83, 102, 113n, 119, 187n, 198–9
Neal, Ralph, medallist, 220; **224a**
Nelson, Admiral Lord, **143a–c**
Nero, Emperor, 6, 106
Nether Alderley, St Mary's Church, 52, 217; **16a**
New, Rev. F. T., **15a**
New College, London, principals (listed), **212a**
Newark, Christ Church, 104, 199, 221; **114a**
Newcastle-upon-Tyne, St Nicholas Church (later Cathedral), 53; **20a**
Newport, Viscount, **54a**
Newth, Dr S., **212a**
Nile, Battle of, **143b, c**
Norfolk, Duke of, **97a**
Northumberland, Duke of, 221; **45b, c**
Northwich, Verdin Technical School, 181; **230a**
Norton, Charles, surveyor, 8, 79, 199

Office of Works, 'attached architects', 199
Old Hall Green, Herts., St Edmund's College, 77, 227; **60a**
Oldham, Blue Coat School, 102, 197, 217; **110a**
Library & Museum, 168; **205a**
Olympia, Temple of Zeus, 54
Onslow, Ven. R. F., **81a, b**
Orchard, William, mason, 48
Ordish, F. W., architect, 142, 199
Orleans, Cornmarket, 106n
Osborn, W. H., **105a**
Ottley, John, medallist, 34, 69, 220–221, 228n; **35c–e, 54b, c, 57a, 62c, 81b, 88a, 95a, 98a, 101a, b, 103a, b, 104a, 105a, 112a, 114a, 132a, 140a, 165v–z, 174a, 175a, b, 182m–o, 187a, 195a**
Ottley, Thomas, medallist, 221; **141a, b**
Outram, Rev. E., 218; **41b**
Owen, Jacob, architect, 89, 199
Oxford, Bishop of, **54a**
Oxford, Christ Church Cathedral, 48, 216; **9a, b**
Divinity School, 48
Martyrs' Memorial, 48; **9b**
University Gymnasium, 150, 207; **177a**

Pagot, E. N., architect, 106n
Paine, J. D., architect, 104, 199
Paley & Austin, architects, 52; *see also* Sharpe & Paley
Palladio, Andrea, 59, 71, 197n
Palmerston, Lord, 2
Papworth, J. B., architect, 103
Paris, Eiffel Tower, 177
St Cloud, project for exhibition building, 147
Park Hall, Staffs., *see* Sedgley Park
Parkinson, Ven. T., **89a**
Parsons, William, architect, 91, 199; **89a**
Pasti, Matteo de, medallist, 1
Paxton, Sir Joseph, 12, 19, 23, 141–2, 147, 158, 199–200, 214, 221, 227; **165c–q, t–z, 171a, c, f, g, j**
Peace of Amiens, 11; **39a**
Pearce, Samuel, **40a**
Pearce & Sons, **204a**
Pearson, F. L., architect, 174n, 200
Pearson, James, **108d**
Pearson, John Loughborough, architect, 48, 174, 200
Pease, Edward, **138a**
Peel, Bt., **54a**
Pennethorne, Sir James, architect, 73
'Penny Black', postage stamp, 74, 228
Perry, James, C., **61a**
Peters, James, publisher, 15, 69, 70n, 221
Phillp, I., engraver, 221; **29a–c**

Phipson, William, **108d, 125a**
Pickop, John, **195a**
Picton, Sir James A., architect, 107n, 195n
Pierce, Edward, 24, 209, 225
Pilkington, William, architect, 77, 200
Pinchback, W., **83a**
Pinches, family, medallists, 221
Pinches, Francis, 221; **197a**
Pinches, John, medallist, 216, 220, 221, 227; **56b, 121a, 171f–i, 173a–c, 182p–r**
memorial medal, **221n**
Pinches, John H., medallist, 176, 221, 224; **221b**
Pinches, Thomas R., medallist, 222; **171c, e**
Piranesi, Giovanni Battista, 2
Pistrucci, Benedetto, medallist, 211, 228
Plumbe, Roland, architect, 72
Plymouth, Other Archer, seventh Earl of, **54a, 78a**
Pocock, William Fuller, architect, 111, 200
Pope, Jacob, **112a**
Portsea, All Saints' Church, 89
Potter, Joseph, sen., architect, 46, 200
Potter, Joseph, jun., architect, 88, 95, 109, 200
Potter, Robert, architect, 95
Pountney, Miss, **186a**
Preston, St John's Church, 54; **23a**
Prevost, I. L., **125a**
Price, F. T. (Sarum), **154a**
Price, Theodore, **108d**
Prince of Wales (later King Edward VII), 166, 215, 225, 227; **161c, 178a, 180a, b, 188a, 189a, 202a, 215a, 216a, 221b, 225a**
thanksgiving for recovery, 11, 215; **39j–l**
Princess of Wales (later Queen Alexandra), **178a, 188a, 202a, 215a, 225a**
Promoli, W. B., publisher, **113b**
Proud, G. L., **105a**
Pryce, Dr R. V., **212a**
*Public Buildings of London*, 61
Pugin, A. W. N., architect, 20, 21, 23, 27, 30, 46, 74, 77, 106, 109, 127, 128, 152–3, 185, 187, 200–1, 202

Railton, William, architect, 119, 201; **143a, b**
Railways:
Chester & Holyhead, (135), 204
Grand Junction, **113a, b**
London & Birmingham, **125a, b**
North Midland, 204
Paris to Le Havre, 204
Railway structures, **113a, b, 125a, b, 164a, b**
Ratcliff, John, **35a–c**
Rathbone, T. W., **125a**
Rathbone, William, **170a**
Rawsthorne, John, architect, 76, 201
Read, R. J. J., 177
Reducing Machine, 33
Reform demonstration, Leeds 1866, **175b**
Rennie, John, engineer (1761–1821), 3, 80, 97, 192, 201
portrait medal, 201, 213; **234a**
Rennie, Sir John, engineer (1794–1874), 97, 201
Repton, Humphrey, 199
Restall, J. A., medallist, 222; **213a**
Rice, Isaac, **83a**
Richard II, King, 55
Richards, Rev. John, **46a**
Richardson, H. H., architect, 177, 205
Richardson, Thos., **138a**
Richmond, Yorks., School, 134, 184; **163a**
Rickman, Thomas, architect, 21, 23, 90, 93, 108, 189, 195, 201–2, 203
Rickman & Hutchinson, architects, 90; **88a, b**. *See also* Rickman, Thomas, and Hutchinson, Henry
Ridley, Sir Matthew White, M.P., **222a**
Rimini, Church of S. Francesco, 1
Ripley, Julia, and Thomas, **184a**
Roberts, Edward, architect, 159n
Robertson, William, **112a**
Robson, E. R., architect, 172, 202
Rock, Jos$^{h}$, **112a**
Rogers, Rev. W., **224a**
Rome, meat market, 6, 7, 106
St John Lateran, 1
Temple of Castor and Pollux, 101
Room, James, **61a**
Room, William, **112a**
Roscoe, William (Roscoe Prize Medal), **119a**
Rose, Henry, architect, 134, 202
Rothschild, Baron de, **139a**
Rothwell, Northants, Board School, **32a**
Market House, 59, 193, 222; **32a**
Roty, L-O., medallist, 33, 214
Roumieu, R. L., architect, 114, 193
Rouw, Peter, the younger, sculptor, 223
Rowles, Henry, **125a**
Royal Academy, 73, 187, 189
Royal Agricultural Society, **56b**
Royal Engineers, prize medal, 24, 191; **233a**
Royal Institute of British Architects, *see* Institute of British Architects
Royal Mint, London, 34
Royle & Bennett, architects, 162–3
Rubens, Peter Paul, 59
Rundell, Bridge & Rundell, **131a**
Russell, Dr, 98
Russell, Lord John, M.P., **97a**
Ryder, Henry, *see* Lichfield & Coventry, Bishop of

Ryland, John, **40a**
Ryland, W. H., **186a**
Rysbrack, Michael, sculptor, 59, 214

S, **228a**
S. K., *see* Kelsey, S.
St Edmund's College, Herts., *see* Old Hall Green, Herts.
Sale, H. B., 222; **191a**
Salisbury, Cathedral, 49, 209, 213, 217; **10a, b**
Diocesan Board of Education, **10b**
Market cross, 45
Salomons, D., **139a**
Salomons, Edward, architect, 148, 202
Salt, Sir Titus, 161, 197
Saltaire, The Institute, 161, 197, 218; **190a**
Salvin, Anthony, architect, 23, 200
Saunders, Charles, architect, 175, 193
Schnitzpahn, Christian, medallist, 222; **182s, u**
Schools, awards or commemoration, **19a, 27a, 31a, 32a, 33a–c, 38a, 39n, 43a, 44a, b, 47a, 50a, 55a, 57a, 59a, 64a, 71a, 86a, 95a, 96a, 99a, 104a, 107a, 110a, 116a–d, 119a, 120a, 126a, 130a, 133a, 134a, 135a, 136a, 137a, 138a, 139a, b, 140a, b, 141a, b, 151a, 156a, 163a, 169a, 172a, 176a, 186a, 192a, 193a, 202a, 219a**
Sunday Schools, **14a, 16a, 17a, 51a, 58a, 62a–c, 66a, 94a, 98a, 100a, 107a, 128a, 132c, 145a, 152a, 174a**
Medical, **93a, 109a, 148a**
Technical, **226a**
Scott, Sir George Gilbert, architect, 2, 21, 45, 46, 47, 48, 49, 50, 51, 53, 118, 120n, 126, 127, 160, 185, 198, 202–3, 209; **142a, 147a**
portrait on medal, 203, 212, 213; **235a**
Scott, Sir Giles G., architect, 87, 159
Scott, Maj. Gen. Henry Young Darracott, RE, 161, 191, 203
Scott, J. Oldrid, architect, 47, 203
Scott & Moffatt, architects, 118, 126, 198; **142a, 147a**. *See also* Scott, Sir George Gilbert, and Moffatt, W. B.
Sedgley Park School, 68, 227; **44a, b**
Sedgwick, Barry, **64a**
Selborne, Lord, **194a**
Seward, A., 222; **184a**
Sforza, Francesco I, Duke of Milan, 1
Shakespeare, William, **28a, b**
Sharpe & Paley, architects, 148, 203
Shaw, Benjamin, **97a**
Shaw, Charles, **108d**
Shaw, John, sen., architect, 94, 203–4
Sheffield, Mount St Mary's College, 128, 194; **151a**
Sheffield—*continued*
St Mary's Church, Bramhall Lane, 95, 200; **100a**
Wesley College, 112, 191, 220; **130a**
Shellard, E. H., architect, 54
Shepton Mallet, St Peter & St Paul, 51, 219; **15a**
Sherborne, Abbey Church, 53, 212; **21a**
Shireburn, family, 5, 58
Showell, John Whitehouse, **61a**
Sibthorp, Col., Charles de L. W., M.P., 140, 141
Siemens, Sir William, 220; **200a**
Sinnott, E. S., engineer, 175
Skipper, Jn°., **83a**
Skipwith, Bt., **54a**
Slater, W., architect, 53
Slavery, **40c**
Small, Robert, **83a**
Smirke, Sir Robert, architect, 23, 51, 73, 94n, 113n, 199
Smirke, Sydney, architect, 51, 125, 153
Smith, Henry (Birmingham), engraver, 222; **186a, 203a**
Smith, Henry, **108d**
Smith, John, M.P., **97a**
Smith, Timothy, **108d**
Smith, W., builder, **112a**
Smith & Hammond, architects, 179
Smyth, Rev. Edward, **83a**
Soane, Sir, John, architect, *Frontis.*, 59, 99, 169n, 188, 190, 199, 204, 207
portrait on medal, *Frontis.*, 11, 24, 213, 228; **106a**
presentation of medal, 24, 99, 204, 210
Society of Jesus, 58, 75
Somerset, Duke of, 168
Southsea, St Paul's Church, 89
St Paul's School, 89, 199; **86a**
Spence, Geo., **83a**
Sperandio, of Mantua, medallist, 1
Spink & Son Ltd., 222; **32a, 132c**
Spooner, Richard, **108d**
Stafford, Marquess of, **54a**
Stamford & Warrington, Earl of, **80a**
Stanley, Rev. Edward, 52; **16a**
Stanley, Lord, M.P., **141a**
Stanley, memorial pew, 52
Startin, William, architect, 98, 204
Stephenson, Robert, engineer, 3, 135, 204, 227; **125a, 164a**
Stevens, H. J., architect, 149, 204
Stockport, St Mary's Church, 80–1, 209, 217; **68a**
Sunday School, 78, 80, 217, 221; **62a–c**
Stoke-on-Trent, St Peter's Church, 95, 149, 205, 221; **98a**
Stonyhurst College, Lancs., 5, 58, 217; **33a–c**

Storie, Rev. J. G., **147a**
Storrs, Rev. John, **90a**
Story, Bishop, 45
Stothard, Alfred Joseph, sculptor, 8, 222; **131a, 146e**
Stratford-upon-Avon, Shakespeare's House, 56, 212, 223; **28a, b**
Street, G. E., architect, 23, 100, 189
Sturge, Joseph, **125a**
Sussex, H.R.H. Frederick Duke of, **70a**
Sutcliff, **40a**
Swan, Rev. Thomas, **61a**
Swinton, St Peter's Church, 100
St Peter's School, 100; **107a**

Talbot, Earl, **54a**
Tate, Bishop, **163a**
Taylor, James, architect, 77
Taylor, J. (Birmingham), medallist, 222–3; **40b, 77a, 142a, 143b, 146w, 147a**
Taylor, Sir Robert, architect, 127n, 198, 200
Taylor, William Joseph, medallist, 111, 217, 220, 221, 223; **28a, 39j, 126a, 134a, 165aa, 171j–l**
Teck, Princess Mary Adelaide, Duchess of, **191a**
Telford, Thomas, engineer, 135, 228
Temple:
allegorical, 7, 54, 190, 226; **24a**
of Castor and Pollux, Rome, 101
on the River Illysus, 88
of Vesta, Tivoli, 99
Teneriffe, Battle of, **143b, c**
Theobalds Park, Herts., 62
Thomas, —, **40b**
Thomas à Becket, St, 44
Thomas, J., stonecarver, 185
Thomason, Sir Edward, 94n, 215, 217, 219, 223; **39b, 108d**
Thompson, Francis, architect, 3, 135, 204
Thompson, William, M.P., **96a**
Thornton, John, 51
Thorpe, James, **114a**
Thorpe, John, 60
Thursby, Col., **210a**
Tiffin, —, **154a**
Tintwistle, Christ Church, 9, 108, 221; **121a**
Tite, Sir William, architect, 23, 61, 104, 125, 204–5, 208; **146a, i–k, u, x, y**
Tivoli, Temple of Vesta, 99
Tooke, T., **125a**
Tooke, William, **97a**
Townsend, Charles Harrison, architect, 23, 177, 205
Trafalgar, Battle of, **143b, c**
Tresham, Sir Thomas, 58, 193
Trubshaw, J. & C., architects, 119, 205
Trubshaw & Johnson, architects, 95, 205
Truro, Bishop of, **216a**
Truro, Cathedral, 21, 174, 200; **216a**
St Mary's Church, 174
Tunbridge Wells, St John's Church, 162, 189, 193, 222; **191a**
Turk, Thomas, **83a**
Turner, John, **108d**
Turnour, Rev. Francis E., **105a**
Tyndall, Thomas, **112a**

Uhlorn, H., **182s–u**

Vanbrugh, Sir John, architect, 14(Pl. 3), 15, 67–8, 195, 205, 208, 213, 227; **42a**
Vaughtons Ltd., medallists, 224; **181a, 219a**
Vertue, Robert and William, masons, 48
Vickers, N. W., architect, 168
Victoria, Queen, 9, 11, 15, 23, 31, 125, 152, 176, 214, 217, 225, 227, 228; **22a, 30a, 35a–e, 53a–c, 75a, 90a, 100a, 121a, 126a, 132c, 146a, b, f–l, o–u, w, x, 150a, b, 153a, b, 155a, 161a–c, 165f–o, q, z, dd, ee, gg, 168a, 173c, 175a, b, 179a, b, d, g, h, 182d, h, j, k, n, o, v, w, 189b, 190a, 211a, 215a, 218a, 221a, b, 225a, 229a, 230a**
Jubilee (1887), 3, 212; **22a, 30a, 121a, 190a, 211a, 215a, 218a, 221b**
Jubilee (1897), 9, 214; **90a, 100a, 132c, 228a, 229a, 230a**
medallic portraits of, **22a, 30a, 35a–e, 53a, b, 75a, 90a, 100a, 121a, 132c, 146a, b, f, j–l, o, q, r, x, 150a, b, 153a, b, 155a, 161a–c, 165h, k, l, q, z, dd, ee, gg, 168a, 173c, 175a, 179a, b, d, g, h, 182d, h, j, k, n, o, v, w, 189b, 190a, 211a, 215a, 218a, 221a, b, 225a, 229a, 230a**
opening of Royal Exchange, 125; **146f–x**
portrait used for 'Penny Black', 74, 228n; **53b**
visit to Aston Hall, **35a–e**
visit to City of London in 1837, 9, 15, 215, 228; **53a–c**
Victoria, Princess Royal, **161c**
Vivian, E. M., **17a**
Vizard, William, **83a**
Vyse, 75n

Waddington, W., & Sons, architects, 171, 205
Wagner, Rev. H. M., **91a**
Wainwright, C., architect, 51; **15a**
Walker, Joseph, **108d**

Walker, J., **125a**
Walsall, St John's Church, 150, 194, 220; **176a**
Walsall Wood, St John's Church, 108, 215; **122a**
Waltham Cross, Herts., Eleanor Cross, 48
Walthew, John, builder, **78a**
Warburton, Henry, **97a**
Ward, Henry, publisher, 224; **1b**
Ward, John, first Viscount Dudley & Ward, 68
Ward, John William, Earl Dudley, and fourth Viscount Dudley & Ward, **54a, 97a**
Ward, Joseph, **83a**
Ward, William, **40c**
Warder, William, **187a**
Warre, Henry, **125a**
Warrington, Bank Hall (now Town Hall), 71, 193; **48a**
Warwick, Earl of, **54a**
Waterhouse, Alfred, architect, 11, 87, 104, 158, 164, 173, 175n, 197, 206
Waterloo, Battle of, 125; **146n, p, t**
Waterlow & Sons Ltd., 176, 224
Watson, 72n
Watt, James, 34, 227, 228
Waymouth, Henry, **97a**
Webb, Sir Aston, architect, 111, 165, 175, 206
Webb, John, architect, 197
Webb, Thomas, medallist, 8, 224; **65a**
Weekes, Henry, sculptor, 125
Wellesley House, Twickenham, 143
Wellington, Arthur Wellesley, first Duke of, 212; **25a**
statue, at Royal Exchange, 125; **146g–i, n, p, t, v, w**
battles, **146n, p, t**
Wetherhead & Co., ironfounders, **78a**
Wesley, John, **127a, b**
Wesley College, *see* Sheffield, Wesley College
Wesleyan Methodism, Centenary 1839, **127a, b**
Westmacott, Sir Richard, **52a**
Westminster, City of, 61
West Bromwich, Christ Church, 92, 193, 221n; **92a**
Whateley, I. W., **88a**
Whetham, G., **17a**
Whiffin, William, **83a**
Whishaw, John, **97a**
Whitaker, John, **66a**
Whitwell, T. S., architect, 82, 206; **72a, b**
Wickham, Rev. W. P. T., **15a**
Wiener, Jacques, medallist, 5, 25, 27, 31, 33, 152, 160n, 213, 216, 222, 224–5; **7b, 8b, 11b, 13d, 39i, 179i, 182s–u**
Wiener, Leopold, medallist, 213, 224, 225; **179i**
Wild, J. W., architect, 23, 115, 206
Wilkins, William, architect, 19, 31, 81, 94, 119, 192, 207; **97a**
Wilkinson, William, architect, 150, 207
Willcox, William, **61a**
William, IV, King, 97, 215, 228; **102a, (125b)**
William of Sens, 44
Williamson, H. H., 119
Willoughby de Broke, Lord, **54a**
Wilson, C. L. N., engineer, 180
Wilson, E., **125a**
Wilson, James, architect, 117, 207
Wilson, Thomas, **97a**
Wilson, W., medallist, 24, 213, 225, 227; **39h**
Wilton, Joseph, sculptor, 73
Wilton, St Mary & St Nicholas, 115, 129, 206, 209, 213, 223; **154a**
Winchester, Geo. Tomline, Bishop of, **83a, 117a**
Winchester, Cathedral, 31, 49, 213, 216, 224; **11a, b**
choir screen, 31, 49, 197; **11b**
College, 11, 33, 55–6, 217; **27a**
500th anniversary, 11; **27a**
Guildhall, 163, 196; **194a**
Windsor, Beaumont Lodge, Old Windsor, 5, 75, 191; **55a**
Windsor Castle, 8, 83, 113, 148, 186, 210, 222; **131a, b**
Windsor & Wolverhampton, H. L. Hobart, Dean of, **101a, b**
Winnington, —, M.P., Bt., **54a**
Wolverhampton, Art Gallery, 171, 188; **209a**
Orphan Asylum, 144; **169a**
St George's Church, 96, 198, 221; **101a, b**
Wood, John, the elder, architect, 70, 71, 207
Wood, John, the younger, architect, 207
Wood, John, **161c**
Woodhead & Hurst, architects, 88, 93, 208
Woodgate & Collcutt, architects, 163, 189
Woodyer, H., architect, 106
Woolaton Hall, 131
Woolfield, Thomas, publisher, **82a**
Worcester Engine Works Company, 167
Worcester, Henry Cornewall, Bishop of, **81b, 158a, 167b**
Worcester, Cathedral, 50, 216; **12a**
Exhibition Building, 167, 222; **203a**
Worsley Hall, 129, 186, 212; **155a**
Worthington, Thomas, architect, 171, 174, 208
Worthington & Elgood, architects, 171, 174; *see also* Worthington, Thomas
Wren, Sir Christopher, architect, 22(Pl. 8), 24, 49, 58, 59n, 61, 66, 159, 195, 196, 205, 208–9, 213, 225, 227; **37a, 39h, i, o**
Wrottesley, —, M.P., Bt., **54a**
Wyatt, James, architect, 45, 46, 48, 49, 192, 200, 201, 203n, 209, 210
Wyatt, Jeffry, *see* Wyatville, Sir Jeffry
Wyatt, John Drayton, architect, 160, 209; **187a**

Wyatt, Lewis William, architect, 80–81, 103, 209
Wyatt, Sir Matthew Digby, architect, 147n, 159n, 203
Wyatt, Thomas Henry, architect, 23, 129, 132, 206, 209; **154a, 160a.** *See also* Wyatt & Brandon
Wyatt & Brandon, architects, **154a, 160a**. *See also* Wyatt, T. H., and Brandon, D.
Wyatville, Sir Jeffry, architect, 8, 83, 99, 113, 148, 191, 209, 210
Wykeham, William, of, 49, 56; **11b, 27a**
Wyon family, medallists, 33, 34, 225
family tree, 226
Wyon, Alfred Benjamin, medallist, 225, 227; **39k, 189a, b, 202a, 206a, 232a**
Wyon, Allan, medallist, 225; **212a**
Wyon, Benjamin, medallist, 5, 6–7, 15, 25, 27, 34, 54n, 85, 213, 215, 222, 225, 226–7, 228n; **24a, 25a, 39h, 42a, 49a, 52a, 53c, 79a, 84a, 96a, 102a, 109a, 118a, 120a, 161c, 172a**
Wyon, Joseph Shepherd, medallist, 34, 225, 226, 227; **39k, 189a, b, 232a.** *See also* Wyon, J. S. & A. B.
Wyon, J. S. & A. B., medallists, 3, 11, 34, 190, 215, 220, 225, 227; **39k, 189a, b, 202a, 206a, 232a**. *See also* Wyon, Alfred Benjamin and Wyon, Joseph Shepherd
Wyon, Leonard Charles, medallist, 213n, 216, 221, 226, 227; **164a, 171f, g**
Wyon, Peter, medallist, 219, 226, 227, 228; **60a**
Wyon, Thomas, the elder, medallist, 219, 226, 227, 228; **44a, 79a**
Wyon, Thomas, the younger, medallist, 80, 226, 227, 228
Wyon, William, medallist, 9, 13, 24, 27, 33, 34, 204, 210, 211, 212, 215, 217, 221, 225, 226, 227, 228; **18a, 26a, 43a, 53a, b, 67a, 73a, 99a, 106a, 111a, 146x**
Wyre Hill Home Mission, **186a**

Yevele, Henry, 48
York, Clifford's Tower, **13a**
York Minster, 26(Pl. 9), 27, 50–1, 213, 216, 224; **13a–d**
choir destroyed by fire (1829), **13b**
Young, C. D. & Co., engineers, 148
Young, H. H., **28a**
Young, Robert, **83a**
Young, T., **125a**